THE PHANTOM PUBLIC SPHERE

A series from the Social Text Collective

Aimed at a broad interdisciplinary audience, these volumes seek to intervene in debates about the political direction of current theory and practice by combining contemporary analysis with a more traditional sense of historical and socioeconomic evaluation.

THE PHANTOM PUBLIC SPHERE

EDITED BY | BRUCE ROBBINS

(for the Social Text Collective)

Cultural Politics, Volume 5

University of Minnesota Press
Minneapolis
London

Arjun Appadurai, "Disjuncture and Difference in the Global Cultural Economy,"
reprinted from *Public Culture* 2, no. 2 (Spring 1990), © 1990 by the Center for
Transnational Cultural Studies, by permission; Lauren Berlant, "National Brands/
National Body: *Imitation of Life*," reprinted from *Comparative American
Identities: Race, Sex, and Nationality in the Modern Text*, ed. Hortense J. Spillers
(New York: Routledge, 1991), by permission; Nancy Fraser, "Rethinking the
Public Sphere: A Critique of Actually Existing Democracy," reprinted from
Habermas and the Public Sphere, ed. Craig Calhoun (Cambridge, Mass.: MIT
Press, 1992), by permission; Fredric Jameson, "On Negt and Kluge," reprinted
from *October* 46 (Fall 1988), by permission.

Published by the University of Minnesota Press
2037 University Avenue Southeast, Minneapolis, MN 55455-3092
Printed in the United States of America on acid-free paper

Library of Congress Cataloging-in-Publication Data
The phantom public sphere / edited by Bruce Robbins.
     p. cm.—(Cultural politics ; v. 5)
     Includes bibliographical references and index.
     ISBN 0-8166-2124-1 (alk. paper). — ISBN 0-8166-2126-8 (pb : alk.
paper)
     1. Mass media—Social aspects. 2. Political sociology.
     3. Culture—Political aspects. I. Robbins, Bruce. II. Series:
Cultural politics (Minneapolis, Minn.) : v. 5.
     HM258.P474   1993
302.23—dc20   92-28619
                                         CIP

Contents

Introduction: The Public As Phantom
Bruce Robbins

There is "nothing particularly new in the disenchantment which the private citizen expresses by not voting at all," Walter Lippmann writes in *The Phantom Public* (1925). Unlike so many others, Lippmann says, he will not blame the citizen for "staying away from the primaries," for "not reading speeches and documents," for "the whole list of sins of omission for which he is denounced": "My sympathies are with him, for I believe he has been saddled with an impossible task and that he is asked to practice an unattainable ideal."

According to Lippmann, citizens cannot be reasonably expected to form themselves into a responsible, well-informed public. An active, enlightened, ever-vigilant force that would participate energetically in, would supervise, or would simply lend its authority to the machinery of the state, and would be and do all this after hours, in the leisure time supposedly left over from work and family — the public in this ideal sense is a hypothesis contrary to any possible fact.[1] There is simply not enough time in the day. "I find it so myself for, although public business is my main interest and I give most of my time to watching it, I cannot find time to do what is expected of me in the theory of democracy; that is, to know what is going on and to have an opinion worth expressing on every question which confronts a self-governing community. And I have not happened to meet anyone, from a President of the United States to a professor of political science, who came anywhere near to embodying the accepted ideal of the sovereign and omnicompetent citizen."

To what he saw as the necessary public incompetence of the

temporally overtaxed private citizen, Lippmann offered an una-
bashedly elitist answer: he recommended a delegation of authority
to specialized, competent experts. Since 1925, this has come to seem
less a solution than an unwitting and unhappy description of a newer
set of problems. But Lippmann's critique of the concept of the public
remains extraordinarily and even strangely to the point.

Today, as in 1925, the public's name once again rumbles prophet-
ically through the best-seller lists. The mass media are again accused
of corrupting the habits of self-reliant critical thought necessary to
democracy. The schools and universities are again accused of failing
in their duty to produce responsible, enthusiastically participatory,
fully informed citizens. Citizenship, readership, cities, spaces, intellectuals, even families — about all of these we hear much the same
story: the story, told in Jürgen Habermas's recently translated *Structural Transformation of the Public Sphere* (1962), of a public sphere
gained (by the liberal bourgeoisie of the nineteenth century) and
then lost (in the epoch of consumerism, mass media, and the expansion of the state into the intimate space of the family).[2] This is more
or less what Richard Sennett tells us about cities in *The Fall of Public
Man* (1974), what Russell Jacoby tells us about intellectuals in *The
Last Intellectuals* (1987), and what Allan Bloom tells us about education in *The Closing of the American Mind* (1987). The list of writings that announce the decline, degradation, crisis, or extinction of
the public is long and steadily expanding. Publicness, we are told
again and again and again, is a quality that we once had but have
now lost, and that we must somehow retrieve.

Taking Lippmann's counsel, however, we can perhaps see that the
appearance of the public in these historical narratives is something
of a conjuring trick. *For whom* was the city once more public than
now? Was it ever open to the scrutiny and participation, let alone
under the control, of the majority? Was there ever a time when
intellectuals were really authorized to speak to the people as a
whole about the interests of the people as a whole? If so, where were
the workers, the women, the lesbians, the gay men, the African-
Americans? Historical efforts to pinpoint some moment of prior
possession of publicness are as vain as Lippmann's search for the
"sovereign and omnicompetent citizen." They uncover, in Stanley
Aronowitz's phrase, a "mythic town square in the sky" for which hard
evidence is not proposed, nor even sought.[3] When Allan Bloom

raises the ghost of Greece, allowing Socrates and the Athenian agora to float for contrastive effect over the modern university, he unintentionally offers a juicy Hellenic term for Aronowitz's "mythic town square" — the *phantasmagoria*: an *agora* (public forum, assembly) that is only a phantasm. For the tradition thus conjured up has nothing to do with the realities and limits of Greek democracy, or with the possibilities to extend our own. It is an attempt to haunt us with the Spirit of the Past, an authoritative survival before which we should bow down in fear, awe, and silence.[4]

Like the less credulous reviewers of *The Closing of the American Mind, Illiberal Education*, and other lucrative jeremiads, Lippmann suggests that their sound and fury are misdirected. Neither education nor the press deserves such vehement attacks, for the attacks — for example, blaming either or both for poor voter turnout — are only proportionate to (indeed, are in part produced by) notions of institutional self-importance that are themselves unwarranted. However grandiose the claims to public service they may (and do) assert, neither institution could ever possibly teach people what they would need to know in order to participate competently in all public issues. "The usual appeal to education can bring only disappointment" (27). It cannot be "assumed that the press should do spontaneously for us what primitive democracy imagined each of us could do spontaneously for himself."[5] Like Foucault's specific intellectual, Lippmann refuses to identify his journalistic, pedagogic role with a quasi-divine omniscience. Speaking for the whole, he argues, is no longer an option: "Modern society is not visible to anybody, nor intelligible continuously and as a whole. One section of it is visible to another section, one series of acts is intelligible to this group and another to that" (42). "[E]ven the successful practice of a moral code would not emancipate democracy. There are too many moral codes" (30). Like the recent champions of identity politics and multiculturalism, Lippmann proposes that we give up the quest "to find a unity which absorbs diversity" (98). We must give up, that is, "the sophistry that the public and all the individuals composing it are one mind, one soul, one purpose" (160). In short, we must recognize, as Lippmann's title announces, that the public is a phantom.

The public is a phantom. Is this, then, what we now believe? For radical critics of various sorts and schools, it might indeed seem to approach the status of a contemporary credo. Along with feminist critiques of universalism, which often begin with the fundamental need to overturn or evade the opposition Jean Bethke Elshtain calls "public man, private woman," and the parallel claim to difference put forward by racial and sexual minorities, many of the strongest traditions that now compose the American cultural left, both residual (*Partisan Review* modernism, Frankfurt School mandarinism) and more recent (French poststructuralism), consign the term "public sphere" to the spectral half-life of a word that abides inside quotation marks, thus leading us back to Lippmann's skepticism and his phantom.[6] Watching the government and the media conspire to construct a "general public" that excludes groups affected by the HIV virus (see Michael Warner's essay in this volume), who among us is not justifiably suspicious of those who claim to speak in the public's name? Who does not wonder whether it is a name anyone can legitimately continue to invoke? When Jacques Derrida refers to public opinion (in a passage quoted in Tom Keenan's essay) as "the silhouette of a phantom," he seems to be summarizing a common sense that extends surprisingly far beyond Lippmann's political presuppositions.

The title of the present volume pays its respects to Lippmann, however, not so much because his position overlaps with today's radical suspicions of the public as because it does so *from the right*, and thus poses an urgent and as yet unanswered challenge to the left. How much of Lippmann's analysis must the left digest? How much can it digest without ceasing to *be* a left? In radical struggles over architecture, urban planning, sculpture, political theory, ecology, economics, education, the media, and public health, to mention only a few sites among others, the public has long served as a rallying cry against private greed, a demand for attention to the general welfare as against propertied interests, an appeal for openness to scrutiny as opposed to corporate and bureaucratic secrecy, an arena in which disenfranchised minorities struggle to express their cultural identity, a code word for socialism. Without this discursive weapon, we seem to enter such struggles inadequately armed. If the phrase "phantom public" still has some power to startle and disorient, if there is some reluctance to see the public melt conclusively into air, the cause may not be vestigial piety so much as the fear that we cannot do without it.

At the same time, this fear is not sufficient reason to act as if the concept of the public can be preserved as is, or even that it can be easily salvaged and refunctioned. In an immediate answer to Lippmann from the left, John Dewey's *The Public and Its Problems* (1927) affirmed Dewey's continuing hopes for participatory democracy, for "the reconstruction of face-to-face communities" (see Stanley Aronowitz's essay in this volume).[7] But "face-to-face communities," as Dewey had to admit, were the least visible of entities in a society as fluid, interconnected, and heterogeneous as our own. "If a public exists, it is surely as uncertain about its own whereabouts as philosophers since Hume have been about the residence and make-up of the self."[8] To most readers, Dewey concedes, "the conditions upon which depends the emergence of the Public from its eclipse will seem close to denial of the possibility of realizing the idea of a democratic public." As Robert Westbrook concludes, in a study that is otherwise quite sympathetic to Dewey, "Dewey's assertion that the local community might be reconstructed in the midst of the Great Society also seemed wistful in the absence of specific suggestions for doing so ... he inadvertently and ironically made almost as good a case as Lippmann that the phantom public would not materialize" (315–16).

Instructively parallel debates took place during the same period in Weimar Germany. In 1922, Ferdinand Tönnies — better known for his diagnosis of the breakdown of "community" and its replacement by "society" (in *Gemeinschaft und Gesellschaft* [1887]) — offered a "critique of public opinion," one ghostly, cosmopolitan substitute for the missing primal cohesiveness. Five years later, Carl Schmitt in *The Concept of the Political* (1927) lamented the weakness of the German state. Both were reacting, like Dewey, to capitalist modernization and its undermining of traditional ways of life. Like Dewey, both offer versions of a narrative in which the public falls while the private rises. (For Hannah Arendt, another major figure in this line, what rises when the public falls is "the social," but the narrative is otherwise much the same.) Yet Dewey called the public that he feared to lose by the name of democracy, while within six years Carl Schmitt's version of the public was to metamorphose into fascism.[9] It should be clear that to tell a story in which the triumph of the private means the defeat of the public is not necessarily to do democracy any favors.

Like Dewey, it seems, leftists of the 1990s do not know how to argue for the democracy we want without mobilizing an image of the public so hazy, idealized, and distant from the actual people, places, and institutions around us that it can as easily serve purposes that are anything but democratic. It is this argumentative blockage that *The Phantom Public Sphere* tries to find a way through. Its contributors share that qualified but steadfast commitment to the concept of the public that any supporter of democracy *must* share. Rather than ditch the public/private dichotomy, however pressing the temptation to do so, they worry it, experiment with it, take it apart and recombine the pieces. They write, that is, according to the political principle that to deconstruct an opposed pair like public and private does not mean doing without what was valued or desirable in the privileged term. On the contrary, as their essays illustrate, it means carefully specifying those desirable elements so as to extricate them as far as possible from the opposition and make them available outside it. As Derrida writes, the fact that "public opinion" is a specter, "present as such in none of the spaces" where it is held to be, does not mean one can "*simply* plead for plurality, dispersion, or fractioning.... For certain socio-economic forces might once again take advantage of these marginalizations and this absence of a general forum." The question is, "How then to open the avenue of great debates, accessible to the majority, while yet enriching the multiplicity and the quality of public discourses, of evaluating agencies, of 'scenes' or places of visibility?"[10]

Derrida calls this question "impossible but necessary." Perhaps the question can be addressed with less sense of inevitable contradiction and impasse if one moves away from the universalizing ideal of a single public and attends instead to the actual multiplicity of distinct and overlapping public discourses, public spheres, and scenes of evaluation that already exist, but that the usual idealizations have screened from view. Thus the contributors to this volume look beyond laments for a lone lost public. They try instead to detect and evaluate publicness that is already there in diverse forms, not a single norm or hypothesis set against contemporary people, places, and institutions but a multitudinous presence among the conditions of postmodern life. Addressing the unfinished business of imagining postmodern democracy, democracy in an age of mass media, technical instrumentality, commodification, and social heterogeneity that does not permit a "reconstruction of face-to-face communities," they ask among other things about a concept of the public that would not be shielded from the inauthentic taint of publicity; about a concept of the public that might respond to the irreducible diversity (and the new connectedness) of identity politics; about a concept of the public that would be adequate to the connectedness of power, the politically unpromising consumer culture of global capitalism.

In a usefully synoptic essay, Jeff Weintraub lays out four distinct ways in which the public is customarily opposed to the private. The first is a liberal-economistic model that defines the public as state administration and the private as the market economy. For the second or "republican virtue" model, which would include Habermas, the public means community and citizenship, as distinct both from state sovereignty on the one side and from the economy on the other. The third is a "sociability" model, as in Richard Sennett and Philippe Ariès, which emphasizes symbolic display and theatrical self-representation but has little if anything to do with collective decision making or state power. The fourth, a model shared by feminist and other historians, opposes a privacy defined largely as the domestic or familial to a publicness defined largely as the economy of wage earners.[11]

This analysis suggests, to begin with, why the familiar rhetoric that seeks to inflame its hearers against a perceived loss or diminution of the public is so potent and profitable. This rhetoric creates an illusion of unity among people who, it now appears, rightly belong on opposite sides. To some, the call to restore or extend the territory of the public will seem an appeal for a stronger, more decisive state power, as in model number one. To others, it will be heard to call for greater popular input and debate, even at some cost to the efficacious singleness of executive power and will, as in model number two. It could even be heard as a call to emphasize the market at the expense of the state.

Thanks to Weintraub's classification, we can also introduce some differences into the common sense about the public-as-phantom. When Lippmann took as his point of departure the private male individual, he aligned himself (as did Dewey, and as Richard Rorty does now) with the liberal tradition, a tradition for which the public has *always* been somewhat ghostly. In Locke's *Two Treatises of Government* (1690), for example, we read of "the Image, Phantom, or Representative of the Commonwealth." Free-market liberalism gives so much to the private sphere of the economy that, not surprisingly, little substance is left for the state, which can only be phantomlike. But this does not mean that the suspicion of the public that emerges from the new, still fragile recognition of multicultural diversity (which many of us welcome) is identical with the suspicion that emerges from liberal pressure for economic privatization (which many of the same people will resist). The apparent agreement between feminists and economic liberals that the public is a phantom in fact conceals two radically opposed notions of the public. For the liberals, the public is the state, while for feminists it has been first and foremost the economy (the domain of wage labor outside the family), that is, the very domain that the liberals wish at all costs to reserve as private. The capitalist economy, which figures as both private (for liberals) and public (for feminists), thus seems to be a crucial place both where the public/private opposition breaks down, and where it demonstrates its resilience as well.

As Kathy Peiss argues in "Going Public: Women in Nineteenth-Century Cultural History," feminists cannot simply equate the public with "the world of men." Nor can they, if and to the extent that women are no longer excluded from that world, go on to declare the public/private opposition obsolete. Activities of "production, barter, and exchange" were a part of "the world of men" which did *not* always exclude women, where "women had long been involved."[12] If we accept the public/private opposition as, in Peiss's words, "a social construction that is contested and renegotiated over time," then we will also see the line between state and market as a continual negotiation of (and over) power. Thus women's power cannot be adequately or confidently measured by their exclusion from the state; their placement on the public/private axis and their power to affect their destiny are complicated by their activities in the market, which is at least potentially a site of hidden, new, controversial, or otherwise interesting publicness. For example, women may be acting as public persons both as voters and, more unexpectedly, as shoppers. And the same holds, to follow out the argument in Andrew Ross's essay, for young African-American consumers of 2 Live Crew's music. State censorship of "obscene" popular culture may be seen as a way of regulating the market for consumer goods and entertainment — a market that, left unregulated, would probably express the often contestatory desires of its diverse publics far better than the culture otherwise available. (It should not be forgotten that the right always *has* regulated the market when its interests encouraged regulation, as in Ronald Reagan's military Keynesianism.) Without celebrating consumerism as such or surrendering to currently fashionable capitalist triumphalism, one must conclude that state intervention is not *inherently* more public — more democratic, more empowering — than the market.

In this sense, the concept of the public both challenges the cultural left, which has often spoken against consumerism, "publicity," and the media in a self-serving and complacent way, and is challenged by the cultural left. The left has largely accepted a model (both Marxist and liberal) according to which the rise and spread of the market displaces what used to be public choices into the private domain of supply and demand — private because ruled by supposedly economic laws, not to be tampered with, not open to choice. This depoliticization of the economy and social life is the reason why demands are so often made for or on behalf of the public in the most abstract sense. In effect, what is demanded is politicization itself — an agent, one might almost say *any* agent, that will choose openly instead of allowing the market to choose surreptitiously. What we accept thereby is the equivalence of the public to the political. But the formula "everything is political" is a blunt instrument. Given a political rhetoric in which appeals to or for the public stand in for appeals to actual goals and values, and in which the abstractness of this substituted public in effect replaces divisive but necessary conflict over particular goals or values, there is no room for radicalism. Expression will tend to be valued as an end in itself, and all the places where expression, scrutiny, and debate are already serving as means to various ends will pass unnoticed.

In proposing that publicness is a quantity appearing in the market as well as the state, and in numerous spots in between, I am suggesting that no sites are inherently or eternally public.[13] The lines between public and private are perpetually shifting, as are the tactical advantages and disadvantages of finding oneself on one side or the other. If, for instance, "the private is everything women have been equated with and defined in terms of *men*'s ability to have," as Catherine MacKinnon writes, and if feminists have therefore wanted to make the private into something public (open to discussion, choice, and change), it is also true, as MacKinnon goes on, that "privacy is everything women as women have never been allowed to be or to have."[14] Thus the power to define and defend a domain of privacy, a domain ordinarily protected from intrusive scrutiny, is another (and perhaps sometimes an equal) object of feminist desire and struggle. During the Senate confirmation hearings of 1991, as Nancy Fraser argues in a sequel to her essay here, Supreme Court Justice Clarence Thomas successfully managed to keep his "character" categorized as private, while inequality of power permitted Anita Hill's character to become a subject of unscrupulous public speculation.[15] Any woman who has suffered from sexual harassment in a public workplace might well prefer to see both her own and her harasser's "private" conduct, outside of that public place, ruled off-limits, rather than see herself obliged to suffer a second round of violation. Here, at least, feminist efforts would seem better aimed at the immediately disputable power to redraw the public/private line rather than at the utopian goal of effacing all such lines.

If power is a common theme that emerges from juxtaposing Weintraub's definitions number one and four, it is also there at the intersection of number two with number three. For one line of feminist thinking, the "republican virtue" model is in substance nothing but the staging of a peculiar aesthetic spectacle that absolutely and arbitrarily separates male and female roles — in other words, a gendered version of the "theatricality" model. Writing in an essay entitled "Men in Space" about the concept of "public space" (one possible translation, and the one chosen in France, for Habermas's *Öffentlichkeit*), Rosalyn Deutsche accuses the concept of a centralizing bias that is implicitly masculinist. As enacted in urban studies, she suggests, it can mean a "high ground of total knowledge" that is "gained by violently relegating others to positions of invisibility" (22).[16] According to Iris Marion Young in "Impartiality and the Civic Public," the malevolent magic of this disappearing act is the very essence of the public. For Young, the point of the concept is to make certain (white, male) bodies disappear, while it makes others into glaringly visible signs of the particular, the self-interested, the merely private: "The theoretical and practical exclusion of women from the universalist public is no mere accident or aberration." Because of the "will to unity" exhibited by "the ideal of the civic public," a public self can have "no particular history, is a member of no communities, has no body" (59–60). Hence "the ideal of the civic public as expressing the general interest, the impartial point of view of reason, itself results in exclusion. By assuming that reason stands opposed to desire, affectivity and the body, the civic public must exclude bodily and affective aspects of human existence" (66).[17]

As Young herself suggests, however, her critique holds only for the notion that there is a single, central public sphere. Since Oskar Negt and Alexander Kluge's pioneering critique of Habermas in 1972, *Öffentlichkeit und Erfahrung* (translated as *Public Sphere and Experience*), theorists have sought to pluralize and multiply the concept. Thus we now speak routinely of *alternative* public spheres and *counterpublics*. For Negt and Kluge, the working class and even children are conceived to possess, at least potentially, public spheres of their own.[18] This move, which reflects the realities of identity politics in an age of mass media, pulls us away from Habermas, but also pulls us away from any simple rejection of Habermas or "republican virtue."

Applied to this proliferation of smaller and seemingly incongruous sites, the vocabulary of the public sphere brings them into the same field of vision with traditional questions of sovereignty. It insists, like Foucault's discussions of micropolitics, that they are invested with power, however marginally or covertly. And at the same time it serves as a critique of monolithic notions of power, including that which some readers extrapolate from Foucault. This nuancing of power is a major benefit of thus rephrasing material more often and less consciously put in other vocabularies. Unlike "hegemony," the public sphere is less on the side of rule, more open to opposing views. Unlike "culture," it is more obviously a site of intersections with other classes and cultures. (In anthropology, the concept of the public sphere has been making some claim to replace the stability and borderedness implied by culture, which encourages a subject/object relation of ethnographer to those studied, with a model of dialogue in which the values of the ethnographer's group too are exposed to scrutiny.) To speak of a working-class public sphere, as Negt and Kluge do, rather than working-class culture, is to stress a site of interaction and continuing self-formation rather than a given or self-sufficient body of ideas and practices distinguishing one group from others. Public sphere invokes "identity," but does so with more emphasis on actions and their consequences than on the nature or characteristics of the actors.

In the struggle to fashion identities outside or after the givenness of "face-to-face" community, as Lauren Berlant demonstrates, both "public" invisibility and "private" visibility can be legitimate objects of cultural and political desire.[19] Miriam Hansen gives the example of the early silent cinema, which was a kind of proletarian counter-public sphere, she suggests, in part because it offered the advantages of invisibility: "More than just 'a chance to come in from the cold and sit in the dark' ... early cinema also provided a social space, a place apart from the domestic and work spheres, where people of similar background and status could find company (not necessarily of their own kin), where young working women could seek escape from the fate of their mothers."[20] Paradoxically, the public's artificial illumination can be a sort of sheltering darkness, a refuge from the tradition-heavy weight of private injury and injustice. This notion is further developed in Michael Warner's contribution to this volume. Warner writes: "The 'public' in this sense has no empirical existence, and cannot be objectified. When we understand images and texts as public, we do not gesture to a statistically measurable series of others. We make a necessarily imaginary reference to the public *as opposed to* other individuals." And yet, as Warner suggests, "the moment of special imaginary reference is always necessary." What one is to others in the glare of publicity, which by one standard might be labeled inauthenticity, can also be thought of as an escape from the burden of self-unity, from the wearisome task of holding together an explosive multiplicity of private and public selves. After all, why must Mr. Smith go to Washington and *remain* Mr. Smith there? For Warner, strategies of self-separation, "disincorporation," or "personal abstraction" offered by the media can serve as tools both of domination and of liberation.

The same point can be made about the media's other apportionings of visibility and invisibility. For Habermas, "The world fashioned by the mass media is a public sphere in appearance only."[21] Yet publicity can be a means of alternative self-fashioning for collectivities that may not otherwise or already enjoy "face-to-face" identity — sites for "public displays of gay affection," for example, and thus of self-formation for "heterogeneous publics of passion, play, and aesthetic interest."[22] As Nancy Fraser observes, even a technologically mediated publicness need not bracket desire and affection, but can be a means of stimulating and sustaining them, in the process nurturing a sense of alternative identity. Both for Berlant and for Warner, re-conceptualizing the public sphere around multiplicity means reconceptualizing sensation and sexuality as public and political — a move from the public's near-fatal abstractness toward a revitalizing of personal experience and a sexualizing of local practice. Marking a similar shift for the emotive politics of class, the authors of "Chatter in the Age of Mechanical Reproduction" — a collaborative essay by the Mass Media Group of the Committee for Cultural Studies at the City University of New York → pointedly take the example of the television talk show, which Habermas himself offered as evidence that true *Öffentlichkeit* has now disappeared.[23]

The point is not simply that the mass media have helped reinvent the notion of the public as an urban space of aesthetic self-presentation, sociability, theatricality, and pleasure. More pertinently, it is that in so doing, the media bring this notion of the public (Weintraub's model number three), which seems to have more to do with aesthetics than with politics, together with the politically participatory thrust of the "republican virtue" model (number two). For the crucial implication is that participation in the making, exchanging, and mobilizing of political opinion — the defining characteristic of "republican virtue" — has to some extent been reinvented or relocated as well, and that it is now discoverable to an unprecedented extent in the domain of culture.

There is nothing new, of course, in affirming that culture is a newly significant site of political contestation. The large history of "Western Marxism" since the 1920s and the rather smaller history of periodicals like *Social Text* since the 1970s are equally incomprehensible without that affirmation. What *is* perhaps new, on the other hand, is the pressure that the concepts of culture and the public sphere exert on each other, the way in which the latter both overlaps with and rubs up against the former. Part of the interest of the concept of the public sphere today, in other words, comes from its capacity to frame and question the notion of "cultural politics" that gives this book series its name.

In the classic form of "civic republicanism," the public is frankly hostile to cultural difference. The Habermasian ideal, which rules out anything that gets in the way of rationality, by the same token rules out differences of ethos. In Dana Polan's words: "Culture, or rather media, becomes a pure and corrupting epiphenomenon imposed on a pristine realm of rational openness in which citizens once communicated transparently." If one recognizes the political importance that culture and media have acquired, both in identity politics and more generally, then one can no longer buy into Habermas's comfortably apocalyptic scenario of the rise of the mass media as the decadence of the public. But the criterion of political power cuts two ways. If the cultural domain of style has become crucial to the constituting and mobilizing of collective (ethnic, sexual) identities, as George Yúdice argues in "For a Practical Aesthetics," there is still no a priori guarantee that cultural self-expression will spill over into further categories of political change, even (what cannot be equated with collective self-expression) into collective empowerment. And it is the question of power, finally, that sets the stakes and the framework for continuing negotiations of public and private.

On the subject of power, Habermas's vision of the public sphere is equivocal. Habermas knows, of course, that to belong to the public sphere has always meant to wield some share of the ruling power. In the medieval period, he reminds us early in *Structural Transformation*, "publicare meant to claim for the lord" (6). His later definition, however, stops short of insisting on any immediate implementation of the opinions produced by the public sphere's free and spirited conversation. The public sphere is "a forum in which the private people, come together to form a public, readied themselves to *compel* public authority to legitimate itself before public opinion" (25–26). It is the place not for the compulsion itself, but only for *readying* oneself to compel. Even that compulsion is only a compulsion for the authorities to legitimate themselves, that is, to engage in further dialogue — not a compulsion to bestow universal suffrage, for example, let alone to redistribute wealth. And yet how can Habermas explain even this anticipatory, as yet unused ability to exert compulsion upon the government without examining the power that those who occupy the public sphere draw from historically specifiable sources, sources other than their wit — from their cultural capital, from their gender and race, from the Industrial Revolution, and so on?[24] For Habermas, as many critics have pointed out, the golden age of the public sphere is the long moment of bourgeois revolution, which is also, and perhaps for that reason, the moment when the press seemed to come closest to exercising power. (For Lippmann, who like Habermas comes out of journalism, the role of the press during the Progressive Era is perhaps a parallel.) Yet this is a power that, while riding piggyback on a rising class, pretends not to be or even to touch power.

How then can the public sphere be made to face the issue of power more directly? For all his indifference to cultural difference, Habermas hesitates before power, mimicking one temptation of identity politics — the valuing of expression for its own sake. That before which he hesitates — the bourgeois revolution as a moment when the bourgeoisie and its press seemed briefly able to speak for everyone — is a power that seems to derive from centralization or totalization. But if this were the source of the public sphere's power — a clause that must I think remain in the conditional — then would the irreducible multiplicity of identity politics mean a resignation to lesser goals, or even to powerlessness? Within the concept of the public sphere, there is an unresolved and perhaps unresolvable tension, between a tight, authoritative singleness (the public as object of a quest for a universal collective subject or a privileged arena of struggle) and a more relaxed, decentered pluralism (publicness as something spread liberally through many irreducibly different collectivities). This tension reproduces the problematic — central to *Social Text* since its inception — of the location of "politics" itself, which is asserted to be both "everywhere" (hence the warrant for specifically *cultural* politics) and more intensely and significantly there at certain times, places, and levels than at others.[25] Faced with an onerous history of distinct spheres — "public" as a term that relegated women to domestic privacy — can we opt for an indistinction in which women (and men) are "always already" in public?[26] Negt and Kluge, faithful in this to Habermas, allow the persistently singularizing or universalizing pressure of the term "public" to throw the value of the separate "camp" into question. On the one hand, they dissent from what has become, in Kluge's phrase, a "universal provincialism." On the other, they declare, "When anyone says something is a whole, we don't trust him."[27] The contradictory appreciations of Negt and Kluge included here, by Fredric Jameson (originally published in *October*) and by Tom Keenan, elaborate this unresolved ambivalence.

One effect of this irresolution should be to send us back to the word *power* itself, a god-term in need of further analysis if ever there was one. (Here Nancy Fraser's distinction between weak publics, concerned with opinion formation, and strong publics, concerned with decision making, is an important step.) Another, related effect is to throw back into question that reflex anti-universalism from which the notion of the public, too, has suffered. Linda Zerilli's discussion of Monique Wittig insists on the need for the "universalizing" emphasis that the term "public" stands in for. Without such emphases, she argues, public space will be filled, uncontested, by others — for example, by the implied norm of heterosexuality. Yet this argument too leaves questions in its wake. Is it true that *some* norm, however implicit, is always in effect? Is the norm-embodying public, like power in traditional formulation, a vacuum-abhorring space that must always be filled one way or the other? Or must we, in order to conceive both terms more accurately, be able to conceive their absence — a society in which the normative, totalizing sense of the public could remain vacant or suspended?

In *Beyond Feminist Aesthetics*, Rita Felski argues, along lines like Zerilli's, that "the present status and influence of the women's movement cannot be adequately accounted for by the notion of a unified and autonomous counter-public sphere which remains separate from the rest of society. Given the complex interpenetrations of state and society in late capitalism, one can no longer postulate the ideal of a public sphere which can function outside existing commercial and state institutions and at the same time claim an influential and representative function as a forum for oppositional activity and debate."[28] As David Harvey suggests in *The Condition of Postmodernity*, capitalism in its flexible postmodern form combines connectedness with individuation. Yet this does not mean, on the other hand, that the individuality of all social groups is produced by capitalism, still less that such individuality must serve capitalism's interests. Nor does it mean that any identity-forming counter-public sphere that does not similarly combine local difference with more-than-local affiliation must remain politically ineffective. Analytically, everything is always connected to everything else. Yet as should be obvious, not all analytic connectedness can or even should find corresponding expression in conscious, voluntary political associations of the sort that the public sphere indicates. Even if capitalism is a whole, it remains to be seen whether it can be seriously challenged only in analogously holistic political forms, rather than in quite asymmetrical ones. No overarching adjudication seems possible here. After a certain point, the subject of the public sphere must become a matter of local investigations into particular collectivities and practical politics.

What then of the attempt to seize "the complex interpenetrations of state and society in late capitalism" not on a national but on an *international* scale? Can the notion of the public sphere be internationalized? In a sense, this is nothing more than the challenge that already faced John Dewey in the 1920s: the problematic possibility, to quote Craig Calhoun's commentary on Tiananmen Square, "of a critical public discourse which escapes the limits of face-to-face interaction. This means, in part, finding ways to make the space-transcending mass media supportive of public life."[29] On the other hand, scale matters. When Carol Breckenridge and Arjun Appadurai named their new transnational journal *Public Culture*, they clearly pulled off a brilliant titling coup. For it is far from obvious that the word *public* can expand to cover the far-flung, multiethnic, dramatically diversified materials that the journal gathers in its pages. How many hours would the day have to have in order for a hypothetical cosmopolitan or a "citizen of the world" to acquire the necessary competence for "public" discussion or decision making on this scale? If the public is something of a phantom under the most manageable of circumstances, when stretched so far it may seem almost invisible.

Yet in Appadurai's hands, the centripetal pressure of the concept usefully forces the mind beyond a stunned appreciation of diversity. Appadurai's essay (originally printed in *Public Culture*) takes up the challenge of reconciling the new density of transnational interactions and syntheses, on the one hand, with the seemingly irreducible heterogeneity of their occasions and effects, on the other. Distinguishing five dimensions of "global cultural flow," or global public culture — ethnoscapes, mediascapes, technoscapes, finanscapes, and ideoscapes — it puts the emphasis on their disjuncture. Flows of ideas and media, for example, do not slavishly follow flows of technology and finance capital, as simple narratives of "global Americanization" once seemed to propose. In a sense, this is a global argument for the relative autonomy of culture. And by the same token, if still more implicitly, it is an argument that the distribution of world power has shifted, and with it the possibilities of transnational democratic interchange. In the immediate aftermath of the cold war, before the North has settled into a definitive, equally polar antagonism with the South, it will be interesting to see whether room indeed exists for an international public sphere — for instance, in the universalizing language of "human rights" — in which decolonization would become a discursive reality.

Unlike the usual narratives of decline, Appadurai's discussion is of a public sphere that is only now for the first time coming into being, if indeed the term remains pertinent. After the televised spectacle of the Gulf War and the Thomas confirmation hearings, the multimedia onslaught against multiculturalism in the schools, the presidential campaign of 1992 that is just beginning as I write — that is, in a time when it is hard to find grounds for optimism about the immediate possibilities for a democratic publicity — this is perhaps the best note to sound in conclusion: the public sphere is an unfulfilled task — in Homi Bhabha's words, a "conversation we have to open up," which would be one step toward the still more utopian goal of forging a community that would take "the complex, often incommensurable fate of the migrant as the basis for a redefinition of the metropolitan public sphere."[30] If it cannot resolve the contradictions that continue to swirl around a concept that must remain both unacceptable and necessary, this volume does try to set tasks like this before the reader, thus pushing the topic of the phantom public and its problems into a less backward-looking conversation.

NOTES

1. Walter Lippmann, *The Phantom Public* (New York: Macmillan, 1927), 20–21.

2. Jürgen Habermas, *The Structural Transformation of the Public Sphere*, trans. Thomas Burger with Frederick Lawrence (Cambridge, Mass.: MIT Press, 1989). Even some of Habermas's more sympathetic critics have conceded that his tale of a public sphere gained and lost should be taken less as an account of historical reality than as a usefully mobilizing fiction. But the usefulness of this fiction as an instantly available appeal against the status quo has to be balanced against the demobilizing effect of making the status quo seem an indivisible, immovable monolith.

3. As the most frequent translation of Habermas's *Öffentlichkeit*, or "publicity," the English phrase "public sphere" has a music that recalls the noun's early celestial connotations.

4. Habermas, *Structural Transformation*: "Since the Renaissance this model of the Hellenic public sphere . . . has shared with everything else considered 'classical' a peculiarly normative power" (4).

5. Quoted in Robert B. Westbrook, *John Dewey and American Democracy* (Ithaca, N.Y.: Cornell University Press, 1991), 297.

6. In Lippmann's antipopulist tradition is, for instance, Harold Rosenberg's

remark that "the public continues to be regarded as a primitive organism, a kind of untouched Nature, with which the fine arts ought constantly to commune." Harold Rosenberg, *The Tradition of the New* (New York: Horizon, 1959), 58.

7. John Dewey, *The Public and Its Problems* (Chicago: Gateway, [1927] 1946), 213.

8. Quoted in Westbrook, *John Dewey*, 308.

9. Ferdinand Tönnies, *Community and Society*, trans. Charles P. Loomis (East Lansing: Michigan State University Press, 1957). Ferdinand Tönnies, *Kritik der öffentlichen Meinung* (Berlin: Springer, 1922). Carl Schmitt, *The Concept of the Political*, trans. and with an introduction by George Schwab (New Brunswick, N.J.: Rutgers University Press, 1976). Hannah Arendt, *The Human Condition* (Chicago: University of Chicago Press, 1958). It would be interesting to pair Arendt with Raymond Williams's *Culture and Society*, which came out in the same year and is also mentioned in Habermas's *Structural Transformation*. Another interesting parallel to Lippmann is F. R Leavis, whose doctoral dissertation, submitted in 1924, was entitled "The Relationship of Journalism to Literature."

10. Jacques Derrida, "La démocratie ajournée," in *L'Autre Cap* (Paris: Minuit, 1991), 103. I have drawn on the translation by Pascale-Anne Brault and Michael B. Nass, *The Other Heading: Reflections on Today's Europe*, which has not yet been published.

11. Jeff Weintraub, "The Theory and Politics of the Public/Private Distinction," forthcoming in essay and book form. I am grateful to Craig Calhoun for the reference and to Jeff Weintraub for permission to quote.

12. Kathy Peiss, "Going Public: Women in Nineteenth-Century Cultural History," *American Literary History* 3 (Winter 1991): 817–28.

13. According to Habermas, there has indeed been a mixing of state and market, public and private, but this mixing spells the end of any oppositional function for the public sphere– and thus of the public sphere itself in the true sense. "Refeudalization" occurs when, "with the linking of public and private realms, not only certain functions in the sphere of commerce and social labor are taken over by political authorities but conversely political functions are taken over by societal powers" (231). As the scope of the public sphere expands, its critical function contracts.

14. Catherine MacKinnon, "Feminism, Marxism, Method, and the State: Toward a Feminist Jurisprudence," *Signs* 8 (1983): 635–58.

15. Nancy Fraser, "Sex, Lies, and the Public Sphere: Some Reflections on the Confirmation of Clarence Thomas," *Critical Inquiry* 18 (Spring 1992): 595–612.

16. Rosalyn Deutsche, "Men in Space," *Artforum*, February 1990, 21–23.

17. Iris Marion Young, "Impartiality and the Civic Public: Some Implications of Feminist Critiques of Moral and Political Theory," in *Feminism as Critique*, ed. Seyla Benhabib and Drucilla Cornell (Minneapolis: University of Minnesota Press, 1987).

18. Oskar Negt and Alexander Kluge, *Public Sphere and Experience: Toward an Organizational Analysis of Proletariat and Middle-Class Public Opinion* (Minneapolis: University of Minnesota Press, forthcoming).

19. To be fair, I should say that Berlant shows how capitalist enterprise, even in the hands of (white) women, liberates them into invisibility only by generalizing the visibility of the black woman as their trademark.

20. Miriam Hansen, "Early Silent Cinema: Whose Public Sphere?" *New German Critique* 29 (1983): 159.

21. *Structural Transformation*, 171.

22. Young, "Impartiality," 75.

23. *Structural Transformation*, 164.

24. See Alan Keenan, "Promises, Promises: The Abyss of Freedom and the Foundation of the Political in Hannah Arendt," unpublished manuscript, on the paradox of the public as both freedom and the power that founds freedom.

25. Richard Rorty's strangely disingenuous attack on the notion of "cultural politics" ("Intellectuals in Politics," *Dissent*, Fall 1991, 483–90) in the name of "the poor" seems of a piece with his liberal loyalty to an unproblematized version of the public/private distinction. See Richard Rorty, *Contingency, Irony, and Solidarity* (Cambridge: Cambridge University Press, 1989), 80–87.

26. See the critique of the phrase "always already" in Diana Fuss, *Essentially Speaking* (New York: Routledge, 1989).

27. Alexander Kluge, interview with Stuart Liebman, *October* 46 (Fall 1988): 44, 46.

28. Rita Felski, *Beyond Feminist Aesthetics: Feminist Literature and Social Change* (Cambridge, Mass.: Harvard University Press, 1989), 171.

29. Craig Calhoun, "Tiananmen, Television, and the Public Sphere," *Public Culture* 2, no. 1 (Fall 1989): 68–69.

30. Homi Bhabha, "Novel Metropolis," *The New Statesman* 16 (February 1990).

Rethinking the Public Sphere
A Contribution to the Critique of
Actually Existing Democracy
Nancy Fraser

Today in the United States we hear a great deal of ballyhoo about "the triumph of liberal democracy" and even "the end of history."[1] Yet there is still a great deal to object to in our own "actually existing democracy," and the project of a critical social theory of the limits of democracy in late capitalist societies remains as relevant as ever. In fact, this project seems to me to have acquired a new urgency at a time when "liberal democracy" is being touted as the ne plus ultra of social systems for countries that are emerging from Soviet-style state socialism, Latin American military dictatorships, and southern African regimes of racial domination.

Those of us who remain committed to theorizing the limits of democracy in late capitalist societies will find in the work of Jürgen Habermas an indispensable resource. I mean the concept of "the public sphere," originally elaborated in his 1962 book, *The Structural Transformation of the Public Sphere*, and subsequently re-situated but never abandoned in his later work.[2]

The political and theoretical importance of this idea is easy to explain. Habermas's concept of the public sphere provides a way of circumventing some confusions that have plagued progressive social movements and the political theories associated with them. Take, for example, the long-standing failure in the dominant wing of the socialist and Marxist tradition to appreciate the full force of the distinction between the apparatuses of the state, on the one hand, and public arenas of citizen discourse and association, on the other. All too often it was assumed in this tradition that to subject the economy to

1

the control of the socialist state was to subject it to the control of the socialist citizenry. Of course that was not so. But the conflation of the state apparatus with the public sphere of discourse and association provided ballast to processes whereby the socialist vision became institutionalized in an authoritarian statist form instead of in a participatory democratic form. The result has been to jeopardize the very idea of socialist democracy.

A second problem, albeit one that has so far been much less historically momentous and certainly less tragic, is a confusion one encounters at times in contemporary feminisms. I mean a confusion that involves the use of the very same expression "the public sphere," but in a sense that is less precise and less useful than Habermas's. This expression has been used by many feminists to refer to everything that is outside the domestic or familial sphere. Thus, "the public sphere" in this usage conflates at least three analytically distinct things: the state, the official economy of paid employment, and arenas of public discourse.[3] Now, it should not be thought that the conflation of these three things is a merely theoretical issue. On the contrary, it has practical political consequences, for example, when agitational campaigns against misogynist cultural representations are confounded with programs for state censorship, or when struggles to deprivatize housework and child care are equated with their commodification. In both these cases, the result is to occlude the question of whether to subject gender issues to the logic of the market and/or the administrative state is to promote the liberation of women.

The idea of "the public sphere" in Habermas's sense is a conceptual resource that can help overcome such problems. It designates a theater in modern societies in which political participation is enacted through the medium of talk. It is the space in which citizens deliberate about their common affairs, hence, an institutionalized arena of discursive interaction. This arena is conceptually distinct from the state; it a site for the production and circulation of discourses that can in principle be critical of the state. The public sphere in Habermas's sense is also conceptually distinct from the official economy; it is not an arena of market relations but rather one of discursive relations, a theater for debating and deliberating rather than for buying and selling. Thus, this concept of the public sphere permits us to keep in view the distinctions between state apparatuses, economic markets, and democratic associations, distinctions that are essential to democratic theory.

For these reasons, I am going to take as a basic premise for this essay that something like Habermas's idea of the public sphere is indispensable to critical social theory and to democratic political practice. I assume that no attempt to understand the limits of actually existing late capitalist democracy can succeed without in some way or another making use of it. I assume that the same goes for urgently needed constructive efforts to project alternative models of democracy.

If you will grant me that the general idea of the public sphere is indispensable to critical theory, then I shall go on to argue that the specific form in which Habermas has elaborated this idea is not wholly satisfactory. On the contrary, I contend that his analysis of the public sphere needs to undergo some critical interrogation and reconstruction if it is to yield a category capable of theorizing the limits of actually existing democracy.

Let me remind you that the subtitle of *Structural Transformation* is *An Inquiry into a Category of Bourgeois Society*. The object of the inquiry is the rise and decline of a historically specific and limited form of the public sphere, which Habermas calls the "liberal model of the bourgeois public sphere." The aim is to identify the conditions that made possible this type of public sphere and to chart their devolution. The upshot is an argument that, under altered conditions of late-twentieth-century "welfare state mass democracy," the bourgeois or liberal model of the public sphere is no longer feasible. Some new form of public sphere is required to salvage that arena's critical function and to institutionalize democracy.

Oddly, Habermas stops short of developing a new, postbourgeois model of the public sphere. Moreover, he never explicitly problematizes some dubious assumptions that underlie the bourgeois model. As a result, we are left at the end of *Structural Transformation* without a conception of the public sphere that is sufficiently distinct from the bourgeois conception to serve the needs of critical theory today.

That, at any rate, is the thesis I intend to argue. In order to make my case, I shall proceed as follows: I shall begin, in section one, by juxtaposing Habermas's account of the structural transformation of the public sphere to an alternative account that can be pieced together from some recent revisionist historiography. Then I shall identify four assumptions underlying the bourgeois conception of public sphere, as Habermas describes it, which this newer historiography renders suspect. Next, in the following four sections, I shall examine each of these assumptions in turn. Finally, in a brief conclusion, I shall draw together some strands from these critical discussions that point toward an alternative, postbourgeois conception of the public sphere.

The Public Sphere: Alternative Histories, Competing Conceptions

Let me begin by sketching some highlights of Habermas's account of the structural transformation of the public sphere. According to Habermas, the idea of a public sphere is that of a body of "private persons" assembled to discuss matters of "public concern" or "common interest." This idea acquired force and reality in early modern Europe in the constitution of "bourgeois public spheres" as counterweights to absolutist states. These publics aimed to mediate between "society" and the state by holding the state accountable to "society" via "publicity." At first this meant requiring that information about state functioning be made accessible so that state activities would be subject to critical scrutiny and the force of "public opinion." Later, it meant transmitting the considered "general interest" of "bourgeois society" to the state via forms of legally guaranteed free speech, free press, and free assembly, and eventually through the parliamentary institutions of representative government.

Thus, at one level, the idea of the public sphere designated an institutional mechanism for "rationalizing" political domination by rendering states accountable to (some of) the citizenry. At another level, it designated a specific kind of discursive interaction. Here the public sphere connoted an ideal of unrestricted rational discussion of public matters. The discussion was to be open and accessible to all; merely private interests were to be inadmissible; inequalities of status were to be bracketed; and discussants were to deliberate as peers. The result of such discussion would be "public opinion" in the strong sense of a consensus about the common good.

According to Habermas, the full utopian potential of the bourgeois conception of the public sphere was never realized in practice. The claim to open access in particular was not made good. Moreover, the bourgeois conception of the public sphere was premised on a social order in which the state was sharply differentiated from the newly privatized market economy; it was this clear separation of "society" and state that was supposed to underpin a form of public discussion that excluded "private interests." But these conditions eventually eroded as nonbourgeois strata gained access to the public sphere. Then, "the social question" came to the fore; society was polarized by class struggle, and the public fragmented into a mass of competing interest groups. Street demonstrations and back room, brokered compromises among private interests replaced reasoned public debate about the common good. Finally, with the emergence of "welfare state mass democracy," society and the state became mutually intertwined; publicity in the sense of critical scrutiny of the state gave way to public relations, mass-mediated staged displays, and the manufacture and manipulation of public opinion.

Now, let me juxtapose to this sketch of Habermas's account an alternative account that I shall piece together from some recent revisionist historiography. Briefly, scholars like Joan Landes, Mary Ryan, and Geoff Eley contend that Habermas's account idealizes the liberal public sphere. They argue that, despite the rhetoric of publicity and accessibility, that official public sphere rested on, indeed was importantly constituted by, a number of significant exclusions. For Landes, the key axis of exclusion is gender; she argues that the ethos of the new republican public sphere in France was constructed in deliberate opposition to that of a more woman-friendly salon culture that the republicans stigmatized as "artificial," "effeminate," and "aristocratic." Consequently, a new, austere style of public speech and behavior was promoted, a style deemed "rational," "virtuous," and "manly." In this way, masculinist gender constructs were built into the very conception of the republican public sphere, as was a logic that led, at the height of Jacobin rule, to the formal exclusion from political life of women.[4] Here the republicans drew on classical traditions that cast femininity and publicity as oxymorons; the depth of such traditions can be gauged in the etymological connection between "public" and "pubic," a graphic trace of the fact that in the ancient world possession of a penis was a requirement for speaking in public. (A similar link is preserved, incidentally, in the etymological connection between "testimony" and "testicle.")[5]

Extending Landes's argument, Geoff Eley contends that exclusionary operations were essential to liberal public spheres not only in France but also in England and Germany, and that in all these countries gender exclusions were linked to other exclusions rooted in processes of class formation. In all these countries, he claims, the soil that nourished the liberal public sphere was "civil society," the emerging new congeries of voluntary associations that sprung up in what came to be known as "the age of societies." But this network of clubs and associations — philanthropic, civic, professional, and cultural — was anything but accessible to everyone. On the contrary, it was the arena, the training ground, and eventually the power base of a stratum of bourgeois men, who were coming to see themselves as a "universal class" and preparing to assert their fitness to govern. Thus, the elaboration of a distinctive culture of civil society and of an associated public sphere was implicated in the process of bourgeois class formation; its practices and ethos were markers of "distinction" in Pierre Bourdieu's sense,[6] ways of defining an emergent elite, setting it off from the older aristocratic elites it was intent on displacing, on the one hand, and from the various popular and plebeian strata it aspired to rule, on the other. This process of distinction, moreover, helps explain the exacerbation of sexism characteristic of the liberal public sphere; new gender norms enjoining feminine domesticity and a sharp separation of public and private spheres functioned as key signifiers of bourgeois difference from both higher and lower social strata. It is a measure of the eventual success of this bourgeois project that these norms later became hegemonic, sometimes imposed on, sometimes embraced by, broader segments of society.[7]

Now, there is a remarkable irony here, one that Habermas's account of the rise of the public sphere fails fully to appreciate.[8] A discourse of publicity touting accessibility, rationality, and the suspension of status hierarchies is itself deployed as a strategy of distinction. Of course, in and of itself, this irony does not fatally compromise the discourse of publicity; that discourse can be, indeed has been, differently deployed in different circumstances and contexts. Nevertheless, it does suggest that the relationship between publicity and status is more complex than Habermas intimates, that declaring a deliberative arena to be a space where extant status distinctions are bracketed and neutralized is not sufficient to make it so.

Moreover, the problem is not only that Habermas idealizes the liberal public sphere but also that he fails to examine other, non-liberal, nonbourgeois, competing public spheres. Or rather, it is precisely because he fails to examine these other public spheres that he ends up idealizing the liberal public sphere.[9] Mary Ryan documents the variety of ways in which nineteenth-century North American women of various classes and ethnicities constructed access routes to public political life, even despite their exclusion from the official public sphere. In the case of elite bourgeois women, this involved building a counter-civil society of alternative woman-only voluntary associations, including philanthropic and moral reform societies. In some respects, these associations aped the all-male societies built by these women's fathers and grandfathers; yet in other respects the women were innovating, since they creatively used the heretofore quintessentially "private" idioms of domesticity and motherhood precisely as springboards for public activity. Meanwhile, for some less privileged women, access to public life came through participation in supporting roles in male-dominated working-class protest activities. Still other women found public outlets in street protests and parades. Finally, women's rights advocates publicly contested both women's exclusion from the official public sphere and the privatization of gender politics.[10]

Ryan's study shows that, even in the absence of formal political incorporation through suffrage, there were a variety of ways of gaining access to public life and a multiplicity of public arenas. Thus, the view that women were excluded from the public sphere turns out to be ideological; it rests on a class- and gender-biased notion of publicity, one that accepts at face value the bourgeois public's claim to be *the* public. In fact, the historiography of Ryan and others demonstrates that the bourgeois public was never *the* public. On the contrary, virtually contemporaneous with the bourgeois public there arose a host of competing counterpublics, including nationalist publics, popular peasant publics, elite women's publics, and working-class publics. Thus, there were competing publics from the start, not just from the late nineteenth and twentieth centuries, as Habermas implies.[11]

Moreover, not only were there always a plurality of competing publics but the relations between bourgeois publics and other publics were always conflictual. Virtually from the beginning, counterpublics contested the exclusionary norms of the bourgeois public, elaborating alternative styles of political behavior and alternative norms of public speech. Bourgeois publics, in turn, excoriated these alternatives and deliberately sought to block broader participation. As Eley puts it, "The emergence of a bourgeois public was never defined solely by the struggle against absolutism and traditional authority, but ... addressed the problem of popular containment as well. The public sphere was always constituted by conflict."[12]

In general, this revisionist historiography suggests a much darker view of the bourgeois public sphere than the one that emerges from Habermas's study. The exclusions and conflicts that appeared as accidental trappings from his perspective, in the revisionists' view become constitutive. The result is a gestalt switch that alters the very meaning of the public sphere. We can no longer assume that the bourgeois conception of the public sphere was simply an unrealized utopian ideal; it was also a masculinist ideological notion that functioned to legitimate an emergent form of class rule. Therefore, Eley draws a Gramscian moral from the story: the official bourgeois public sphere is the institutional vehicle for a major historical transformation in the nature of political domination. This is the shift from a repressive mode of domination to a hegemonic one, from rule based primarily on acquiescence to superior force to rule based primarily on consent supplemented with some measure of repression.[13] The important point is that this new mode of political domination, like the older one, secures the ability of one stratum of society to rule the rest. The official public sphere, then, was — indeed, is — the prime institutional site for the construction of the consent that defines the new, hegemonic mode of domination.[14]

Now, what conclusions should we draw from this conflict of historical interpretations? Should we conclude that the very concept of the public sphere is a piece of bourgeois masculinist ideology, so thoroughly compromised that it can shed no genuinely critical light on the limits of actually existing democracy? Or should we conclude, rather, that the public sphere was a good idea that unfortunately was not realized in practice but that retains some emancipatory force? In short, is the idea of the public sphere an instrument of domination or a utopian ideal?

Well, perhaps both. But actually neither. I contend that both of those conclusions are too extreme and unsupple to do justice to the material I have been discussing.[15] Instead of endorsing either one of them, I want to propose a more nuanced alternative. I shall argue that the revisionist historiography neither undermines nor vindicates "*the* concept of the public sphere" *simpliciter*, but that it calls into question four assumptions that are central to a specific — *bourgeois masculinist* — conception of the public sphere, at least as Habermas describes it. These are as follows:

1. the assumption that it is possible for interlocutors in a public sphere to bracket status differentials and to deliberate "as if" they were social equals; the assumption, therefore, that societal equality is not a necessary condition for political democracy;
2. the assumption that the proliferation of a multiplicity of competing publics is necessarily a step away from, rather than toward, greater democracy, and that a single, comprehensive public sphere is always preferable to a nexus of multiple publics;
3. the assumption that discourse in public spheres should be restricted to deliberation about the common good, and that the appearance of "private interests" and "private issues" is always undesirable;
4. the assumption that a functioning democratic public sphere requires a sharp separation between civil society and the state.

Let me consider each of these in turn.

Open Access, Participatory Parity, and Social Equality

Habermas's account of the bourgeois conception of the public sphere stresses its claim to be open and accessible to all. Indeed, this idea of open access is one of the central meanings of the norm of publicity. Of course, we know, both from the revisionist history and from Habermas's account, that the bourgeois public's claim to full accessibility was not in fact realized. Women of all classes and ethnicities were excluded from official political participation precisely on the basis of ascribed gender status, while plebeian men were formally excluded by property qualifications. Moreover, in many cases, women and men of color of all classes were excluded on racial grounds.

Now, what are we to make of this historical fact of the nonrealization in practice of the bourgeois public sphere's ideal of open access? One approach is to conclude that the ideal itself remains unaffected, since it is possible in principle to overcome these exclusions. And, in fact, it was only a matter of time before formal exclusions based on gender, property, and race were eliminated.

This is convincing enough as far as it goes, but it does not go far enough. The question of open access cannot be reduced without remainder to the presence or absence of formal exclusions. It requires us to look also at the process of discursive interaction within formally inclusive public arenas. Here we should recall that the bourgeois conception of the public sphere requires bracketing inequalities of status. This public sphere was to be an arena in which interlocutors would set aside such characteristics as differences in birth and fortune and speak to one another as if they were social and economic peers. The operative phrase here is "as if." In fact, the social inequalities among the interlocutors were not eliminated, but only bracketed.

But were they really effectively bracketed? The revisionist historiography suggests they were not. Rather, discursive interaction within the bourgeois public sphere was governed by protocols of style and decorum that were themselves correlates and markers of status inequality. These functioned informally to marginalize women and members of the plebeian classes and to prevent them from participating as peers.

Here we are talking about informal impediments to participatory parity that can persist even after everyone is formally and legally licensed to participate. That these constitute a more serious challenge to the bourgeois conception of the public sphere can be seen from a familiar contemporary example. Feminist research has documented a syndrome that many of us have observed in faculty meetings and other mixed-sex deliberative bodies: men tend to interrupt women more than women interrupt men; men also tend to speak more than women, taking more turns and longer turns; and women's interventions are more often ignored or not responded to than men's. In response to the sorts of experiences documented in this research, an important strand of feminist political theory has claimed that deliberation can serve as a mask for domination. Theorists like Jane Mansbridge have argued that

> the transformation of "I" into "we" brought about through political deliberation can easily mask subtle forms of control. Even the language people use as they reason together usually favors one way of seeing things and discourages others. Subordinate groups sometimes cannot find the right voice or words to express their thoughts, and when they do, they discover they are not heard. [They] are silenced, encouraged to keep their wants inchoate, and heard to say "yes" when what they have said is "no."[16]

Mansbridge rightly notes that many of these feminist insights into ways in which deliberation can serve as a mask for domination extend beyond gender to other kinds of unequal relations, like those based on class or ethnicity. They alert us to the ways in which social inequalities can infect deliberation, even in the absence of any formal exclusions.

Here I think we encounter a very serious difficulty with the bourgeois conception of the public sphere. Insofar as the bracketing of social inequalities in deliberation means proceeding as if they do not exist when they do, this does not foster participatory parity. On the contrary, such bracketing usually works to the advantage of dominant groups in society and to the disadvantage of subordinates. In most cases, it would be more appropriate to unbracket inequalities in the sense of explicitly thematizing them — a point that accords with the spirit of Habermas's later "communicative ethics."

The misplaced faith in the efficacy of bracketing suggests another flaw in the bourgeois conception. This conception assumes that a public sphere is or can be a space of zero-degree culture, so utterly bereft of any specific ethos as to accommodate with perfect neutrality and equal ease interventions expressive of any and every cultural ethos. But this assumption is counterfactual, and not for reasons that are merely accidental. In stratified societies, unequally empowered social groups tend to develop unequally valued cultural styles. The result is the development of powerful informal pressures that marginalize the contributions of members of subordinated groups both in everyday life contexts and in official public spheres.[17] Moreover, these pressures are amplified, rather than mitigated, by the peculiar political economy of the bourgeois public sphere. In this public sphere, the media that constitute the material support for the circulation of views are privately owned and operated for profit. Consequently, subordinated social groups usually lack equal access to the material means of equal participation.[18] Thus, political economy enforces structurally what culture accomplishes informally.

If we take these considerations seriously, then we should be led to entertain serious doubts about a conception of the public sphere that purports to bracket, rather than to eliminate, structural social inequalities. We should question whether it is possible even in principle for interlocutors to deliberate as if they were social peers in specially designated discursive arenas, when these discursive arenas are situated in a larger societal context that is pervaded by structural relations of dominance and subordination.

What is at stake here is the autonomy of specifically political institutions vis-à-vis the surrounding societal context. Now, one salient feature that distinguishes liberalism from some other political-theoretical orientations is that liberalism assumes the autonomy of the political in a very strong form. Liberal political theory assumes that it is possible to organize a democratic form of political life on the basis of socioeconomic and sociosexual structures that generate systemic inequalities. For liberals, then, the problem of democracy becomes the problem of how to insulate political processes from what are considered to be nonpolitical or prepolitical processes, those characteristic, for example, of the economy, the family, and informal everyday life. The problem for liberals, thus, is how to strengthen the barriers separating political institutions that are supposed to instantiate relations of equality from economic, cultural, and sociosexual institutions that are premised on systemic relations of inequality.[19] Yet the weight of circumstance suggests that in order to have a public sphere in which interlocutors can deliberate as peers, it is not sufficient merely to bracket social inequality. Instead, it is a necessary condition for participatory parity that systemic social inequalities be eliminated. This does not mean that everyone must have exactly the same income, but it does require the sort of rough equality that is inconsistent with systemically generated relations of dominance and subordination. *Pace* liberalism, then, political democracy requires substantive social equality.[20]

So far, I have been arguing that the bourgeois conception of the public sphere is inadequate insofar as it supposes that social equality is not a necessary condition for participatory parity in public spheres. What follows from this for the critique of actually existing democracy? One task for critical theory is to render visible the ways in which societal inequality infects formally inclusive existing public spheres and taints discursive interaction within them.

Equality, Diversity, and Multiple Publics

So far I have been discussing what we might call "intrapublic relations," that is, the character and quality of discursive interactions within a given public sphere. Now I want to consider what we might call "interpublic relations," that is, the character of interactions among different publics.

Let me begin by recalling that Habermas's account stresses the singularity of the bourgeois conception of the public sphere, its claim to be *the* public arena in the singular. In addition, his narrative tends in this respect to be faithful to that conception, casting the emergence of additional publics as a late development symptomatic of fragmentation and decline. This narrative, then, like the bourgeois conception itself, is informed by an underlying evaluative assumption, namely, that the institutional confinement of public life to a single, overarching public sphere is a positive and desirable state of affairs, whereas the proliferation of a multiplicity of publics represents a departure from, rather than an advance toward, democracy. It is this normative assumption that I now want to scrutinize. In this section, I shall assess the relative merits of single, comprehensive publics versus multiple publics in two kinds of modern societies — stratified societies and egalitarian multicultural societies.[21]

First, let me consider the case of stratified societies, by which I mean societies whose basic institutional framework generates unequal social groups in structural relations of dominance and subordination. I have already argued that in such societies, full parity of participation in public debate and deliberation is not within the reach of possibility. Two questions are to be addressed here, then: What form of public life comes closest to approaching that ideal? What institutional arrangements will best help narrow the gap in participatory parity between dominant and subordinate groups?

I contend that, in stratified societies, arrangements that accommodate contestation among a plurality of competing publics better promote the ideal of participatory parity than does a single, comprehensive, overarching public sphere. This follows from the previous section, where I argued that it is not possible to insulate special discursive arenas from the effects of societal inequality; and that where societal inequality persists, deliberative processes in public spheres will tend to operate to the advantage of dominant groups and to the disadvantage of subordinates. Now I want to add that these effects are exacerbated where there is only a single, comprehensive public sphere. In that case, members of subordinated groups have no arenas for deliberation among themselves about their needs, objectives, and strategies. They have no venues in which to undertake communicative processes that are not, as it were, under the supervision of dominant groups. In this situation, they are less likely than otherwise to "find the right voice or words to express their thoughts," and more likely than otherwise "to keep their wants inchoate." This renders them less able than otherwise to articulate and defend their interests in the comprehensive public sphere. They are less able than otherwise to expose modes of deliberation that mask domination by "absorbing the less powerful into a false 'we' that reflects the more powerful."

This argument gains additional support from the revisionist historiography of the public sphere, up to and including very recent developments. This history records that members of subordinated social groups — women, workers, peoples of color, and gays and lesbians — have repeatedly found it advantageous to constitute alternative publics. I propose to call these *subaltern counterpublics* in order to signal that they are parallel discursive arenas where members of subordinated social groups invent and circulate counterdiscourses, so as to formulate oppositional interpretations of their identities, interests, and needs.[22] Perhaps the most striking example is the late-twentieth-century U.S. feminist subaltern counterpublic, with its variegated array of journals, bookstores, publishing companies, film and video distribution networks, lecture series, research centers, academic programs, conferences, conventions, festivals, and local meeting places. In this public sphere, feminist women have invented new terms for describing social reality, including "sexism," "the double shift," "sexual harassment," and "marital, date, and acquaintance rape." Armed with such language, we have recast our needs and identities, thereby reducing, although not eliminating, the extent of our disadvantage in official public spheres.[23]

Let me not be misunderstood. I do not mean to suggest that subaltern counterpublics are always necessarily virtuous; some of them, alas, are explicitly antidemocratic and antiegalitarian; and even those with democratic and egalitarian intentions are not always above practicing their own modes of informal exclusion and marginalization. Still, insofar as these counterpublics emerge in response to exclusions within dominant publics, they help expand discursive space. In principle, assumptions that were previously exempt from contestation will now have to be publicly argued out. In general, the proliferation of subaltern counterpublics means a widening of discursive contestation, a good thing in stratified societies.

I am emphasizing the contestatory function of subaltern counterpublics in stratified societies in part in order to complicate the issue of separatism. In my view, the concept of a counterpublic militates in the long run against separatism because it assumes an orientation that is *publicist*. Insofar as these arenas are *publics* they are by definition not enclaves—which is not to deny that they are often involuntarily enclaved. After all, to interact discursively as a member of a public—subaltern or otherwise—is to attempt to disseminate one's discourse into ever-widening arenas. Habermas captures well this aspect of the meaning of publicity when he notes that however limited a public may be in its empirical manifestation at any given time, its members understand themselves as part of a potentially wider public, that indeterminate, empirically counterfactual body we call "the public at large." The point is that, in stratified societies, subaltern counterpublics have a dual character. On the one hand, they function as spaces of withdrawal and regroupment; on the other hand, they also function as bases and training grounds for agitational activities directed toward wider publics. It is precisely in the dialectic between these two functions that their emancipatory potential resides. This dialectic enables subaltern counterpublics partially to offset, although not wholly to eradicate, the unjust participatory privileges enjoyed by members of dominant social groups in stratified societies.

So far, I have been arguing that, although in stratified societies the ideal of participatory parity is not fully realizable, it is more closely approximated by arrangements that permit contestation among a plurality of competing publics than by a single, comprehensive public sphere. Of course, contestation among competing publics supposes interpublic discursive interaction. How, then, should we understand such interaction? Geoff Eley suggests that we think of the public sphere (in stratified societies) as "the structured setting where cultural and ideological contest or negotiation among a variety of publics takes place."[24] This formulation does justice to the multiplicity of public arenas in stratified societies by expressly acknowledging the presence and activity of "a variety of publics." At the same time, it also does justice to the fact that these various publics are situated in a single "structured setting" that advantages some and disadvantages others. Finally, Eley's formulation does justice to the fact that, in stratified societies, the discursive relations among differentially empowered publics are as likely to take the form of contestation as that of deliberation.

Let me now consider the relative merits of multiple publics versus a single comprehensive public for egalitarian, multicultural societies. By egalitarian societies I mean nonstratified societies, societies whose basic framework does not generate unequal social groups in structural relations of dominance and subordination. Egalitarian societies, therefore, are classless societies without gender or racial divisions of labor. They need not be culturally homogeneous. On the contrary, provided such societies permit free expression and association, they are likely to be inhabited by social groups with diverse values, identities, and cultural styles, hence to be multicultural. My question is: under conditions of cultural diversity in the absence of structural inequality, would a single, comprehensive public sphere be preferable to multiple publics?

To answer this question we need to take a closer look at the relationship between public discourse and social identities. *Pace* the bourgeois conception, public spheres are not only arenas for the formation of discursive opinion; in addition, they are arenas for the formation and enactment of social identities.[25] This means that participation is not simply a matter of being able to state propositional contents that are neutral with respect to form of expression. Rather, as I argued in the previous section, participation means being able to speak "in one's own voice," thereby simultaneously constructing and expressing one's cultural identity through idiom and style.[26]

Moreover, as I also suggested, public spheres themselves are not spaces of zero-degree culture, equally hospitable to any possible form of cultural expression. Rather, they consist in culturally specific institutions — including, for example, various journals and various social geographies of urban space. These institutions may be understood as culturally specific rhetorical lenses that filter and alter the utterances they frame; they can accommodate some expressive modes and not others.[27]

It follows that public life in egalitarian, multicultural societies cannot consist exclusively in a single, comprehensive public sphere. That would be tantamount to filtering diverse rhetorical and stylistic norms through a single, overarching lens. Moreover, since there can be no such lens that is genuinely culturally neutral, it would effectively privilege the expressive norms of one cultural group over others, thereby making discursive assimilation a condition for participation in public debate. The result would be the demise of multiculturalism (and the likely demise of social equality). In general, then, we can conclude that the idea of an egalitarian, multicultural society makes sense only if we suppose a plurality of public arenas in which groups with diverse values and rhetorics participate. By definition, such a society must contain a multiplicity of publics.

This need not, however, preclude the possibility of an additional, more comprehensive arena in which members of different, more limited publics talk across lines of cultural diversity. On the contrary, our hypothetical egalitarian, multicultural society would surely have to entertain debates over policies and issues affecting everyone. The question is: would participants in such debates share enough in the way of values, expressive norms, and, therefore, protocols of persuasion to lend their talk the quality of deliberations aimed at reaching agreement through giving reasons?

In my view, this is better treated as an empirical question than as a conceptual question. I see no reason to rule out in principle the possibility of a society in which social equality and cultural diversity coexist with participatory democracy. I certainly hope there can be such a society. That hope gains some plausibility if we consider that, however difficult it may be, communication across lines of cultural difference is not in principle impossible — although it will certainly become impossible if one imagines that it requires bracketing of differences. Granted such communication requires multicultural literacy, but that, I believe, can be acquired through practice. In fact, the possibilities expand once we acknowledge the complexity of cultural identities. *Pace* reductive, essentialist conceptions, cultural identities are woven of many different strands, and some of these strands may be common to people whose identities otherwise diverge, even when it is the divergences that are most salient.[28] Likewise, under conditions of social equality, the porousness, outer-directedness, and open-endedness of publics could promote inter-cultural communication. After all, the concept of a public presupposes a plurality of perspectives among those who participate within it, thereby allowing for internal differences and antagonisms, and likewise discouraging reified blocs.[29] In addition, the unbounded character and publicist orientation of publics allow for the fact that people participate in more than one public, and that the member-ships of different publics may partially overlap. This in turn makes intercultural communication conceivable in principle. All told, then, there do not seem to be any conceptual (as opposed to empirical) barriers to the possibility of a socially egalitarian, multicultural so-ciety that is also a participatory democracy. But this will necessarily be a society with many different publics, including at least one public in which participants can deliberate as peers across lines of differ-ence about policy that concerns them all.

In general, I have been arguing that the ideal of participatory par-ity is better achieved by a multiplicity of publics than by a single public. This is true both for stratified societies and for egalitarian, multicultural societies, albeit for different reasons. In neither case is my argument intended as a simple postmodern celebration of mul-tiplicity. Rather, in the case of stratified societies, I am defending sub-altern counterpublics formed under conditions of dominance and subordination. In the other case, by contrast, I am defending the possibility of combining social equality, cultural diversity, and parti-cipatory democracy.

What are the implications of this discussion for a critical theory of the public sphere in actually existing democracy? Briefly, we need a critical political sociology of a form of public life in which multiple but unequal publics participate. This means theorizing the contes-tatory interaction of different publics and identifying the mecha-nisms that render some of them subordinate to others.

Public Spheres, Common Concerns, and Private Interests

I have argued that in stratified societies, like it or not, subaltern counterpublics stand in a contestatory relationship to dominant publics.
One important object of such interpublic contestation is the appropriate boundaries of the public sphere. Here the central questions
are, what counts as a public matter and what, in contrast, is private?
This brings me to a third set of problematic assumptions underlying
the bourgeois conception of the public sphere, namely, assumptions
concerning the appropriate scope of publicity in relation to privacy.

Let me remind you that it is central to Habermas's account that the
bourgeois public sphere was to be a discursive arena in which "private persons" deliberated about "public matters." There are several
different senses of privacy and publicity in play here. "Public," for
example, can mean (1) state-related; (2) accessible to everyone; (3)
of concern to everyone; and (4) pertaining to a common good or
shared interest. Each of these corresponds to a contrasting sense of
"private." In addition, there are two other senses of "private" hovering just below the surface here: (5) pertaining to private property
in a market economy; and (6) pertaining to intimate domestic or
personal life, including sexual life.

I have already talked at length about the sense of "public" as open
or accessible to all. Now I want to examine some of the other senses,[30] beginning with (3) of concern to everyone. This is ambiguous
between what objectively affects or has an impact on everyone, as
seen from an outsider's perspective, on the one hand, and what is
recognized as a matter of common concern by participants, on the
other hand. Now, the idea of a public sphere as an arena of collective
self-determination does not sit well with approaches that would appeal to an outsider perspective to delimit its proper boundaries.
Thus, it is the second, participant's perspective that is relevant here.
Only participants themselves can decide what is and what is not of
common concern to them. There is no guarantee, however, that all
of them will agree. For example, until quite recently, feminists were
in the minority in thinking that domestic violence against women
was a matter of common concern and thus a legitimate topic of public discourse. The great majority of people considered this issue to
be a private matter between what was assumed to be a fairly small

number of heterosexual couples (and perhaps the social and legal professionals who were supposed to deal with them). Then feminists formed a subaltern counterpublic from which we disseminated a view of domestic violence as a widespread systemic feature of male-dominated societies. Eventually, after sustained discursive contestation, we succeeded in making it a common concern.

The point is that there are no naturally given, a priori boundaries here. What will count as a matter of common concern will be decided precisely through discursive contestation. It follows that no topics should be ruled off-limits in advance of such contestation. On the contrary, democratic publicity requires positive guarantees of opportunities for minorities to convince others that what in the past was not public in the sense of being a matter of common concern should now become so.[31]

What, then, of the sense of "public" as pertaining to a common good or shared interest? This is the sense that is in play when Habermas characterizes the bourgeois public sphere as an arena in which the topic of discussion is restricted to the "common good" and in which discussion of "private interests" is ruled out.

This is a view of the public sphere that we would today call civic republican, as opposed to liberal-individualist. Briefly, the civic republican model stresses a view of politics as people reasoning together to promote a common good that transcends the mere sum of individual preferences. The idea is that through deliberation the members of the public can come to discover or create such a common good. In the process of their deliberations, participants are transformed from a collection of self-seeking, private individuals into a public-spirited collectivity, capable of acting together in the common interest. On this view, private interests have no proper place in the political public sphere. At best, they are the prepolitical starting point of deliberation, to be transformed and transcended in the course of debate.[32]

Now, this civic republican view of the public sphere is in one respect an improvement over the liberal-individualist alternative. Unlike the latter, it does not assume that people's preferences, interests, and identities are given exogenously in advance of public discourse and deliberation. It appreciates, rather, that preferences, interests, and identities are as much outcomes as antecedents of public deliberation, indeed are discursively constituted in and through it. However, as Jane Mansbridge has argued, the civic republican view contains a very serious confusion, one that blunts its critical edge. This view conflates the ideas of deliberation and the common good by assuming that deliberation must be deliberation *about* the common good. Consequently, it limits deliberation to talk framed from the standpoint of a single, all-encompassing "we," thereby ruling claims of self-interest (and group interest) out of order. Yet, this works against one of the principal aims of deliberation, namely, helping participants clarify their interests, even when those interests turn out to conflict. "Ruling self-interest [and group interest] out of order makes it harder for any participant to sort out what is going on. In particular, the less powerful may not find ways to discover that the prevailing sense of 'we' does not adequately include them."[33]

In general, there is no way to know in advance whether the outcome of a deliberative process will be the discovery of a common good in which conflicts of interest evaporate as merely apparent or, rather, the discovery that conflicts of interests are real and the common good is chimerical. But if the existence of a common good cannot be presumed in advance, then there is no warrant for putting any strictures on what sorts of topics, interests, and views are admissible in deliberation.[34]

This argument holds even in the best-case scenario of societies whose basic institutional frameworks do not generate systemic inequalities; even in such relatively egalitarian societies, we cannot assume in advance that there will be no real conflicts of interests. How much more pertinent, then, is the argument to stratified societies, which are traversed with pervasive relations of dominance and subordination. After all, when social arrangements operate to the systemic profit of some groups of people and to the systemic detriment of others, there are prima facie reasons for thinking that the postulation of a common good shared by exploiters and exploited may well be a mystification. Moreover, any consensus that purports to represent the common good in this social context should be regarded with suspicion, since this consensus will have been reached through deliberative processes tainted by the effects of dominance and subordination.

In general, critical theory needs to take a harder, more critical look at the terms "private" and "public." These terms, after all, are not simply straightforward designations of societal spheres; they are cultural classifications and rhetorical labels. In political discourse, they are powerful terms that are frequently deployed to delegitimate some interests, views, and topics and to valorize others.

This brings me to two other senses of "private," which often function ideologically to delimit the boundaries of the public sphere in ways that disadvantage subordinate social groups. These are sense (5) pertaining to private property in a market economy; and sense (6) pertaining to intimate domestic or personal life, including sexual life. Each of these senses is at the center of a rhetoric of privacy that has historically been used to restrict the universe of legitimate public contestation.

The rhetoric of domestic privacy seeks to exclude some issues and interests from public debate by personalizing them or familializing them; it casts these as private-domestic or personal-familial matters in contradistinction to public, political matters. The rhetoric of economic privacy, in contrast, seeks to exclude some issues and interests from public debate by economizing them; the issues in question here are cast as impersonal market imperatives or as "private" ownership prerogatives or as technical problems for managers and planners, all in contradistinction to public, political matters. In both cases, the result is to enclave certain matters in specialized discursive arenas so as to shield them from general debate. This usually works to the advantage of dominant groups and individuals and to the disadvantage of their subordinates.[35] If wife battering, for example, is labeled a "personal" or "domestic" matter and if public discourse about this phenomenon is canalized into specialized institutions associated with, say, family law, social work, and the sociology and psychology of "deviance," then this serves to reproduce gender dominance and subordination. Similarly, if questions of workplace democracy are labeled "economic" or "managerial" problems and if discourse about these questions is shunted into specialized institutions associated with, say, "industrial relations" sociology, labor law, and "management science," then this serves to perpetuate class (and usually also gender and race) dominance and subordination.

This shows once again that the lifting of formal restrictions on public sphere participation does not suffice to ensure inclusion in practice. On the contrary, even after women and workers have been formally licensed to participate, their participation may be hedged by conceptions of economic privacy and domestic privacy that delimit the scope of debate. These notions, therefore, are vehicles through which gender and class disadvantages may continue to operate subtextually and informally, even after explicit, formal restrictions have been rescinded.

Strong Publics, Weak Publics: On Civil Society and the State

Let me turn now to my fourth and last assumption underlying the bourgeois conception of the public sphere, namely, the assumption that a functioning democratic public sphere requires a sharp separation of civil society and the state. This assumption is susceptible to two different interpretations, depending on how one understands the expression "civil society." If one takes that expression to mean a privately ordered, capitalist economy, then to insist on its separation from the state is to defend classical liberalism. The claim would be that a system of limited government and laissez-faire capitalism is a necessary precondition for a well-functioning public sphere.

We can dispose of this (relatively uninteresting) claim fairly quickly by drawing on some arguments of the previous sections. I have already shown that participatory parity is essential to a democratic public sphere and that rough socioeconomic equality is a precondition of participatory parity. Now I need only add that laissez-faire capitalism does not foster socioeconomic equality and that some form of politically regulated economic reorganization and redistribution is needed to achieve that end. Likewise, I have also shown that efforts to "privatize" economic issues and to cast them as off-limits with respect to state activity impede, rather than promote, the sort of full and free discussion that is built into the idea of a public sphere. It follows from these considerations that a sharp separation of (economic) civil society and the state is not a necessary condition for a well-functioning public sphere. On the contrary, and *pace* the bourgeois conception, it is precisely some sort of interimbrication of these institutions that is needed.[36]

However, there is also a second, more interesting, interpretation of the bourgeois assumption that a sharp separation of civil society and the state is necessary to a working public sphere, one that warrants more extended examination. In this interpretation, "civil society" means the nexus of nongovernmental or "secondary" associations that are neither economic nor administrative. We can best appreciate the force of the claim that civil society in this sense should be separate from the state if we recall Habermas's definition of the liberal public sphere as a "body of private persons assembled to form a public." The emphasis here on "private persons" signals (among other things) that the members of the bourgeois public are not state officials and that their participation in the public sphere is not undertaken in any official capacity. Accordingly, their discourse does not eventuate in binding, sovereign decisions authorizing the use of state power; on the contrary, it eventuates in "public opinion," critical commentary on authorized decision making that transpires elsewhere. The public sphere, in short, is not the state; it is rather the informally mobilized body of nongovernmental discursive opinion that can serve as a counterweight to the state. Indeed, in the bourgeois conception, it is precisely this extragovernmental character of the public sphere that confers an aura of independence, autonomy, and legitimacy on the "public opinion" generated in it.

Thus, the bourgeois conception of the public sphere supposes the desirability of a sharp separation of (associational) civil society and the state. As a result, it promotes what I shall call *weak publics*, publics whose deliberative practice consists exclusively in opinion formation and does not also encompass decision making. Moreover, the bourgeois conception seems to imply that an expansion of such publics' discursive authority to encompass decision making as well as opinion making would threaten the autonomy of public opinion — for then the public would effectively become the state, and the possibility of a critical discursive check on the state would be lost.

That, at least, is suggested by Habermas's initial formulation of the bourgeois conception. In fact, the issue becomes more complicated as soon as we consider the emergence of parliamentary sovereignty. With that landmark development in the history of the public sphere, we encounter a major structural transformation, since sovereign parliament functions as a public sphere within the state. Moreover, sovereign parliaments are what I shall call *strong publics*, publics whose discourse encompasses both opinion formation and decision making. As a locus of public deliberation culminating in legally binding decisions (or laws), parliament was to be the site for the discursive authorization of the use of state power. With the achievement of parliamentary sovereignty, therefore, the line separating (associational) civil society and the state is blurred.

Clearly, the emergence of parliamentary sovereignty and the consequent blurring of the (associational) civil society/state separation represents a democratic advance over earlier political arrangements. This is because, as the terms "strong public" and "weak public" suggest, the "force of public opinion" is strengthened when a body representing it is empowered to translate such "opinion" into authoritative decisions. At the same time, there remain important questions about the relation between parliamentary strong publics and the weak publics to which they are supposed to be accountable. In general, these developments raise some interesting and important questions about the relative merits of weak and strong publics and about the respective roles that institutions of both kinds might play in a democratic and egalitarian society.

One set of questions concerns the possible proliferation of strong publics in the form of self-managing institutions. In self-managed workplaces, child care centers, or residential communities, for example, internal institutional public spheres could be arenas of both opinion formation and decision making. This would be tantamount to constituting sites of direct or quasi-direct democracy wherein all those engaged in a collective undertaking would participate in deliberations to determine its design and operation.[37] However, this would still leave open the relationship between such internal public spheres-cum-decision-making-bodies and those external publics to which they might also be deemed accountable. The question of that relationship becomes important when we consider that people who are affected by an undertaking in which they do not directly participate as agents may nonetheless have a stake in its modus operandi; they therefore also have a legitimate claim to a say, through some other (weaker or stronger) public sphere, in its institutional design and operation.

Here we are again broaching the issue of accountability. What institutional arrangements best ensure the accountability of democratic decision-making bodies (strong publics) to *their* (external, weak, or, given the possibility of hybrid cases, weaker) publics?[38] Where in society are direct democracy arrangements called for and where are representative forms more appropriate? How are the former best articulated with the latter? More generally, what democratic arrangements best institutionalize coordination among different institutions, including among their various coimplicated publics? Should we think of central parliament as a strong superpublic with authoritative discursive sovereignty over basic societal ground rules and coordination arrangements? If so, does that require the assumption of a single weak(er) external superpublic (in addition to, not instead of, various other smaller publics)? In any event, given the inescapable global interdependence manifest in the international division of labor within a single shared planetary biosphere, does it make sense to understand the nation-state as the appropriate unit of sovereignty?

I do not know the answers to most of these questions and I am unable to explore them further in this essay. The possibility of posing them, however, even in the absence of full, persuasive answers, enables us to draw one salient conclusion: any conception of the public sphere that requires a sharp separation between (associational) civil society and the state will be unable to imagine the forms of self-management, interpublic coordination, and political accountability that are essential to a democratic and egalitarian society. The bourgeois conception of the public sphere, therefore, is not adequate for contemporary critical theory. What is needed, rather, is a postbourgeois conception that can permit us to envision a greater role for (at least some) public spheres than mere autonomous opinion formation removed from authoritative decision making. A postbourgeois conception would enable us to think about strong *and* weak publics, as well as about various hybrid forms. In addition, it would allow us to theorize the range of possible relations among such publics, thereby expanding our capacity to envision democratic possibilities beyond the limits of actually existing democracy.

Conclusion: Rethinking the Public Sphere

Let me conclude by recapitulating what I believe I have accomplished in this essay. I have shown that the bourgeois conception of the public sphere, as described by Habermas, is not adequate for the critique of the limits of actually existing democracy in late capitalist societies. At one level, my argument undermines the bourgeois conception as a normative ideal. I have shown, first, that an adequate conception of the public sphere requires not merely the bracketing, but rather the elimination, of social inequality. Second, I have shown that a multiplicity of publics is preferable to a single public sphere both in stratified societies and in egalitarian societies. Third, I have shown that a tenable conception of the public sphere would countenance not the exclusion, but the inclusion, of interests and issues that bourgeois masculinist ideology labels "private" and treats as inadmissible. Finally, I have shown that a defensible conception would allow both for strong publics and for weak publics and that it would theorize the relations among them. In sum, I have argued against four constitutive assumptions of the bourgeois conception of the public sphere; at the same time, I have identified some corresponding elements of a new, postbourgeois conception.

At another level, my argument enjoins four corresponding tasks on the critical theory of actually existing democracy. First, this theory should render visible the ways in which social inequality taints deliberation within publics in late capitalist societies. Second, it should show how inequality affects relations among publics in late capitalist societies, how publics are differentially empowered or segmented, and how some are involuntarily enclaved and subordinated to others. Next, a critical theory should expose ways in which the labeling of some issues and interests as "private" limits the range of problems, and of approaches to problems, that can be widely contested in contemporary societies. Finally, our theory should show how the overly weak character of some public spheres in late capitalist societies denudes "public opinion" of practical force.

In all these ways, the theory should expose the limits of the specific form of democracy we enjoy in contemporary capitalist societies. Perhaps it can thereby help inspire us to try to push back those limits, while also cautioning people in other parts of the world against heeding the call to install them.

NOTES

1. This essay is reprinted with permission from *Habermas and the Public Sphere*, ed. Craig Calhoun (Cambridge, Mass.: MIT Press, 1992). I am grateful for helpful comments from Craig Calhoun, Joshua Cohen, Tom McCarthy, Moishe Postone, Baukje Prins, David Schweikart, and Rian Voet. I also benefited from the inspiration and stimulation of participants in the conference on "Habermas and the Public Sphere," University of North Carolina, Chapel Hill, September 1989.

2. Jürgen Habermas, *The Structural Transformation of the Public Sphere: An Inquiry into a Category of Bourgeois Society*, trans. Thomas Burger with Frederick Lawrence (Cambridge, Mass.: MIT Press, 1989). For Habermas's later use of the category of the public sphere, see Jürgen Habermas, *The Theory of Communicative Action*, vol. 2, *Lifeworld and System: A Critique of Functionalist Reason*, trans. Thomas McCarthy (Boston: Beacon, 1987). For a critical secondary discussion of Habermas's later use of the concept, see Nancy Fraser, "What's Critical about Critical Theory? The Case of Habermas and Gender," in Fraser, *Unruly Practices: Power, Discourse and Gender in Contemporary Social Theory* (Minneapolis: University of Minnesota Press, 1989).

3. Throughout this paper, I refer to paid workplaces, markets, credit systems, etc., as "*official* economic system institutions" so as to avoid the androcentric implication that domestic institutions are not also "economic." For a discussion of this issue, see Nancy Fraser, "What's Critical about Critical Theory?"

4. Joan Landes, *Women and the Public Sphere in the Age of the French Revolution* (Ithaca, N.Y.: Cornell University Press, 1988).

5. For the public/pubic connection, see the *Oxford English Dictionary* (second edition, 1989) entry for "public." For the testimony/testicle connection, see Lucie White, "Subordination, Rhetorical Survival Skills and Sunday Shoes: Notes on the Hearing of Mrs. G.," *Buffalo Law Review* 38, no. 1 (Winter 1990): 6.

6. Pierre Bourdieu, *Distinction: A Social Critique of the Judgment of Pure Taste*, trans. Richard Nice (Cambridge, Mass.: Harvard University Press, 1984).

7. Geoff Eley, "Nations, Publics, and Political Cultures: Placing Habermas in the Nineteenth Century," in *Habermas and the Public Sphere*, ed. Craig Calhoun. See also Leonore Davidoff and Catherine Hall, *Family Fortunes: Men and Women of the English Middle Class, 1780–1850* (Chicago: University of Chicago Press, 1987).

8. Habermas does recognize that the issue of gender exclusion is connected to a shift from aristocratic to bourgeois public spheres, but, as I argue below, he fails to notice its full implications.

9. I do not mean to suggest that Habermas is unaware of the existence of public spheres other than the bourgeois one; on the contrary, in the preface to *Structural Transformation* (xviii), he explicitly states that his object is the liberal model of the bourgeois public sphere and that therefore he will discuss neither "the plebeian public sphere" (which he understands as an ephemeral phenomenon that existed "for just one moment" during the French Revolution) nor "the plebiscitary-acclamatory form of regimented public sphere characterizing dictatorships in highly developed industrial societies." My point is that, although Habermas acknowledges that there were alternative public spheres, he assumes that it is possible to understand the character of the bourgeois public by looking at it alone, in isolation from its relations to other, competing publics. This assumption is problematic. In fact, as I shall demonstrate, an examination of the bourgeois public's relations to alternative counterpublics challenges the bourgeois conception of the public sphere.

10. Mary P. Ryan, *Women in Public: Between Banners and Ballots, 1825–1880* (Baltimore: Johns Hopkins University Press, 1990) and "Gender and Public Access: Women's Politics in Nineteenth Century America," in *Habermas and the Public Sphere*, ed. Craig Calhoun.

11. Eley, "Nations, Publics, and Political Cultures."

12. Eley, "Nations, Publics, and Political Cultures."

13. I am leaving aside whether one should speak here not of consent *tout court* but rather of "something approaching consent," or "something appearing as consent," or "something constructed as consent" in order to leave open the possibility of degrees of consent.

14. The public sphere produces consent via circulation of discourses that construct the "common sense" of the day and represent the existing order as natural and/or just, but not simply as a ruse that is imposed. Rather, the public sphere in its mature form includes sufficient participation and sufficient representation of multiple interests and perspectives to permit most people most of the time to recognize themselves in its discourses. People who are ultimately disadvantaged by the social construction of consent nonetheless manage to find in the discourses of the public sphere representations of their interests, aspirations, life problems, and anxieties that are close enough to resonate with their own lived self-representations, identities, and feelings. Their consent to hegemonic rule is secured when their culturally constructed perspectives are taken up and articulated with other culturally constructed perspectives in hegemonic sociopolitical projects.

15. Here I want to distance myself from a certain overly facile line of argument that is sometimes made against Habermas. This is the line that the ideological functions of the public spheres in class societies simply undermine the normative notion as an ideal. This I take to be a non sequitur, since it is always possible to reply that under other conditions, say, the abolition of classes, genders, and other pervasive axes of inequality, the public sphere would no longer have this function, but would instead be an institutionalization of democratic interaction. Moreover, as Habermas has often pointed out, even in existing class societies, the significance of the public sphere is not entirely exhausted by its class function. On the contrary, the idea of the public sphere also functions here and now as a norm of democratic interaction we use to criticize the limitations of actually existing public spheres. The point here is that even the revisionist story and the Gramscian theory that cause us to doubt the value of the public sphere are themselves only possible because of it. It is the idea of the public sphere that provides the conceptual condition of possibility for the revisionist critique of its imperfect realization.

16. Jane Mansbridge, "Feminism and Democracy," *The American Prospect*, no. 1 (Spring 1990): 127.

17. In *Distinction*, Pierre Bourdieu has theorized these processes in an illuminating way in terms of the concept of "class habitus."

18. As Habermas notes, this tendency is exacerbated with the concentration of media ownership in late capitalist societies. For the steep increase in concentration in the United States in the late twentieth century, see Ben H. Bagdikian, *The Media Monopoly* (Boston: Beacon, 1983). This situation contrasts in some respects with countries with state-owned and -operated television. But even there it is doubtful that subordinated groups have equal access. Moreover, political-economic pressures have recently encouraged privatization of media in several of these countries. In part, this reflects the problems of state networks having to compete for "market share" with private channels airing U.S.-produced mass entertainment.

19. This is the spirit behind, for example, proposals for electoral campaign financing reforms aimed at preventing the intrusion of economic dominance into the public sphere. Needless to say, within a context of massive societal inequality,

it is far better to have such reforms than not to have them. In light of the sorts of informal effects of dominance and inequality discussed above, however, one ought not to expect too much from them. The most thoughtful recent defense of the liberal view comes from someone who in other respects is not a liberal. See Michael Walzer, *Spheres of Justice: A Defense of Pluralism and Equality* (New York: Basic Books, 1983). Another very interesting approach has been suggested by Joshua Cohen. In response to an earlier draft of this essay, he argued that policies designed to facilitate the formation of social movements, secondary associations, and political parties would better foster participatory parity than would policies designed to achieve social equality, since the latter would require redistributive efforts that carry "deadweight losses." I certainly support the sort of policies that Cohen recommends, as well as his more general aim of an "associative democracy"; the sections of this paper on multiple publics and strong publics make a case for related arrangements. However, I am not persuaded by the claim that these policies can achieve participatory parity under conditions of social inequality. That seems to me to be another variant of the liberal view of the autonomy of the political, which Cohen otherwise claims to reject. See Joshua Cohen, "Comments on Nancy Fraser's 'Rethinking the Public Sphere'" (unpublished manuscript presented at the meetings of the American Philosophical Association, Central Division, New Orleans, April 1990).

20. My argument draws on Karl Marx's still unsurpassed critique of liberalism in Part I of "On the Jewish Question." Hence, the allusion to Marx in the title of this essay.

21. My argument in this section is deeply indebted to Joshua Cohen's perceptive comments on an earlier draft of this paper in "Comments on Nancy Fraser's 'Rethinking the Public Sphere.'"

22. I have coined this expression by combining two terms that other theorists have recently used with very good effects for purposes that are consonant with my own. I take the term "subaltern" from Gayatri Spivak, "Can the Subaltern Speak?" in *Marxism and the Interpretation of Culture*, ed. Cary Nelson and Larry Grossberg (Urbana: University of Illinois Press, 1988), 271–313. I take the term "counterpublic" from Rita Felski, *Beyond Feminist Aesthetics* (Cambridge, Mass.: Harvard University Press, 1989).

23. For an analysis of the political import of oppositional feminist discourses about needs, see Nancy Fraser, "Struggle over Needs: Outline of a Socialist-Feminist Critical Theory of Late-Capitalist Political Culture," in Fraser, *Unruly Practices*.

24. Eley, "Nations, Publics, and Political Cultures." Eley goes on to explain that this is tantamount to "extend[ing] Habermas's idea of the public sphere toward the wider public domain where authority is not only constituted as rational and legitimate, but where its terms are contested, modified, and occasionally overthrown by subaltern groups."

25. It seems to me that public discursive arenas are among the most important and underrecognized sites in which social identities are constructed, deconstructed, and reconstructed. My view stands in contrast to various psychoanalytic accounts of identity formation, which neglect the formative importance of post-Oedipal discursive interaction outside the nuclear family and which therefore cannot explain identity shifts over time. It strikes me as unfortunate that so much of contemporary feminist theory has taken its understanding of social identity from

psychoanalytic models, while neglecting to study identity construction in relation to public spheres. The revisionist historiography of the public sphere discussed earlier can help redress the balance by identifying public spheres as loci of identity reconstruction. For an account of the discursive character of social identity and a critique of psychoanalytic approach to identity see Nancy Fraser, "The Uses and Abuses of French Discourse Theories for Feminist Politics," in *Revaluing French Feminism: Critical Essays on Difference, Agency, and Culture*, ed. Nancy Fraser and Sandra Bartky (Bloomington: Indiana University Press, 1992).

26. For another statement of this position, see Nancy Fraser, "Toward a Discourse Ethic of Solidarity," *Praxis International* 5, no. 4 (January 1986): 425–29. See also Iris Young, "Impartiality and the Civic Public: Some Implications of Feminist Critiques of Moral and Political Theory," in *Feminism as Critique*, ed. Seyla Benhabib and Drucilla Cornell (Minneapolis: University of Minnesota Press, 1987), 56–76.

27. For an analysis of the rhetorical specificity of one historical public sphere, see Michael Warner, *The Letters of the Republic: Publication and the Public Sphere in Eighteenth-Century America* (Cambridge, Mass.: Harvard University Press, 1990).

28. One could say that at the deepest level, everyone is mestizo. The best metaphor here may be Wittgenstein's idea of family resemblances, or networks of crisscrossing, overlapping differences and similarities, no single thread of which runs continuously throughout the whole. For an account that stresses the complexity of cultural identities and the salience of discourse in their construction, see Nancy Fraser, "Uses and Abuses." For accounts that draw on concepts of *métissage*, see Gloria Anzaldúa, *Borderlands—La Frontera: The New Mestiza* (San Francisco: Spinsters Books, 1987) and Françoise Lionnet, *Autobiographical Voices: Race, Gender, Self-Portraiture* (Ithaca, N.Y.: Cornell University Press, 1989).

29. In these respects, the concept of a public differs from that of a community. "Community" suggests a bounded and fairly homogeneous group, and it often connotes consensus. "Public," in contrast, emphasizes discursive interaction that is in principle unbounded and open-ended, and this in turn implies a plurality of perspectives. Thus, the idea of a public, better than that of a community, can accommodate internal differences, antagonisms, and debates. For an account of the connection between publicity and plurality, see Hannah Arendt, *The Human Condition* (Chicago: University of Chicago Press, 1958). For a critique of the concept of community, see Iris Young, "The Ideal of Community and the Politics of Difference," in *Feminism and Postmodernism*, ed. Linda J. Nicholson (New York: Routledge, Chapman and Hall, 1989), 300–323.

30. In this essay, I do not directly discuss sense (1) state-related. In the next section of this essay, however, I consider some issues that touch on that sense.

31. This is the equivalent in democratic theory of a point that Paul Feyerabend has argued in the philosophy of science. See Feyerabend, *Against Method* (New York: Verso, 1988).

32. In contrast, the liberal-individualist model stresses a view of politics as the aggregation of self-interested, individual preferences. Deliberation in the strict sense drops out altogether. Instead, political discourse consists in registering individual preferences and in bargaining, looking for formulas that satisfy as many private interests as possible. It is assumed that there is no such thing as the

common good over and above the sum of all the various individual goods, and so private interests are the legitimate stuff of political discourse.

33. Mansbridge, "Feminism and Democracy," 131.

34. This point, incidentally, is in the the spirit of a more recent strand of Habermas's normative thought, which stresses the procedural, as opposed to the substantive, definition of a democratic public sphere; here, the public sphere is defined as an arena for a certain type of discursive interaction, not as an arena for dealing with certain types of topics and problems. There are no restrictions, therefore, on what may become a topic of deliberation. See Seyla Benhabib's account of this radical proceduralist strand of Habermas's thought and her defense of it as the strand that renders his view of the public sphere superior to alternative views. Benhabib, "Models of Public Space: Hannah Arendt, the Liberal Tradition, and Jürgen Habermas," in *Habermas and the Public Sphere*, ed. Craig Calhoun.

35. Usually, but not always. As Josh Cohen has argued, exceptions are the uses of privacy in *Roe v. Wade*, the U.S. Supreme Court decision legalizing abortion, and in Justice Blackmun's dissent in *Bowers v. Hardwick*, the decision upholding state antisodomy laws. These examples show that the privacy rhetoric is multivalent rather than univocally and necessarily harmful. On the other hand, there is no question but that the weightier tradition of privacy argument has buttressed inequality by restricting debate. Moreover, many feminists have argued that even the "good" privacy uses have some serious negative consequences in the current context and that gender domination is better challenged in this context on other discursive grounds. For a defense of "privacy" talk, see Cohen, "Comments on Nancy Fraser's 'Rethinking the Public Sphere.'"

36. There are many possibilities here, including such mixed forms as market socialism.

37. I use the expression "quasi-direct democracy" in order to signal the possibility of hybrid forms of self-management involving the democratic designation of representatives, managers, or planners held to strict standards of accountability through, for example, recall.

38. By hybrid possibilities I mean arrangements involving very strict accountability of representative decision-making bodies to their external publics through veto and recall rights. Such hybrid forms might in some, though certainly not all, circumstances be desirable.

The Public's Fear; or, Media As Monster in Habermas, Negt, and Kluge
Dana Polan

Oprah. Today's subject of debate: the labeling of records and CD's for imputed obscenity. The two most interesting guests: the infamous Tipper Gore, champion of labeling practices; the infamous Ice T, a rapper whose songs have been targeted by Gore as particularly immoral. In the middle, Oprah, liberal mediator, voice of reason. The "discussion" starts. It breaks down. Everyone talks over everyone else. Debate turns into a tactical game of who can talk louder than an opponent. Audience members join the yelling. Oprah watches confusedly, helplessly, waiting, so it might seem, for a commercial break to give her a chance to restore some order. Finally, Oprah demands that Tipper be given the floor. Tipper begins calmly, with seeming reasonable liberalness (her own self-description is "liberal"). Tipper suggests that the function of bringing all groups on a show like Oprah's can be to open up dialogue, to allow views to be heard and evaluated rationally. She is willing to talk rationally with Ice T. We must get beyond strife, she argues, we must all work together to . . . She is cut off as the image cuts to the program credits. The show is out of time. The very call for a space of open public discussion is closed by the structural demands of that media form in which most discussion today takes place. Reason reveals itself to be what it really is: a show, a spectacle in which truth is not a content but, à la Russian Formalism, a *device*, an alibi to get excitement going, to make a scene. One watches really more for the excitement, the good fight, than for the enunciating of reasoned positions.

I saw this episode of "Oprah Winfrey" as I was reading Jürgen

Habermas's *The Structural Transformation of the Public Sphere*, the translation (by Thomas Burger, with Frederick Lawrence) of his 1962 *Habilitationsschrift*, and the relation of the book and the television show seems to me highly symptomatic of the simultaneous relevance and anachronism of Habermas's analysis for cultural study today.

On the one hand, the Habermas book seems made precisely to explain what happens to rational intervention in an age of media dominated by shows like "Oprah." The media here are readable as a degradation, and for those readers who are used to thinking of Habermas as a *social* or *political* thinker, but only rarely as a *cultural* one concerned with the specific role of cultural phenomena in the social totality, *The Structural Transformation of the Public Sphere* can help revise our standard image of Habermas and suggest his contribution to a cultural study. Indeed, what is very striking about the work is the sheer physicality of its analyses of the realm of everyday life: this is a book that is very close to the lived ordinariness of culture — culture as the pages of books and newspapers, as the shape of television shows, as the space of common interactions. To take just one example, Habermas situates the family's loss of cultural capital in the modern age in relation to transformations in the very materiality of family space.[1] His discourse on this materiality resembles nothing so much as that in recent investigations of the everyday semiosis of architecture and adds to those investigations a Foucauldian panoptic twist:

> This surreptitious hollowing out of the family's intimate sphere received its architectural expression in the layout of homes and cities. The closedness of the private home, clearly indicated to the outside by front yards and fence and made possible on the inside by the individualized and manifold structuring of rooms, is no longer the norm today, just as, conversely, its openness to the social intercourse of a public sphere was endangered by the disappearance of the salon and of rooms for the reception of visitors in general. . . . Thin walls guaranteed, if need be, a freedom of movement protected from sight but not from hearing; they too assumed functions of social communication difficult to distinguish from social order. (p. 157)

On the other hand, it is important to note the constant movement by which Habermas presents culture as a type of media and so offers no analysis of why cultural spectacles (like "Oprah") grip us. This slide — from culture to media — is not Habermas's alone. In the age of new forms of culture — of television, of radio, of cable television, of mediatized ideas, of the blurring of all this so that what we know in ourselves of, say, *Teenage Mutant Ninja Turtles*, of what cultural meaning they have for us, is indistinguishable from what television, convenience stores, movies, videos, lunch pails, and so on and on have told us they mean for us — it is easy to assume that culture and media are the same. But all too often, the linguistic substitution of one for the other brings with it a semantic shift; in thinking of culture as media we lose some of the things we might take culture to be about.

I need to be clear about this point. I am not at all trying to go back to that Culture and Society tradition that would see Culture as a thing apart, a thing above. Nor do I want to deny that cultural production today is often intimately connected with media. But equating cultural productions (whether high or popular) with media productions runs the risk of missing the ideological and cultural specificity of cultural production. Media theory is primarily a theory of the quantitative: who owns how many of the channels of communication, how much gets transmitted. Such an approach misses the meanings and coun-termeanings that are transmitted.

We might, for example, note the distance of media theory — with its traditional question of who's doing what to whom and to what effect? — from cultural study as it is coming to be constituted today: culture here is not an imperial and imperialist takeover of mind, a pure blanketing (as in the title of Edward Said's *Covering Islam* — media as an imposition from without), a descending of false signals onto a pristine identity, but rather culture comes to be seen as a complicated negotiation of inside and outside, of internal and external — a battle of meaning, a battle within meanings, such that we cannot talk any longer of original experiences overladen with media distortions. We might note, for example, the almost complete absence in media theory of any notion of the unconscious: in media theory, human subjects are pure vessels into which are poured all the clichés of communication practice — media theory's psychology is Pavlovian (see its endless references to "needs and gratifications") and not Freudian. In this respect, many post-Lukácsian theories of the loss of proletarian consciousness still remain pre-Freudian even when they claim to turn to Freud for an explanation of why people seem to choose against their own best interests (see, for example, the work of the Frankfurt School on the authoritarian personality or on the Weimar working class). Desire here is never anything but negative, and never anything but a yearning imposed from without through the medium of the media.[2] If Lukács was not able to account for the gap between real and imputed class consciousness, later critics can account for it all too easily by blaming the monster of the media. Against this, today's cultural studies emphasizes the simultaneous regressive and progressive role of fantasy and desire and of culture's embodiment of them. To take just one example, a book like Linda Williams's *Hard Core*, on pornography, is fully symptomatic of cultural studies approaches in its emphasis on pornography as something that users can negotiate, reshape to their own needs, consume in ways that potentially exceed the interests of their media producers (the filmmakers and, beyond them, their Mafia financiers).[3]

In these terms, Habermas's *Structural Transformation* is still a work of *media* theory. It may not be accidental that this first work of Habermas's appears as his most concrete, most grounded in the ordinary. The course of Habermas's writing career — where he increasingly comes to value the role of a public sphere of rational reconstruction of social values, where he comes (in *Knowledge and Human Interests*) to deal explicitly with Freud but only to rewrite him as a hermeneutician, as the theorist of past experiences, not of future-oriented fantasies — suggests that for Habermas all this stuff that goes on in everyday life, behind closed doors, thin windows, and so on, is really contingent. If the bourgeois public sphere begins to be transformed by the modern age, this has nothing to do with its own nature, but with things that happen to it from without. Culture, or rather media, becomes a pure and corrupting epiphenomenon imposed on a pristine realm of rational openness in which citizens once communicated transparently. Habermas may present everyday culture in all its detail in his first book only to pinpoint all the forces that a new rational reconstruction of value would have to overcome. For all his emphasis here on the materiality of everyday activities, Habermas takes the new practices of cultural space as not the reality of human nature, but as something that detours human nature from its rational nature. The story that *Structural Transformation* sets out to tell is a tragic rise-and-fall myth — the public sphere arose in reaction to the artificialities of the old aristocracy, but it lost out to the new artificialities of a mediatized world — but the movement of his whole career sets out to reinscribe that tragedy within comic celebration: Habermas's own patient dissections of society will serve as the new basis on which a rational, transparent public sphere can be reerected.

Of course, Habermas is clever enough to remember that the supposedly pristine space of eighteenth-century bourgeois reason was itself run through with distortion — most especially in the gap between the disinterested reason of public debate and the real economic interests that this debate depended upon. He reminds us (and himself) that bourgeois society's reasoners were representatives of a system of exchange. But even here, economic interest seems contingent. Yes, only certain people are part of the public sphere, and, yes, the things they evaluate have a bearing on their capitalist efforts, but the sphere of reason bears nonetheless a certain degree of relative autonomy from the origins and interest of its members. This relative autonomy allows Habermas's glance back at the eighteenth century also to be a wishful restorative glance forward to a new structure of social relations that would allow the public sphere to come back into its own. It is this relative autonomy that allows the Marxist Terry Eagleton to find in Addison and Steele a reason that avoids the faddishness of superficial jargons of the new and that can give intellectuals a proper place in social reconstruction.[4]

One of the most famous and telling critiques of the promotion of the eighteenth-century bourgeois society as the site of the public sphere comes from Oskar Negt and Alexander Kluge in their *Public Sphere and Experience*.[5] Negt and Kluge's hesitations are two-sided, even as they hold out a belief in a public sphere per se (Kluge: "[Our notion of *Öffentlichkeit*, or publicness] is not really opposed [to Habermas's]. It is a response as part of a process of discussion. We quite agree with him about the necessity of the process of enlightenment, of the need for a new encyclopedia").[6] On the one hand, Negt and Kluge work hard to show that the bourgeois public sphere was much more run through by the interests of capitalist exchange than Habermas wants to admit. In other words, they challenge the notion of that realm's purity. Indeed, intriguingly and polemically in opposition to those scholars (like Erich Fromm) who want to see fascism as an outcome of misguided proletarian longings, Kluge and Negt argue boldly that it is precisely the bourgeois public realm that may have to be held accountable for fascism. As Kluge puts it:

Our point of departure always remains the public sphere of 1933 that could be conquered by the National Socialists. This must be fortified in different ways so that it cannot be conquered. If the public sphere, that is, the container for the political, was inadequate and conquered by the Nazis, then it is useless to study the achievements of the eighteenth and nineteenth centuries and to repeat and defend the old conception of the public sphere, as Habermas does, for no moral resistance was objectively possible within it.[7]

On the other hand, if Negt and Kluge suggest how the bourgeois public realm was a besmirched realm, not worthy of the mantle of history, they take an additional polemic step and argue that if there is anything really resembling a public realm, it is the realm of *proletarian* productivity. Starting, then, from many of the same Enlightenment principles as Habermas, Kluge and Negt imagine a very different history of the public, of its discourse, of its possibilities.

And yet, the very way Kluge, in his interview with Stuart Liebman, describes the power of the proletarian public sphere suggests a limit to the very conception of a politics today based on principles of supposedly open and rational investigation, whether that of the bourgeois public sphere or a proletarian counter-public space. Just after his assertion of the inadequacies of the Habermasian model after the rise of fascism, Kluge posits an alternative: "We must look into the production sphere, where the potential for resistance is hidden."[8]

Here we can see glimpses of a myth of purity not so far from Habermas's. There is, in Kluge and Negt, a romanticism of the moment of production that assumes that moment undergoes corruption when it becomes only a step in the process of exchange. To be sure, as Fredric Jameson argues, this romanticism may finally be a rhetorical tactic for Negt and Kluge, their projection backward of a pristine realm of work before exploitation actually was a way of projecting forward a utopian hope (as Kluge's very emphasis on "potentials for resistance" suggests).[9] But even if it is rhetorical — and Jameson's own analysis suggests that the image of the primal is not just tactical in Kluge and Negt — the emphasis in *The Public Sphere and Experience* on production as a sphere where one could be in an unalienated relation to the senses leads almost as if by a natural current of induction to another emphasis, close to Habermas: on culture equated with media and imagined and feared as a monstrous force of distortion that strengthens the alienations of exchange. Indeed,

Kluge and Negt can seem even more bleak than Habermas in their image of a contemporary world infiltrated by media at every level. Even Jameson, who wants to read their work for its utopian impulses, is forced to term *The Public Sphere and Experience* somewhat of a failure in its discovery that the much-vaunted proletarian public realm has itself lost out to media: as Jameson put it, "we set out, Negt and Kluge tell us, to project a proletarian public sphere and found ourselves reduced to writing a critique of the limits of the bourgeois public sphere."[10]

Again, we have to note the distance of some of Negt and Kluge's suppositions from those that guide cultural studies today. As with Habermas, the very notion of a transparent realm of open interaction can only sit uncomfortably with psychoanalysis's assumptions that no interaction is transparent, is not run through with fantasy, aggression, desire, rivalry. To be sure, Kluge and Negt's *Public Sphere* does have a psychology, but it seems primarily a corporeal, tactile one in which the primary human psychological state (the human production) is imagined as relatively unproblematic and another (the producer caught up in the web of exchange) is imagined as coming onto the scene to distort basic needs. Symptomatically, as the book moves forward, Negt and Kluge increasingly come to imagine fantasy in the age of media control as only perverted, escapist fantasy: the worker turns to fantasy to stay alive in the world of alienated labor, but this turn remains unconscious, a quietist means for the worker to consciously work while unconsciously being elsewhere. In contrast to the enabling assumptions of today's cultural studies, Kluge and Negt's work cannot emphasize the potentially contradictory role of desire and fantasy in the work of hegemony and counterhegemony.

Indeed, the very emphasis on a resistance in the *production* moment and not in that of consumption is contrasted by cultural studies' emphasis on the subcultural refashionings, precisely within consumption, of the dominant culture's offerings (see, for example, Dick Hebdige's notion of semiotic guerrilla warfare).[11] Culture can be empowering not only in its use value, but also its reuse. Ironically, there seems to be a gap in this respect between Kluge as social theorist and as cultural worker. On the one hand, Kluge's artistic efforts, especially in television production, seem geared, as Miriam Hansen points out, to democratizing media at the level of *production* — for example, his television series in which alternative media producers are chosen to present works of five or fewer minutes.[12] On the other hand, this question of media access, of returning production to the producers, does not remain indifferent to questions of specific form and content and is indeed quite concerned to discover how new patternings of image and sound might lead to new spectator relationships.

Kluge gives a nice glimpse of this spectatorial work (which is not fully reducible to production or consumption) at the end of the interview with Stuart Liebman:

> In the popular scene there are networks. You make a picture; the clothes are worn by other people, real people; you see the film on television; then there is often a book made after the film. At the end you have something of a network of products. . . . You can now throw on the same subject, the same human experience, the literary "light" by writing a novel, a cinematic "light" by making a film, or a discursive "light" by writing an essay. Each of the three approaches yields a different impression, different perspectives on the same subject. . . . I would say that the differences narrated in the different forms provoke the spectator to work toward a truth.

I find these comments heartening. Coming from someone whose most famous work on media is bleak and fearful, they suggest another attitude, one of open and willing experimentation, an ability to engage in media, to work through culture. But this necessitates a virtual reshaping of the model of the public sphere. To "*provoke* the spectator to work toward *a* truth . . ." The intellectual's role here is no longer the Habermasian one of assuming truths to be fully constituted objects that a knower can know through transparent and rationally evolved conduits of intellectual perception. Knowledge is not in objects, waiting for the intellectual to call it forth through reason. Knowledge is produced in the provocation not of *the* truth, but of *a* truth.

In seeming to confirm our very worst fears of the loss of the public under the pressures of media, Habermas consigns himself to the most outmoded form of Enlightenment thinking. Habermas can talk of space, of materialities, of concrete experiences of everyday life only because his framework figures these from the start as symptoms of a monolithic fall from reason. Ironically, the more Habermas says about media, the less he is able to offer us anything useful or productive for our engagements with culture today.

NOTES

1. Jürgen Habermas, *The Structural Transformation of the Public Sphere*, trans. Thomas Burger (Cambridge, Mass.: MIT Press, 1989).

2. For a representative example, see Erich Fromm, *The Working Class in Weimar Germany: A Psychological and Sociological Study*, trans. Barbara Weinberger (Cambridge, Mass.: Harvard University Press, 1984).

3. Linda Williams, *Hard Core: The Frenzy of the Visible* (Berkeley: University of California Press, 1989).

4. Terry Eagleton, *The Function of Criticism: From the Spectator to Post-Structuralism* (London: Verso, 1984).

5. Negt and Kluge, *The Public Sphere and Experience*, forthcoming, University of Minnesota Press.

6. Stuart Liebman, "On New German Cinema, Art, Enlightenment, and the Public Sphere: An Interview with Alexander Kluge," *October* 46 (Fall 1988): 42.

7. Liebman, "On New German Cinema."

8. Fredric Jameson, "On Negt and Kluge," *October* 46 (Fall 1988): 151–77.

9. See, for example, 162–63: "[Kluge and Negt's] observation will be misused or misunderstood if it is taken to be the development of a conservative or nostalgic ideological vision of the past. It poses, rather, an empirical question about the actually existing utopian imagination and, thereby, about the possibility of the development of a political vision of change and action."

10. Jameson, "On Negt and Kluge," 157.

11. Dick Hebdige, *Subcultures: The Meaning of Style* (New York: Methuen, 1979).

12. Of her many essays on Kluge, see, for example, Miriam Hansen, "Reinventing the Nickelodeon: Notes on Kluge and Early Cinema," *October* 46 (Fall 1988): 179–98.

On Negt and Kluge

Fredric Jameson

Nine years separate the two collaborative works of Oskar Negt and Alexander Kluge,[1] and what first strikes the materialist reader (the reader of physical books, rather than of "ideas") is something like a typographic revolution that, along with the postmodern, the end of the sixties, and the defeat of the left, intervenes between them. The first book already clearly suffered under the constraints of classical discursive form, its six official chapters, which set forth to establish a theory of the "proletarian" public sphere, finding themselves forced against their will to produce the rudiments of a theory of the bourgeois public sphere instead. Here already, everything began to flee into the footnotes and appendices: three "excurses" and some twenty separate "commentaries" now filling up a third of a five-hundred-page volume, into which already a few illustrations begin to emerge. Elsewhere in "First World" theoretical zones, new ideologies of the heterogeneous and of difference begin to inspire "rhizomatic" notions of form: Deleuzian "plateaus" are laid out side by side in separate and seemingly unrelated chapters, while the two stark columns of *Glas* dare you to figure out when to jump back and forth and which thread to hold onto. Expensive journals often explore these possibilities more dramatically; and the discontinuities of Kluge's stories and films perhaps more definitively bar the way back to the traditional essay or treatise, closing the road with a landslide of rubble ("you can imagine the problem of antagonistic realisms in terms of the analysis of the site of an explosion. The explosion scattered objects across a wide area. The force of the explosion, in other words what really moved, is no longer present ..." [348]. Benjamin's "dialectical constellations" or montages — like Pound's ideograms — seem genealogically to present a family likeness, although in these predecessors the "heap of images" was perhaps too insistently accompanied by the strong hint that there was a *right* way of putting them all back together. Yet Kluge's own aesthetic (and that of *Geschichte und Eigensinn*, which is something of a theoretical film) is decidedly post-Benjaminian rather than post-Brechtian, and (despite Kluge's long personal association with Adorno) the present volume finds its genealogical ancestor in Benjamin's enormous and fragmentary *Passagenarbeit*, or at least in what one imagines this last might have become (an imaginative effort itself interestingly modified by the present book and its appearance). Here is, for example, what Kluge says about one of his films:

> [It] does not produce statements but *proportions*; an *object* one can argue with. Our point of departure is the following observation: that there is no immediate form of sense experience, or at least no organized form, that can encompass the various individual areas of work and milieus of production. Only a spurious public sphere offers such order and unity, as in the media.... The question is: how does one proceed with a disordered reality, with mixed experiences? How does one learn in the middle of errors. How do we operate with distorted objective and subjective impressions...? You have to deal with *reality as raw material*.... Our opinion is that the viewers can use this film to test their own concepts of what is public and what is realistic.[2]

The segmentation in Kluge's stories, however, is not merely perspectival and cinematographic (a fifteen-minute sequence of experience juxtaposed with a paragraph foreshortening eight years); it also projects qualitative leaps into incommensurable dimensions, and it is this particular reading experience that is prolonged in *Geschichte und Eigensinn*, where notes on Marx's "mode of production" (he dozed much of the day on the sofa, with people coming in and out, wrote nasty comments in the margins, strewed his papers with tobacco spots), disquisitions on *Blitzkrieg* and on the *Chanson de Roland*, illustrations drawn from evolutionary theory and the history of automata, anecdotes about Kant, quotes from the letters to Fliess, studies of domestic labor, the history of prices, the politics of the German romantics, and on-the-spot readings of fairy tales succeed one another unpredictably, in competition with an extraordinary collection of hundreds of images drawn from medieval manuscripts, films, workers' newspapers, ads, graphs, scientific models, newsreel photographs, pictures of old furniture, science fiction illustrations, penmanship exercises and reconstruction of Roman roads or Renaissance battles. Typography meanwhile enters the scene by reclassifying these various chapters, sections, paragraphs, notes, and digressions (themselves following a variety of numeration systems) by way of alternate typefaces, frames and blocks, and, most dramatically, the black pages with white type that interleaf the more "normal" experiments (sometimes, as with the alternation of color and black-and-white in the *Heimat* series, by Kluge's former cameraman Edgar Reitz, one has the feeling that it is the shift that counts, and not any stable one-to-one correspondence between the content and the mode of representation: Proust already said as much about the alternation of imperfect and preterite in Flaubert's tenses).

Authority is therefore here displaced and transformed; reading is still an exercise, a training, a socialization, and a pedagogy, but there is very little of the terroristic or the disciplinary in this one, nor even the dialectical imperative of the older montage, where, as in Godard, you are still warned to find or guess the proper standpoint. Here the gaps and leaps suggest a different associative process from our own; or at least trust presupposes the existence of such an alternative somewhere that it might be interesting to try to approximate, if not to learn. Indeed, the emphasis on learning is here so ubiquitous that we are willing to entertain the possibility of some utopian way of establishing relations between these themes and exhibits that is not Negt and Kluge's private style or methodological property, but that remains to be invented.

Yet, as they never tire of reminding us, the experience of production is distinct from and incommensurable with its instruments or its products: political economy, capitalogic, deal with this last, but it is more difficult, and fraught with indirection, to seek, as here, to write a "political economy of labor power" (139). This also means that it will be structurally perverse to seek to convey this book by way of the various "theories" it throws up in passing, as we shall have to do here, patiently turning back into a "system" what wanted to be a way of doing things, or even a habit, in some strong positive sense. Thinking here (including "theory," which throughout this book means Marxism) is therapeutically reduced to a component of action, itself considered as a form of production, as we shall see shortly.

A similar qualification must be registered at this point about language, and in particular about our words for concepts, about which Negt and Kluge have some relatively uncanonical positions. One of the ways in which the story of modern thought can be told, indeed, is as an exploration of the consequences of a radical linguistic skepticism, in which Nietzsche's philological sophistication and the Sartrean attack on ordinary language in *Nausea* culminate paradoxically in a philosophical privileging of language in structuralism and poststructuralism that seals the diagnosis and confirms language itself (in forms that range from Western syntax to Kantian grids of discursive epistemes) as a new equivalent of ideology itself and as the source of all error, a formulation now however utterly misleading insofar as it implies the possibility of truth (that is to say, of getting outside of language itself). How to produce philosophical concepts under these circumstances slowly shifts about into the problem of the status of a new "theoretical" language or discourse, about which the only general agreement turns on the requirement that it be radically provisional and abolish itself in the process (meanwhile, the equally influential current discussions of essentialism and antiessentialism or antifoundationalism would seem better grasped as an indictment of master linguistic codes rather than of "beliefs," about which no one is very clear whether they exist any longer). Fulfilled or unfulfillable, however, the mission of philosophy in this situation continues to turn around the ambition to create a language that escapes this condition, in no matter how provisional or neologistic a fashion.

This impulse is, for example, at work in that tradition of German philosophical speculation that is perhaps most alien to the other national cultures to its west, namely what Jean Paulhan used to call the "proof by etymology,"[3] the inspection of the roots and radicals of contemporary German for traces of some older and more primal mode of thinking, which is then also affirmed to be a more primal mode of relating to being itself. The procedure is defended on the grounds of some more direct, unmixed, unmediated relationship to the tribal language than is the case with the Romance languages or English, for example; and it allows German philosophy to assert its claim to parity with Greece, where Socrates (or Plato) often argued in a similar way, transforming "folk etymology" into the avenue of philosophical reason (a more distant, but related, analogy is to be found in China, where the written character offers similar evidence of older, "truer" meanings). The misuse of such arguments in Heidegger will make their recurrence in the left thinking of Negt and Kluge perplexing (thinking — *begreifen* — as related to *greifen*, grasping or gripping in the production process [20–22]) until it is understood that not "nature" or "being" is here appealed to, but rather what Marx called the "naturwüchsig", or the significantly different structure of earlier, simpler social formations.

On the other hand, this "method" need have nothing of the religious solemnity of Heidegger's stylistic rituals:

> In Kluge's segment of *Deutschland im Herbst*, we already saw Gabi Teichert digging with a spade for German history. These scenes have been transferred to *Die Patriotin*, where digging for the German past and for German history has become the central metaphor. The figurative language of "digging for the treasures of the past" Kluge here takes absolutely literally, rendering it visually in the concrete image of a physical excavation of the frozen earth. What results is a kind of surrealistic image-pun in the tradition of Buñuel or Karl Valentin, which has the effect of distancing the viewer: who is then brought to observe the eccentric activities of Gabi Teichert less with empathy than with critical skepticism. So also when she translates the knowledge contained in fat historical tomes into sense perceptions and in that spirit "works on" old folios, something also "literally" illustrated: she dissects the history books with saws, drills, and hammers, and dissolves their pages in orange juice in order to choke them down. She thus "bores her way into history," "assimilates history into herself," etc. — all unrealistic dream images that are grounded on linguistic figures. As she participates in illegal excavations of the old city wall as a part-time archaeologist, she hopes to "grasp" [*be-greifen*] the past in the form of prehistoric utensils, that is to say, to be able to "take hold" of it and to "understand" it all at once.[4]

About such "efforts" to restore the purity of philosophical language, however, whether by way of fresh invention or of linguistic archaeology, two further things now need to be observed. Whatever the crisis of philosophical discourse owes to the metaphysical or ontological doubtfulness of language itself, that crisis can also be read in socioeconomic terms as a local result of intensified commodification, in which abstract philosophical terms (now seen as something like the private property or brand names of their producers) enter the force field of commodity reification, where their increasingly rapid transformation into cultural objects and images equally rapidly undermines their philosophical legitimacy (along with that of philosophy itself). This is also what is meant when this or that philosophical concept is described as outmoded or old-fashioned (a reproach that would have sounded very strange indeed in traditional philosophy); it seems to me also to be what Paul de Man had in mind when he reflected on the "thematization" that was the fate of philosophical themes and concepts in modern times.

Other solutions remain possible, however, in the contemporary proliferation of ephemeral or provisional theoretical codes and discourses, solutions that do not (in some outmoded or old-fashioned way) propose the invention of truer ones, or the return to purer ones. Such is, for example, the notion of *transcoding* as a contemporary alternative to traditional philosophical critique: what is implied here is that the various "master terms" or "master codes" govern and name distinct, often contiguous and overlapping zones of the real, such that a systematic alternation between them or comparison of their signifying capacities results, not in the emergence of any new linguistic or terminological synthesis, but nonetheless in a kind of mapping out of the raw materials in which the real consists (Hjemslev's linguistic "substance"). The process is analogous to the problem of translation in the realm of the natural languages, which all project at least minimally distinct cognates of the meaning a translated sentence is supposed to share with its original. What is philosophical about translation is then not the effort to reproduce a foreign utterance as the *same*, but rather its deeper experience of the radical differences between the various natural languages.

Transcoding imposes itself at once with Negt and Kluge's first book, *Öffentlichkeit und Erfahrung* (1972), whose title can only imperfectly be translated as *Experience and the Public Sphere*. The motivation for the English equivalent is clear enough, insofar as the substantive "publicity" has already long since been captured by a specialized segment of that larger public domain the German *Öffentlichkeit* renders; while the notion of a "sphere" or "zone" — transferable to other dimensions of social life, such as culture — has already seemed to generate interesting theoretical problems in its own right (which the term would not do in German). Meanwhile, the topic itself can be said in some sense to "belong" to Jürgen Habermas, whose first book, *Strukturwandel der Öffentlichkeit* (1962, *The Structural Transformation of the Public Sphere*), offers a history of the emergence of the institutions of the early bourgeois media, including their philosophical and juridical theorization, from a perspective that will remain constant throughout Habermas's work: namely, that the values of the bourgeois revolutionary period remain universal ones, which it would be improper to analyze in terms of the functional ideology of a specific social class, and whose palpable limits and failures are not internal but the result of the historical blocking of the utopian promise of the bourgeois revolutionary process that has remained incomplete and unrealized. This perspective is not shared by Negt and Kluge, for whom the tendential monopoly of the public sphere in modern times is very intimately related to the class function of the bourgeois concept of the public and to the nature of the institutions that emerged from it, and who propose, in contrast, the idea and the value of a radically different type of collective openness and communication, which they call "the proletarian public sphere."[5]

Transcoding means, however, something more than mere translation: and to appreciate its significance we need to return to the other term of their title, *Erfahrung* or experience, in order to measure the deeper implicit claim of the concept of the "public sphere" to govern a far greater area of social life than is the case with Habermas, whose early work tends to reduce the new topic to that relatively specialized institutional material that is the history of the nascent media (newspapers, public opinion, "representative" or parliamentary debate, and so forth), and whose later philosophical development (speech acts, communicative action) makes it clear that he is as suspicious of phenomenological concepts such as that of experience as anyone on the other side of the Rhine. (Negt and Kluge can therefore be aligned with antistructuralist defenses of the notion of experience that range from E. P. Thompson and Raymond Williams to Sartre, but with some unexpected differences and modifications, as will become clear when we examine the prolongation of this idea and value in their later work.)

What is significant about Negt and Kluge's extension of the notion of the public sphere, however, is that, while continuing to include the institutional referents of Habermas's history (in their contemporary forms, such as television), they seek to widen it in such a way as to secure its constitutive relationship to the very possibility of social or individual experience in general. The structure of the "public sphere" is now seen as what enables experience, or on the other hand limits and cripples it; this structure also determines that fundamental modern pathology whereby "experience" is itself sundered, its uneven torn halves assigned to stereotypical public expressions on the one hand, and on the other to that zone of the personal and the private, which seems to offer shelter from the public and the political at the same time that it is itself a social fact that those produce. At once, therefore, *Öffentlichkeit* becomes something like a "named concept," centrally in competition with a host of other concepts that range from Freud's talking cure to the very notion and language of "democracy" itself, in its political as well as its social forms: "workplace democracy," for example, would now very much constitute a central and ineradicable space of the "proletarian public sphere," and the political stake in transcoding can now be measured by way of a comparison between the relative weight of the political rhetoric of democracy and that of the new discursive space of *Öffentlichkeit*.

The originality of Negt and Kluge, therefore, lies in the way in which the hitherto critical and analytic force of what is now widely known as "discourse analysis" (as in Foucault's descriptions of the restrictions and exclusions at work in a range of so-called discursive formations) is now augmented, not to say completed, by the utopian effort to produce discursive space of a new type. But this redramatizes the philosophical problem of the creation of a new language or terminology in a way that relates it to the very issue of the public sphere itself: for there are social and historical reasons why a new and more adequate philosophical language — which is to say a new *public* language — is lacking. The forms and experiences to which such a language correspond do not yet themselves exist: the very absence of a proletarian public sphere problematizes the attempt to name it, except in the gaps in our present discourse, something that holds even more strongly for the conception of "work" and of "production" Negt and Kluge attempt to produce in *Geschichte und Eigensinn*, which they also describe as a "political economy of labor power [*Arbeitsvermögen*]" (136–43). But even in Marxism these words designate a restricted or specialized zone of human activity: work or labor or production only insofar as those can be "realized" in value as such (as in "the reproduction of the worker's labor power"). The inaugural separation of use from exchange *value* in the first pages of *Capital* (and the subsequent use of this term to designate only this last) means that Marx will write a political economy of labor, a capitalogic, and not that anatomy of its demiurgic underside, the anthropology of human productive power, attempted here. *Öffentlichkeit und Erfahrung* was in that sense a failure: we set out, they tell us, to project a proletarian public sphere and found ourselves reduced to writing a critique of the limits of the bourgeois public sphere. *Öffentlichkeit* will, however, return in the later work in the climactic concept of a "public productional sphere" (*Produktionsöffentlichkeit*), which is identified with history itself.

The new book therefore itself partially transcodes the older one: but it flings down a more fundamental discursive challenge to current doxa, not merely in its ongoing commitment to the category of experience (including the anthropological dimension of the description of a whole range of bodily, psychological, and cultural "capacities"), but above all in its most unseasonable foregrounding of the category of production itself (which the authors understand in a very different way from the fashionable and metaphorical, often cultural, uses of this term in the Althusserian and post-Althusserian period). Is a concept of production absolutized in this fashion and extended to all of human activity still a "productionist" one in the bad sense? The judgment will be more adequately made, however, on the success of the language experiment itself, and on the capacity of a language of production to articulate a wide range of materials normally governed by other languages or codes, most notably the psychoanalytic realm, the area of desire, fantasy, the intimate, the unconscious, but also that very different order of realities that is history and historical events (here most specifically German history). We are familiar with cognate experiments in the first of these areas in Deleuze and Guattari (occasionally referred to in these pages); the second would seem to stand in some conflict with what we have termed the anthropological dimension of this work, in the sense in which philosophical anthropologies (unless they posit "aggressivity" or the "will to power" as components of human nature, as in sociobiology) generally involve an implicit commitment to positivities, thereby setting the violence and the catastrophes of history beyond their reach.

The problem of history is to be sure registered in the title of the second work, but not yet the concept of production (nor even that of labor power), which is oddly and substitutively "represented" by the untranslatable word, *Eigensinn*, which Miriam Hansen has registered in its most common acceptance as the English *obstinacy*, but which Andrew Bowie more searchingly tries to render as *willful meaning*;[6] to which I will add my own suggestion, *self-will*, which restores the component of ownness or primal property to the other variants and balances the (perfectly correct) insistence on the arbitrary and the stubborn with the coexisting connotation of an immanent logic, a drive or impulse remaining faithful to itself and pursuing its own line of force, its own specific trajectory, which is then also, as on Bowie's reading, its meaning. I gloss the term this way to remove the henceforth misleading overtones of the word *self* in my version: not that it will not be a question of "identity" in this work, but that identity — collective or individual — is rather to be achieved in the future: the self, if you like, of Marx's *Gesamtarbeiter* or collective worker, and not of any current or preceding construction of the subject (such as the Freudian structure, where, Negt and Kluge suggest, the psychic functions operate in something of the fashion of bourgeois parliamentary representation [382]). It is not therefore some primal "self" that has *Eigensinn*, but rather a whole range of historically acquired and developed skills, drives, and capacities, each of which makes its own "stubborn" demands and has its own distinct "meaning." Such forces, however, can be residual or emergent; they often fail to be used to capacity, and their unemployment generates specific pathologies, as does their equally possible repression, alienation, or diversion. What also generates social pathology is their multiplicity, which is to say the permanent possibility for contradiction or for a harmful coordination among them: this is for example what explains the circumstance (so often dramatized for us by Kluge's fables) that a "capacity" that is a splendid natural force in its own right may, in the historical accident of combination with other equally valuable forces, have deadly or indeed deathly effects.

What is implicit in this first appeal to some deeper meaningful logic, if not of the human instincts then at least of the socially and historically constructed human drives and powers, is a repudiation of vanguard left politics that is explicitly stressed in both of Negt and Kluge's books. *Eigensinn* or labor power, labor capacity, is then in that sense something like a Gramscian "good sense," inherent in the collectivity, and scarcely needful of the supplement of intellectual or vanguard political stimulus. That it may often seem to need that, however, is the effect of a deeper natural conservatism in the human organization, related to the requirements of shelter, protection, and subsistence: a number of pages in both books, indeed, systematically analyze historical crises in the labor movement from this perspective, and such analyses are clearly crucial to their project, which could still, in 1972, appeal to conceptions of cultural revolution, but which in 1981 speak from a situation of left discouragement and pessimism, in which Negt and Kluge wish to assert a hope of a longer, geological or evolutionary, type, a hope that retains from cultural revolution its pedagogical impulse and its drive toward self-formation and self-reconstruction.

Geschichte und Eigensinn is organized around three enormous subsections: "The Historical Organization of Labor Capacity"; "Germany as a Public Productional Sphere [*Produktionsöffentlichkeit*]"; "The Power of Relationality [*Gewalt des Zusammenhangs*]." It will be misleading, but indispensable, to describe these sections as follows: The first sets in place the elements of what I have called Negt and Kluge's "anthropology," namely their "political economy of labor power" — something that involves not only the labor process, but also evolutionary materials and an interest in the coexistence of a variety of temporal rhythms and cycles (individual, historical, and biological). The second section then attempts to confront the "peculiarities" of German history by way of these new production categories: its formal problem lies therefore in the conceptual gap between the language of historical events and a conceptuality of production whose scale and focus is clearly very different from historiography and often felt to be incommensurable with it. The final section, which also includes a disquisition on war as a kind of production, and a lengthy engagement with existential experience and psychoanalytic materials, can best be grasped as the attempt to produce a new active ethical and political value that is also a working concept, namely that of relationship or relationality itself. Theoretical positions emerge in each of these lengthy sections, and I will try to convey some of them: but they are not "argued," as the philosophers might put it, and the form of presentation is no longer that of the philosophical treatise or discursive essay. Rather, we might describe the book as a kind of conceptual film (if by film we have Kluge's own in our mind's eye).

The crucial mediatory concept in the introductory "anthropological" section, which must be abstract enough to function for a variety of different kinds of materials, but also contain within itself the force of an event (trauma, change, scar, transformation, an irrevocable that also brings the future with it), is the still classical Marxian notion of *Trennung* — separation, division, in Marx above all the historical "separation" of the producer from the means of production (as well as from the production and from production itself as my own activity). This is of course for Marx the central structural feature of that historical catastrophe at the very origin of capitalisim, namely "so-called primitive accumulation." Not only is there, therefore, already in Marx a mediation between a form of production and a historical event; Negt and Kluge will also generalize this event — primitive accumulation — along with its structural concept — *Trennung*, division and separation — into a more general historical and philosophical one, which designates all the catastrophes of history, most crucially at its beginning and in the destruction of traditional agricultural and communal societies. The concept of separation then becomes available for other kinds of materials: in the traditional Marxist literature, for the division of labor, for the separation between manual and intellectual labor, for the fragmentation of the psyche into distinct "faculties," and finally for the notion of reification itself (in Lukács primarily a matter of the "Taylorization" of social life); here in Negt and Kluge the primary emphasis seems to lie on the separation of the various work powers or capacities from one another, with results that will be clear later on. It will be objected that such a concept implicitly or explicitly tends to valorize the phenomenon of "unification" on which it necessarily depends: that may be so, and Negt and Kluge's vision of communal life on the land would certainly seem to provide evidence of historical nostalgia; but they explicitly repudiate conceptions of the dialectic that aim at restoring some primal unity (42–44: "What kind of reality would the reappropriation of something lost have?"). Far from perpetuating the longing for reunification, therefore, the fact and the concept of *Trennung* will have the very different effect of generating relationality as such, the ceaseless establishment of new connections and relationships. This too has its formal analogy in Marx, in the emergence, from the historical catastrophe of industrial wage labor, of the historically new value and social relationship he calls *cooperation* (192, and see below).

The other concept that emerges from this enlarged and generalized notion of "primitive accumulation" evidently turns around what is thereby accumulated: in this "political economy of labor power" that will be very precisely "dead labor," stored labor, the human labor of the past—a mysterious capital of human productive activity most dramatically in Marx associated with machinery and industrialization, in which that amassing of the labor time of preceding generations that necessarily characterizes all of human history knows a sudden quantum leap. In its larger redeployment here in Negt and Kluge, "dead labor" means tradition generally, cultural capital *and* habitus all together (to use Bourdieu's terminology), and very much includes the reproduction of acquired characteristics and of archaic character structures and the historical levels of the psyche. Dead labor is, however, for Negt and Kluge a baleful concept,[7] which can account for the violences of history and its seemingly cyclical, irrepressible disasters (and which thereby helps them avoid the ideological and anthropological temptation to posit negative forces within "human nature," such as aggressivity and the will to power). In this negative inflection of the notion of stored labor they approach the Sartrean idea of the "practico-inert" (developed in the *Critique of Dialectical Reason*), where human praxis, successfully invested in the transformation of the object world, then "magically" returns upon human beings with an autonomous power of its own, as destructive fate and the now incomprehensible and antihuman "counterfinality" of a History beyond all human control. Any comparison between these two cognate philosophical projections needs to register the difference in emphasis between Sartre's central category of praxis—as realized human activity of any type—and Negt and Kluge's notion of labor power or capacity, which stresses potentiality and the subterranean formation and exercise of a variety of capabilities. Sartre's vision of counterfinality is thereby incomparably more dramatic and vivid than Negt and Kluge's, but also relatively monolithic, subsuming a whole range of historical disruptions beneath the single named concept. In Negt and Kluge, however, dead labor can have a variety of distinct historical results: in German history, the Ur-trauma of the peasant wars, but also the initial disintegration of communal production at the dawn of feudalism, and the great "lost opportunity" of the anti-Napoleonic war of national liberation of 1811.

But their assessment of these historical events involves a reading of the Marxian "modes of production" that must first be laid in place. Characteristically, their attention to the various modes of production will be directed by their interest in the specific capacities and forms of labor power developed in each. Their first schema (165–210), then, isolates those three different moments of production, which are agriculture, handicraft, and industrial work; and to specify these as distinct kinds of labor (as well as different historical dominants or moments of social development) is to begin to imagine how capabilities needed and developed in one form might undergo a kind of sedimentation in the succeeding one, leaving traces and scars in layers on subjectivity and the body, on experience and in history itself. Like a swimmer's muscles mobilized during wartime for the digging of trenches and then used to make a living in the postwar era by way of acrobatic spectacles, historically developed capabilities persist, unused, misused, or readapted, occasionally interfering with one another or symptomatically marking and deforming the gestures current in some new kind of daily life.

Labor on the land is clearly for Negt and Kluge the "natural" form of human social life; or rather (since propositions of this type are alien to their work) it is at least the oldest form — the foundation but also the starting point — of the European and specifically the German social formation:

> We can only measure the comprehensive potentialities of field work by way of their modern transformations. Since all producers today derive via their ancestors from the peasant class, there is something like a "peasant in me." This component of contemporary labor capacity — in a certain hindsight the latter's foundation — reveals itself (and reveals itself today, as distinct from its *historical* representations) as *versatile* [*wendig*], working in a *nonfragmented* way, developing more concrete visions and intimations of *collective life* than the other,

later modes. The subtle component of properly "*spiritual*" activity follows the logic of a *peasant* or *gardening* mode of production. Labor capacity that aims at emancipatory processes or economic consciousness must necessarily deploy some vision of original property that stems from the history of agriculture. The idea of the "natural" qualities of a product and the development of human measures of time and temporality also derive from that source. In contrast, actual agricultural work today is in this country a subset of the industrial process. (174)

The observation will be misused or misunderstood if it is taken to be the development of a conservative or nostalgic ideological vision of the past: rather, it poses an empirical question about the actually existing utopian imagination, and thereby about the possibility of development for a political vision of change and action. What is asserted here and throughout is that *Eigentum* designates something more fundamental and necessary than property (the literal meaning of the word) in the juridical sense of forms of private property that come into being historically and can also be done away with. *Eigentum* — now in the more etymological sense of ownness, what belongs to me or us, what informs *Eigensinn* — is not a matter of possession but of place and space and of our relationship to what Marx called "the body of the earth." The consequence is that for Negt and Kluge the vision of a purely urban utopia is impossible,[8] and that the utopian imagination will always have to come to terms in one way or another with the demands of this the oldest layer of consciousness or labor capacity. What must then be stressed is not merely that this is also an urgent political issue — for there can be no development of any genuine political movement or praxis without a vision of the future and of radical change — but also that, in the postmodern era, characterized by the atrophy of the historical imagination in general and of the capacity to project the future in particular, the analysis of the way in which the utopian imagination functions is very much on the agenda.

In contrast, Negt and Kluge's devaluation of handicraft is to be read against a situation in which intellectuals are as a rule strongly drawn to this mode, which seems to offer an idealization of their own professional activities and of writing and cultural production in general[9] (the authors' more comprehensive discussion of the derivation of the work of intellectuals from more general productive capacities is to be found in the chapter entitled "On certain striking deviations in the functioning of intelligence" [415–88]). Handicraft can then be seen to project values of métier and craftsmanship whose darker side is less often stressed: not merely the extension of labor to nonnatural products, nor even the tendential "liberation" from time and space, from the earth and from the seasons, but above all some historically new principle of competition that arises from the work of small producers,

> each of whom finds his point of honor in the effort to distinguish his activity from that of everyone else. This principle of competition determines a general expansion of production. . . . Such tendential expansion is deeply embedded in handicraft, even to the point of self-destruction. The guilds then necessarily try to correct this impulse, by a limitation on products and a restriction on the choice of possible trades or callings. (175)

The very values of craftsmanship itself, then, lead dialectically to competition and to a limitless drive to overproduce commodities that foreshadows the market system itself and its structure and rhythms.

> The craftsman must work at two kinds of things at once: (1) his product and (2) the conviction in his client . . . that *his* product is indispensable and *uniquely* useful. This is a conviction the fieldworker does not particularly need to arouse. But what happens in handicraft labor is that, where painstaking effort is not visible, where the métier does not self-consciously make its presence felt, the activity ceases to be thought of as a matter of craftsmanship and stops being a viable profession. Professional honor must be present in the thing, like a payment for it — some first payment, which includes the recognition of its style and specificity, only then to be followed by the second one, in cash. (176)

Professional jealousies, pride, and competition, as well as the limitless dynamic of sheer commodity accumulation, are therefore already implicit in this mode, as the vices inherent in its virtues.

The industrial mode, and the nature of industrial labor, needs less attention since it has been so carefully examined from Marx himself on down. In a very different spirit from Negt and Kluge, Sartre's essentially urban perspective often led him to celebratons of the anti- and postnatural consciousness generated by work with machinery —

an insistence clearly an essential feature of any consequent "worker-
ism" or "workerist" ideology. The specific forms of the alienation
of factory work — and in particular its specific divisions or *Tren-
nungen* — are more vividly reflected in contemporary theory: particularly in Harry Braverman's fundamental analysis of Taylorism and
its effects, an analysis whose relevance for culture and intellectual
work has not been lost on contemporary theory, but is not particularly stressed by Negt and Kluge, even though they include a striking
analysis of a subsegment of production in a steel mill (202–7). The
unique and historically new capacity developed by factory work is,
however, cooperation; and the emergence of this new form of labor
will then allow Negt and Kluge to stage the final section of their book
in terms of the relationality that now issues from it.

Modes of production are, however, generally discussed and debated more historically, in terms of those formations named feudalism, capitalism, the Asiatic mode, and so forth. In order to understand how the preceding discussion can be related to that type of
historical category, and also in order to grasp how war can sometimes stand as a grisly caricature of cooperative labor on a national
scale, we must now (to borrow one of Negt and Kluge's favorite
expressions) pass through the "needle's eye" of German history.

It has the same starting point, namely the primacy of peasant experience and of the specific capacities developed through labor on
the land. Meanwhile, the German experience is determined by the
spatial situation of central Europe, thus offering all the peculiarities
of a land-based and landlocked collectivity. Experience, however, if
the word means anything, must designate not merely the kinds of
problems and dilemmas or crises confronted, but also what is
learned from those repetitive solutions, and what is transmitted in
the form of habit and pedagogy: but where are we to find the traces
of such experience and the codification of these collective learning
processes?

In fairy tales, which are not merely the repository of peasant utopian wishes ("those who don't believe in fairy tales were never in
distress [*Not*]" — 619 n. 48), but also preserve the most characteristic
collective experience of danger or menace, along with the age-old
solutions devised to ward it off. Fairy tales in Germany are thus a
collective testimony equivalent to but significantly different from the

myths and sea-based epic legends of the Mediterranean classical world, to which it is instructive to compare them. For the activities, the skills, strengths, and capacities celebrated, preserved, and transmitted by the Greek stories — those well-known "virtues" of shrewdness and cunning, resourcefulness and wiliness, of which Odysseus is the prototype — are the professional attributes of a world of commerce and trade, of merchant ruse and imperial diplomacy; they are shipboard attributes, augmented by ultimate recourse to the sea, to sail-borne flight or the return, at night, with muffled oars. For a peasantry, however, such narratives are problematic and unserviceable: unlike the great ships, "house, farmyard, and field cannot evade their dangers" (752). Meanwhile, for a peasant storytelling, for which "the dimension of production (or its impoverishment) is the determinant moment," tales of exploration and maritime adventure may look rather different and find their perspectives inverted.[10] So it is, for example, that the protagonist of the Argonaut myth is from the Greek standpoint Jason and his crew, a focus that relegates the peasant experience — the landed population of Colchis — to the position of the Other: they are here the prize and the object of exploitation, the story is not told for them, and this radical reversal of a peasant perspective is most evident in the inhumanity and monstrousness with which the figure of Medea herself emerges, a figure who from the indigenous point of view (compare the role of Malinche or Pocahontas in the New World) takes on the attributes of the patriot and the guerrilla, of Judith and of the struggles of wars of national liberation. From this pespective the Argonauts are not mere adventurers. Their function is to bring exchange and the market, to spell the doom of the older agricultural and communal system: "various episodes taken together make up the equivalent of what is, for *production*, the separation of labor power from the land and from the commune, namely primitive accumulation. From the perspective of goods distribution or the exchange relationship, there emerges an analogous mark of forced learning, of the introjection by violence" (747).

Within the peasant environment, therefore, and specifically within the world of the German fairy tale, this violence of commerce, this forcible "opening" and threat from without, will be registered in very different narrative forms and demand the development of very different kinds of essentially defensive skills. In "The Wolf and the Seven Little Kids," a premium is placed on powers of discrimination or judgment:

> What the enemy is is no longer clear. It becomes exceedingly difficult to decide whether the flour-covered paw of the wolf or the high-pitched voice belong to the other, or whether the mother (end or means) may not actually have a pelt covered with flour or a high-pitched voice, and so forth. The mind is thus directed, not toward adventure as such, but rather toward a more decisive question: how can I distinguish the enemy exactly, where are the boundaries between the inside and the outside, between safe and unsafe? All German myths, as testimony of historical experience, take as their content the question about the How of wishes, and tell the story of this central uncertainty: how can we know about the outside from within the inside? . . . This also shows how difficult it was, on the basis of the German relationship to history, to ascertain what was being let inside with Hitler. (754–55)

The originality of these analyses of Negt and Kluge, which prolong Benjamin's thoughts on collective narrative in *The Storyteller* in new and unforeseeable ways, consists in a hermeneutic that, although registering the function of the tale to reflect the collective situation in a twofold positive and negative way (it incorporates utopian hope or wish; it inscribes historical catastrophe), now strikes out in a third interpretive path, rereading the text as collective pedagogy, as the transmission now, not merely of experience, but also of collective vocational training. The instinctive recall of Brecht, whenever the pedagogical function of literature is invoked in the contemporary period, should not be allowed to distract us from some basic differences in emphasis: the content of Brecht's pedagogy is for one thing very different from Negt and Kluge's insistence on the learning of skills and capacities, while his reading of the texts of the past most often stresses bad pedagogy in the spirit of negative ideological critique (see the splendid sonnets on *Hamlet* and on Kleist). This is not to say that for Negt and Kluge a lesson, even well learned, cannot be without mixed consequences:

> The prototypical fairy tale that tries to rework this historical experience [an ideal dream of happiness that finds no encouragement in the social facts themselves] in a way propitious for wish fulfillment is Sleeping Beauty: an evil witch — but on top of everything evil out of

disappointment and therefore not merely evil, but also, in some
sense, a comrade — has set princess and castle, including all its
inhabitants and workers, in a magic sleep. Impenetrable hedges now
surround it. But at the very outset a good witch has also sworn an
oath, etc., etc. The main thing is simply to have the patience to
endure the thousand-year rhythm in which change takes place. So
when it turns out that the prince looks like Bismarck, Hindenburg,
Hitler, or Adenauer, it isn't out of stupidity that you made a mistake
and believe in the awakening kiss, nor out of lack of experience
(some of the princes are obviously very old, others come from
distant peripheral areas of the Reich and are very unaristocratic), but
rather out of the urgent need to give objective expression (however
improbably) to the ongoing immemorial work of wish fulfillment. It
must be somehow applied, and applicable! Even if those who pretend
to be princes are false a hundred times over! (619 n. 48)

This first strand of analysis of the German situation, therefore — a
kind of cultural investigation — retains the significance of the peasant
world, whose endemic crises and dangers it confronts with the specific *habitus* or labor capacity developed in peasant life, which is
evidently not altogether equal to the task of overcoming the former.

The same story is then told again, on the level of the various historical modes of production, and in particular in terms of the crisis
of feudalism, in a more concrete way in which historical events and
catastrophes now make their formal appearance. Indeed, Negt and
Kluge develop a provocative analysis of feudalism (559–65) in which
they suggest that what gives other national situations and histories
their productive dynamism — not merely their capacity to "evolve"
into capitalism but especially to generate active political movements
of all kinds — is the essentially impure or mixed nature of the feudalisms implanted there. The various feudalisms of Italy, France, and
England are never indigenous or autochthonous, but the result of
various kinds of foreign intervention: in Italy the German emperors,
in France the Franks, in England the Normans — these importations
mark the new socioeconomic system in such a way that its own specific internal contradictions cannot take deep root, making it susceptible to radical historical modification and change. But Negt and
Kluge follow Marx — in that section of the *Grundrisse* often re-
named "precapitalist modes of production" — in seeing feudalism as
a dialectical but nonetheless organic outgrowth of the communal
structure of the German tribes: feudalism is thereby at home in

Germany in a way very different from the Western histories, with the consequence that "the capitalistic principle found no original intro-jection [*originäre Verinnerlichung*] in our country" (893):

> The basic rule is this: where a social formation *originates*, it continues
> to bear all its contradictions and the essentials of its evolutionary
> emergence within itself. It therefore does not develop systematically
> into its fullest form, since those very contradictions and laws of
> emergence by definition tear apart its absolute principle. In this
> sense no original prototype, but rather the feudal structure that
> William the Conqueror and his barons brought with them to England,
> stands as the most perfect realization of a classic feudal constitution.
> (562–63)

Replaced within the current "modes of production" debate, the anal-ogy might well be the history of the capitalist mode, whose "indig-enous" form in England remained notoriously unaccompanied by any "pure" political development of a triumphant bourgeoisie and a middle-class state (as in France).

However one judges this new theory of "transition," it will in Negt and Kluge have two different lines of consequence. One has to do with what is often called the national character: "In the German con-figuration of the feudalism/capitalism form, the principle of abstrac-tion [for Negt and Kluge, as for the Marxist tradition generally, a more general description of the essentially abstract "logic of capital"] ap-pears as that of uncertainty in the application of power; by the same token, its specific principle of production can be described as an ideal of completeness and thoroughness [*Gründlichkeit*]" (564). We will return to this *habitus*, which combines arbitrariness with a com-pulsive work ethic, shortly.

The other, historical result of the contradictions in German feu-dalism is an event: the catastrophe of the Peasant Wars, the Ur-trauma of German history and one of those "resolutions" of class struggle about which Marx was probably thinking when in the *Manifesto* he evoked, as an alternate outcome to the "revolutionary reconstitution of society at large," the possibility of "the common ruin of the con-tending classes."[11] For this common ruin is very specifically what the Peasant Wars achieve:

> The peasant wars end with the political victory of a coalition made up
> of city burghers and feudal lords, but from an economic perspective

all three of the classes involved in the struggle — peasants, lords,
cities — all know defeat. In the future no one of the three classes will
ever be able to establish its independent political dominion.
Economic and political determinants drift apart. (556)

Negt and Kluge stress the cultural consequences of the catastrophe;
and it is logical, in light of their valorization of the land and of peasant labor, that they should isolate as a supreme symptom the way in
which peasant culture is stigmatized and repressed in Germany in
the succeeding centuries, giving rise to an artificial culture based on
what Bourdieu calls "distinction." Even the emergent middle classes
now want to be "refined," have manners, transcend the body, and
acquire "culture" and "taste" in their new ideological senses. Another fairy tale, "The Three Brothers," showing the absurdity of a
competition for arbitrary new skills when the upshot will be to live
all together in the old home after all, is in this respect cautionary. It
proves to dramatize

> the distance that now divides collective life, the simple house on
> simple soil, from "simple" activity. Simplicity is not so easy to achieve.
> One's own soil and collective life correspond rather to a complex
> psychic structure and remain the high point and the prize toward
> which all labor power strives. On the human or individual scale, such
> values then become ever more distant and difficult to realize, and for
> that reason you have to work ever harder and take more pains. This
> is very precisely the developmental path of the introversion of labor
> capacity in Germany. (632)

This is then the point at which the tendential repudiation of peasant
culture, the radical turning away from peasant "labor capacity" and
the repression of the "peasant in me," dialectically generates the
German form of that principle of abstraction that has been mentioned above (and which is for Negt and Kluge a virtual Thanatos or
death drive within capitalism as well as in German history). The
stress is not on the features of some national identity or national
character (which then in the pluralism of human cultures and collective identities takes its rather unique and grisly place), but rather
on the failure of national identity, and on what they call "national
loss" (*Nationalverlust*, 538), seen not in terms of collective psychology but as a subset of a general loss in reality itself (see below).
There emerges a specific form of German "inflexibility" that ranges

across a host of historical and cultural embodiments as well as a variety of linguistic expressions, from the work ethic of painstaking thoroughness (*sich Mühe geben, Gründlichkeit*: see above) to the terrible righteousness of Kleist's Michael Kohlhaas (and of Luther and Kant) and beyond to the inexorability (*Unerbittlichkeit*) of resistance and obedience to the state in the last weeks of World War II, or the implacable strategy of the Baader-Meinhof Red Army Faction in the mid-1970s *fiat justitia pereat mundus!* Let justice prevail even though the world itself should go under:

> Even if civil society were to dissolve itself with the consent of all its members (for example, if a people who inhabited an island decided to separate and to disperse to other parts of the world), the last murderer in prison would first have to be executed in order that each should receive his deserts and that the people should not bear the guilt of a capital crime through failing to insist on its punishment.... 'It is better that one man should die than that the whole people should go to ruin.' For if justice perishes, there is no further point in men living on earth.[12]

These chilling words of Kant are more deeply and figurally inscribed at the very center of *Geschichte und Eigensinn* in the form of the shortest and most dreadful of all the Grimm fairy tales, "The Willful Child" (*Das eigensinnige Kind*), whose obstinacy, first expressed in disobedience and then in a kind of psychosomatic illness, persists after death (a hand stubbornly emerging from the grave) and must be chastised posthumously by the mother before rest is found. In the German history section, then, the enigmatic *Eigensinn* of Negt and Kluge's title (interpreted philosophically in our various translations above) now takes on ironic literality, not only now formally posing the question of the relationship between history and inflexible self-will in Germany itself, but also raising the now current issues of the relationship in the past and the dead in Germany today, and in particular the much-discussed question of the "work of mourning" (Freud's expression *Trauerarbeit*) needed to exorcize that past (rather than to repress it). For this particular fairy tale, however, the Greek equivalent comes as a rebuke (765–69): for the stubbornness of Antigone is a heroic form of political resistance with a social and collective resonance utterly lacking in the German story. Antigone's

Eigensinn remains, to be sure, deadly, but it is a deathly outcome that, as Hegel showed us, is now consecrated as tragedy, which is to say, as contradiction and as the unavoidable blocking of historical development; it has none of the shame that oddly clings to the Grimm tale, where the child seems pathological, but even the mother (in Negt and Kluge a nurturing, sheltering figure associated with the primal commune) becomes strangely ambivalent and repulsive, as she shatters the child's dead arm with her rod.

How, in the third section of this book, relationship, relationality as such, affords the diagnosis of such symptoms, let alone a prescription for their transcendence, must now in conclusion be sketched in. What must most urgently be related is surely what we conventionally dissociate as the public and the private, the political and the psychic, the realm of the socioeconomic, with its language of production, and that of the psychoanalytic, with its languages of desire and fantasy. The act by which these dimensions are related will be, as a whole range of currents in contemporary thought testifies, a punctual and discontinuous one, a provisional exchange of energies, a spark struck across, and will no longer present the appearance of the older systematic attempts at a formal Freudo-Marxian synthesis, in which Freud's findings are somehow built into Marx once and for all in some new total system. What underlies the provisionality of the new "relational" approaches is no doubt the feeling that dimensions that are objectively sundered in our social order cannot finally be reassembled and put back together by an effort of pure thought.

Here too, in one sense Negt and Kluge prolong and correct Habermas, whose "synthesis" of Marx and Piaget[13] aimed to substitute a cognitive evolution for the discontinuous violence of social revolution. In Habermas issues of desire, the unconscious, and sexuality are no longer much in evidence, but Piagetian psychology still affords in his work a kind of bridge between the "objective" historical and social situation and the "subjective factor," the kinds of individual dispositions and mental equipment necessary for social change and for the inauguration of a new stage in social development. In Negt and Kluge, the Piagetian reference is reduced to one of many constellations of illustrative or analogical materials, along with Freud, evolutionary theory, anatomy, cultural archaeology, and the rest: but Habermas's great theme of the cognitive — here transformed into the pedagogical and the formative — is centrally maintained, and offers a utopian response to the classical Frankfurt School critique of bourgeois "enlightenment" as such (a critique that remains an embarrassment for Habermas himself, since he is concerned, as we have seen, to promote the utopian possibilities inherent in precisely that bourgeois Enlightenment and the bourgeois concept of Reason).

As for desire and fantasy, however, their status in contemporary theory seems to result from the feeling everywhere today that narrative, image, fantasy, and embodied symptom are no longer mere subjective epiphenomena of one sort or another but objective components of our social world, invested with all the ontological dignity of all the other hitherto "objective" social materials presented by economics, politics, and historiography. What is even more significant is that such hitherto subjective or psychological phenomena are now increasingly seen as having epistemological and even practical functions: fantasy is no longer felt to be a private and compensatory reaction against public situations, but rather a way of reading those situations in its own right, of thinking and mapping them, of intervening in them, albeit in a very different form from the abstract reflections of traditional philosophy or politics. Deleuze and Guattari's two-volume *Capitalism and Schizophrenia* (which so often comes to mind in reading this other collaboration) testifies to the richness of such explorations, as does Theweleit's related *Männerphantasien* (both are invoked in these pages). Along with the traditional idea of Reason, however, one of the casualties of this new valorization of fantasy (which surely corresponds both to historical changes in the structure of society and to the media apparatus of late capitalism) is the traditional concept of ideology and ideological analysis (essentially still the false-consciousness, or base-and-superstructure model, not often appealed to here): into the breach opened in this area, a whole range of new "ideologies of Desire" have flowed. It is certain that, in the spirit of their antivanguard political positions, Negt and Kluge's utopian work implicitly rejects the negativity of traditional forms of "ideology critique"; equally certain that, particularly if we augment the theoretical collaboration with Kluge's own stories and films, the primacy of the "subjective factor" is here everywhere affirmed, but as historical fact. Just as in Marx capital itself has a *Heisshunger* (voracious appetite) for the realization of value, so Negt and Kluge identify a comparable appetite and lust for the "private," the "intimate," and the "subjective" in modern society:

> Relationships are to be found in all public areas that have been structured as private enclaves. But the libidinal relationships encapsulated in private contacts in the narrower sense reach the most bewildering levels of intensity of all social relationships. . . . The disintegration of the traditional public sphere programmed into the current crisis system therefore leads not merely to the strengthening of forces intent on constructing alternate or proletarian public spheres. It also simultaneously encounters this other tendency toward the private accumulation of the work of relationship [*Beziehungsarbeit*], a kind of voracious appetite of the work of relationship, the private search for happiness. (877)

This compensatory reading of the subjectification of modern life is, however, in Negt and Kluge complicated by their (properly post-1960s) insistence on the importance of "intimacy" as such: "intimacy is the practical touchstone for the substance of the public sphere" (944). This emphasis now reconnects the materials of *Geschichte und Eigensinn* with the program of the earlier work and its projection of an alternative, proletarian public sphere, about which it is now affirmed that the latter can only be tested (politically as well as theoretically) by its capacity to handle the whole raw material of the private or intimate (or, using our own narrower terminology, to transcode this last).

The earlier work, however, which necessarily dealt extensively with the commodification of fantasy in contemporary media (and also in fascism), took a somewhat simpler and populist position on the transformation of the subjective in some new proletarian public sphere. Drawing on Basil Bernstein's notion of the "restricted code" of working-class language (which he sees as essentially situation-specific), and driven by a related critique of the "principle of abstraction" in the bourgeois media, *Öffentlichkeit und Erfahrung* stressed the bodily and sensual/sensuous (*sinnlich*) requirements of proletarian consciousness (as well as the ways in which these sensuous necessities are appropriated and displaced by the dominant media).

The emphasis on the bodily is maintained in the later volume (most strikingly in the Bourdieu-like diagnosis of the repression of a corporeal peasant culture by bourgeois "distinction"), but the analysis of fantasy itself is here far more complexly articulated. Negt and Kluge propose indeed at one point a sixfold differentiation of the coordinates or dimensions of social consciousness: horizontal, vertical, functional, irrational, imaginary, and revolutionary (511). The first two of these coordinates or capacities still designate the immediate individual possibilities for thinking and for mapping out a given situation, observing it from across a wide perspective, or on the other hand digging in it,[14] reading it diachronically or synchronically, much as in the successive volumes of *Capital* Marx shows that processes can be described either as cycles or as simultaneous interlocking operations. But both *horizontal* and *vertical* dimensions remain bounded by the horizon of the immediate situation. What is structurally not fully perceptible within that set of immediate coordinates — such as, for example, the multifarious prolongations of social institutions and firms whose significance and operations I cannot deduce on the basis of my phenomenological contact with their public facade — falls under the category of the *functional*, which requires a different kind of evidence and different kinds of thinking or analysis: "I must here measure in order to orient myself; here *immediate* forms of essential relationship no longer exist unless I can manage to produce them myself. Here therefore orientation finds itself dominated by synthetic conducts. Immediate impressions are as misleading as 'obviousness' of hegemonic categories" (513).

The functional is therefore already the place of alienated reality in the strict sense of the term; but also that of scientific analysis, and of the correction of appearance and ideological distortion by theory. The next three coordinates, however, clearly move us into the whole area of the "libidinal," or of fantasy and "subjectivity"; and the originality of Negt and Kluge here is to have articulated this whole area in a new and complex way whose threefold system usefully complicates and differentiates the usual dualisms (such as the De-leuze-Guattari binary opposition between the paranoid and the schizophrenic — the molar and the molecular, the statist and the nomadic — which are there somewhat too easily assimilated into the value opposition between the fascist and the revolutionary, respectively). One also has the sense that, with the appearace side by side of the hitherto generally synonymous terms of the *irrational* and the *imaginary*, we have cut back through the sedimented philosophical and psychoanalytic connotations of these words to their original mathematical senses where "irrational" designates quantities that, although existent, have no objective embodiment in reality (that is to say, they correspond to no *ratios* or integers), while "imaginary" designates negative quantities to be taken into account in computations but that cannot be thought of as corresponding to any particular existent: the distinction would be what obtains between π and the square root of minus one, for example.

> If the functional is the coordinate of my determination from the outside, the *irrational* is the sum of *direct* answers, compromises (or balancing acts), evasions, furnished by the *antirealism of motives*; the imaginary is then the coordinate of reality loss, historical loss, identity loss, and — something of the greatest interest in the present context — national loss. But if the determination from the outside [the functional] still includes a dimension of human praxis (diverted but continuing to realize itself), i.e., alienated *labor*, inverted *life*, false *consciousness*, including their reification and elaboration on higher levels, and if the irrationality produced by that dimension and its production process is still present within it, the *dimension of the imaginary* is on the contrary determined by the becoming unreal and the loss of objectification. Attention exclusively directed to the functional and the irrational, which aims at protesting the loss of natural relations in spatial and temporal contexts and in human arrangements, tends generally to overlook this antidimension of the loss of solid ground and the conjuring into nothingness of real time. The *dimension of the revolutionary*, simultaneously virulent in all the other dimensions, where it has, however, failed to realize itself, stands in the sharpest antagonism possible to this particular dimension of the antiworld and the imaginary: much more sharply than it does to the functional or the irrational, which to be sure set barriers to the revolutionary, but also lend it new substance and content. (511–12)

These distinctions will be clarified by Negt and Kluge's discussion of the concept (which is to say the experience) of "reality," articulated into the axis of determinacy (or indeterminacy) and that of objectivity (or the dissolution of the boundaries of the object) (343). As the preceding passage suggests, however, the Real has not one but two opposites: the antireal and the unreal, the refusal to accept reality in protest and revolt, and that very different kind of reality loss designated above by the term *imaginary*, in which the very substance of the world and our active relations with it drain away, leaving us in a passive floating relationship to an only feebly cathected phantasmagoric outer world. The point of such distinctions, finally, is to confront and come to terms with the ambivalence of mass political commitment, both retrospectively (in the mass popular adherence to nazism) and today, where everyone seems intent on assuring us that the masses have become consumers or at the very least have been definitively depoliticized. The systematic reinterrogation of nazism as a successful appeal to the working classes, which began in the 1960s (often including a return to Wilhelm Reich's early works on the subject), and which constitutes the central motive power of the Deleuze-Guattari works mentioned earlier, obviously becomes meaningless when the distinction between reactionary and progressive impulses is abandoned; the problem lies in maintaining this distinction as a symmetrical dualism. In effect Negt and Kluge maintain the drive toward a utopian transformation of present circumstances by way of their "revolutionary" coordinate while articulating what used to be called "reactionary" (on the basis of its effects) into a variety of different coordinates whose constellation varies historically.

As for the present, the authors explain repeatedly that *Geschichte und Eigensinn* emerged directly from the reflections on the labor movement that took up so large a part of the earlier work (389). Even though the later volume also concludes with an explicit discussion of aspects of working-class politics, however, it is clearly pitched at a more general theoretical level and in terms of a longer (not to say more evolutionary) time scale, moving beyond the immediate question of the here and now toward the problems of tradition, collective pedagogy, collective habitus, and also of the scars of the past: not the least interesting moment, indeed, of *Öffentlichkeit und Erfahrung* involved the lessons of defeat (in the process repudiating the facile triumphalism discernable in so much left retelling of history). Mao Zedong, they remind us, describes the "Internationale" in one of his poems as a "tragic song," a memorial of bloody failures; and they quote the closing fragment of *Dialectic of Enlightenment*[15] to telling effect: "Stupidity is a scar ... good will turns to evil when it suffers repeated violence," adding:

Yet social sensibility needs the resistance upon which it works and from which it works itself out in order to constitute itself as experience. Learning processes based on defeat must therefore be undertaken in terms of two distinct kinds of experience: a destructive and an emancipatory one. When only one is present, a mistake in the analysis can generally be detected.[16]

Lernprozesse: this word, along with the term *Lebenslauf* (individual life history, as in the title of Kluge's first book of stories), is probably the most insistent recurrent terminological signal in Kluge's work, as well as in this collaboration. Life trajectories are those units of passionate existential experience that have been reduced and compressed into glacial, well-nigh statistical anecdotes by the mass of history itself: a woman fleeing the American bombs and hiding in the cellar of a bombed-out house, a superannuated high school teacher writing a memoir of Charlemagne in the debacle of May 1945, juridical cases, compulsive thefts and flights, postwar survivals in which both rubble and unexpected affluence are equally bewildering for the subjects in question, who often, in Kluge's stories and films alike, seem quietly aberrant and bereft of the social habits that might have given their movements a certain stability, even in the absence of individual motivations and ambitions. Anecdote is here what binds the individual to the collective and historical by problematizing the connection: it can scarcely teach lessons, save to raise the supreme riddle of how we learn anything in the first place. In this sense, the one optimistic note in Kluge's first film (*Abschied von gestern*) — "You can't learn not to learn" — often seems wildly premature.

Yet it suggests that "learning," whatever it is, is not a conscious or voluntary process and that some first step consists in discovering what has in fact been learned, in detecting the powers and habits, the capacities (*Arbeitsvermögen*) that have already been accumulated, in the body, in the unconscious, in the collectivity. Relationality — which we have seen is Negt and Kluge's ultimate practical message or slogan — is far from proposing any organic synthesis of those capacities; and indeed their proposal for the making of connections sometimes has a remarkably postmodern ring:

But these multiple languages of the various relationships cannot be reduced to anything unified. Nor do the capacities for autonomy require complete translation in the detail. They can perfectly well accommodate untranslatability and even the incomprehensibility of these various languages among each other, provided the untranslated is grasped as relationship. (1088)

Yet it would be well to think of relationality (even here) in the light of the value of *Öffentlichkeit* proclaimed in the earlier work—a bringing into the open, an expressing and making public, not quite to be reduced either to Habermas's notion of communication on the one hand nor to the mere establishment of new kinds of institutions on the other. The relationship, then, between "relationality" and the "public sphere" might best at first be grasped by way of the blocking of both and the limits and boundaries built into our current social arrangements:

> For conveying the rigidity of the social compartmentalization of experience, nothing better occurs to us than the prison. Here we have the institution of the visitors' room: the only point of contact between the realm of experience of those inside and of those outside, even though ultimately each prisoner belongs to both. But in industry provision is not made even for this kind of visitors' cell as a place of exchange of those points of contact the worker needs, as an organism that exists indivisibly inside and outside all at once. (795 n. 5)

A politics of *Öffentlichkeit* would necessarily begin from this situation and this image, and it would clearly also be a cultural politics in that wider sense in which Negt and Kluge once used the term "cultural revolution" (oddly, there is very little discussion of culture as such or even specifically cultural production in *Geschichte und Eigensinn*).

As for "labor capacity" itself, however, which constituted something like the official theme or topic of the book, relationality here also means judgment or discrimination (a power that must itself, as in the fairy tale illustrations, be developed in its own right): it involves not merely the assessment of a given force or power in and of itself (craftsmanship, perseverance, courage, etc.), but also the way in which it intersects with other forces and the kinds of combinations within which it is applied. Judgment of this kind is a well-nigh juridical matter, and above and beyond the "accident" of Kluge's personal profession, there is therefore a deeper significance in the considerable role played by lawyers, law courts, and legal judgments in his stories and films. For a capacity such as "reliability" (*Verläss-lichkeit*) is finally, in concrete history, exceedingly ambivalent: combined with other contradictory "capacities" the devotion to duty of a bomber pilot or technician can figure in very different kinds of stories: on the one hand, in what seems to be the Ur-trauma of Kluge's stories, the bombing of his own town of Halberstadt on April 8, 1945, when he was thirteen years old;[17] on the other hand, the "unreliability" of the technician who told on Nixon and Kissinger when he discovered that the targets assigned were in fact located on the far side of the Cambodian border (700–703).

In such examples, the whole issue of the personal and of individual and collective pedagogy veers around into the ethical, but in some new way that no longer needs that term and its history and that redirects our attention from the putative qualities of individual talents and forces it to the more urgent matter of their combinations. *Arbeitsvermögen* thus becomes a new way of raising the issue, not of virtue as such, but of the original Aristotelian "virtues," of which Alisdair MacIntyre's book *After Virtue* reminds us that they are multiple and collective, and demand a rethinking of the individualist traditions of conventional moral philosophy.

New learning processes would be required for such a reinvention, for which *Geschichte und Eigensinn* tries to give us some new names. The task cannot even be begun, however, without a vivid awareness that there also exist *Lernprozesse mit tödlichem Ausgang* — learning processes that have deadly outcomes (the title of one of Kluge's collections of stories). That other outcomes, other learning processes, are at least conceivable is what the present volume asks us to imagine.

NOTES

1. *Öffentlichkeit und Erfahrung: Zur Organisationsanalyse von bürgerlicher und proletarischer Öffentlichkeit* (Frankfurt: Suhrkamp, 1972); *Geschichte und Eigensinn* (Frankfurt: Zeitausendeins, 1981). All page numbers given in the text refer to this second volume.

2. Alexander Kluge and Edgar Reitz, "In Gefahr und grösster Not bringt der Mittelweg den Tod," *Kursbuch* 41 (1975): 42–43.

3. *La Preuve par l'etymologie* (Paris: Minuit, 1953).

4. Anton Kaes, *Deutschlandbilder* (Munich: Edition text und kritik, 1987), 48.

5. In both books, Negt and Kluge use the term *proletarian* in its most general sense: "proletarian, i.e., separated from the means of production, designates not merely the labor characteristics of the industrial proletariat, but all similarly restricted productive capacities," *Geschichte und Eigensinn*, 445, n. 16.

6. And see, on Kluge more generally, Miriam Hansen, "Space of History, Language of Time: Kluge's *Yesterday Girl* (1966)," in *German Film and Literature: Adaptations and Transformations*, ed. Eric Rentschler (New York: Methuen, 1985), 193–216; and "The Stubborn Discourse: History and Story-Telling in the Films of Alexander Kluge," in *Persistence of Vision* 2 (Fall 1985): 19–29; and also Andrew Bowie, "Alexander Kluge: An Introduction," *Cultural Critique* 4 (Fall 1986): 111–18; "*Geschichte und Eigensinn*," *Telos* 66 (Winter 1985–86): 183–90; and "New Histories: Aspects of the Prose of Alexander Kluge," *Journal of European Studies* 12 (1982): 180–208.

7. "Only in wartime is the abrupt liquification of dead historical labor translated into a real acceleration. The thousand-year-old city of Magdeburg burned down in two days during the Thirty Years' War. But as far as the historical process is concerned hardly anything was brought into movement during the Thirty Years' War. In particular, no social relationship expressed itself in any real way in the burning of Magdeburg." *Geschichte und Eigensinn*, 276.

8. Here once again their thought finds some resonance in that of Raymond Williams: the claims of an urban versus a pastoral utopia have been dramatized most richly in science fiction, particularly in the "debate" between Samuel Delany and Ursula Le Guin.

9. As, for example, in Roland Barthes's description of the handicraft aesthetic of the early modern, in particular in Flaubert and Baudelaire (*Writing Degree Zero* [London: Cape, 1967]).

10. Contemporary studies of the literature of modern imperialism—also essentially a literature of adventure—are relevant here: see, for example, Edward Said, "Kim, The Pleasures of Imperialism," in *Raritan* 7, no. 2 (Fall 1987): 27–64.

11. Marx and Engels, *Basic Writings*, ed. L. Feuer (New York: Doubleday, 1959), 7.

12. Immanuel Kant, *The Metaphysics of Morals*, in *Kant's Political Writings*, ed. H. Reiss (Cambridge: Cambridge University Press, 1970), 156, 155 (quoted in this form in Kluge's story "Hinscheiden einer Haltung," in *Lebensläufe* [Hamburg: Fischer, 1964], 26).

13. In *Zur Rekonstruktion des historischen Materialismus* (Frankfurt: Suhrkamp, 1976).

14. Digging, part of the peasant "labor capacity," is often associated in fairy tales with finding buried treasure: being lucky, where the German word for good fortune, *Glück*, is also the word for happiness; on happiness itself, see the very remarkable pages in *Geschichte und Eigensinn*, 924–30, which in many ways prolong Adorno.

15. "On the Genesis of Stupidity," in Adorno and Horkheimer, *Dialektik der Aufklärung* (Frankfurt: Fischer, 1986), 228–30.

16. *Öffentlichkeit und Erfahrung*, 404–5.

17. See, for example, the "second notebook" in his *Neue Geschichten* (Frankfurt: Suhrkamp, 1977), 33–106.

Is a Democracy Possible?
The Decline of the Public in the American Debate
Stanley Aronowitz

To dissenting and oppositional intellectuals the 1920s were a turning point. The "American celebration," always an intrinsic feature of American nationalist ideology, seemed to reach a fever pitch with the election of the deeply conservative and isolationist Warren Harding; the ascendancy of a new era of religious fundamentalism; the crushing of the Great Steel Strike in 1919 and the wave of subsequent lost strikes — in the midst of unparalleled prosperity — in textiles, the needle trades, and metal fabricating industries; and the turn of the Democratic Party from its promise of a New Freedom to an adjunct of the national consensus. Leading philosophers and critics such as Thorstein Veblen, John Dewey, and especially Walter Lippmann were convinced that republican democracy was in crisis. They spent much of the postwar era trying to understand it and find the strategic grounds for political reconstruction.

The consensus among most of these writers was that industrialism and urbanism had produced a palpable decline of the democratic "public." There was also agreement that the key to this deterioration of public life was to be found not in the surface evidence of a new conservatism, labor struggles, or the religious revival that, notoriously, challenged the legitimacy of natural science to explain human and cosmological evolution. Instead, these postwar developments were themselves symptoms of the increasing mediation of reality by newspapers, film, and radio. These new media provided only partial and often distorted information, and the public's capacity to make political decisions suffered accordingly. Knowledge of public events had become impossibly fragmented, everyday life had become increasingly privatized, and, perhaps most importantly, the whole society had become absorbed in an orgy of consumption. For these critics, the survival of democracy itself was at stake. For if one could not presuppose, even in theory, the existence of a public capable of grasping both large (national and international) and local public issues, then the institutions of democracy were fated to wither, regardless of the formal guarantees of participation provided by open primaries, general elections, and even membership in political parties.

Recall that for Jefferson, the possibility of a public of decision makers hinged on the efficacy of public education that could provide to its people a broad cultural formation in which the individual, schooled in the tools of language, the intellectual and artistic traditions of civilization, and a thorough knowledge of contemporary public issues was literally *trained for citizenship*. For Dewey, the school became the moral equivalent of the education afforded aristocrats and upper middle classes as a matter of right. For Jefferson and Dewey both, genuine democracy presupposed such citizenship training. By the early twentieth century, however, Dewey seemingly had reason to be alarmed, and Lippmann to more than doubt that an active democratic public was possible. Their despair can be traced to a long-standing assumption concerning the relation of high to "mass" entertainments — more globally to the degree that mass media dominate our intellectual as well as our aesthetic lives.

In what follows, I will dispute their fundamental premise: the claim that the cultivation of aesthetic and intellectual "taste" is a necessary concomitant, if not a prerequisite, of citizenship. I will argue that this profoundly undemocratic expectation has subverted the development of a genuine theory of the public sphere. For it assumes that, lacking education, the "people" are fated to be inherently incapable of governing themselves. At the same time, most theorists and critics in this mode recognize that mediated knowledge and popular culture are an inevitable consequence of what Benjamin calls the age of the mechanical reproducibility of art, and others have called "mass" society. Once one posits that industrialization, especially technological transformation, *entails* massification, fragmentation, and degradation, the logical outcome is that democracy is all but impossible, all protestations to the contrary notwithstanding.

It is now necessary to delve a little deeper into the precise nature of the connection between questions of political and social rule and those of culture. The theory of mass culture implies the theory of the massification of society and the transformation of the conception of the *polis*. We have lost, it suggests, a public sphere consisting in its ideal form of individuals who, because they are freed from the banalities of everyday life, can in consequence know the common interests and legislate in their behalf. And we have entered an age of mass passivity where citizenship consists merely in giving consent through the ritual of voting. The ultimate referent of mass society is the historical moment when the "masses" make the (still) contested demand for the full privileges of citizenship, despite the fact that they are obliged to work at mundane tasks, are typically untrained for the specific functions of governance, and are ensconced in the routines of everyday life. In this discourse, the term "masses" does not connote those on the lower rungs of the social and economic ladder (in Ortega's terms, the working class). More apposite is the distinction between those in all the classes of the third estate condemned to active participation only in the labor process and commerce or in the vagaries of privatized existence (the family in its broadest connotation), on the one hand, and on the other the elite of intellectuals and modern aristocrats who are able to employ their leisure in the cultivation and dissemination of civilization, with all of the baggage associated with that term — aesthetics, ethics, and, of course, political and social knowledge and the responsibility that is consequent upon it.

Plainly, the masses include the mass of the middle classes. Indeed, for de Tocqueville and Ortega on the right, as for Veblen on the left, the urban middle class is invariably the bearer of cultural degeneration. For the high cultural intellectuals the banal existence of "mass man" disqualifies the "people" for making aesthetic and philosophical judgments. To the contrary, good taste must be protected from the masses of those engaged in commerce no less than the productive classes lest civilization itself degenerate. According to these theorists, the "masses" are subject to a division of labor that limits their vision to the particular interests of their family and community.

Moreover, as Lippmann cogently argues, their ability to transcend the conditions of their own upbringing and immediate environment is virtually nonexistent. For him privatized existence compounds the problems of systematically distorted communications offered by mass media and professional politicians.

What is at stake is whether a larger conception of democracy than that of representative, republican government — that is, a polity that can take control over economic and political life — is at all desirable, much less possible in a world increasingly dominated by standardization, fragmentation, and escapist pleasure, what Herbert Marcuse calls "repressive desublimation." In short, despite the pervasiveness of democratic ideology since the French Revolution, intellectuals left and right have questioned its consequences in terms that are remarkably consistent since de Tocqueville's lament.

Perhaps the most subtle and influential American treatise against the concept of mass democracy was Walter Lippmann's *Public Opinion* (1922). Lippmann had been a socialist but discarded this allegiance in the wake of the Great War, when he discovered his own nationalism, and also the dangers of placing primary, much less exclusive, reliance on the decision-making power of the democratic *polis*. Lippmann's crucial argument presupposes a social and, more specifically, an epistemological premise: that there is a profound chasm between "the world inside our heads" and reality. The world inside our heads is shaped by various stereotypes promulgated by habit and tradition but also by newspapers, magazines, and the statements of politicians. The vast public forms its opinions according to these stereotypes, which shape what we see: "For the most part, we do not first see, and then define, we define first and then see. In the great blooming, buzzing confusion of the outer world we pick out what our culture has already defined for us, and we tend to perceive that which we have picked out in the form *stereotyped for us* by our culture" (emphasis added).

This process is made all but inevitable by the fact that, individually, we occupy only a small part of the world — our family, our work, our friends are the context and the substance of what we call "experience." We may belong to organizations such as civic groups and labor and business organizations, or even be professionals, such as engineers, physicians, and attorneys. Yet, according to Lippmann, none of us is exempt from perceiving the world as a series of stereotypes given to us by the culture. Thus, unlike most other critics of mass culture who carefully distinguish between educated minorities and the masses, he is not concerned to reproduce a picture in which the mass public is fundamentally different from "trained observers." Unlike his master Plato, whose allegory of the cave places the philosopher in a qualitatively better position to see reality than the mass of people, Lippmann *universalizes* the problem of shadow knowledge to embrace all of humanity insofar as it acts as private individuals. Given the necessary distortions in perception, there are bound to be necessary distortions of judgment mediated, in the main, by particular interests, by the fragmentation of everyday existence, and by the distortions of media representations. The "buzzing confusion of the outer world" is the mode of existence of humans. Although Lippmann is most interested in the problems of political democracy, specifically how the public may function as the *legitimating* base of any nonauthoritarian system of governance, his argument rests at its most profound level on what might be described as a *social epistemology* in which "culture" is the crucial determinant of the ways of seeing social reality. His sources — the art critic Bernard Berenson and anthropologist A. van Gennep — are much clearer about the Kantian premises of this argument. If there is no chance that the public can "see" beyond its own "self-contained community" or the distorted communications of the news media or even "education and institutions" that can sharpen the differences between images and reality, "the common interests very largely elude public opinion entirely and can only be managed by a specialized class whose personal interests reach beyond the locality" (195). This is usually an irresponsible arrangement when the specialized class lacks the disinterest as well as the expert intelligence required to identify the public interest and act rationally to serve it. Yet in the absence of a theory of social transformation that can account, if not for the immediate prospect, at least for the *possibility* of a democratic and competent public able to intervene in or control processes of governance, Lippmann is obliged to fall back on the hope of creating a professionally competent public bureaucracy that is, at the same time, responsible to what he later was to term the "phantom" public.

The conclusion of Lippmann's discourse is both tortured and ironic. Clearly, he recognizes the danger of placing such extraordinary power in the hands of experts who, as his previous examples amply showed, were not typically more reliable than the broad public. But by providing stability without which no intelligent and effective government can exist, the trained, expert bureaucracy may help unite "reason and politics." In the end, he argues that we must retain democratic institutions such as elections if only because the alternative, a self-contained oligarchy, is worse. Thus, the public must be consulted and, periodically, must "intervene" to keep the technical bureaucracy honest and assert its own needs, but the creation of a genuine public sphere, as in the political theory that derived its conception of democracy from the Athenian example, is utterly out of the question. In the end, embarrassed by his own reference, Lippman turns to Plato's words in book five of *The Republic* as his epigraph: "Until philosophers are kings, or the kings and princes of this world have the spirit and power of philosophy, and political greatness and wisdom meet in one . . . cities will never cease from ill — no, nor the human race." For Lippmann, Socrates' decision to "retire in anger" in the face of the utopianism of his demand upon a state whose goverance was propelled by the destructive effects of "culture" was no longer an acceptable alternative. Whatever their pitfalls, only the humanistic and technical intellectuals could provide hope that reason would control political life, and that culture, which, in this discourse, is the determining agent of social distortions, could be subordinated to intelligence. Only then could the "common interests" be revealed and become the basis of public life.

Lippmann appropriates John Dewey's concept of *intelligence* as the standard against which the current confusion of public life could be measured as well as the goal to which it must aspire. Yet Dewey himself, however much he admired the power of Lippmann's analysis of our contemporary malaise, was constrained to reject his conclusion that the time had come to abandon the ideology of popular democracy for a more realistic democratic elitism. To be sure, in his book-length reply to Lippmann's assertion that the modern democratic state is in crisis, Dewey accepts Lippmann's judgment that the public has been severely weakened, if not destroyed, by the ascendancy of mass culture. The difference between the two positions consists of Dewey's stubborn faith that democracy can be reconstructed through an act of *will* that promotes the revival of community.

Dewey begins his crucial chapter "The Eclipse of the Public" with this somber statement: "Optimism about democracy is today under a cloud." To Carlyle's celebrated comment "Invent the printing press and democracy is inevitable," Dewey adds "Invent the railway, the telegraph, mass manufacture and concentration of population in urban centres, and some form of democratic government is, humanely speaking, inevitable" (304). Yet, for Dewey, the historical experience of industrial and urban democracies is no cause for celebration, and surely no cause for the self-congratulation that he saw in the America of the 1920s.

Democracy may entail industrialism, urbanism, and technological change, but, according to Dewey, its roots are agrarian: "American democratic polity was developed out of genuine community life, that is, association in the local and small centres where industry was mainly agricultural and where production was carried on mainly with hand tools." Here he stresses "pioneer conditions" to account for the stability of early American democracy. These conditions "put a high premium upon personal work, skills, ingenuity, initiative and adaptibility, and upon neighborly sociability." Therefore, public institutions such as schools developed under local conditions and the appropriate form of governance of these institutions, given the ecological and economic basis of association, was direct participation among citizens, through the town meeting, in the decisions affecting these public goods.

"We have inherited . . . local town-meeting practices and ideas. But we live and act and have our being in a continental national state." Yet our political structures do not hold the national state together. According to Dewey, in modern industrial society "we are held together by non-political bonds, principally those of communications — railways, commerce, mails, telegraph and telephone, newspapers" (306). But while these instrumentalities create a fragile unity, they are not sufficient to maintain a genuine democratic polity: "It seemed almost self-evident to Plato — and to Rousseau later — that a genuine state could hardly be larger than the number of persons capable of personal acquaintance with one another" (306).

Here Dewey sounds the theme that animates much of American philosophy and art since the United States embarked, in the 1850s, on its century-long journey to world power. American democracy was born of the necessity arising from the conditions of its settlement. In order to negotiate their relationship with an obdurate nature that did not yield its fruits easily, the "pioneers" were obliged to share social and political power. The people who occupied this "virgin land" were fiercely individual and cherished, above all other values, their freedom. But, in the interest of survival and then prosperity, they were obliged to constitute a political system based on the principle that all who engaged in the labor of making of this wilderness that was America a civilized community shared equally in its governance.

This system of direct as opposed to representative democracy flourished on a foundation of face-to-face interaction among people who, whatever their differences, understood and therefore trusted one another within the limitations of any political relation. In the first half century of the American republic, the root site of this remarkable public life was New England. Dewey gives the example of the school district: "They get a schoolhouse built, perhaps with their own labor, and hire a teacher by means of a committee, and the teacher is paid from the taxes. Custom determines the limited course of study, and tradition the methods of the teacher modified by whatever personal insight and skill he may bring to bear" (306).

What impresses is the informality of the process; the state is constituted through the face-to-face interactions of its members. One can extrapolate from this example the formation of committees to build and maintain a local road, another to oversee the work of the tax collector, a third to develop a water and sanitation system, and so forth, and a community where final disposition of the recommendations of these subbodies is made by the town meeting. (Here, of course, the question of who gets to vote is not discussed by Dewey. We know that the franchise in this democracy is reserved for male property owners. While the evidence for women's protest against their exclusion is scant, we do know that the "crowd" of tenants and wage laborers who were typically denied the franchise frequently responded to decisions that affected them, but over which they had no control, with protests, often in the form of disrupting the town meeting.) This political idyll was short-lived. Dewey recounts that "the temper and flavor of the pioneer evaporated" when "the wilderness [was] gradually subdued; a network of highways, then of railways unite the previously scattered communities. . . . Our modern state-unity is due to the consequences of technology employed so as to facilitate the rapid and easy circulation of opinions and information, and so as to generate constant and intricate interaction far beyond the limits of face to face communities" (306–7).

Of course, the United States was a pioneer in the democratization of the political system, even as it forged a breathtakingly vast communications system that facilitated the spread not only of information but also of goods. Universal white male suffrage was enacted without the struggle that the English and other European workers conducted to win similar rights. With this technologically based communications revolution came a new *culture*. For thinkers of Dewey's generation, the ability of technology to maintain national unity was purchased at an enormous cost. "The public seems to be lost. . . . If a public exists, it is surely as uncertain about its own whereabouts as philosophers since Hume have been about the residence and make-up of the self" (308). If a free society *means* not only the right but also the ability of its citizens to participate beyond voting in the decisions that affect their lives, then to the extent that mass communication and its culture have replaced the "face-to-face" community, American democracy is, indeed, in serious trouble. For democracy is the same as community life itself, where the idea of community entails participation among equals, at least for the purposes of public activity.

For Dewey, as much as for Lippmann and other postwar writers, political apathy and the absence of intelligent political discourse among those who participate in elections and other public forms on the basis of "habit and tradition" or self-interest are a function of

the power of bread and circuses to divert attention from public
matters. . . . The members of an inchoate public have too many ways
of enjoyment, as well as of work, to give much thought to
organization into an effective public. Man is a consuming and sportive
animal as well as a political one. What is significant is that access to
means of amusement has been rendered easy and cheap beyond
anything known in the past. And these amusements — radio, cheap
reading matter and motor car[—]with all they stand for have come
to stay.

Dewey is forced to admit that there are no certain paths to the formation of an articulate public. With the complexity and heterogeneity associated with industrialization and urbanism, the conditions for community life have been disrupted, perhaps forever. Moreover, while his framework of analysis is democratic rather than aristocratic, his invocation of a rural culture upon which to mount a critique of contemporary society leads to nostalgia rather than reconstruction, for he is hard put to find redeeming features in urban, industrial society precisely because it engenders massification. Dewey describes contemporary American society as a mass society, constituted by the vast information networks whose volume and complexity overwhelm individuals and all but drive them to retreat to the other, "instinct"-induced activities such as consumption and amusement. In current language, privatization is the consequence of massification. But, if these implements of mass culture are here to stay and, since these judgments were rendered in the 1920s when consumer society was still in its infancy and before television and VCRs became the main sources of information, it is hard to see how the public may be reconstituted short of some unforeseen cataclysmic event that recreates the wilderness in which small groups of survivors may, finally, form democratic communities.

Finally, Dewey rejects the inevitability of the coming of Mass Man with its implication that only the rich and powerful and their intellectual retainers or, in its liberal technocratic version, experts, can be effective in solving social problems. However, since "human nature" is itself complex (we are pleasure seekers as well as moral agents — the two for him are incompatible on the social level), we are compelled to recognize that democracy and freedom are not given by historical law. They are moral imperatives, the achievement of which depends on whether we have the will to employ our innate reason to suppress those features of human character that, especially since the nineteenth-century scientific and technological revolution, have proven to be both powerful and amoral.

Like Veblen, whose roots are in the Scandinavian immigrants who transformed the plains and prairies of the American Midwest using their inherited artisanal skills and their communal ties, Dewey has a deeply religious native American heritage. More specifically, he has a faith that social problems can be solved only when the individual is both the end and the means of human activity. This aim can be attained through the development of what might be described as an *intentional* culture, the deepest source from which habit and tradition, the actual governors of public activity, are formed. Instead of submitting to habit, this culture would stress the unity of head and hand. That is, it would promote the application of intelligence —

whose instrument is the scientific method — rather than science's technological applications, to regulate our relations with nature and among ourselves.

Dewey tried to define a radical democratic vision of the future in which individuals, constituted as an independent and articulate public, could stem the tide of both totalitarianism and authoritarian democracy. In the early thirties he worked with Paul Douglas (later a U.S. senator from Illinois), Reinhold Niebuhr, Norman Thomas, and others to form a third party as a practical vehicle to promote a new public life against the apathetic and narrowly self-interested political parties. This party failed when the progressive George Norris refused to run in 1932. Yet Dewey's commitment to social action never waned. He intervened throughout his life in practical political issues — trade unionism for teachers as well as industrial workers, schools (as well as education), and the defense of the rights of persecuted minorities, notably Leon Trotsky and his Soviet followers. Despite his fundamentally pessimistic analysis of modern culture, Dewey displayed an almost classic "optimism of the will," one that could only be grounded in ethical rather than logicoscientific theory. This ethical dimension was rooted in a faith for which the main local precedent was the New England town meeting, one signifier of a beloved community of individuals who, through dialogue and debate, were able to grasp common interests.

The mass society/mass culture debate begins with the French Revolution when, in the perception of representatives of the ancien régime, the "masses come to power." For political and social theorists, even those like Madison and Jefferson who were key figures in the American Revolution, the necessary limits to the unthrottled power of the people were provided by the system of checks and balances that were designed to prevent representative bodies broadly linked to insurgent dispossessed classes from capturing the state. The executive branch and, especially, the court were to be the institutional expression of the best and the brightest of the new society, to which Jefferson added the provision of universal public education as the best guarantor of a responsible and active citizenry.

In this respect Dewey, although following this program, became an advocate of the link between citizenship and education *only* in consequence of the development of urban, industrial capitalism. For his historical reflection on *direct* democracy presupposed no conditions on citizenship. In a democracy, schools are to be the instrument of *Bildung* (self-formation) where the individual, regardless of social origin, may choose to imbibe the legacy of Western culture — not only literacy, but also history, government, literature, and, most of all, the ambiguous skill called "critical" thinking. The contract between a democratic state and its people was to be fulfilled, primarily, in terms of the educational system at a time when distorted communication had become a normal means by which the population received information.

In the past century, Dewey has veritably become *the* American philosopher of education precisely for his insistence on education as the condition for informed citizenship and the fulfillment of the dream of social equality. This aim, rather than that of narrow occupationally oriented training, pervaded all of his proposals for school reform, even those that advised that children learned best through practices that were broadly "vocational" rather than rote. He accepted the judgment of his fellow intellectuals that industrialism and urbanism tend ineluctably toward massification. Consequently, one may no longer (if we ever could) rely on the "free," private individual to constitute an effective polity without the mediation of the state to provide universal cultural formation. Eighteenth-century political philosophy posited the separation of the private from the public sphere as a necessary condition for the ability of individuals to make their collective voices heard in public affairs. Dewey, although retaining his ultimate reliance on individuality for preserving the common good, reluctantly advocated the development of the interventionist state to assure such an eventuality in the light of the wanton intervention of pernicious private interests in public affairs. Like many other liberals of his generation who held similar views, Dewey saw state intervention, though far removed from collectivist aims, as the last best hope for individual freedom. This, of course, distinguishes modern liberalism from state socialism, even as they both insist upon public ownership of public goods such as schools.

As Dewey correctly saw, state intervention in education can accomplish a great deal. What schools cannot do, however, indeed what is in the last analysis a worse than futile quest, is "prepare" young people for responsible citizenship. This judgment derives not merely from my assessment that, from the child's standpoint, schooling is chiefly a ritual performance whose crucial requirement is to get by. It also stems from the judgment that, as Lippmann observed, the program of linking a democratic *polis* to the "elevation" of the masses through cultural formation is fundamentally flawed.

It would be excessive to claim that Dewey relies exclusively on schooling to make democracy work to insure popular power. Yet, in concert with intellectuals of the left as well as the right, his acceptance of the argument that the unintentional consequence of "progress" has been to crush the *capacity* of the individual to retain his or her sovereignty in the wake of the concentration of cultural as well as economic power in fewer hands places his call for the revival of direct democracy in serious jeopardy. For if popular sovereignty is not unconditional, but must presuppose the successful transmission of Western culture through school (the most democratic institution of mass society), then we have arrived at a position in which the concept of democracy is significantly compromised.

In light of the sordid history of the revolutionary movements of the twentieth century, it is quite difficult to invoke, without qualification, one of their crucial precepts: that the masses of peasants and workers are capable of self-rule prior to the achievement of mass literacy, and certainly before their collective and individual acquisition of the gems of high culture. That self-rule would entail a radical reduction of the duration of compulsory wage labor, freeing women from the exclusive burdens of the home, and massive efforts to provide the tools by which scientific, technical, and political knowledge can be gained goes without saying. But what is at issue in all appeals to the "people" is their deep suspicion, not without reason, of the educated classes who appear to be gatekeepers of a distant culture and are often the barriers to popular political and social participation. Since the French Revolution the concept of privilege has never been confined to economic property but has typically included cultural property. Hence, together with the antagonism between classes based on the criterion of property ownership, there has also been a persistent historical gulf between intellectual and manual labor. For a century and a half, since the advent of mass public schooling, the democratic promise that education may be a leveler of class distinctions has been vitiated by devices such as IQ tests that have produced, in every major country, a fairly rigid streaming or tracking system; and, of course, political philosophers and cultural critics have never ceased to impose sanctions on popular participation but have, instead, insisted that politics and art are too important to be entrusted to the masses.

Despite the rhetoric of popular sovereignty, revolutionary leaderships — parties and military groups — often violated the assumption of the revolution that it would be not only for the immense majority, but also by and of them. This gap between a rhetoric of popular democracy and an oligarchic political practice has its roots in both the American and French revolutions. And, as we know, in Russia the soviets were, as it turned out, more or less permanently disbanded in the wake of the exigencies of foreign invasion, civil war, and famine. The Chinese and Cuban revolutions periodically made attempts, with varying degrees of seriousness, to create forms of popular participation. In Cuba, neighborhood committees, factory councils, and other bodies have provided some democratic outlets for popular expression, but not unambiguously because of their police function. And, notwithstanding its grave repressive distortions, the Cultural Revolution raised to the level of public discussion the question of the degree to which the revolution had been betrayed by its functionaries and intellectuals — raised the question, but, as it turned out, in the service of an elite counter to that of the party technocrats.

It is only the revolutionary councils of the Paris Commune of 1871, the soviets in 1905, and some of those formed in 1917 that afford a glimpse of what a developed proletarian public sphere might entail. These were, among other things, both forums for hammering out revolutionary policy *and* organs of administration — of the economy and of civil society, in the Gramscian sense. Different and opposing views of political parties, groups, and individuals were articulated without fear of reprisal because, however imperfectly, these institutions made the fundamental assumption that their participants were speaking in good faith. These forums, usually of small units of workers, soldiers, and sailors and (perhaps the unknown aspect of the revolution of 1917–21) of anarchist-inspired peasants as well, approximated the conditions of face-to-face interaction from which Dewey derived his own democratic alternative. In these conditions, there was no presumption that citizenship crucially depended on literacy or on any other high cultural formation.

On the contrary. While the existence of peasants, workers, and artisans able to read and write was firmly established in all urban centers and in rural districts as well, the criteria for citizenship in a situation of popular participation are shared histories of oppression and shared modes of life, not high cultural formation or literacy. I want to suggest that these commonalities are one form of specification of what Dewey was to call *experience*. Theirs was the experience of exclusion by the higher orders, including intellectuals, from processes of public life. For the excluded, the prerequisite of education as a *condition* of participation in the public sphere was (and is) taken as a rationalization for privilege, however sincerely it may be held.

Since the intellectuals have, with some exceptions, traditionally associated themselves with power — either the political and economic kind or, in a different register, high culture — one might expect that there would be a countertendency to valorize the oral culture of the lower orders, an anti-intellectual populism that, in context, appears to represent the spirit of the insurgency. In fact, the rebellion of the Paris Commune and the rebellions it inspired in the twentieth century are expressions of subaltern groups, a form of speech that requires no formal educational preconditions.

Of course, this conception violates a major precept of ancient Greek democracy, which presupposed equals of homogeneous cultural formation. This has remained an ideal of even the most passionate democrats, such as Dewey. Nevertheless, Dewey regarded it as only one aspect of citizenship, and it is entirely inconceivable as anything but an ideology of exclusion in the contemporary world marked by both heterogeneous class and cultural formation. It was precisely the requirement of literacy as a condition of voting that was resolutely opposed by the black freedom movement in the twentieth century, even as the movement fervently fought for expanded educational opportunities for blacks.

To be sure, democratic populism discovers its limits at the moment when rebellion transforms itself into administration. The historical record of the revolutions of the past two hundred years makes this crystal clear. The Bolsheviks, for example, discovered that to *re-*

tain state power, as opposed to seizing it, requires a huge army of soldiers and an even larger army of bureaucrats and technically trained cadres. Consequently, mass education becomes a priority of the new regime. Among Western capitalist states, despite the widely held view that a vast army of technically trained and literate workers was necessary for scientifically based industrial development, the imperative of mass, universal education was not a rational discovery of the employer class, but was the outcome of a determined century-long struggle by workers' movements in alliance with social reformers. For these movements, literacy was not only a crucial form of cultural capital (there were those in the workers' movements who resisted acquiring it), but also an important dimension of political and social emancipation. The employers and the reigning politicians of the liberal states were not easily persuaded that the advantages of schooling outweighed the risks of an educated working class that might, by virtue of its education, discover its own capacity for self-rule.

Thus, it is far from the case that schooling is historically rejected by movements for economic and social emancipation. For these movements, knowledge is, indeed, ineluctably linked to power. Even as they protested the monopolies of knowledge held by intellectuals and capitalist rulers, they understood its importance for their own aspirations, especially for full participation in the public sphere. As E. P. Thompson, George Rudé, and many others have shown, the written word as much as oral tradition was among the weapons of working-class emancipation. However, this is different from the proposition held by, say, Jürgen Habermas as much as by Jefferson and Dewey, that the public sphere could be constituted only by those qualified by a certain cultural formation. Perhaps inadvertently, this utopian proposal is parallel to Jefferson's admonition that popular democracy presupposes popular education: the playing field can be leveled only on condition that each citizen possesses an equivalent cultural formation, that is, has access to the civilizing process once reserved for the aristocracy. For Jefferson, democracy presupposes universal *Bildung* (high cultural formation) just as for Habermas its realization hinges on a universal pragmatics universally internalized. In order to achieve this end, speakers must acquire communicative "competence," a euphemism for what has been described (by Basil Bernstein) as an "elaborated code." In addition, speakers agree to abide by rules. And, perhaps even more important, they share a series of values upon which linguistic and moral interaction is not possible.

Now, it is not difficult to show that this prescription is both gendered and rooted in certain assumptions about class. Indeed, Habermas's early study *Structural Transformation of the Public Sphere* is precisely a critique of the failed project of citizenship under bourgeois stewardship. Published in 1962, when Habermas was still under the influence of Adorno, it was an exemplary work of critical theory insofar as it offered both a historical and an immanent critique of the taken-for-granted features of liberal democratic culture. But in his later search to resolve the legitimation problems of late capitalist democracies, Habermas was constrained to abandon his penetrating insight that the concept of the public sphere was itself a central ideology of liberal democratic regimes. Instead, he substituted a positive theory, the theory of communicative action, that could account for its possibility. In order to accomplish this objective, on the assumption that conflict was built on the structural barriers to understanding, Habermas chose to limit himself to those problems that bear on the moral formation of individuals and groups rather than the issues bearing on inequalities of economic and political power. By thus bracketing the "power" and "interest" from the public sphere and specifying that "reason" is a presupposition of public communication, Habermas provides a moral justification for a conception of the public that is fundamentally exclusionary.

If democracy hinges on education — whether in the details of high art or the semantic and syntactical complexities of language — then Lippmann's suggestion that the idea of direct and persistent citizenship has been foreclosed is entirely reasonable. Moreover, the public sphere is always a *restricted* space — restricted, in Habermas's model, to people like himself, those who have undergone the rigorous training of scientific and cultural intellectuals. Among the moral, if not the practical, elements of this formation is the separation of knowledge from interest, manifested in the ability of the intellect to transcend the materiality of the body, including emotion. For only those individuals who have *succeeded* in screening out the distorted information emanating from the electronic media, politicians, and the turmoil of everyday life are *qualified* to participate in social rule.

If all cultural formation is embodied and interested, however, then no such antidemocratic exclusions can ever be admissible — in which case both optimistic palaver about universal "truths" and pessimistic narratives about public decline may be dispensed with. What cannot be jettisoned is an urgent effort to reconstitute subaltern publics that will once again, in the wake of the most blatant power grab in this century, discover their own historicity.

Chatter in the Age of Electronic Reproduction
Talk Television and the "Public Mind"

Paolo Carpignano, Robin Andersen, Stanley Aronowitz, and William DiFazio

A conventional wisdom has consolidated around the question of mass media and politics and the public sphere. Its history is long, its variations are numerous. And yet there is a common ground, a mutual acceptance of basic premises, shared by practicing politicians, conservative ideologues, and leftist cultural critics. Its unquestionable truism is that the mass media today *are* the public sphere and that this is the reason for the degradation of public life if not its disappearance. Public life, the argument goes, has been transformed by a massive process of commodification of culture and of political culture in particular by a form of communication increasingly based on emotionally charged images rather than on rational discourse, such that political discourse has been degraded to the level of entertainment, and cultural consumerism has been substituted for democratic participation.[1] The culprit might be the corruption of basic values, or the evil of capitalism that reduces even our consciousness to a commodity, but critics reserve their ultimate disdain for the degenerate state and corrupting nature of television. Television has been portrayed by most cultural critics in images that recall Spengler's dark ruminations about the decline of the West. It is apparent from this state of conventional wisdom that we are still in the thrall of powerful conceptions of the mass media first fashioned by American social critics, especially Walter Lippmann, Edward Bernays, and John Dewey, in the 1920s and the Frankfurt School in the following decades.

Evidence confirming that political communication has indeed acquired the nature of a spectacle seems to be overwhelming. It is enough to point, for confirmation, to the most potent metaphor in recent political life: an actor turned president. What better exemplification can one find of the spectacularization of public life, of the transformation of the public into a spectator? A pivotal formulation of the media paradigm is evidenced therefore in the conception of the media audience as a passive spectator, the receptor of a battery of ideologically informed images dished out by a media machine that is ineluctably bound up with corporate and state power.

Recently some writers have insisted that alongside the hegemonic messages themselves, there exists a counterculture of resistance. Because of the discursive nature of power, hegemonic messages are discursively constituted and resisted at the level of (television) readership. In most formulations, however, the traditional distinction between the production and consumption of cultural product remains, even in the more nuanced models.[2] So, despite resistances, the main threads of the legacy of progressive liberalism and critical theory remain: television contains both degraded propaganda and subversive elements within a paradigm that views the media as perhaps the key ideological apparatus of the state, displacing family, school, religion, and the electoral machinery. In short, with important variations the framework for understanding media has remained intact for at least seventy years, if not longer.

It is obvious that to refute such overwhelming consensus and such weight of argumentation is an impossible task, especially in the short space of an article. We would like, however, to pose some questions and to advance some hypotheses that might shift the argument in a different direction.

First of all, it could be easily argued that spectacle and politics have always been inseparable. Those who have raised this point have pinpointed many instances in the history of political thought where there has been a profound awareness of this common ground, from Machiavelli to de Tocqueville. But most importantly, the relationship between politics and spectacle is not so much in the histrionics that characterize their rhetorics, but in the very communicative form that they deploy. For representative politics is built on the same separation of performance and audience that characterizes the structure of theatrical communication at least since early modern times, when modern theater was born. It is not by chance, as it has been observed, that representative politics comes into being historically and geographically in concomitance with the birth of Elizabethan theater.[3] That representative politics is a performing art should not be a sufficient reason for justifying its decay in recent time. And that the spectacle form of modern politics is historically related to the social relationships instituted by the development of the market and the commodity form should come as no surprise to anybody who has some familiarity with, for instance, Marx's analysis of commodity fetishism. Most importantly, it is on the structural separation between performance and audience that the ideological category of the public is constructed. The public is the undifferentiated mass, the recipients of political messages (as well as the abstract subject of political rights) beyond class antagonism.

What is then the reason for the degradation of the public sphere? Is it the excess of spectacularization and commodification? Or should we not try to reverse the question, and say that the crisis of representational politics, at least in this country, is not so much that politics has become a spectacle, but that *the spectacle form itself is in crisis?* Put in a different way, the crisis of representational politics could be read as the crisis of a communicative model based on the principle of propaganda and persuasion. This is not to say that these communicative strategies are not used anymore, are not attempted in many instances of political practices. It is important to understand, however, that the age of propaganda is exhausted because it is based on a mass-media system that has been dramatically transformed by the changes in social communication. Propaganda and persuasion have a long history in this country and are based on the theories of social engineering of consensus developed in the twenties, reaching their most massive and sophisticated application in the thirties and forties, promoting the social policies of the New Deal and the World War II effort. It is important to emphasize that the propaganda mode of communication is based on a structural separation between the source of the message and the audience. It is the control over the channels of disclosure that makes the public an audience; the consensus is measured in terms of the efficacy of the effect of the message.

Institutionally this means the establishment of the press as the fourth estate, asserting its independence and autonomy from external controls. If the pretension of propaganda is the circulation of the truth, the ideology of the press is the ethics of objectivity, the professional code of the reporter. The two are the poles of the checks and balances, a dialectic based on the same form of communication. The structure in which the audience is the recipient of information about events remains fundamental to news reporting. In this sense the reception of the news is not very different from that of other forms of the mass media, for example the film, the other major communication form of the age of persuasion.

It is our contention that the present crisis of the public sphere is the result of, among many other factors, a crisis of legitimacy of the news as a social institution in its role of dissemination of information about and interpretation of events (i.e., the social construction of public life). This phenomenon is historically related to the development of new social relationships of communication embodied in the television medium that have progressively undermined the structural dichotomy between performance and audience. More than any other television genres, the new talk shows exemplify the transformation of these relationships that radically shifts the framework within which the apparatuses of mass communication and popular culture operate. They call into question the very structure of the separation between production and consumption of cultural products; they problematize the distinction between expert and audience, professional authority and layperson. Ultimately they constitute a "contested space" in which new discursive practices are developed in contrast to the traditional modes of political and ideological representation.

I

A recent advertisement for Channel 9 News in New York, posted on city buses and in subway cars, declares, "You don't just watch the news, you experience it." Channel 9 invites viewers into the editorial room to observe reporters who are preparing reports about to go on the air, as if they were participating in the editorial process themselves. Thus television viewers no longer passively receive messages constructed anonymously, they partake in the experience of reporting them. This backstage invitation is clearly a formatting gimmick, but this particular format reveals the crisis of electronic journalism.

The development of the presentation of news as information has produced a separation between information and experience, and it is experience itself that is now commodified on Channel 9.

Walter Benjamin introduced the problems posed by the historical development of information within the context of the decline of storytelling: "Little by little narration has been expelled from living speech."[4] The communicative practice of modernity has progres- sively substituted the shared experience of living speech with the reproduction and distribution of information. Daily life used to be the basis of shared experiences, transmitted from generation to gen- eration. Information, the primary matter of the printing press, turned life experiences into an endless plethora of newspaper headlines. But in so doing it expropriated knowledge of experience. The knowledge of events acquired through the consumption of infor- mation prevailed over the narration of experience. Living speech was silenced as a source of counsel and ultimately of wisdom. Informa- tion has created a world rich in events but devoid of shared experi- ence. Relegated to the realm of reported events, experience takes place outside of us, lives an autonomous life, acquires the nature of a spectacle. But along the way, the communication of events loses narrative authority. As Benjamin noted, experience is the source of authority. Information has no authority because it does not "author" experience, it simply reports the event. Information has status only if it can be verified, and verifiability is the last semblance of authority. Journalistic rituals of legitimacy developed to fill the void left by the demise of authority.

The mass media, and more specifically the professionalization of journalism, grew up to claim the institutional authority once embod- ied in living speech. Historically, it was precisely this development, the dissemination of information as news, that provided the raw material for the development of the "public sphere."

Out of the new institutions of European capitalist "civil society" a modern public sphere was born during the seventeenth and eigh- teenth centuries. As Habermas has shown, a new and independent cultural sphere was established on the basis of new cultural practices and institutions of communication, from coffeehouses to salons, from literary society to the press.[5] These new communications insti- tutions allowed for the creation of a "philosophy of discourse" that was central to liberal democratic practices. The literary public sphere provided an uninhibited exchange of ideas and opinions, and this cultural activity was independent from the singularly private economic interests of individuals and also from the domination of the state. The new sphere of cultural activities resulted in the transformation of political life, which could now be based on the independent formulation of a "public opinion," and these opinions in turn had an independent influence on the state. The material basis for the development of this new social category was the commercialization of cultural production. It is the capitalist market that poses the conditions for the formulation of a new social arrangement and provides the infrastructure for the circulation of cultural commodities, in particular the "published word," which was becoming the "decisive mark" of the new epoch.

Thus the new public sphere was born out of several contradictions. Although claiming equality of status against the ranks of traditional society, the new public was in reality made up of a new emerging class of intellectuals and technicians (as part of the very limited "reading public") who actually articulated the theoretical category of publicity and applied them to civil society as a whole.[6] It followed that the principle of acceptability and inclusiveness of the public was in practice founded on the general access to cultural commodities provided by the "natural" extension of the market. This meant that even the early generations of the public, although conscious of being a part of a larger public that potentially extended to include humanity as a whole, related to its generality in terms of representation or in the form of an audience.[7]

Habermas's account of the subsequent demise of this short-lived public space underscores the decline of the newly formed independent modes of communication. As capitalism develops, the once liberating cultural sphere that fostered open debate and independent thought becomes increasingly penetrated by special interests and an interventionist welfare state. The commodification of cultural products, which is accelerated through the use of public relations strategies by private interests, transforms the practices of the public sphere into a form of "manipulative publicity." As capitalism develops, the "critical publicity" characteristic of a once relatively egalitarian public sphere is lost. The transformations of the public sphere result in a decline of public involvement in political life and the now "uncritical masses" use the media, dominated by the state and commercialism, as a "tranquilizing substitute for action."

Whether Habermas's view of the process of commodification of culture stands up to the subsequent development of social relations of communications we will examine in the later part of this article. What is important to notice now is that the notion of public from its very inception carries a heavy ideological burden in the sense that, by definition, it transcends the dichotomy of class struggle by implicitly subsuming the proletariat in the form of public as audience.

This contradiction explodes at the very beginning of "mass society" and in the United States before anywhere else. It is not by chance that the debate over the redefinition of the public and of public opinion within the context of public relations takes place in the United States in the 1920s. The preceding two decades had witnessed profound social transformations. Mass production and mass immigration had changed the configuration of the American working class. A new mass of unskilled workers was raising the demands of material well-being irrespective of the rule of industriousness and the codes of the old trades. The social paternalism of the Progressive Era was shattered by the one-sided demands of a new working class unwilling to share in the civic-mindedness and republican virtue of Americanism. It is at this point, after the struggles have reached their peak around the end of World War I, that the idea of the public begins to lose its political significance and that it has to be reinvented to fit the new requirements of the new phase of social relations. Significantly, Bernays entitles the first chapter of his book on the foundations of the science of public relations "Organizing Chaos."[8] In the preceding years, in their debate over the faith of the public, John Dewey and Walter Lippmann had identified its changed nature and acknowledged its deterioration if not its disappearance. Lost in the disintegration of "organic society," caught in the technological process of mass production, which had displaced the rationality of civic associations with the irrational search for material well-being, diverted from political concerns "by the increase in number and cheapness of amusements," the public seemed to have degenerated into a "phantom."[9] For Dewey, it is possible to reconstitute a genuine public of a democratic society on the condition that it is reestablished on the basis of a communicative practice of local communities and of a "face to face relationship by means of direct give and take ... the local is the ultimate universal."[10] Yet technology and science may provide the basis upon which increasingly privatized industrial activities may be transformed into the "Great Community" in which information can be widely disseminated as never before.

Lippmann, on the contrary, favored the development of a spirited, responsible elite as a surrogate for public opinion and the action of the masses. While he was unwilling to shed the trappings of liberal democracy, he urged that the elite seek its legitimacy, but not guidance, from the public: "I have conceived of public opinion to be not the voice of God, nor the voice of society, but the voice of the interested *spectators* of actors."[11]

Gone is the optimism about the automatic mechanism of the market of rational ideas and opinions. The public as spectator is no longer the result of a spontaneous circulation of social messages. The public becomes an objective, it has to be produced. Publicity becomes a strategy for organizing consensus. Circulation gives way to engineering. Propaganda, Bernays observes, "takes account not hardly of the individual, nor even of the mass mind alone, but also and especially of the anatomy of society, with its interlocking groups, formations and loyalties."[12] Thus the formulation of public opinion becomes an act of governing. Public opinion becomes a matter of public relations. And the science of public relations does not assume a public sphere as a given, it intervenes in shaping it. Bernays again: "Those who manipulate this unseen mechanism of society constitute the invisible government which is the true ruling power of our country."[13]

If the public is a spectator, then the mechanism of distribution of information becomes the guarantee for the functioning of a democratic society. As an institution, the press assumes the ideological connotation that the public once had. But where the ideology of the public was humanity, the ideology of the press is objectivity.

Historically the legitimacy of the news is tied to the institutionalization of journalism as a profession. The journalist/reporter becomes the prototypical technical intellectual of mass society. Legitimacy of the news can be conceived only in terms of a relationship between the event and the reporter. Reporting is unearthing the event. Thus in the long and formidable tradition of American journalism, reporting takes the form of investigating.

Where in the Progressive Era the role of the press was identified with the heroics of individual journalists, with the development of the mass media as an industry and the introduction of broadcasting, the media have come to coincide with the formulation of public opinion. The definition of what is newsworthy is tantamount to the definition of what is public. And public opinion is the independent variable of the welfare state, much like demand in the economy of the Keynesian state. The media as a fourth estate, as check and balance of the discursive power of the state, correspond to the subsumption of social conflict within the dynamics of balanced growth. For this reason journalism as an institution becomes the pole of the dialectic of democratic society. The golden age of propaganda requires the heroics of Ed Murrow. Not surprisingly, the bulk of theories concerning the news are examinations of the journalistic profession. Thus, what they celebrate as the rise of journalism as an institution of a democratic society (with its codes of conduct and its professional and institutional boundaries always and inevitably betrayed) is in fact the practice of legitimation of information.

It is the crisis of the welfare state that exposes the shortcomings of the dialectics of information. The more the complexity of subjective practices emerges, the less it can be subsumed under the dynamics of public opinion. The news media cannot encompass the variety of subjective practices under the common denominator of the public, in a common negotiation of social meanings. The crisis of democracy, which political science attributes to the unreconcilable interplay of interest groups, undermines the model of universal communication that the media traditionally guaranteed by playing the ideological role of social mediator. In fact, the media can be the site of the public sphere to the extent that social mediation is conceived within the political realm. But the confrontation today is between politics and the refusal of politics of which the drop in voter turnout, or the "dealignment," is but a symptom. Public opinion and the general interest are now a total attribute of the state. The media that had become the embodiment of the public sphere are now reduced to the function of mouthpiece of officialdom. The "we" of the media is the official voice of the state. If Ted Koppel or Thomas Friedman seems a surrogate secretary of state, and James Baker a surrogate anchorman, it is because their difference is in the formalities of their roles and not in the substance of their performances.

The widespread phenomenon of the refusal of politics in the United States (note also the low voter turnout in recent elections in Hungary and Colombia) severely compromises the status of media as a mediator. As slavish media reportage of the U.S. invasion of Panama in December 1989 demonstrates, the vestiges of a bourgeois public sphere that could still be represented during the Vietnam War era, especially on interventionist issues, has all but disappeared.

The press, especially television, demonstrated a total inability to distinguish its own voice from that of an invading state power. Television instead became the voice of the military, disseminating endless Pentagon official statements and press releases. Many journalists referred to "our troops" and commonly used "we" when reporting U.S. government actions and strategy. Soldiers in uniform stood before maps of Panama, and slick graphics illustrated how the U.S. troops reached Panamanian war zones. The only visual footage of the invasion itself came from television crews shepherded by Army public relations officials. The networks allowed the U.S. government to control their images and present a version of the invasion so obviously "official" that it was indistinguishable from state-controlled media.

Political discourse has come to emphasize statecraft, with the axis of debate turning on the tensions between the executive and legislative branches, or on macro level concepts that subsume national and international issues under the rubric of "Western democratic capitalism." National television news coverage is dominated by a macrodiscourse that has become detached from actual public concerns, as noted by John Fiske:

> If there is no relevance between a text and the everyday lives of its
> readers, there will be little motivation to read it. . . . News may well be
> watched out of a vague moral sense that we ought to know what is
> going on in the world, but if it lacks these microconnections, it will
> be watched halfheartedly and will be rapidly forgotten — which,
> indeed, is the fate it frequently suffers.[14]

The identification of the media with the official "public" discourse increases the contradictory reading of the news. Because of its very nature, television lives this contradiction more than any other media.

There is no doubt that, at least in its early stages, television reproduced the established communicative relations of the information form. What usually passes for the golden age of television is in reality the last stage of "radio days" with the addition of a visual backdrop and a telegenic announcer. But, as the news format evolved and began to use the full range of the communicative potential of the medium, the news acquired its own specific character.

The first attempt at counteracting the crisis of legitimacy of the news was the creation of an "authority figure," a news narrator. The reintroduction of orality and gesture, the appearance of personal proximity, gave the reporter the aura of an "electronic storyteller." The anchor, the star investigative reporter, became the staple of television news and documentaries.

Furthermore, the need to exploit the immediacy and the "nowness" of the medium gave television the ability to bring events into private lives in a way that no other technology had previously achieved. In the early 1960s in particular, when television news was only beginning to learn how to make sense of the new image world, the world itself became more opaque. It seemed to burst open with the struggles, hopes, and desires of people responding to the contradictions of postwar abundance and change, amid stagnant social and cultural configurations. The medium grew up within and responded to the social historical forces that propelled its development. The boundaries of history and video representation blurred as the interactive nature of visual social representation became a powerful historical prodigy. Television did not sit on the sidelines, recording the tumultuous decade to play it back as a simple reflection, but rather became part of the stage itself, an important actor whose influence was not yet wholly grasped. The television medium was imbedded within an institutional fabric not yet solidified, and improvisation and spontaneity characterized an extended experimental phase. Television news reporting expanded from fifteen minutes to a half hour in 1963, and the increased air time opened more avenues for trial and error. Some habitual patterns were already set. Early Vietnam coverage carried the banner of official pronouncements against communism, and opponents of the war were ruthlessly marginalized as violent extremists. But the contradictions of the decade were not contained over time and all issues. Television was an actor in the civil rights movement and brought images of brutality — dogs, water hoses, and police nightsticks — to those not living in the South, thus contributing to the circulation of new discursive practices.

The effectiveness of some of the television interventions, in spite of the ideological construction of the reporting, illustrates an important feature of this medium. The object of the video camera is not the narration but the presence of a place. The film camera assembles fragments, details; the video camera monitors unlimited spaces. The electronic editing is not sequential, but angular, space encompassing. Perception becomes a logistical problem.[15] As technology becomes more sophisticated, "being there" replaces the event. News events are not wired, they are monitored. They are not scenographed, they are scenologized. As a consequence, the event loses status, and its fall from grace inevitably brings down the reporter. Lately this phenomenon has become quite striking and its communicative consequences more evident. For reporting and visuals are increasingly becoming two independent, often divergent texts. The spatial presence develops independently from the interpretative "noise."

This is not to say that television displays a contradiction between the truth of images and the interpretation of reporting. It should be clear that all television images are constructed no matter how "live" they might be. Their "framing" is not an ideological device that betrays the mediatory nature of television. Those who lament that the interpretative framework of television programs denies the potentiality of the medium ultimately have a conception of electronic technology as neutral. In this view, television could establish an "unmediated," direct relationship with reality if it were not for the ideologically charged framing of the events. The livelike quality of events, it is maintained, is only a way of authenticating a mediatory relationship with reality.

In fact, there is no distinction in terms of truth between live pictures and framed events, not because the equation between live and real is ideological but because reality as such is socially constructed. The specificity of the television medium lies elsewhere. The textual divergence we have identified relates to two different modes of relationship with the medium. The "mediating" narrative of reporting establishes a relationship between a recipient of information and an

event. The watching of a live space establishes a relationship between an act of monitoring and a happening. In other words, the
reporting induces receivership (no matter how critical or partial);
the monitoring entails a form of *reverse manipulation* that is structurally independent from the narrative of the text viewed. The more
the news is forced to emphasize its livelike quality, the more the
scanning of places will be privileged over reporting events. At times
the crisis of interpretation becomes apparent even to the textual con-
structors themselves, as when Ted Koppel admits on the air that he
should say nothing, but simply run the live video of Nelson Mandela
being released from prison. The liveness and nowness are not just a
gimmick to authenticate an ideological reality but also, and primarily,
a response to the use of television as a monitoring device.

When Michael Deaver concentrated the Reagan White House public relations strategy on the creation of media events, he was responding precisely to this form of communicative practice. The old
model of propaganda was based on the control of information reported by the news media. The Deaver strategy, instead, reached
inexorably beyond the realm of ideological mediation on which the
news operates and into the terrain of the monitoring practices of
television viewers.

The predicament of television news has resulted in at least two
major changes in the nature of reporting. The first is that the act of
reporting has acquired the same status as the event to be reported —
thus the endless series of programs devoted exclusively to industry
self-analysis. All networks have their own media analysts. The Jeff
Greenfields of the media cover the news as a world in itself, not to
mention the numerous panels on media responsibility and, most
conspicuously, the coverage of the "spin doctor" phenomenon in
election campaigns. The newsroom becomes the location of a happening and the reporting of the events becomes the plot of the situation (the difference between "Murphy Brown" and "Eyewitness
News" might be only in the intensity of laughter).

The second consequence is that the reporting tends to become
increasingly conversational. Having lost any interpretative legitimacy,
television journalists resort to a style of presentation that emphasizes
their presence in a collective group discussion, as if their reporting
were tantamount to voicing an opinion. In a current news program
aired in New York and New Jersey, "Nine Broadcast Plaza," the news

reporting takes place in a studio where journalists-hosts discuss events with an audience as they are reported. The dividing line between a news program and a talk show has disappeared.

II

Another way of looking at the ideology of the public is to look at the way the public actually appears on television, both as audience and as repository of public discourse. These two roles are often indistinguishable and for this reason we will examine them together. As it will become clear, however, there are television formats in which the public also becomes a presentation of common sense.

By "public on television" we mean people who laugh and applaud situation comedies or variety shows, who cheer at sports events, who are interviewed by reporters "in the street." Most importantly, they are the audiences and participants of talk shows, especially those that invite audience participation.

They are not celebrities, they do not follow a script, they do not appear as reporters or experts. They appear as themselves (as their anonymous selves), as a segment of what is usually referred to with a touch of redundancy as "the general public."

Although readily identifiable, the public on television does not have a homogeneous identity. In fact, it is possible to trace a typology of publics with different roles, functions, and uses. The most elementary and rudimentary form of public on television is what can be called the "audible public." This is the mostly invisible studio audience of variety shows and sitcoms. Its existence is revealed by background noise, mainly applause and laughter, that is much like a sound effect. Its presence is atmospheric, its utterances rhythmic, like the tempo of a musical score. It is used to delimit the various segments of a show, to underline the punch line of a joke, or to mark the finale of a narrative crescendo. The effect is often less than spontaneous. In fact, the edited-in laughter of the sitcom often sounds awkward, and the applause somewhat contrived (everyone knows of the existence of the applause sign). Yet the need to underscore the narrative flow explains only in part the background sound presence of an audience. Instead, the most important role that the audible public is playing is that of creating the appearance of a live show. If it is in the nature of television to "present itself as a relay of what is happening,"[16] the sound of laughter and applause provides, in the most elementary form, the sense of that happening. The realism of a sitcom is not only in the narrative sequence of the story but also in the fact that the story is displayed in front of a public and that it is monitored as an event, which ultimately constitutes the "situation." Thus the sound of the studio audience is not an ornament or an inducement, it is an essential component of the specificity of the television medium expressed in that particular show and codified in the claim of the oxymoron in the final credits, "taped live."

A second type of public on television is the visible but inarticulate public. This is, for example, the public of a televised sport event. Individual members are hardly distinguishable. What is essential is the totality of the crowd, its massive presence, its noise and chants, its proverbial and sometimes literal "roaring." The public here is cast in a specific role of spectator, visible but distant. On occasion, however, the camera will zoom in and highlight funny hats, strange customs, unusual gestures. Various signs are displayed by the fans. Some refer to the game or to the teams. Others are addressed directly to the network or to the commentators who acknowledge them as they appear on screen in the lull between plays. A sort of dialogue is thus established, fragmentary and inarticulate, but a visible mark of a presence nonetheless.

Then there is the public in shows like "Candid Camera" and its numerous clones. Here the public appears as "real people," engaged in apparently normal daily activities but confronted with unusual situations. The comedic situation of course consists in the fact that these people are not aware of being on camera. This creates a superimposition of divergent contexts and a transgression of meanings that become the source of laughter. The people are acting without a script, they are provoked in their spontaneity, but the plot is written and arranged elsewhere. Here the public on television is fully articulate, in fact the protagonist, but scripted within a very strict set of circumstances that reduces its role to that of an object of hilarity. A variation of this format can be found in the people interviewed by David Letterman in his periodic forays among the "common people" of New York. Here the presence of the camera is acknowledged from the beginning, and the public becomes not an object of hilarity but an object of ridicule.

The public of news and documentary programming is the "edited public." Here people are asked to play the part of "public opinion." They are those who inevitably claim to be shocked by the news that their quiet neighbor has just been accused of burying parts of a human body in his basement. They are those who are interviewed back to back by the reporter and give nicely symmetrical opposite opinions on any given subject as if the world were always perfectly divided in two. And they are those who represent a random sample of opinion of the crowd demonstrating in Wenceslaus Square and who happen to speak a perfect English, sometimes with a British accent to give Continental flair. The "edited public" is utterly predictable and serial. It is a projection of the reporter, who uses it to underscore the reporting by creating "visuals" to make the presentation more dramatic, but without adding anything to the story. In other words, it is a journalistic artifact, the creation of the editing room.

Only on the talk show does the public on television gain full recognition and, in its latest incarnation, the role of protagonist. Of course, the public on talk shows is not a unique example of an active audience. Game shows, for instance, require the active participation of contestants in the studio as well as of the home viewers. But the talk show is the only program that proclaims its intention (one might say the pretension) of presenting issues for public debate and, it will be our contention, the only program whose discursive format is conversation rather than commentary or debate. For this reason it is necessary to analyze the talk show public in greater detail.

It is not surprising that the talk show is one of the oldest and most durable genres of American television. From an economic point of view, its revenue potentials are much greater than its minimal cost of production. As a commercial venture, it is a perfect promotional showcase for products of all kinds — movies, records, books, celebrities, and even other talk shows. As a self-referential and typically intertextual program, the talk show is an essential infrastructure in the strategies of television programming. Its ultimate strength, however, is in its popularity and in its ability to establish a bond of familiarity with television audiences.

In its most consolidated and stable format, the talk show consists of a public rite of hospitality.[17] The set is decorated as a sort of living room. The protagonist of the show (who also gives the show its name) is called a host, and the people who appear on the program are called guests. And although the narrative of the show is based on the expectation of unexpected, spontaneous behavior, the common denominator is an atmosphere of shared activity. As in any rite, the unproffered rules are well defined, and so is the main cast of characters: the host, the band leader, the sidekick. Everything is fine-tuned to maximize the feeling of a joyous private affair among friends. In the words of one television critic, the talk show acts as a "substitute saloon" for an atomized television audience.[18]

Yet the most interesting aspect of the talk show format is that it brings to its most mature form some of the specific features of the television aesthetic. Its mode of expression is primarily based on orality; conversation is the thread that links the different parts together. Its immediacy is in its livelike quality and in the sense of a real time progression. Its content spans the "marvelous world of the ordinary," to use Paddy Chayevsky's characterization of television. The mandatory parade of celebrities does not exclude the emphasis on the personal. In fact, the very rule of television exposure mandates the revelation of the intimate, ordinary side of stardom. More than any other format, however, the talk show requires the de facto or implied presence of the audience. In fact, the measure of success of a talk show is the rate of implied participation communicated to the audience (in the studio or at home). Johnny Carson's trademark, the sardonic and silent gaze at the camera/audience in response to an outrageous statement by one of his guests, makes the viewer an accomplice to the joke and a participant in the show. The viewer is not only addressed directly, as in the case of many other television formats (by the news anchor, the game show host, or anybody who utters "we'll be right back"), but also invited to sit in, as a guest during the monologue or as cohost when the officially invited guests make their appearance, in a communal living room — a mass invitation to a private affair.

This sense of participation in a communal event is made possible by the particular spatial perception that the show conveys. The framing of the screen is not the visual space of the camera but the physical space occupied by the show and to which the public is invited. The camera is not so much a conveyor of a visual reality as the instrument of our presence, the viewers' presence. The editing strives to reveal the place rather than narrate it. On the David Letterman show, what appears to be a transgression of formal requirements is instead the fulfillment of the vocation of the talk show format. Nothing is left out of our view: the camera operators, the technicians, the electricians. We see the corridors that lead to the studio, the cables on the ground. We see the guests being made up in the waiting room, the cue cards held behind the camera. The camera itself becomes a protagonist, installed on the head of a monkey or propelled across the studio ceiling on a wire before falling on the host's head. In this way the limitation of theatrical space vanishes and the sense of participating and belonging is enhanced.

A distinct change in the character of the talk show came about when the studio audience was introduced as a major player. Phil Donahue is usually recognized as the inventor of the new format. The proliferation of this type of show in recent years — Oprah Winfrey, Geraldo Rivera, Morton Downey, Jr., Sally Jessy Raphael — testifies to the success of the formula. The difference from the old format is immediately visible. The living room gives way to a sort of town assembly. The spatial dichotomy between the lineup of guests on one side and the spectators on the other (the traditional theatrical structure) is superseded by a compact amphitheater where the visual planes are not defined by the back and front of the camera. The camera encompasses the whole space and follows the interactivity among all the members of the gathering. The public is not in the dark of an orchestra pit. In a sort of democracy of lighting, everybody is brought on stage and given a share of illumination.

The hosts are deprived of their spatial authority. The desk behind which they used to sit had constituted the visual focus of the show. Now hosts are let loose with microphone in hand, running from place to place to catch a speaker, to give voice to a position expressed by members of the audience. The host is not a member of the panel, except in the sense that it is his or her show. The role is more that of an intermediary (Phil), a counselor (Oprah), or an instigator (Morton). Not that the host is less of a celebrity. The shows after all bear the hosts' names. If anything, they gain status, being often the only celebrity on the show, and their performance may become the main object of watching. But the performance is judged not on the basis of congeniality with individual guests but on the basis of the host's handling of the topic of the show. The show is now built around a topic, and the topic becomes the headline of the show, its fulcrum. Johnny Carson will advertise his show on the basis of its participants, Geraldo on the shock effect of a forbidden subject.

None of these innovations in the format of the talk show would be significant if it were not for the change in the role of the studio audience. In the old format the public is acknowledged, talked to, made fun of, included in the monologue or in some sketches, but its presence is ultimately peripheral, incidental. Its role is well defined as that of spectator. The show is not about the public, it is put on for the public. In some news shows, like, for example, Ted Koppel's town meetings, some members of the audience are given an opportunity to express their opinions. Politely they line up behind a microphone, they wait for their turn, they speak their mind, many times reciting a prepared statement because they have been previously selected as representative of this or that position, and hence they contribute to what is presented as an exercise in electronic democracy. In fact they are no more than polite witnesses to and occasional commentators on a well-orchestrated, balanced, and high-ground debate of luminaries sitting in a panel arrangement (always the same, no matter the topic, as if they were permanent members of a crew flying in formation, high priests of the panel circuit).

The novelty introduced by the new kind of talk show is that the public is literally on center stage. Being a protagonist does not mean to have a starring role. The public is by definition a nonstar. But the show is constructed around the audience. The value of a topic is measured on the basis of what kind of participation, what kind of arousal it creates (how many people will literally stand up). The whole point of the show is the invitation, sometimes the provocation, to become involved in the argumentation. The show is ultimately defined by that involvement. The concern is not only the proverbial how it will play in Peoria but also how a miniature Peoria will play as a show. The success of the show is in the degree to which it is capable of eliciting commonsense reactions on the part of the public on television.

Leaving aside for a moment the detailed phenomenology of talk show studio audiences — the variation in their composition (Phil's middle-class white women, Morton's working-class New Jerseyites,

Oprah's racially conscious mix) and their functions (Phil's quietly
moral sitters, Morton's assault team, Oprah's chatterers) — it is necessary now to turn to some general considerations about the consequences that the presence of the public on talk shows has for the
textual reading of such a format.

The first critical impact is on the notion of audience. Audience
analysis has a long, rich, and complicated history, and it is not our
intention to examine it here. At the risk of generalizing, however, it
is worth noticing for our purpose that at the heart of the notion of
audience there exists a dichotomy between the ideas of spectacle
and public. This structural relationship can, of course, be traced back
to the birth of the theater in early modern times when the audience
comes into being as a separate entity, superseding the traditional
communal representations of the sacred dramas and of the carnivals.
Today, the terminology and the metaphors used to characterize this
relationship are quite different. Much critical work has been based
on the idea that the concept of audience is problematic if not out-
right obsolete. The idea, dear to "effect theories," of an audience as
a passive recipient of preproduced messages has been replaced by
the more dynamic concept (borrowed from literary criticism) of the
reader. In this version of reception theory applied to television, the
viewers are giving meaning to what they see. They are located in a
material and social situation that conditions those meanings. They
are producers of texts, makers of meanings and pleasures. They have
control over meanings and also over the role those meanings play
in their lives. This is the result of a negotiation that takes place between the text and its socially situated viewers.[19] It is, in Eco's words,
a form of "aberrant decoding": the meanings are more determined
by the social situation of the decoder than by that of the encoder.[20]
The process is facilitated by the very character of television, which
tends to offer open texts, to facilitate diverse modes of reception,
and to invite complicity.

Yet even this semiotic reading presupposes that the production of
what we, as viewers/public, see on television is separate from the
production of the meaning we ascribe to the text. Dialectically related as they may be, in Baudrillard's words they are "separated entities of the structural communication grid," and therefore intrinsically "irresponsible."[21]

The public on television adds another dimension to this process by short-circuiting the dichotomy. For the act of viewing a text becomes an act of viewing an act of viewing. The text incorporates the "responsibility." The viewer's production is already in the text that has to be decoded. The aberrant decoder is decoding an aberration, for the studio audience is participating not just in viewing a text, but also in writing its script. The studio audience is not just a reader but a writer as well. Hence the viewers at home monitor a space where a negotiating of textual meanings is in progress — much the same process as their personal negotiations with the screen. What then is the difference, apart from the obvious fact that there are different individuals involved? Can the public on television in this case be considered an extension of the viewing public, a segment of a generalized collective of common discourse? Can their relationship be considered a form of participation? After all, the public on television is no more a representation of the viewing public than each person is a representation of himself or herself. The answer to these questions is premature because so far we have dealt only at the level of forms. What is certain, though, is that the talk show is the most eloquent example of the crisis of theatricality. What appears to be a spectacularization of common sense constitutes in fact the very crisis of the spectacle form.

If the common sense produced by the talk show is, as we have seen, formulated rather than represented, and in a process not dissimilar to that of the television viewer, then the only difference might seem to be in the fact that it is flashed out on a screen, not unlike the "truisms" of Jenny Holzer's installations. Without getting entangled in the quagmire of postmodern discourse, but being aware of the problematic raised by the notion of crisis of rationality, it is important to observe that the experience of electronic communication is indeed based on the tactile, shocking effect that Benjamin attributed to reproduced images. Thus, our common sense is formed through a process that has less to do with the inductive and deductive processes of rational inquiry than with "the selective choice and variable employment of abstract scientific paradigms, more or less immediately available through a certain degree of socialization of knowledge."[22]

If what has been said so far makes any sense, then it is possible to formulate a new criterion to deal with the social formation of common sense. Common sense in this perspective would not be limited to a set of assumptions derived from life experiences that are used to confront, challenge, or resist, from the outside, the dominant ideology conveyed by television. Common sense could also be conceived as a product of an electronically defined common place that, by virtue of being electronically reproduced, can be considered a public space. In its most elementary form, going public today means going on the air.

Before we can determine if that common place is a political space, that is, a power relationship, and if the talk show qualifies to be such a place, we have to answer an inevitable objection. Since the audience of a talk show is selected and coached, the host's personality is dominant and determines a well-defined structure of authority, and, most importantly, the program is ultimately framed in conformity with the institution it belongs to; a talk show is as ideologically charged as any other program on TV. And even worse, the sense of interactivity conveyed by the show is an illusion of reciprocal response that increases the impotence of an atomized and silenced home audience by transferring to a proxy — staged debate — the real need for response.

First of all, it should be noticed that the selecting and the coaching have less to do with the framing of an ideological message than with the orchestration of "theatrical" requirements. In fact we know that almost any position is accepted as long as it performs well. Secondly, the authority structure of a talk show is not different from that of any informal group, as democratic and nonauthoritarian as it may claim to be. (Even a consciousness-raising group, or the Civic Forum meeting in the Theater of the Magic Lantern has an authority structure based on power, charisma, etc.) Thirdly, and most importantly, the outcome of the talk show format is diametrically opposed to that of a debate.

Debates are still the most common format that news programs use to express opinions. The news debates not only are more structured than the talk show conversational style in terms of their allotment of time, argumentations, and viewpoints, but also are organized around the methodological premise of a structural balance. What is usually intended for balance is "a matter of official political institutions. . . . There is no operational concept of balance in relation to ordinary people."[23] The debaters are either government officials or representatives of recognized institutions, and as such they inhabit the sphere of newsworthiness. (In a new twist in the recent proliferation of debates, the moderator proposes a story line, a fictitious narrative, and the debaters play the roles assigned to them. They are asked to cease to be themselves and to become the embodiment of institutions: Dan Rather of the press, Elliott Abrams of the State Department, and Charlie Rangel of the Congress. If it is present at all, the public is presented as another institution.) The debate is conceived and executed as a rational exchange of conflicting viewpoints. Each participant is supposedly given a chance to respond, to flex, to amalgamate in an orchestration directed by an inquisitive moderator. Though the object is not agreement, the implied dynamics consist of variations on a given totality. The totality is the debate form itself, that is, the ideology of public discourse, where agreement is not always attainable but communication is always possible, and television is the ultimate terrain of social consensus because it embodies the universality of communication.

Morton Downey's talk show is a far cry from the civility and rationality of Ted Koppel's "Nightline." It is not the violence of the confrontation, be it true or simulated, however, that differentiates talk shows from news debates. The apparent purpose of a news debate is to inform. The purpose of the talk show, in contrast, is not cognitive but therapeutic. The structure of the talk show is not a balance of viewpoints but a serial association of testimonials. The orchestration is not dialectical in the sense that individual interventions are not predisposed to follow a logical argumentative line. More often than not they are inconsequential. The statements are repetitive and sometimes assume the aura of a ritual. In the end there is no resolution, the show provides no conclusions. In fact, the real confrontation is between those who espouse therapeutic solutions and those who keep open the continuity of a discursive practice.

It is not by chance that the original transformation of the talk show, with the participation of the public in the conversations, seemed to be directed at including women, at dealing primarily with women's issues. Still today most of these types of talk shows deal with topics that are considered of interest to women. In the network programming schedules they occupy the time targeted for women's programs, right after the soaps. The popularity of these shows is a result not only of the transformation of the social agenda in this country during the past twenty years, following the changes in the role of women in the family and in society and the awareness brought about by women's struggles, but also of the fact that women's struggles have redefined the relationship between the public and the private. The result of the politicization of the private is a transformation in the nature of the political. And the means of expression of these new areas of political struggle are quite different from those of formal politics. They rely more on the circulation of discursive practices than on formal political agendas.

In this sense, the talk show can be seen as a terrain of struggle of discursive practices. The politicization of private issues is not the invention of the feminist movement. The welfare state is the historical embodiment of the socialization of politics. The social policy of the welfare states intervenes in every aspect of civil society. The private becomes social and the social political. The emergence of social movements and social struggles is acknowledged as long as they can be channeled into the dynamics of political forces. The social becomes political when it is assimilated into categories of general interest. The welfare state is the ultimate dialectical state.

Similarly, the mostly liberal-minded experts on talk shows converse about sexuality, the disintegration of the family, health problems, criminality, and so forth, in terms of societal ills, deviations. They prescribe cures, they practice therapies. Thus the sexually explicit becomes titillation, the politically unorthodox becomes a freak show. That is why it is so easy to dismiss talk shows as a spectacle of forced exaggerations. But because of the nature of the format that we have tried to describe, what is conceived as a confrontational device becomes an opening for the empowerment of an alternative discursive practice. These discourses do not have to conform to the dictates of civility or the general interest. They can be expressed for what they are: particular, regional, one-sided, and for that reason politically alive. Few other shows on television today can make that claim.

The process of formation of common sense is illustrated by the dynamics that the talk show institutes between the experts and the public. The confrontation is not between scientific knowledge expressed by the panel of experts and the "natural" immediacy of ordinary people. In fact, the sort of experts appearing on these shows espouse theories that are based on practical knowledge. Very often they are social workers or therapists, and in fields that are intrinsically dependent on the evaluation of commonsense practices. Also, it is in the nature of the show to discourage the use of data or theories that are not immediately explicable and plausible. Any attempt to the contrary would be interrupted or limited by the host and shouted down by the public. Those who consider this a trivialization of intellectual discourse do not take into account the fact that what is expressed is a refusal not of knowledge but of expertise. The talk show rejects the arrogance of a discourse that defines itself on the basis of its difference from common sense. On the other hand, the common sense of the ordinary public is not at all based on a set of natural intuitions consolidated with life experiences that are brought into balance with that of experts. The experts' common sense shows its conventionality, its social training, its knowledge of television conventions of speech and gestures. If they appear artificial it is because artificiality is the basis of our linguistic experience conditioned and transformed, at least in part, by television. These technical and artificial conventions have become an inseparable part of our negotiation of individual and collective meanings. In debate the authority of the expert is replaced by the authority of a narrative informed by lived experience. This process counteracts endless news reports that announce that the public cannot possibly understand or affect the world and must therefore defer to the experts. "Because crack can overwhelm parental instincts, the nation is giving birth to a new underclass of youths unlike any seen before, experts say"[24]: this typical headline assures us that we cannot understand this new breed of people and we should leave it to the "experts."

A good example of the vicissitudes of expertise on talk shows based on audience participation is the Morton Downey, Jr., show. Arrogant and conservative, Downey physically threatens his guests, the women sexually, the men with "wiping the floor up" with them. He shouts down experts and orchestrates his audience in a cacophony of hoots and grunts. Whether he agrees or disagrees with the experts on the show, they are to be the object of derision. The working class is going to have its day. No longer can experts shut down discourse with scientific studies and endlessly boring statistics and legalisms. Downey calls his regulars "loudmouths," and a good part of the show is dedicated to their views. "These are called the loudmouths, these are where the people speak their piece because all of the experts haven't done squat for us," he says. "Audience, keep kicking ass."

Neither his nor the audiences' arguments are ever the result of rational, empirically verified, objective evidence; they are simply asserted, commonsense, based on their own experience. The experts are treated with anger and moral disdain. Thus an antiwar activist leads the audience to respond not with an argument but a group singing of "America the Beautiful." He sometimes finds his expert guests so repulsive that he has them forcibly removed.

Of course Downey's real concern is to create controversy. Of course he is authoritarian, reactionary. But Downey provides a forum for the disenfranchised, especially young white men (working and lower middle class) who are not represented in the current knowledge-based commodity culture. Even leftists such as Lenora Fulani, the squatters from Thompson Square Park, lesbian separatist Sonia Johnson, and others who are totally absent on television in the United States, can be on the show. From a working-class perspective, Downey is trash television because he trashes middle-class university- and business-based expertise. The show is like a street fight, and even the experts are forced to bare their knuckles as if they were truck drivers or dock wallopers.

The concerns and values of the audience can no longer be reduced to scientific facts. The audience cannot simply be treated as know-nothings. Their lives are not trivial and their concerns must be taken seriously. Thus, Downey provides a forum for common sense (workers have it but experts do not) and reduces the expert to just another member of the audience. Thus in a recent show on the massacre of Chinese students in Tiananmen Square, an expert from the Heritage Foundation, Steve Mosher, gets his five minutes to put his conservative position across, but later in the show Mosher is in the audience fighting for his say with an anarchist squatters' group. The squatters win and get more time.

Finally, more than any other television format the talk show exploits the intertextual nature of the medium. Thus the shows cannot be examined individually. The significance is not in a particular topic. Nor can talk shows be read selectively, according to one's political preference. If what we said is correct, there is no reason to differentiate a liberal talk show from a conservative one, say a Donahue from a Downey. As a social phenomenon the talk show should be analyzed in the context of the proliferation of local call-in shows, talk radio, and the like, a network whose significance in local political organizing is only lately becoming apparent. It should be linked theoretically to the spread of interactive technology that is reshaping much of our communicative experience. Seen in this context, the talk show begins to appear as a current of accumulated social discourse, a readily available data base of acquired discursive practices that can shed new light on the problematic of the public. The crisis of the bourgeois public sphere is fully visible and displayed in front of our eyes. The crisis of representational democracy is the crisis of the traditional institutions of the public sphere — the party, the union, and so forth — and, most importantly, the present mass refusal of politics. If we think about the reconstitution of a public sphere in terms of the revitalization of old political organizations and maintain a definition of politics as basically a form of management of the state, then the embryonic discursive practices of a talk show might appear interesting but ultimately insignificant in the grand scale of political agendas. But if we conceive of politics today as emanating from social, personal, and environmental concerns, consolidated in the circulation of discursive practices rather than in formal organizations, then a common place that formulates and propagates common senses and metaphors that govern our lives might be at the crossroads of a reconceptualization of collective practices.

NOTES

1. For a good example of the convergence of these critical perspectives see the recent Bill Moyers PBS series "The Public Mind" where, for instance, the difference between the arguments of a Michael Deaver and a Neil Postman is hardly noticeable.

2. For a classic position on the role of consumption in mass society, see Hannah Arendt, "Society and Culture," in *Culture for the Millions*, ed. N. Jacobs (Totowa, N.J.: Van Nostrand, 1961), 46.

3. Jean-Christophe Agnew, *Worlds Apart* (Cambridge: Cambridge University Press, 1986).

4. Walter Benjamin, "The Storyteller," in *Illuminations* (New York: Harcourt Brace & World, 1968), 83–109.

5. Jürgen Habermas, *The Structural Transformation of the Public Sphere* (Cambridge, Mass.: MIT Press, 1989).

6. Habermas, *Structural Transformation*, 23.

7. Habermas, *Structural Transformation*, 27.

8. Edward Bernays, *Propaganda* (New York: Horace Liveright, 1928).

9. Walter Lippmann, *The Phantom Public* (Harcourt Brace, 1925).

10. John Dewey, *The Public and Its Problems* (New York: Holt, 1927), 218.

11. Clinton Rossiter, *The Essential Lippmann*, ed. James Lare (New York: Random House, 1963), 92, our emphasis.

12. Bernays, *Propaganda*, 28.

13. Bernays, *Propaganda*, 9.

14. John Fiske, *Reading the Popular* (Boston: Unwin Hyman, 1989), 187.

15. Paul Virilio, *Logistique de la perception* (Paris: Gallimard, 1984).

16. John Fiske, *Television Culture* (New York: Routledge, 1988), 22.

17. Brian Rose, *TV Genres* (Westport, Conn.: Greenwood, 1985), 341.

18. Quoted in Rose, *TV Genres*, 343.

19. Fiske, *Reading*, 17.

20. Quoted in Fiske, *Reading*, 65.

21. Jean Baudrillard, *For a Critique of the Political Economy of the Sign* (St. Louis, Mo.: Telos, 1981), 129.

22. Paolo Virno, *Convenzione e materialismo* (Rome: Theoria, 1986), 35, authors' translation.

23. John Ellis, *Visible Fictions* (London: Routledge & Kegan Paul, 1982), 229.

24. *New York Times*, March 17, 1990.

Windows: of vulnerability
Thomas Keenan

> ... *(and does a window form part of the inside of a building*
> *or not? ...)*
>
> —Jacques Derrida

1.0 "Loos asserted to me one day: 'A cultivated man does not look out of the window; his window is made of frosted glass; it is there only to give light, not to let the gaze pass through.'" (Le Corbusier)[1]
2.0 ...
3.0 "Move me away from the windows at least!" (*Lethal Weapon 2*)

"Simple glass as a membrane filling probably will not last out this century as the dominant window material, and it will take the decorative-holes-in-cave-walls concept with it as it disappears. The idea of static facade is now being challenged by the concept of animated thermal barrier. The poets' charming metaphors of windows as "eyes to the soul" may soon be written into architectural specifications, if present laboratory research proves successful. There are now experimental models of windows that not only blink of their own accord but also send back messages. The reader should not ignore these experiments as flights of poetic nonsense — animated windows are now operating in Japan."[2]

3.1 On a hillside along Mulholland Drive above Los Angeles rests a house that looks like an eye. A one-hundred-foot wide, gently flat-

Photo by Julius Shulman

tened oval of an eye; a bridge on steel struts, a vast facade of window glass, and a softly curving eyelid of a roof. Somehow "the poets' charming metaphors of windows as 'eyes to the soul' " have been literalized, "animated" into an entire house, and attached prosthetically to the "face" of the cliff. The inhabitants of the eye might even become strangely incidental, their "views" oddly irrelevant, occupying as they do nothing but a machine for looking itself. The house stands out on the hill as a hooded aperture, not so much a platform or a container for viewing as the very technology of the gaze. It looks like an eye.

And yet, what the house asks us to question is exactly the reading of this phrase, "looks like." Does it *look*, like an eye, or does it simply figure, look *like*, the eye that architecture has always desired for its houses and its humans? Does the eye of the house — its south elevation is virtually nothing but a window — frame a view for its occupant, overlooking, as they say, the canyon that it dominates? Or does the window rather open the house out, let light in, invent the interior and expose its occupant to the intrusion of an uncontrollable exteriority? The question can be reduced to that — to light or to see? — and its response remains to be . . . seen?

The house, designed by Los Angeles architect John Lautner as a "residence for Mr. and Mrs. Russell Garcia," dates from December 1959.[3] It is as ferocious in its commitment to letting light in as it might seem to be in allowing a gaze to pass through. It poses a remarkable challenge to a traditional humanism of architecture, taking up as it does that discourse's most privileged figure and reinscribing it as a technology for the admission of light. Light enters this strange eye from all four sides — or more accurately, from seven of eight sides, since the house is split through its center by an opened space that separates it into halves (carport above and bedrooms below on the east side, living and dining rooms and kitchen on the west). With the exception of the entrance to the carport, all of the walls are windows, including horizontal bands along the sides, the vast surface (reaching as high as eighteen feet) on the south, and the "interior" exterior surfaces that define the cut that opens through the middle. The open outside at the center, limited only by the terrace, the roof, and these inner windows, punctures and traverses the space with nothing but light. The open center marks the place of the pupil, the eye's aperture, and exposes it as an unshuttered void.

3.2 Lautner's Mulholland Drive house stars in Richard Donner's 1989 film *Lethal Weapon 2*, in which it houses some lethal South Africans committing crimes with apparent impunity as well as diplomatic immunity. Mel Gibson and Danny Glover must visit the house on no fewer than three separate occasions before the racist miscreants are eradicated. The film luxuriates less in the views from the house, of which there are none, than in the fact that the excess of windows both opens the house to surveillance from the exterior and allows interior scenes to be shot with all the brightness of the open sun. The windows flood the house with light, of such intensity that it seems almost to constitute on its own the open space before the cameras. The effectively unbounded interior is nothing other than the result of this lighting.

But the film seems to attach most significance to the blatant precariousness of the building's perch on the hillside; it is referred to in the credits simply as the "stilt house."[4] Gibson's first encounter with it sends him over the rail of the terrazzo balcony, dangling dangerously and looking like nothing so much as the steel columns denied their base in the earth. And in fact, the film seems to reserve its most invested counterlethality for the violent spectacle of the removal of the house's foundations. As sidekick Joe Pesci is being bloodied by the South African thugs inside, Gibson below hitches a rope from his pickup to the base of the struts and starts pulling. When the house begins to shake, the terrified Pesci specifies rigorously the articulation between window and foundation, shouting against the threat of collapse the unexpected but precise imperative: "Move me away from the windows at least!" No sooner has Glover extracted him from the building — through a window, of course — than it loses its last support and tumbles down the hill in flames.

3.3 This house is a risk, not simply *at* the empirical risk so easily thematized and exploited by the film. It asks: what house would not like to be an eye? and then puts that desire into play. The house risks architecture's investment in the window as a certain experience of foundation, as a platform for the human subject. It performs this coincidence of window and foundation — *as* the house — with such rigor that it exposes that articulation itself to a certain instability. What if the opening of the aperture that allows sight were to become uncontrollable, if the regulated light that makes seeing possible were to *over*expose the interior — which it opens — to the exterior against

"... in giving it the chance for reflection, that is, also for *dissociation*.... An empty place for chance; the invagination of an inside pocket. The time for reflection is also the chance for turning back on the very conditions of reflection, in all senses of that word, as if with the help of a new optical device one could finally see sight, one could not only view the natural landscape, the city, the bridge and the abyss, but could view viewing.... Then the time of reflection is also an other time, it is heterogenous with what it reflects and perhaps gives time for what calls for and is called thought.... The chance for this event is the chance of an instant, an *Augenblick*, a 'wink' or a 'blink,' it takes place 'in the twinkling of an eye,' I would rather say, 'in the twilight of an eye' ..." (Jacques Derrida)[5]

which it defines itself? The opening risks the more violent opening of the distinction between inside and outside, private and public, self and other, on which the house of the human is built. This predicament of disarticulation structures all domestic space as such, but it proves determinant for this house. The Garcia house runs this risk, without letting us decide whether its foundations have finally given way. But the exposure to risk offers us in turn the chance to think about the light in the eye, about the window in all its forms as an event or a gift of light — the chance of a blink, the twilight of an eye.

3.4 And what comes before sight? What comes through a window?

4.1 "*Vulnerable* ... from Latin *vulnerare*, to wound, from *vulnus*, wound" (*American Heritage Dictionary*)

4.2 "*Window* ... An opening in a wall or side of a building ... to admit light or air, or both, and to afford a view of what is outside or inside.... 1667 Milton, *P.L.* IV. 191 'As a thief ... in at the window climbs.' ... 1687 Boyle ... 'The wounds that we quietly suffer to pierce our Breasts, would open you Windows into our hearts' " (*Oxford English Dictionary*)

5.0 "a pitiless, blinding light that destroys all calm and sense of protection..." (M. H. Baillie Scott)[6]

5.1 Beatriz Colomina has recently exposed this "little-known fragment of Le Corbusier's *Urbanisme* (1925)":

> Loos asserted to me one day: "A cultivated man does not look out of the window; his window is made of frosted glass; it is there only to give light, not to let the gaze pass through."[7]

When a window "gives light [*donner de la lumière*]," what happens? What is the force of the gift, and what arrives with this light?

5.15 In a series of articles,[8] Colomina has focused our attention on the political and psychological stakes of debates in the architectural discourse of this century about the form of the window, and has begun to dislodge the humanist paradigm that has dominated that discourse for so long. Analyzing the texts, drawings, and buildings of Le Corbusier and Loos in particular — and especially the debate between Le Corbusier and Auguste Perret on the "horizontal window" — she has argued convincingly that their windows, oriented toward the entrance of light rather than the presentation of a painterly view, finally correspond not to the "traditional space of perspectival representation" but to the technological "space of photography," not to the form of the human but to something that displaces it.[9] What is at stake is not so much the opposition between eye and

camera, though, but the possible interference of light in the look of
the human and its eyes (whether organic or technical). Whether the
gaze is aimed toward the exterior or redirected through the interior
of these buildings, and who would seem to possess these looks,
are finally less important than the threat that the hyperbolic admission of light poses to looking as such, to the looking that it of course
makes possible. When Le Corbusier "demonstrates ... that the
fenêtre en longuer illuminates better, by relying on a photographer's
chart that gives times of exposure" (21), his diagram charts precisely
the danger of overexposure, of an interruption in seeing as the light
floods in.

5.2 The disputes about the shape of the window can be summarized
briefly as follows. The humanist window, the "window-door," is the
vertical frame that matches and houses the standing, looking, representing figure of the subject. And if what enters through the enlarged windows that reinforced concrete construction allowed is, as
the early-twentieth-century critic M. H. Baillie Scott cringed, " 'inside,
a pitiless, blinding light that destroys all calm and sense of protection' " and if in particular, as Bruno Reichlin puts it, "Le Corbusier's
horizontal window tears a hole in [what Benjamin called] 'the protective covering of the private person' " that is the interior, then what
is threatened by the arrival of not simply "more light" but "too much
light" is precisely the security of the individual subject and the
interior(ity) that grounds its seeing.[10] Humans, it seems, need windows — but of a certain sort.[11]

Humans, because they are essentially upright, first of all are seeing
beings, seeing ahead, from their heads, and their actions are human
to the extent that they derive and follow from what they see. What is
elsewhere presents itself before the human subject for sight and cog-
nition. (This was Heidegger's "anti-humanist" argument in "The Age
of the World Picture" and other texts.) Human knowledge stems
from the gaze, and the window perhaps even more than the mirror
gives form to this tenacious ideologeme.[12] Evidently, we learn from
Colomina and Reichlin, the length and horizontality of Le Corbusier's window band cuts across the human form and disfigures it,
mutilates the upright installation of the one who stands. The shape
of the window transforms the topography, and the figure is denied
the stance, at once protective and projective, of the *Vorstellung*, the

grounded position of a subject for and before whom objects — including of course the subject itself — are represented in a frame.[13]

5.25 The interest and the tension here reside not in the competition between architects, between one orientation of the window and another, nor even in the historical transformations of these wall apertures. Instead, the question is simply that of the interpretation of windows — philosophical, ideological, everyday. At stake in every understanding of the window is an interpretation of architecture and of politics, an implicit setting and definition of the terms in which they will be elaborated, practiced, and contested. In the careful shorthand of the quotation attributed to Loos, and in its insistence on taking sides, we are given a simple figure with which to gauge the intensity and implications of the questions.... To give light, or to let the gaze pass through?

5.3 The more light, the less sight, and the less there is in the interior that allows "man" to find comfort and protection, to find a ground from which to look. The light, while not exactly absent or available for representation, is not present either — it surprises and blinds the present, disrupts the space of looking and opens an interior, opens it to a force over which it can exert little control. The window can breach, tear open, the "protection" that is the human subject, overcome it with a violence that proves remarkably resistant to knowledge (especially that of vision) or representation. Something displaces, disfigures, or even blinds the human who tries to look, and it can be alternately figured as technology or, perhaps more disquietingly, as the violence of the light.[14]

5.4 What is at stake for us in thinking that we look out, that we gaze (know, dominate), from a ground and through a window, and in forgetting the entrance or the "gift" of that light? The philosophical history of the subject or the human is that of a light and a look, of the privilege of seeing and the light that makes it possible — there would be no humans without the light that allows us to see, whether into the *Lichtung* that lets the other appear or into the otherwise invisible center of the self, and that sometimes blinds us, to remind us of our humanity. "The entire history of our philosophy is a photology," as Derrida has written.[15] But what would "too much" light do, beyond the reassuring symmetries of self and other, human and transcendent, inside and outside? How might such light disturb these topologies? Where does the light come from, and what can we do about it?

5.5 That light can also be the dark side, as it were, of the humanist interpretation of the window and its framed figure is shown of course by Bentham's Panopticon project. Foucault, in *Surveiller et punir*,[16] has analyzed the mechanism by which the window in its structured brilliance works to produce or constitute the human subject, to invent the interiority of the prisoner as something to be attended to and regulated on one's own, in the uncertain absence of the jailer. Which means that the well-lit cell has as its singular object

> "The peripheric building is divided into cells, each of which extends the whole width of the building; they have two windows, one on the inside, corresponding to the windows of the [central] tower; the other, on the outside, allows the light to traverse the cell from one end to the other. . . . By the effect of backlighting [*contre-jour*], one can observe from the tower, standing out precisely under the light, the small captive silhouettes in the cells of the periphery. . . . It is at once too much and too little that the prisoner should be constantly observed by an inspector: too little, for what matters is that he knows himself to be observed; too much, because he actually has no need of being so. . . . Unverifiable: the inmate must never know whether he is currently being looked on; but he must be sure that he may always be so. . . . He who is subjected to a field of visibility, and who knows it, assumes responsibility for the constraints of power; he makes them play spontaneously upon himself; he inscribes in himself the power relation in which he simultaneously plays both roles; he becomes the principle of his own subjection." (Foucault, 200–203)

the production precisely of this "one's own." The subject comes into being as a ghostly silhouette, the target and the source of peculiar gazes that function by *not* seeing — the prisoner can never see the jailer, but only the jailer's possibility, and therefore the jailer need not see the prisoner. This play of nongazes, under the steady enlightenment of a cell whose walls are windows, converges in that strange obligation of self-surveillance that is the prisoner. The terrifying economy of the panoptic structure lies in the fact that this autosurveillance itself can do without seeing, requiring only light as the possibility of sight. In it, I must make myself something *more* than what I see, something *within* that can be known. The parallel windows of the cell define an interiority that is in turn doubled "within" the prisoner; uncertain about my exposure to sight, but brightly illuminated, I study myself as the subject constituted by these windows ... windows that define "a cell of visibility in which the inmate will find himself caught as 'in the glass house of the Greek philosopher' " (249). But the human being *is* this glass house, this inward-turned and hence nonseeing eye: "just a gaze. A gaze which inspects, and which each individual, feeling it weigh on him, will end by interiorising to the point of observing himself, each individual thus exercising this surveillance over, and against, himself."[17] "Just a gaze" means a strangely gazeless gaze, dependent on the architecture of light, a simulacular sight that takes its (only) cue from the effect of illumination and reproduces its nonpresence with a look that, try as hard as it might, could never see. For this look, only light—without sight—is required.

5.6 When we look, even without seeing, we reaffirm our humanity, our responsibility for ourselves, even in detention. The soul of the Panopticon, unlike Leibniz's, must have windows, opening for the admission of a light that constitutes the self as a unique interiority. Still ... the figure of the human as prisoner — secure captive of self-knowledge and of a closed interiority, of peace and quiet, looking without seeing — is challenged, disfigured, by the blinding light of another window.

6.0 ...

7.0 It is said that in 1826 one Nicéphore Niépce "took the first photograph, an eight-hour exposure through a window of his house in Châlon-sur-Saône," and that the back of this print calls it "the heliograph. The first results spontaneously obtained by the action of light."[18] This curious duplication—the photograph is a window, through a window — repeats itself regularly in the history of the technologies of these "words of light."[19] Not only in the infancy of cinema,[20] but later again at the birth of the television age, the earliest practitioners and promoters found themselves looking out yet another window. In *Here Is Television, Your Window to the World*, Thomas Hutchinson recalls that "the first television picture of a distant location was thrilling. ... But what good was there in seeing if there was nothing to look at? At the Radio and Television Show in

Berlin in 1938 one of the sets showed a vista of a Berlin street. A camera had been focused out the window but few people were interested. You simply don't stand on a street corner and watch traffic for very long."[21] And contemporary technologies of the image have either substituted the screen for the window altogether ("The world constructed by the media seems to be a valid surrogate for 'real life' whatever that is. I decided that aiming my camera at the television set was just as reasonable as aiming it out the window," says artist John Baldessari[22]) or simply become impatient with the mediation still implied by the figure of the window in an age of computerized virtual reality ("where is the window?" asks one prophet of its doom, in order to answer that it has been "shattered" with our newfound ability to enter "a virtual place").[23]

7.1 If Hutchinson found himself unable to resist the figure of the window, he nevertheless remained somewhat divided over the question of its direction. Does a window belong to the inside or the outside? In *Here Is Television, Your Window to the World*, he split the difference:

> Television actually is a window looking out on the world. Radio brought sound to the home — television adds the visual image. . . . Television means the world in your home and in the homes of all the people in the world. (x–xi)

In which direction does this window "face"? Looking out *onto* the world, presenting a view of the distant (tele-vision)? Or does it intrude *into* the home, all the homes, transforming the space, transporting the "world" into the homes of the world — opening them up and facilitating the arrival of the image and the other? "See, here it is," wrote Keats. To the extent that this new window serves as a vehicle for light, as something that "brings" the entire outside into one of its parts, by processing it as an image or an electronic light signal, the event of the television confirms the residual tension in the window. The trace of that disjunction (gaze out, light in) can be found in the confusion over inside and out ("looking out on the world," "the world in your home"), in the double incorporation by which television at once contains the world and is then recontained by the home, a home that can then be reintegrated into the world home-system to the extent that "all" the homes share this new inhabitant — the television light.[24]

7.15 The common — although just how common remains to be seen — light can of course give rise to an effect of differentiation that may exceed even the cunning of its spokespeople. In *The Medium Is the Massage* McLuhan and Fiore quote *Variety* ("Ice Boxes Sabotage Capitalism") quoting Sukarno: "The motion picture industry has provided a window on the world, and the colonized nations have looked through that window and have seen the things of which they have been deprived. It is perhaps not generally realized that a refrigerator can be a revolutionary symbol — to a people who have no refrigerators."[25]

7.2 That this televisual lighting is an architectural question can be quickly confirmed by reference to Bruno Funaro, then assistant dean at Columbia University's School of Architecture, speaking at the U.S. Chamber of Commerce in November 1956.[26] He begins with a survey of the paradoxical status of the window at mid-century:

> Today we are faced with what appears to be a dilemma: modern building technology has, on one hand, made unlimited windows possible. With the outer surface of buildings freed from structural commitments, windows can be placed anywhere, everywhere. On the other hand, modern technology has replaced with more reliable means many of the services which were performed by windows and which were their reason for being. Now that we can have them, we are not so sure that we really want them. (63)

Yet they persist, and Funaro's lecture turns around and around the question: why do humans want windows? After a brief investigation of their history and aesthetic dimensions, he returns to the technological challenges to the window's functions (e.g., daylight has been replaced by "fluorescent lights," air by "air conditioning"), concluding with the central issue of what we might call the "vision thing":

> The scientists tell us that it is essential to focus the eye occasionally on a distant view, also that people psychologically need a visual contact with the outside. Windows may take care of these requirements, but rather poorly, especially when the glass is heavily tinted to reduce glare or when the shades are pulled down. I do not see why these functions could not be much better performed by electronic devices. Imagine each desk equipped with its own TV window through which the office worker may look down the street and "stretch" his eyes, no matter how distant his desk is from the outer wall. The climax of this horrible thought would be a closed TV

office circuit which offers the opportunity to Washington office workers
to feast their eyes occasionally on sunny Biscayne Boulevard. (64)

Although he immediately calls this a "joke," Funaro is obviously en-
tranced by this new view. So fascinated, or perhaps blinded, as to fail
to notice that all the light in his office is not coming from those
fluorescent fixtures. The television emits a different glow, and the
strange quotation marks around "stretch" perhaps signal a certain
hesitation about the effect of that light on the eyes of the human
figure. These eyes are being stretched in another direction, horribly,
and the terrified response is this fantasy of the "closed circuit" that
aims to keep the invasive procedure that is the television under control by limiting it to a "view," to be turned off and on occasionally...
8.0 "It is old-fashioned to assume as they did in the 1930s that these
struggles will be determined in the streets when there is a mass
medium in every house that acts as a kind of window. Against such
a power to convince millions through television, all conventional
means are powerless." (Alexander Kluge)[27]
8.1 Has the political theory of democracy ever seriously questioned
the figure of the window, by which it organizes and secures its inaugural distinction between public and private? With a handful of
exceptions (Lefort, Kluge, Mouffe and Laclau, Derrida), the answer
is no. The window implies a theory of the human subject as a theory
of politics, and the subject's variable status as public or private
individual is defined by its position relative to this window. Behind
it, in the privacy of home or office, the subject observes that public
framed for it by the window's rectangle, looks out and understands
prior to passing across the line it marks — the window is this possibility of permeability — into the public. Behind it, the individual is a
knowing — that is, seeing, theorizing — subject. In front of it, on the
street for instance, the subject assumes public rights and responsi-
bilities, appears, acts, intervenes in the sphere it shares with other
subjects. The window defines the place and the possibilities of the
subject and contains a theory of politics within a theory of this
subject.

But what comes *through* a window? For if the window is the opening in the wall constitutive of the distinction between public and
private, it is also the breaching of that distinction itself.
8.2 The "public sphere" cannot simply be a street or a square, some-

place where I go to become an object or instead heroically to reassert my subjectivity, some other place out into which I go to "intervene" or "act." If it is anywhere, the public is "in" me, but it is all

"A 17-year old Brooklyn youth . . . was killed early yesterday morning by a stray bullet as he peered out the window of a friend's apartment, the police said. The teen-ager, Tango Gillard, had gone to the window when he heard the sound of gunfire and a bullet struck him in the head at 2:20 A.M., the police said." (*New York Times*, June 17, 1991)[28]

"For children, the local television news is the widest window on the world just beyond their home, their street and their school. And when they peer through that window, they shudder at a landscape of violence and danger. 'Like, on the news, people get hurt — some bullets come in the arm,' said 8-year-old Nisera Cekic, sitting on a seesaw at the Austin Street Playground in Forest Hills, Queens. 'It makes me sad.' " (*New York Times*, September 11, 1990)[29]

that is not me in me, not reducible to or containable within "me," all that tears me from myself, opens me to the ways I differ from myself and exposes me to that alterity in others.

8.3 The public is not the realm of the subject, but of others, of all that is other to — and in — the subject itself. We can never hope to think the peculiarity of what is public if we persist in figuring it as the unstructured open into which the previously private subject strides or from which it retreats, or worse yet as simply another "face" of that humanity. The public is not a collection of private individuals experiencing their commonality, nor the view organized for and by the human of what might gather it together. The public is the experience, if we can call it that, of the interruption or the intrusion of all that is radically irreducible to the order of the individual human subject, the unavoidable entrance of alterity into the everyday life of the "one" who would be human. The public — in which we encounter what we are not — belongs by rights to others, and to no one in particular. (That it can in fact belong to specific individuals or corporations is another question, to which we will return.) Publicity tears us from our selves, exposes us to and involves us with others, denies us the security of that window behind which we might install ourselves to gaze. And it does this "prior to" the empirical encounter between constituted subjects; publicity does not befall what is properly private, contaminating or opening up an otherwise sealed interiority. Rather, what we call interiority is itself the mark or the trace of this breach, of a violence that in turn makes possible the violence or the love we experience as intersubjectivity. We would have no relation to others, no terror and no peace, certainly no politics, without this (de)constitutive interruption.

8.35 The well-known "glare of publicity" is precisely this *light* — "glare," after all, shares its root with "glass," and is nothing other than "an intense and blinding light" (*American Heritage Dictionary*) — in the window. Publicity is the intervention of the utterly nonhuman or nonsubjective, always already at work "within" us, at least to the extent that we speak and write in a language — "the peculiar possession of the public," as Wimsatt and Beardsley said[30] — that is finally beyond our control. Something *else* arrives through this window, something other than the human.

8.4 Today, and tonight, publicity has found another mode of access. As Alexander Kluge has emphasized, "It is old-fashioned to assume as they did in the 1930s that these struggles will be determined in the streets when there is a mass medium in every house that acts as a kind of window. Against such a power to convince millions through television, all conventional means are powerless" (40). To think — and perhaps to intervene in — this kind of window and its other light implies a radical reorientation of our conventional categories of

---

"In 1976, when Reagan first seriously ran for president, we learned that ten- to twenty-second sound bites on the evening news constituted our window to the voter. So I saw as my responsibility making that television window as appealing as possible. It wasn't my job to worry about words. I worried about what was around Reagan's head inside the picture; I wanted people to have something pleasing and attractive to look at." (Michael Deaver)[31]

---

space and time, inside and outside, now and then. The television window, a pocket of somewhere and somewhen else, has entered our living and working space and time behind the back of the political theorist, who continues to stare out of the window in search of the disappearing public realm. It emits what Paul Virilio has called "another light," "an indirect public lighting,... an artificial light which has now finished off electrical lighting just as it had once supplanted the daylight."[32] If the *porte-fenêtre* had allowed the passage of people between indoors and out, and the second "specialized window" had interrupted that access with an excess of light, then this "third window" opens another sphere altogether:

> The *third window* ... is the television screen, removable and portable window which opens onto a "false day," that of the speed of luminous emission, introverted opening which no longer gives onto neighboring space but beyond, beyond the perceptive horizon.[33]

The beyond from which this indirect light enters breaks utterly with the present of any given subject or group of subjects, neither here nor there nor anywhere accessible to intuition or perception. It is emitted from beyond the horizon of anything reducible to humanity, from the placeless place of . . . others.

8.5 The erosion of the security of the private sphere figured by the opening of the window, and with it the classical definition of the public sphere as well, forces us to reconsider the space and time, as well as the agencies, of political action in terms that can no longer be content to accept the restrictions imposed by the thought of publicity as presence. What if the peculiarity of the public were — not exactly (its) absence, but — the rupture in and of the subject's presence to itself that we have come to associate with writing or language in general? If language exceeds the subject, opens a window to the other in the monad, what becomes of the public that was once defined in opposition to this private self?

In this sense, all those books and articles mourning the loss or disappearance of the public sphere in fact respond to, if in the mode of misrecognition, something important about the public — that it is not here.[34] The public sphere is structurally elsewhere, neither lost nor in need of recovery or rebuilding but defined by its resistance to being made present.

And somehow doubly elsewhere, as Jacques Derrida has insisted when he responded to a question about public opinion[35] by defining it, today, as "the silhouette of a phantom":

> How to identify public opinion here? Does it take *place?* Where does it give itself to be seen, and as such? The errancy of its own body is also the ubiquity of a spectre. But it is not present as such in any of these spaces.... It does not speak in the first person, it is neither object nor subject ("we" or "one"), it is cited, it is ventriloquized. (105–6)

The public takes the form of nothing so much as a foreign body — nothing personal, nothing to be perceived in the present of a subject, but something that comes from a distance, an interruption, an alien arrival that disturbs the masterable surroundings of the subject. This flickering ghost light, the twilight or the trilight of something blinking uncontrollably, constitutes an opening — a *glasnost* or *Öffentlichkeit* of sorts. But the space and time of this openness must above all not be confused with the freedom philosophy has always associated with the human subject. In public, exposed to the blinding light of the other, I am without precisely the self-possession that would otherwise constitute my freedom. The enlightenment of this other light opens me not by freeing me but by exposing me, to all that is different in and beyond me.

8.8 Neither absent nor captive, I am in public a "hostage" of the other. As Blanchot has written, following Lévinas, of the "disaster," "it is the other who exposes me to 'unity,' causing me to believe in an irreplaceable singularity, as if I must not fail him, all the while withdrawing me from what would make me unique: I am not indispensable; in me anyone at all is called by the other. The responsibility with which I am charged is not mine, and because of it I am no longer myself."[36]

8.9 "It is the dark disaster that carries the light" (17).

9.0 ...

10.0 "He jests at scars that never felt a wound / But soft, what light through yonder window breaks?" (*Romeo and Juliet*, II.ii.1–2)

10.1 If architecture has anything to do with language, if it like the unconscious is "structured like a language," then the axis of the simile cannot be humanity, and certainly not some supposed power of expression, signification, representation, or communication. Indeed, each of these functions is in turn rendered possible and put in irrecuperable jeopardy by what we call language. Language gives no stable ground to humanity, makes no room for our signs and representations. If we do so, if we make images and express ourselves, we

ABC News

do so only at the risk of the selves we so desperately long to present and represent. For language intervenes in the lives of those who seek to use it with a force and a violence that can only be compared to . . . light, to the tear of the blinding, inhuman, and uncontrollable light that comes through a window — something soft, that breaks.
. . .

NOTES

1. Cited by Beatriz Colomina, "Intimacy and Spectacle: The Interiors of Adolf Loos," *AA Files* 20 (Autumn 1990): 5. Here and elsewhere I have sometimes slightly modified the existing translations of texts written in French and German.

2. Forrest Wilson, "Covering Holes in the Wall: Window Membranes over the Years and into the Future," *Architecture* 77, no. 8 (August 1988): 95. That "the poets" have always considered the eyes as windows to the soul, and not the other way around, is extensively documented in *The Macmillan Book of Proverbs, Maxims, and Famous Phrases*, ed. Burton Stevenson (New York: Macmillan, 1948), 732–33. This has not stopped one Jocasta Innes, "London designer," from "call[ing] windows 'the eyes of a house' " (91), as we learn in Ann Dermansky, "Points of View," *Elle Decor* 2, no. 6 (August 1991): 86–97 — an article whose two punning subtitles ("windows are for more than looking out of" and "when windows look their best") gently qualify the optimism of its title, and that nevertheless reiterates that "windows frame views" even while warning that "shades or blinds are often necessary, for privacy or for keeping out the dawn" (97).

3. My thanks to Laura Kurgan for showing me this house, to the staff of John Lautner's office, especially Duncan Nicholson, for access to drawings and photographs, and to Julius Shulman for his photographs. My information here comes from drawings dated December 4, 1959. In an unpublished project list supplied by his office, Lautner has described the Garcia residence, which was completed in 1962, in these terms: "Laminated wood arched roof to blend in the hills and give free framed views. Clear span for simple uncluttered foundation." The only published reference to the house that I have been able to locate occurs in Esther McCoy's "West Coast Architects V: John Lautner," *Arts and Architecture* 82, no. 8 (August 1965): 22–27.

4. The film is not alone in this attention; compare Reyner Banham's reading of another Lautner house, Chemosphere, also off Mulholland Drive, in *Los Angeles: The Architecture of Four Ecologies* (Harmondsworth: Penguin, 1971), 104.

5. Jacques Derrida, "The Principle of Reason: The University in the Eyes of Its Pupils," trans. Catherine Porter and Edward P. Morris, *Diacritics* 13, no. 3 (Fall 1983): 19–20.

6. Cited by Bruno Reichlin, "The Pros and Cons of the Horizontal Window: The Perret–Le Corbusier Controversy," *Daidalos* 13 (September 1984): 76–77.

7. Colomina, "Intimacy and Spectacle," 5.

8. See Colomina, "Intimacy and Spectacle," as well as "Le Corbusier and Photography," *Assemblage* 4 (October 1987): 6–23; "*L'Esprit Nouveau*: Architecture and *Publicité*," in *Architectureproduction*, ed. Beatriz Colomina (New York: Princeton Architectural Press, 1988), 56–99; "Domesticity at War," *Ottagono* 97 (December

1990): 24–47; and "The Split Wall: Domestic Voyeurism," in *Sexuality and Space*, ed. Beatriz Colomina (New York: Princeton Architectural Press, 1992), 73–128.

9. Colomina, "Le Corbusier and Photography," 20.

10. Reichlin, "Pros and Cons," 76–77; for further extensive analyses of Le Corbusier's windows, see also Reichlin, "The Single-Family Dwelling of Le Corbusier and Pierre Jeanneret at the Weissenhof" and "The Pavillon Church," in *In the Footsteps of Le Corbusier*, trans. Hanna Hannah, ed. Carlo Palazzolo and Riccardo Vio (New York: Rizzoli, 1991), 37–57 and 58–71.

11. Besides Colomina and Reichlin, see Georg Kohlmaier and Barna von Sartory, *Houses of Glass: A Nineteenth-Century Building Type*, trans. John C. Harvey (Cambridge, Mass.: MIT Press, 1986 [Munich 1981]), 20–24, on the "troublesome window" with its "onslaught of light," and Georges Teyssot, "'Water and gas on all floors,'" *Lotus International* 44 (1984): 83–94, esp. on the "floods of light" (87) that put the stable individual into disorienting motion. That this remains a practical trouble for even the most banal architectural discourse can be readily measured by the attention paid to light in the "Windows, Outside and In" section of a recent *New York Times* ad supplement, which worries that "if a window is on the first floor and overlooked by passersby, ... the view in must be excluded, ... [or] even that too much light comes in the windows so that it will need filtering" ("From House to Home," advertising supplement to the *New York Times*, September 15, 1991, 10A).

12. Theodor Adorno puts the two into provocative juxtaposition in his reading of Kierkegaard's "window mirror," in *Kierkegaard: Construction of the Aesthetic*, trans. Robert Hullot-Kentor (Minneapolis: University of Minnesota Press, 1989), 41–42; see also Diana Agrest, "Architecture of Mirror/Mirror of Architecture," *Architecture from Without* (Cambridge, Mass.: MIT Press, 1991), 139–55.

13. See Colomina, "Le Corbusier and Photography," 18–21. On "man" as the being that represents and sets up the world for view as an image, the subject of *Vorstellung*, see Martin Heidegger, "Die Zeit des Weltbildes," in *Holzwege* (Frankfurt am Main: Vittorio Klosterman, 1972), 82–83; "The Age of the World Picture," in *The Question Concerning Technology*, trans. William Lovitt (New York: Harper & Row, 1977), 129–30.

14. See (as it were) Paul de Man, "Shelley Disfigured," in *Deconstruction and Criticism* (New York: Seabury, 1979), 55–56 and 65.

15. Jacques Derrida, "Force and Signification," *Writing and Difference*, trans. Alan Bass (Chicago: University of Chicago Press, 1978), 27. On this "metaphor" of "light," see also "White Mythology," in *Margins—of Philosophy*, trans. Alan Bass (Chicago: University of Chicago Press, 1982), 207–71, esp. 245–57, and for a reading of the "blinding of wounding" that can stem from that heliotropic light, Andrzej Warminski, "Prefatory Postscript," in *Readings in Interpretation: Holderlin, Hegel, Heidegger* (Minneapolis: University of Minnesota Press, 1987), xlvii.

16. Michel Foucault, *Surveiller et punir* (Paris: Gallimard, 1975); *Discipline and Punish*, trans. Alan Sheridan (New York: Random House, 1977). References are to the English text, although the translations have sometimes been slightly modified.

17. "L'Oeil du pouvoir," discussion among Foucault, Jean-Pierre Barou, and Michelle Perrot, in Jeremy Bentham, *Le Panoptique* (Paris: Pierre Belfond, 1977), 19; "The Eye of Power," in *Power/Knowledge*, trans. Colin Gordon (New York: Pantheon, 1980), 155.

18. Allen S. Weiss, "Cartesian Simulacra," *Persistence of Vision* 5 (Spring 1987): 55–61. The quotation is on p. 56; the photograph is reproduced on the next page. My thanks to Tom Levin for calling this to my attention.

19. Eduardo Cadava, "Words of Light: Theses on the Photography of History," *Diacritics* (1992): forthcoming.

20. See Friedrich von Zglinicki, *Der Weg des Films, Die Geschichte der Kinematographie und ihrer Vorläufer* (Berlin: Rembrandt, 1956), 265, cited in Anke Gleber, "Briefe aus Berlin," *Monatshefte* 82, no. 4 (Winter 1990): 452–65.

21. Thomas H. Hutchinson, *Here Is Television, Your Window to the World* (New York: Hastings House, 1946), 214. I learned about Hutchinson in Lynn Spigel's "Installing the Television Set," *Camera Obscura* 16 (January 1988): 11–47.

22. Quoted in "Guide to Room 5," John Baldessari exhibition, Whitney Museum of American Art, New York, 1991. Thanks to Deborah Esch for passing this along.

23. Regina Cornwell, "Where Is the Window? Virtual Reality Technologies Now," *Artscribe* 85 (January–February 1991): 52–55: "The window as a cultural metaphor has been with us since at least the Renaissance. Then the painting was thought to be a window, representing the external world or the imagination, for edification, instruction, or pleasure. The film screen is often spoken of as a window opening onto the world and even onto other worlds. Television transmits the world onto screens in our livingrooms and bedrooms. While the computer screen seems the next likely candidate for the window metaphor, somehow the window seems to have shattered in face of recent developments in computer technology and applications for what has come to be called virtual reality. . . . Do we step into the computer? Where is the window? While goggles and gloves replace screen . . . , no need to talk about interface or conversation, to anthropomorphise a place. We are in a place now, a virtual place" (52, 54).

24. On this "cryptic topology" (a "haunting" where "the part includes the whole") and "the double overrun of these two inner borders [in a] . . . double invagination," while " 'the light was going mad, the brightness had lost all reason,' " read Jacques Derrida, "Living On," in *Deconstruction and Criticism*, 156–57, 166, and 89.

25. Marshall McLuhan and Quentin Fiore, *The Medium Is the Massage* (New York: Bantam, 1967), 131. I am grateful to Suju Vijayan for supplying this reference.

26. Bruno Funaro, "Windows in Modern Architecture," in *Windows and Glass in the Exterior of Buildings* (Washington, D.C.: National Research Council, Building Research Institute, 1957), 63–66.

27. Alexander Kluge, "On New German Cinema, Art, Enlightenment, and the Public Sphere," interview with Stuart Liebman, *October* 46 (Fall 1988): 40.

28. Jacques Steinberg, "Recovering from Wounds, Youth Is Slain by Stray Shot," *New York Times*, June 17, 1991, B2.

29. Dennis Hevesi, "TV News: Children's Scary Window on New York," *New York Times*, September 11, 1990, B1.

30. W. K. Wimsatt, Jr., and M. C. Beardsley, "The Intentional Fallacy," *The Sewanee Review* 54, no. 3 (1946): 468–88 at 470.

31. Michael Deaver, "Sunny Side Up," interview by Ken Adelman, *The Washingtonian*, December 1989, 99.

32. Paul Virilio, "The Work of Art in the Electronic Age," *Block* 14 (1988): 4 (Colomina cites this interview in "Domesticity at War," 35); "La Lumière indirecte,"

Communications 48 (1988): 52. See also "La Troisième Fenêtre," *Cahiers du Cinéma* 322 (April 1981): 35–40; "The Third Window," trans. Yvonne Shafir, in *Global Television*, ed. Cynthia Schneider and Brian Wallis (New York: Wedge Press; Cambridge, Mass.: MIT Press, 1988), 185–97.

33. Paul Virilio, *L'Espace critique* (Paris: Christian Bourgois, 1984), 99; *The Lost Dimension*, trans. Daniel Moshenberg (New York: Semiotext[e], 1991), 79.

34. "Whatever Became of the Public Square?" *Harper's* 1682 (July 1990): 49–60; Richard Sennett, *The Fall of Public Man* (New York: Knopf, 1977).

35. Jacques Derrida, "La Démocratie ajournée," in *L'Autre cap* (Paris: Minuit, 1991), 103.

36. Maurice Blanchot, *L'Ecriture du désastre* (Paris: Gallimard, 1980), 35, 28; *The Writing of the Disaster*, trans. Ann Smock (Lincoln: University of Nebraska Press, 1986), 18, 13.

The Trojan Horse of Universalism: Language As a "War Machine" in the Writings of Monique Wittig
Linda Zerilli

> *One must understand that men are not born with a faculty for the*
> *universal and that women are not reduced at birth to the particular.*
> *The universal has been, and is continually, at every moment,*
> *appropriated by men. It does not happen by magic, it must be done. It*
> *is an act, a criminal act, perpetrated by one class against another. It*
> *is an act carried out at the level of concepts, philosophy, politics.*[1]
>
> — Monique Wittig

Monique Wittig is a unique and often lone voice in French feminist theory. Despite all the scholarly attention that has been lavished upon Continental poststructuralist thinkers, her works, which elaborate an ungendered, universal theory of the subject, have been largely neglected in contemporary debates about feminism, anti-foundationalism, and the political public sphere.[2] This neglect, as we shall see, is more than an academic oversight: it is symptomatic of the presumed ontological categories of heterosexuality that organize, legitimate, and give meaning to the political relations of society and that are all too often inadequately interrogated by their postmodern critics; it is indicative of the blind spot in many French feminist theories of postmodernism — theories that purport to critique but in subtle ways reproduce gender as the central category of albeit fractured identities and of the subject in process; and it is expressive of the general silence that surrounds any serious discussion about universalism in contemporary feminist theory.

In a recent article on the postmodern feminist bugaboo called essentialism, Naomi Schor put the last point succinctly when she wrote that the "universal and universalism may well be one of the most divisive and least discussed issues in feminism today."[3] In certain respects, of course, universalism has been on the broader feminist critical agenda for quite some time. Early feminist critiques of traditional political theory, for example, contended that women were not and could not be included in Enlightenment notions of the citizen. The universalist, that is, generic theory of citizen man, they argued, was a political chimera that concealed reductive because functionalist (Okin), privatized (Elshtain), and sexualized (Pateman) images of citizen woman.[4] Focusing on the silenced and repressed aspects of a political theory, these critics sought to delimit the cultural authority of an academically sanctioned tradition that claimed to speak a universal political language. They called for new theories of politics that would reflect historical and contemporary modes of women's civic activism; they demanded a more inclusive understanding of the public sphere that would incorporate the voices of women.

Students of postmodernism, however, approach the problem of universalism and gender from a slightly different angle. Focusing on the collapse of metadiscourses, they take up Lyotard's claim that the "grand narratives of legitimation" are no longer credible.[5] Narratives that tell stories about the march of progress and reason, about the dialectical development of Spirit (Hegel), and about the triumph of the working class (Marx) have lost (more or less) their cultural authority; this is a familiar statement on the postmodern condition. For feminists who reject humanist theories of the subject, extending the critique of universalism as metanarrative to reveal its structural androcentrism has been especially important; and the elaboration of "feminine difference" as subversive of the masculine claim to universality has been absolutely central to that critique. As we shall see, in the poststructuralist context of feminist theory, to pursue a critical strategy that would seek fuller or equal representation for women in dialogical structures of language and politics must founder on the very phallogocentrism of representation itself. For the "feminine" is not the position from which women might claim the universal status of the subject. Instead, to quote Luce Irigaray, the "feminine" is the "hole in men's signifying economy," the "lack" that "might cause the ultimate destruction, the splintering, the break in their systems of 'presence,' of 're-presentation' and 'representation.' "[6]

The result of these critiques of representation, however, has been to strike universalism from the feminist theoretical agenda, to assume that the very idea of the universal can no longer be entertained by those feminists who are sympathetic to or who advance the critical project of postmodern theory.[7] The debunked political narrative of universalism, in short, has become the accepted critical position from which feminists articulate decentralized notions of community and radical pluralized concepts of citizenship. Whatever the theoretical fruit of these arguments — and some of them will be discussed here — the feminist critique of universalism has become a prisoner of its own judgment. For if universalism and the universal, as Schor noted, have not been discussed much in feminist poststructuralist circles recently, this results from the uncritical assumption that to utter these words with any degree of seriousness is to rearticulate the metapolitical narratives of the Enlightenment. Stated somewhat differently, to speak the word *universal*, to paraphrase Virginia Woolf, is to reflect citizen man back to himself at twice his original size. Indeed universalism and the universal, as Schor writes of essentialism, have "been endowed within the context of feminism with the power to reduce to silence, to excommunicate, to consign to oblivion."[8]

Within the conceptual, academic, and, to some extent, artificial split that has emerged between "humanist" and "poststructuralist" feminists, those who are either reluctant to abandon or who would critically deploy the language of universalism in an attempt to articulate feminist politics and theories of the subject are too often dismissed as theoretically antiquarian or politically naive. Thus it is not uncommon in the feminist literature to find that so-called humanist feminist theorists, such as Simone de Beauvoir, stand accused of allowing themselves to be seduced by the Hegelian Spirit, the Absolute Subject.[9] Apart from the injustice that such readings do to as challenging a theorist as Beauvoir, the assumption that universalism has been rightfully and thoroughly disgraced as a political category for feminist theory has led to a different kind of seduction: a willingness to embrace French theories of difference for fear of remaining trapped in that looking glass of androcentrism. More specifically, as I will contend later, gender as "the enforcement of sex in language," an enforcement that, Wittig writes, deprives women of the "authority of speech," has been reconstituted in the works of some French feminists under the radical guise of *écriture féminine* (Cixous), *parler femme* (Irigaray), and the maternal semiotic (Kristeva).[10]

The texts of French feminism most widely read in this country (those of Hélène Cixous, Luce Irigaray, and Julia Kristeva) have been addressed critically, extensively, and from virtually every conceivable angle by feminist scholars. Some of these critiques, especially those that bring the charge of essentialism against French theorists of difference, are misdirected because they confuse the French concern with theorizing the "feminine feminine" (difference) with the "phallic feminine" (sameness). The result is a reductive account of the challenge that such theories pose to dominant modes of representation and of subjectivity. For example, to conflate French and American notions of difference, to identify, say, Irigaray's attempt to theorize feminine difference with that of Carol Gilligan,[11] is to confuse the overarching French understanding of the "feminine," which concerns the heretofore unsaid and unrepresented of patriarchal discourse, with the American attempt to revalue the represented but derided voices of women. Whatever problems may be involved in the trans-Atlantic translation of their conceptual categories, however, French feminist theories of difference pose difficult questions for feminist theory as political theory, as a theory of citizenship, and as a theory of counterpublics organized around collective speaking subjects.

In this essay I address the twin problems of difference and universalism in feminist theory focusing largely but not exclusively on the theoretical and fictional writings of Monique Wittig. In Wittig's account, notions of gender as sexual difference, however one conceptualizes the latter, remain tied to oppressive discourses of heterosexuality, to what Wittig identifies as political and cultural emanations of the "straight mind."[12] Heterosexuality, she contends, be it naturally, socially, or discursively theorized, gives the lie to universalism; but so too does universalism give the lie to gender as sexual difference. Whereas French theorists of difference use the feminine to deconstruct the universal, Wittig will employ the universal to deconstruct the "feminine." Working within a poststructuralist context and with a materialist theory of language, however, Wittig negotiates critically the related problems raised by those who would critique androcentrism by reconstituting the "female" subject as a whole, positive, and unified identity as well as those raised by the liberal feminist search for an androgynous citizen self. Moreover, as we shall see, it is her radical and unflinching critique of a heterosexual episteme that allows Wittig to deploy the universal in ways that suggest challenging directions for feminist political theory.

I

The preceding discussion introduces large and difficult claims about politics, language, and feminist theory — claims that this essay can only begin to address. For to talk about French feminist and postmodern theories of the subject is to enter a series of complex and critical debates in which the meanings of such terms as "the subject" are themselves continuously contested. To introduce the problems of difference and universalism for feminists, then, I would like to begin with a concrete and, in my view, telling example of how the question of universalism has been formulated in the feminist literature: with the provocative article in *Differences* by Naomi Schor, noted above. Although her argument addresses the problem of essentialism in contemporary feminist criticism through a close reading of Irigaray, Schor tackles as well the theoretical quagmire of "saming" and "othering" that structures what she sees as the scholarly silence concerning universalism in feminist theory. Introducing the voice of Monique Wittig into this debate, I hope to show, allows us to move beyond the restrictive and politically problematic idea of feminine difference as an alternative to androcentric conceptions of universalism and of the speaking subject.

Schor set up the debate over "saming" and "othering" in feminist theory by contrasting the work of Luce Irigaray with that of Simone de Beauvoir. What unites these theorists, Schor correctly notes, is their critical concern with "the appropriation of subjectivity by men." Thus Beauvoir's famous statement in *The Second Sex* that "he is the Subject, he is the Absolute," is expressed as well by Irigaray's claim that "any theory of the 'subject' has always been appropriated by the 'masculine.' "[13] What distinguishes these two theorists, however, is their very different notions of the subject. Beauvoir's "Subject," with its "impressive capitalized S, reinforced by the capitalization of Absolute, its homologue," writes Schor, is not comparable with "Irigaray's subject, with its lower case s and the relativizing quotation marks that enclose both subject and masculine" (43). Whereas "Beauvoir's subject is the familiar Hegelian subject . . . , a heroic fig- ure locked in a life and death struggle with the not-self, chiefly the environment and the Other," Irigaray's "is a diminished subject that bears little resemblance to the sovereign and purposeful subject of existentialist philosophy" (43–44). Because she rejects as illusory *any* notion of the universal, Irigaray cannot share in Beauvoir's pro- ject to include women "fully in the privileges of the transcendent subject" (45). Indeed for Irigaray, Schor writes, "the goal is for women to achieve subjectivity without merging tracelessly into the putative indifference of the shifter" (45).

If Beauvoir was concerned to reveal the mechanisms of "other- ing," the processes by which patriarchy relegates all women to the fixed place of the "absolute Other," Irigaray is keen to demonstrate the related but significantly more troubling process of "saming," a process that "denies the objectified other the right to her difference, submitting the other to the phallic laws of specularity" (45). On Schor's reading, moreover, the twin problems of othering and sam- ing reflect the very different categories of *"homo faber"* and *"homo parlans,"* which, she argues, organize, respectively, the feminist cri- tiques of Beauvoir and Irigaray: "For Irigaray — and this displace- ment is crucial — the main attribute of the subject is not activity but language," Schor writes (44). Thus the speaking subject of Irigaray's feminist discourse is a subject who speaks "a sexually marked lan- guage, a parler femme" (45). In Irigaray's view, writes Schor, "to speak woman is above all not to speak 'universal' " (45).

In Schor's account of the debate between Beauvoir and Irigaray, "each position has its own inescapable logic": "If all difference is attributed to othering then one risks saming, and conversely: if all denial of difference is viewed as resulting in saming then one risks othering" (46). However, readings of Beauvoir but especially of Irigaray that lament the inability of each to avoid the problems raised by the critique of the other theorist are themselves misreadings, she contends. For Irigaray, in particular, is involved in a theoretical undertaking that defies any attempt to *define* woman by speaking her difference. That is a task better left to men, as Irigaray herself notes. Instead the question of woman's difference becomes the "question of the difference within difference" (47). And it is Irigaray's "wager," writes Schor, "that difference itself can be reinvented, that the bogus difference of misogyny can be reclaimed to become a radical new difference that would present the first serious historical threat to the hegemony of the male sex" (47).

Schor's sympathetic and intelligent reading of Irigaray points to the problems involved in assuming that to speak of women's difference is necessarily to speak in an essentialist tongue. This is the same problem of conflating the "feminine feminine" (difference) with the "phallic feminine" (sameness) noted above. But if Schor would rightfully "de-hystericize" the debate over essentialism that rages in contemporary feminist theory, pointing instead to the complexity with which Irigaray enacts what Mary Ann Doane calls a "defamiliarized version of femininity" (47), she does so by enacting a familiarized reading of Beauvoir, one that aligns this unreconstructed "existentialist feminist" unambiguously with that other source of hysteria in postmodern critical thinking, universalism. Thus it comes as no surprise to the reader of Schor's article that Beauvoir is left behind in the first pages as the author moves on to presumably more radical theories of subjectivity as they are articulated in the works of Irigaray.

My quarrel with Schor, then, concerns, first, what is to be gained by setting up Beauvoir as the straw woman of postmodern feminism, and, second, whether Beauvoir does in fact "give herself away" when she writes that women can achieve greatness (i.e., subjectivity) in the world only at the expense of their so-called difference (47). As I have argued elsewhere, the radical teaching of *The Second Sex* is not simply that woman is Other; nor is it that woman ought to share in the properties of the Hegelian Subject, capitalized or otherwise.[14] Beauvoir's brilliant insight was to see that gender effects a division in the speaking subject, male and female, a division that fractures the masculine claim to universalism and that denies women their subjectivity. For Beauvoir, however, the solution is not *parler femme* quite simply because there can be no unambiguous voicing of the "female self," or of the heretofore unrepresented "feminine feminine," because there can be no gendered self that does not split, once again, the "female" subject into self and Other.

Beauvoir's difficult task, I contended, was to take up this "ambiguous situation" assigned to woman and to locate herself not simply as *homo faber* but also as *homo parlans* squarely yet indefinitely within the discursive space she discovered between the historical speaking subjects called women and the patriarchal monolith called

Woman. For Beauvoir, the ambiguity that inheres in being and not being a woman is the troubling but productive tension that makes the feminist critique of universalism both possible and necessary. In Beauvoir's hands, however, it is a critique that does not simply reinscribe women into a circle of specularity but also enables them to reformulate what universalism must mean if it is to be what it claims to be, universal.

The difference that Beauvoir located between femininity as patriarchal ideology and femininity as a complex and contradictory component of women's psychic social existence, then, is crucial to a feminist critique of universalism and it is necessary for a feminist rethinking of the universal. French theorists who follow more closely in the tradition of Beauvoir, for example those who write in the French feminist journal *Questions féministes*, have pointed to the *néoféminité* that, they argue, shapes the discourse of those who write in journals such as *Psychoanalyse et politique*.[15] While these debates are too complex to discuss in detail here, we might note that the central concern of neglected (in this country) French feminists such as Colette Guillaumin, Monique Plaza, Christine Delphy, and, as we shall see shortly, Monique Wittig, is to point out how political questions of social and economic inequality are eclipsed in French feminist discourse by the overriding obsession with writing the feminine. My purpose here, however, is not to summarize or to adjudicate, as if either were possible, what can only be construed as another artificial dichotomy in French feminist theory. Instead, I want to address the related political questions of universalism and of speech by turning to the critique of heterosexuality and language elaborated in the writings of Monique Wittig.

II

In a 1981 article on French feminist theory, Hélène Vivienne Wenzel writes perceptively that "Wittig's works take the reader on a journey through time and space, self and other, language and culture, to arrive ultimately at a genesis of a new language, and its redefinition of woman."[16] In Wenzel's view, Wittig disrupts the phallogocentrism of dominant theories of the subject by displacing man himself, by exiling him to the outlands of her fictional universe. All "female worlds," she argues, allow Wittig to radically reconceptualize women as speaking subjects; for it is on narrative landscapes where man has no existence that women can begin to "constitute themselves as speaking/naming subjects of their own discourse."[17]

Similarly, in a more recent article on Wittig's novel *Le Corps lesbien*,[18] Namascar Shaktini has written that Wittig displaces the "absolute central metaphor" of the phallus with that of the lesbian body. Shaktini, however, who locates the "token 'presence' " of the phallus in the center of Wittig's book, suggests that the novel exposes "the essentially metaphorical nature of the phallus, and the political nature of metaphor."[19] Like Wenzel, Shaktini reads such novels as *Le Corps lesbien* as political interventions into patriarchal discourse, an intervention in which the phallic subject is displaced by being replaced with the lesbian subject.

The importance of these readings for feminist theorists lies in their fundamental appreciation for the radical implications of Wittig's critique of heterosexuality. If Wittig herself has been banished to the outlands of contemporary feminist theory, this results, at least in part, from the assumption that her writings can be slotted neatly into a phantom school of feminist thought called "lesbian theory" or "lesbian fiction."[20] The violence done to Wittig's work is similar to that done to the writings of Beauvoir. For "taxonomies" of feminism, as Donna Haraway has argued, such as "lesbian feminism" or "existentialist feminism," or, for that matter, "postmodern feminism," can create artificial dichotomies between feminist discourses that seriously impede constructive political debates about subjectivity for women.[21]

However, to suggest, as Wenzel does, that "gender difference is not at all an issue" in Wittig's fiction risks overlooking both important conceptual issues that link her novels to her political essays[22] and the relationship of the reader, who exists in a larger matrix of heterosexual social relations, to the text. Focusing first on the political essays and later on her novels, I will argue that Wittig does not create the possibility of universalism for women by getting rid of men with a stroke of the feminist pen; instead she deconstructs the terms of heterosexual discourse, male and female, men and women, by deploying the universal to reveal the lie that gender speaks in the name of universalism and the lie that the universal speaks in the name of gender.

"Language as a whole gives everybody the same power of becoming an absolute subject through its exercise," writes Wittig in "The Mark of Gender."[23] There is, perhaps, no statement in all of Wittig's writings that distinguishes her position on language from that of Irigaray quite so boldly as this one. Implicitly refuting the critique of Irigaray, Wittig's theory of language refuses to identify the category of the subject with the masculine. As Judith Butler has argued of Wittig, "The very plasticity of language, for her, resists the fixing of the subject position as masculine."[24] But gender, writes Wittig, "works upon this ontological fact (of equal access to subjectivity through language) to annul it as far as women are concerned and corresponds to a constant attempt to strip them of . . . [their] subjectivity" ("Mark," 6). In contrast to Irigaray, then, Wittig asserts that gender, as a "mark" of women's difference *only*, is both a "linguistic index of the political opposition of the sexes"[25] and a powerful device deployed through the practices of speaking and writing that sustains the fiction not so much of the universal or of the subject but of woman as a sexed being, of the category of sex as definitive of those individuals called women.

In "The Mark of Gender," Wittig elaborates the division that gender effects in those individuals called "women" as speaking subjects. "Gender," she argues, "takes place in a category of language that is totally unlike any other and which is called the personal pronoun" ("Mark," 4). We tend to think that such pronouns are neutral, for "I" or "you" — setting aside the third-person singular "he" or "she" for a moment — seem to be unmarked positions in language that allow each speaker to enter language in the same way and that designate its locutors. But in reality, she points out, "as soon as gender manifests itself in discourse, there is a kind of suspension of the grammatical form. A direct interpellation of the locutor occurs" ("Mark," 5). In French this gendered marking of the subject/speaker occurs because the locutor is required to proclaim its gender in the correct use of past participles and adjectives. But even in English, where such marking does not occur, a woman is still put upon to "make her sex public" ("Mark," 5).

Gender, as we shall, see, is not only a grammatical but a sociological, political, and material category of language, according to Wittig. Beauvoir — to whose critique of gender and language Wittig is herself indebted — spoke to the latter point when she wrote that be-

cause the social context of a conversation in patriarchal society positions the "female" speaking subject as a "woman," that subject is
denied what Wittig calls "the abstract form, the general, the universal," a form that the class of men has appropriated for itself. Thus,
Beauvoir wrote in *The Second Sex*, whatever she, the author, says,
she is certain to be reminded that she thinks the way she does because she is a woman. For Beauvoir, the only defense was to reply,

> "I think thus and so because it is true," thereby removing my
> subjective self from the argument. It would be out of the question to
> reply: "And you think the contrary because you are a man," for it is
> understood that the fact of being a man is no peculiarity.[26]

The removal of her "subjective self," of course, refers to the problem of being and not being a woman noted above. For Beauvoir, in
other words, the problem of speaking for women is the problem of
speaking "I" when this "I" (which in her as in Wittig's view constitutes the speaker as an absolute subject) is referred back by the in-
terlocutor as a marked "I," a position in language that, in theory,
allows the locutor to make a claim to the universal but that, in conversation, reinscribes the "female" speaking subject in the particular.
But, for Beauvoir, to deny that one is a woman, to say "I think thus
and such because it is true," is to deny one's own self-conception, to
negate not one's natural but one's social and psychic existence as a
"woman."

Rejecting strictly "nominalist" theories of "woman" as self-delusions,
Beauvoir argues that to say "I am a woman" is the "truth" on which
all further dialogue about language, gender, and subjectivity "must
be based."[27] Negotiating the universal and the particular, Beauvoir
both retains the idea that "woman is, like man, a human being" and
insists that "such a declaration is abstract. The fact is that every concrete human being is always a singular, separate individual."[28] Thus
to decline to accept the albeit ambiguous and mythic but nevertheless psychic power of that patriarchal monolith called Woman, she
contends, "does not represent a liberation for those concerned, but
rather a flight from reality."[29] For a woman, then, to counter particularism by denying her "subjective self" and asserting truth is to
claim the abstract form on the terms of an androcentric universalism.

Thus, far from seeking to occupy unambiguously the masculine
position in language, as some critics would have it,[30] Beauvoir

showed the impossible position in which women stand in relation to discourse. She conceptualizes discourse, however, in terms not of inherently phallogocentric structures of language but of context: the social, political, and economic context of gender relations in which a conversation takes place — a context that marks and inscribes both sex (female) and gender (woman) on the speaking subject; a context, moreover, in which the locutor, if she is "a woman," must inscribe as well sex and gender on herself (must say, "I am a woman") if she is to make a claim to subjectivity without merging into the "Man" that lurks behind the universal. Wittig, as we shall see, refuses to say "I am a woman" while advancing Beauvoir's critical project of rethinking the relationship of the particular to the universal.

Beauvoir's understanding of the body as a "situation," as Butler points out, suggests that the relation of sex to gender is an arbitrary one that is discursively constructed and legitimated as natural.[31] Wittig extends and, to some extent, radically transforms Beauvoir's critique by focusing on the ways in which the bodies of "women," defined as "female" bodies, are ascribed social meaning through a heterosexual imperative, through what Adrienne Rich called "compulsory heterosexuality."[32] According to Wittig, heterosexuality assumes the status of an ontological category in language, which obscures the socially constructed category of sex itself.

For Wittig, gender, as an element of language, does not simply reflect but constitutes, in crucial ways, heterosexuality as ontology; and it does so through a series of repeated acts over time, acts that produce the category of sex as a reality effect. Sex, in short, is a "fetish," an "imaginary formation,"[33] constructed in daily linguistic practices as if sex were the foundation of those practices. Language produces and re-produces sex and gender as part of the "immediate given, the sensible given."[34] "Language casts sheaves upon the social body, stamping it and violently shaping it," writes Wittig ("Mark," 4). To destroy the category not only of gender but also of sex in language, as we shall see, is a political task of the utmost importance. Indeed, Wittig is critical of the sex/gender dichotomy in much feminist theory because such a dichotomy leaves unquestioned the belief that there is a "core of nature which resists examination, a relationship excluded from the social in the analysis — a relationship whose characteristic is ineluctability in culture, as well as in nature, and which is the heterosexual relationship."[35]

Putting sex in nature, gender in society, Wittig suggests, enabled feminists to interrogate the cultural construction of femininity; but this strategy also allowed dominant discourses to acknowledge the distinction without rethinking the foundations of their diverse theoretical enterprises and their concepts of subjectivity. In Wittig's view, then, heterosexuality remained the "universal" category of such varied discourses as psychoanalysis, anthropology, sociology, and linguistics: "Thus one speaks of *the* exchange of women, *the* difference between sexes, *the* symbolic order, *the* unconscious, desire, *jouissance*, culture, history" ("The Straight Mind," 107). What these discourses share, she suggests, is an ontological assumption: the "obligatory social relationship between "man" and "woman" ("Straight," 107). Stated more precisely, heterosexuality is *the* metanarrative of modern discourse; a patriarchal story of origins and of social transition that insures that even radical (although inadequate) ideas of bisexuality, such as those of Freud, and of the social construction of sexuality must eventually give way to the immanent tale of "men" and "women."

As I suggested earlier, although the ontology of heterosexuality proclaims the difference between men and women, it turns out, as Beauvoir understood, that only women are "different," for "being a man is no peculiarity." But the "concept of difference," argues Wittig, "has nothing ontological about it" ("Straight," 108). "Man and woman are political concepts of opposition, and the copula which dialectically unites them is, at the same time, the one which abolishes them" ("Straight," 108). To invoke "difference" when speaking of "women" — whether one speaks of women's difference as voiced but socially derided, in the American context, or of the "feminine" as the unrepresentable, in the French — is to recreate a "mythic formation." Indeed Wittig insists that to speak of women's "difference" is to "throw dust in the eyes of people"[36] by imputing to what is a historical and political category[37] an archaic, mythological status.

By posing the problem of speaking for women as a material and political question, Wittig, following the insights of Beauvoir, is able to interrogate language and the structuralist and poststructuralist discourses that analyze it as political issues that concern not only the material oppression of women but also the individual responsibility of those who proclaim and reinscribe heterosexuality as ontology. Discourses of heterosexuality, she argues, "speak about us [lesbians,

women, and homosexual men] and claim to say the truth in an apolitical field, as if anything of that which signifies could escape the political in this moment in history" ("Straight," 105). Such discourses
"oppress us in the sense that they prevent us from speaking unless
we speak in their terms": "you-will-be-straight-or-you-will-not-be"
("Straight," 105, 107).

Wittig insists that individuals take responsibility for the meanings
they produce, specifically for the oppressive meanings they ascribe
to those persons denied their subjectivity by being defined as
women. Like Beauvoir, as we shall see, Wittig is critical of those theories of language that shift the question of responsibility from politics to the phallogocentric structures of language itself. But because
Wittig works from a notion of the subject as universal and of language as offering the possibility of universality, and because she suggests that volition is central to understanding the re-production of
heterosexual discourses, her critique of heterosexuality as ontology
opens itself up to charges of humanism, to postmodern critiques of
the subject, such as those suggested by Irigaray.

In what follows, I want to address the difficulties raised by poststructuralist accounts of the subject and to inquire whether Wittig
does in fact, as Judith Butler has persuasively argued, fall back into
the same metanarratives of the Subject that some feminist critics have
located in the work of Beauvoir. For if Wittig assumes that there is a
presocial core called the "person," which only subsequently comes
to be marked as "female" or "woman," then her materialist theory
of language and her critical deployment of the universal, which seek
to reveal the lie of universality as a politically contingent rather than
inherently structural component of language, must reinscribe the
category of the natural—a category that Wittig herself disclaims as
illusory and oppressive.

III

The political question of language and responsibility, as we know,
is a thorny one for feminists who work within the field of post-
Saussurian linguistics. For the concept of the subject as the origin of
meaning, it has been argued, is itself an ideological construction. As
Louis Althusser put it, "The category of the subject is only constitutive

of all ideology in so far as all ideology has the function (which defines it) of 'constituting' concrete individuals as subjects."[38] Ideology, according to Althusser, "interpellates" individuals, addresses itself to them directly, allows them to imagine a set of relationships to the real material relations in which they live, allows them to imagine that they are subjects, the source of all meaning. Althusser's insight, of course, was to examine ideology as more than a set of illusions; for ideology is both real and imaginary — real in that it speaks to the ways in which individuals live their relationships to the actual material conditions that govern their lives, and imaginary in that ideology prevents them from understanding the social relations of power that constitute those relationships.

Developments in linguistic theory have complicated and extended Althusser's critique to account for illusory notions of the subject as the origin of meaning. Advancing the work of Saussure, theorists such as Emile Benveniste have argued that it is language that allows for subjectivity; language enables the subject to posit itself as an I, as the subject of a sentence. But that consciousness of self, of "I," is only possible through processes of contrast and differentiation, through distinctions such as "not I" or "you." "And so it is literally true," writes Benveniste, "that the basis of subjectivity is in the exercise of language. If one really thinks about it, one will see that there is no other objective testimony to the identity of the subject except that which he himself gives about himself."[39]

Similarly, but from a slightly different angle, Jacques Lacan argues that the subject cannot be viewed as the origin of meaning primarily because speaking, which involves learning a series of different subject positions, requires that the child enter a symbolic order that he or she does not constitute but that constitutes him or her as a subject. Thus the subject does not construct language; language constructs the subject. But if that subject is a decentered subject, argues Lacan, this results from the twin processes of "misrecognition" in the "mirror-stage," a process in which the child identifies with an image that is illusory because whole and unitary,[40] and from the split occasioned by the child's entry into the symbolic order, a split between the "I" of discourse, the subject of the utterance and the "I" who speaks, the subject of the enunciation. The self that speaks and the self that is represented, in short, are not the same I.[41]

Wittig both takes up and criticizes the insights of these theories. For her, the problem with theorists like Lacan is that they situate the problem of speaking for women outside conscious structures and institutions of the social domination of women and within unconscious processes generated by the subject's entry into the symbolic order. By making language into a "fetish," Lacan, in particular, obscures the material, political, and historically contingent character of language, she contends.

In Wittig's view, moreover, Lacan's theory of language allows one to evade critical questions of responsibility for meaning by offering individuals the specious structuralist excuse that might be stated as follows: "Language made 'me' say it" or, what amounts to the same thing, "Language prevented me from representing it," with "it" being "the feminine."[42] As we saw in the more deconstructive approach of Irigaray, for women, this amounts to saying that language forces me to deny my own subjectivity because, in order to speak "I," "I" must reaffirm the status of the phallus as the master signifier. Wittig's own critique of how accepted critiques of phallogocentrism can circumvent the traditional humanist concern with questions of responsibility is one that deserves more attention in the context of feminist poststructuralist debates about the *politics* of language and subjectivity.

The division of the subject in language, in Wittig's view, involves specific and political gender issues that cannot be accounted for fully by the initial split occasioned in the mirror stage of "misrecognition" or by the subject's entry into language. That Lacan, for example, contends that those who do not accept the phallus as the master signifier are doomed to schizophrenia is for Wittig an elision of the central political question of domination. Wittig reads Lacanian categories like the symbolic order as ideological constructs that, in Althusser's theory of ideology, "interpellate" individuals not only as subjects but as heterosexual subjects, as "men" and "women." Without the oppositions contained in the terms "male" and "female," "men" and "women," it is implied, there is no culture (Lévi-Strauss), no language (Lacan), and no meaning (Saussure); and heterosexuality is the "origin" of all three.

Nevertheless, the absence of the unconscious as a meaningful category for thinking through political problems of gender, language, and subjectivity is a disturbing one in Wittig's writings. She seems to assume that language can in fact fully represent the subject of the enunciation as a whole, unitary being — a position firmly rejected by Lacan. Moreover, at times she seems to underscore voluntarist notions of what it means to break off what she calls the "heterosexual contract," that is, to imply that the latter can be broken by the individual choices that primarily lesbians but also gay men make to disassociate themselves from it. In this sense, she deploys the terms "homosexual" and "heterosexual" as binary, absolute, and oppositional categories. To be a lesbian, to dissociate oneself from the heterosexual contract, is to be both a "not-woman" and a "not-man" according to Wittig. The category of lesbian is not a third gender but a transvaluation of sex/gender as the so-called core of one's identity. This is an important and radical assertion, and I will return to it later.

In the context of voluntarist understandings of power and identity, however, I would agree with Judith Butler that Wittig underestimates the fundamental incoherence and impossibility of heterosexuality as identity.[43] Because she rejects unequivocally psychoanalytic explanations of the subject, Wittig does not extend her own claim that heterosexuality is a "fetish," that to be a "man" or a "woman" is a phantasmatic construct. And as identities, "man" and "woman" can never be "secured" but must continually be reproduced through the very mechanisms of language and the social institutions that Wittig herself has identified as oppressive. Thus, by positing a disturbingly monolithic view of heterosexuality Wittig neglects its precarious character, its internal instability. This may have the unintended consequence of shoring up heterosexuality as a unified identity that can either be chosen or refused in its entirety.

Whatever its shortcomings, however, Wittig's theoretical focus on the ways in which discourses, while purporting to explain, actually reproduce gender as sexual difference as heterosexual myth allows feminists to question the social, political, and intellectual mechanisms that deny women that moment of the becoming of the subject through language. Agreeing with Benveniste's understanding of language and subjectivity, Wittig writes that "It is when starting to speak that one becomes I." She qualifies, however:

> This act — the becoming of *the* subject through the exercise of
> language and through locution — in order to be real, implies that the

locutor be an absolute subject. For a relative subject is inconceivable, a relative subject could not speak at all. I mean that, in spite of the harsh law of gender and its enforcement upon women, no woman can say I without being for herself a total subject — that is, ungendered, universal, whole. ("Mark," 6)

By invoking the universal category of the subject, argues Judith Butler, Wittig "confirms rather than contests the normative promise of humanist ideals" inasmuch as she advances a presocial, prediscursive notion of the subject, called "person," which only subsequently comes to be marked as a woman. In this view of the subject, its core (person) is distorted, so to speak, in being named as "female" or "woman." Thus, in Wittig's account, argues Butler, the destruction of the category of sex, as the destruction of an attribute only, would restore women as universal subjects. Retaining the category of the subject as agent, Butler writes, Wittig's "humanism" assumes that there is a "doer behind the deed," that, to paraphrase Nietzsche once again, there is some "Being" behind "doing."[44]

To assume that there is a presocial, prediscursive subject, argues Butler, compromises the otherwise radical critique of identity that characterizes Wittig's fictional writings. Wittig's "foundationalist fiction" of the subject allows her to interrogate the limits of universalism, but it also places her in the paradoxical situation of reaffirming the oppressive fiction of an "authoritarian" because absolute subject. Whereas novels such as Le Corps lesbien and Les Guérillères[45] strive to decenter the subject and, thus, to suggest that gender and identity cannot be understood in terms of "being" but rather as "performance," her essays embrace disturbing, if not totalitarian, notions of "sovereign speech acts" (Gender Trouble, 118).

But even the radical possibilities of Wittig's novels, Butler argues, which "follow a narrative strategy of disintegration, suggesting that the binary formulation of sex needs to fragment and proliferate to the point where the binary is itself revealed as contingent" (Gender Trouble, 118), are finally contained by her self-conscious deployment of the literary text as what Wittig herself called "a war machine."[46] The latter, writes Butler, seeks "to preempt the position of the speaking subject and its invocation of the universal point of view" (Gender Trouble, 119). In so doing, however, Wittig directs her attack on "the splitting of universal and particular in the name of a recovery of a prior and essential unity of those terms," Butler contends. Hence "destruction is thus always restoration — that is, the destruction of a set of categories that introduce artificial divisions into an otherwise unified ontology" (*Gender Trouble*, 119).

In Wittig's own account, her fictional strategies are informed by her understanding of Marx's claim that each new class that fights for power must, if only to reach its goal, represent its interests as the common interests of all members of the society. Understood as a political strategy, this claim assumes that there is in fact a group, called women, a "We" whose presumably common interests can be expressed in language because they exist in an empirically, although not naturally, constituted social reality. Likewise, Wittig contends that the universalizing of those interests would ultimately destroy their material basis by dissolving the category of sex in language. Thus the narrative strategy of "universaliz[ing] the point of view of a group condemned to being particular" ("Mark," 7) is effected through the "neuter" *on* (one) in *The Opoponax*,[47] through the third-person pronoun *elles* in *Les Guérillères*, and, finally, in the first person written as *j/e* in *Le Corps lesbien*. In the latter text, the split *j/e*, writes Wittig, "is not an I destroyed but an I so powerful that it can attack the order of heterosexuality" by lesbianizing "symbols," "gods and goddesses," "men and women" ("Mark," 11). The lesbian subject comes to occupy an absolute position in speech, an "I" that "reorganizes the world" from its point of view, an "I" that "lays claim to universality" ("Mark," 6).

In Wittig's writings, then, argues Butler, "there appear to be two orders of reality, two orders of ontology": "Socially constituted ontology emerges from a more fundamental ontology that appears to be pre-social and pre-discursive" (*Gender Trouble*, 115). Whereas sex is socially constituted, its destruction through authoritative speech acts, through the conscious appropriation of the universal by women, assumes that there is a prediscursive reality to which the *j/e* of *Le Corps lesbien*, for example, returns in asserting its claim to speech. If sex "violates a pre-social ontology of unified and equal persons," then *j/e* restores the "right" to an "I" to women by inserting itself violently in language, by attacking the category of sex in language. But this assumes that there is in fact some place beyond sex and beyond power to which this *j/e* might return in asserting its ontological right to language, a language that is itself positioned outside relations of power. Thus does Wittig's "I" assume what Butler calls "god-like dimensions" (*Gender Trouble*, 117); the sovereign self reappropriates the entire world from its point of view.

Butler's powerful yet sympathetic critique of Wittig raises important questions about the limits of universalism as a category for feminist theory. These problems include the difficulty of postulating a "we" noted earlier. Wittig places herself "within the traditional discourse of the philosophical pursuit of presence" and asserts that speaking, if it is to be meaningful, must invoke a "seamless identity of all things," Butler contends (*Gender Trouble*, 118). This "we" displaces the heterosexual episteme only to replace it with a homosexual episteme, which in turn assumes that homosexuality is "unconditioned by sexual norms" — a view rejected by many gay and lesbian theorists (*Gender Trouble*, 121). Moreover, in Butler's view, the implicit separatism that such a view advances creates serious problems for feminist politics, a critical position also articulated in an article by Susan Suleiman.[48]

My own position here is that readings of Wittig that label her a separatist — even intelligent ones such as those of Suleiman and Butler — acknowledge only to circumscribe the radical and deconstructive power of her work within a critique of her "humanism." In fact, reading Wittig as a separatist makes it far easier to associate her with the kind of humanism that both of these feminist critics would reject. Thus, writes Butler, even more damaging to Wittig's call for women to assert themselves as absolute speaking subjects in fictional worlds in which men have no existence is the manner in which Wittig affirms the very category of the universal subject that, in Butler's view, is itself an oppressive fiction. Would it not be wiser to pursue the radical decentering of the subject? she asks. Instead of replacing the universalist pretensions of the "straight mind" with what might be called those of the homosexual mind, feminists, and especially lesbians, would do better to play out the dissonant possibilities that exist in what Beauvoir understood as being and not being a woman, possibilities that are not outside of but that inhere in the fundamental incoherence of gender identity itself.

To address these problems in Wittig's writings I want to return to the category of the lesbian subject and to her theory of the literary text as a "war machine." Wittig's "subject" I will argue is not so much a return to an ontological right of speech or to a prediscursive fiction before the intrusion of gender in language. Instead her fiction deploys the universal as what she herself calls a "Trojan horse," a simulacrum of Being and of the universal that not only pulverizes "old forms and formal conventions" ("Trojan," 45) but effects as well a radical decentering of the subject as it has been conceptualized by the straight mind.

IV

"When I say that it is quite possible for a work of literature to operate as a war machine upon the context of its epoch," writes Wittig in "The Trojan Horse," "it is not about committed literature that I am talking."[49] Committed literature, for example "*écriture féminine*" ("Trojan," 46), she argues, is limited in its transformative power for primarily two reasons. The first concerns the question of what happens to the writer if one's work is "banned by the group" or if the structures of oppression have been overthrown. Would the writer then be dismissed as reactionary or quite simply have nothing left to say? she asks ("Trojan," 46).

More troubling, however, is the second problem that Wittig associates with committed literature, namely the marginalization of the writer's works that is effected through their containment in existing forms and conventions. One has only two choices in one's work, contends Wittig: "either reproducing the existing forms or creating new ones" ("Trojan," 46). Although these mutually opposed possibilities apply to both "straight" and "minority" writers, for the latter the choice becomes far more difficult to negotiate. Disturbed as they are by the social invisibility of their subject, "minority writers" are concerned to voice "that which calls for a hidden name, that which dares not speak its name."

> Writing a text which has homosexuality among its themes is a gamble. It is taking the risk that at every turn the formal element which is the theme will overdetermine the meaning, monopolize the whole meaning, against the intention of the author who wants above all to create a literary work. Thus the text which adopts such a theme sees one of its parts taken for the whole, one of the constituent elements of the text taken for the whole text, and the book becomes a symbol, a manifesto.[50]

When a literary text becomes a manifesto, Wittig argues, it not only "ceases to operate as literature," it also fails to realize its unique potential to carry out "the only political action that it could: introducing into the textual tissue of the times by way of literature that which it embodies" ("Point," 65–66). If a committed text attracts attention to a particular social problem, so too does it compromise its power as literature. Thus the text that is identified as a gay or lesbian text is categorized as particular, as expressive only of those groups who identify themselves as gay or lesbian. Particularism condemns a text to silence; it insures that the committed text will be dismissed, neglected, fall out of print, or "only be interesting to homosexuals"; it results in the failure of a work "to change the textual reality within which it is inscribed" ("Point," 65).

Wittig's remarks about committed literature are at first startling. She seems to underscore those definitions of literature that have contained it within canonical notions of the Great Books. Yet her argument turns on an understanding of the universal that can only with great difficulty be identified with that of chivalric defenders of The Literary Tradition. The text that has become a political symbol, she insists, "loses its polysemy, it becomes univocal" ("Point," 65). This loss of multiple meanings and multiple significations occurs because the "minority writer" has failed to make the "minority point of view universal" ("Point," 66). To make a point of view universal, however, involves but certainly cannot be reduced to making a particular group visible. Stated more precisely, to make a group truly visible one must make it universal, otherwise that group recedes into the "already there," into the "what-goes-without-saying" ("Point," 67), into the matrix of heterosexuality. The committed text, in other words, stands in danger of being appropriated by the straight mind to enforce those very binary categories of male and female, men and women, self and other, that deny "minority writers" their subjectivity.

Understanding Wittig's literary strategy for universalizing the point of view of those condemned to the particular involves grasping the distinction she draws between "letter and meaning," terms that she invokes in place of "signifier and signified." Whereas the latter pair "describe[s] the sign in relation to the terms of the reality being referred to," letter and meaning "describe the sign solely in relation to language" ("Point," 67). In a work of literary experimentation there can be an "equilibrium" of letter and meaning. The writer may attempt to eliminate meaning in favor of the letter or the letter may be made the meaning, the signifier the signified — despite, as Roland Barthes argues, the efforts of an author at "pure" literary experimentation ("Point," 67). Minority writers in particular, writes Wittig, "are menaced by meaning, even when they are engaged in formal experimentation." What may be only a formal element in their work imposes itself as "meaning *only* for straight readers" ("Point," 67). Thus even experimental practices of writing may be contained and interpreted as committed literature. If, as Wittig contends, "meaning hides language from sight" ("Point," 68), then the task of the writer who would contest existing forms must be to make apparent how language constitutes meaning. Such writers must concern themselves with the letter, with the "concrete" of language. The problem with language, in other words, lies in its abstract character and in the meanings that hide the very processes that generate meaning from us — for example, how a pronoun used to designate a subject position in language becomes instrumental in "activating the notion of gender" ("Mark," 5). Language cannot be seen; one "sees and hears only meaning" ("Point," 68). This is especially true with words like "woman" or "women," words that Wittig refuses to use in her work.

To make language visible is to engage in a process of defamiliarization, a process that, however, attempts not to make a reader see the "things" of daily life differently but to force the reader to see "words" differently: "as a writer, I would be totally satisfied if every one of my words had on the reader the same effect, the same shock as if they were being read for the first time" ("Trojan," 48). Words, if they are to effect a political displacement of reality, must be deployed by the writer such that they preempt meaning in the mind of the reader. Wittig calls this "dealing a blow with words" ("Trojan," 48); it is the literary text as a war machine.

Marcel Proust and Djuna Barnes, Wittig argues, transformed literature because they deployed words in such a way that homosexuality became "the axis of categorization from which to universalize." But the minority "subject" of their work, she contends — and this is crucial — is not the same as the "straight subject." The "constituted subject" of Proust's and Barnes's literary practice "is not self-centered as is the straight subject. Its extension into space could be described as being like Pascal's circle, whose center is everywhere and whose circumference is nowhere" ("Point," 65). This "fracturing" and de-centering of the subject is necessary if the text is to displace the totalitarian because exclusively male subject of compulsory hetero-sexuality, if the text is to produce the homosexual subject as the universal subject as a reality effect.

To produce the minority as universal subject, the "writer must first reduce language to be as meaningless as possible in order to turn it into a neutral material — that is, raw material" ("Trojan," 47). Words can act as a "Trojan horse," Wittig suggests, because the reader "recognizes" them, takes them into her or his cognitive world, much as the Trojans took the horse into their city, completely unaware that words, like that horse, are a "war machine." More precisely, because they are familiar words can enter the consciousness of the reader as signs that seem to refer to real objects; they can, in short, be adopted by the reader as "real," as the already known, but also combined, organized, and deployed by the writer in ways that explode the real, the referent, for which they were thought to stand. While Wittig's choice of the phallic Trojan horse as a metaphor for lesbian writing may seem curious, it is actually appropriate. For what changes must take place in the mind of the reader, we might ask, when out of the phallic horse comes not the male warrior but the lesbian subject?

Wittig employs the Trojan horse strategy of writing in several ways. Although she uses names and characters, she dissociates the universal subject of *on*, *elles*, and *j/e* from any "person" in her novels. In *Les Guérillères*, for example, the "I" of discourse, the subject of the utterance cannot be identified with the "I" who speaks, the subject of the enunciation. Indeed the latter, as we shall see, is dissolved into the fabric of the text itself. The novel, which tells a "story" of the war waged by modern Amazonians, breaks with traditional narrative form by constituting itself in descriptive fragments written in the present tense.[51] These fragments are themselves interrupted repeatedly by pages on which are printed names that do not correspond to any individual characters in the novel:

METTE KHDIOTA MICHAELA
PHANO HUGETTE LELIA
SIDONIA OMAYA MERNEITH

INIBRINA WUANG QUIANG
ASPASIA HANNA LETTIA
NORA BENOÎTE RADEGONDE[52]

As Nina Auerbach has noted, "Though these names take on their own incantatory life, the empty resonance of their sound is also the death of the real people we used to read novels to meet."[53] Actually, according to Toril Moi, Auerbach's reading of these names as being spoken by *someone* is a misreading. For "Wittig's text in fact nowhere indicates that the names are spoken by anyone: the 'ritualistic chanting' represents Auerbach's own attempt to attribute the fragmented text to a unitary human voice."[54] In Wittig's terms, the text would become "univocal," it would lose its "polysemy" and hence its force as literature. Auerbach, Moi contends, longs for an end to the war, for a time when "it would be possible to return to the individuality of Meg, Jo, Beth, and Amy,"[55] the characters in *Little Women*, another text examined by Auerbach.

"When the text no longer offers an individual grasped as the transcendental origin of language and experience," writes Moi, humanist feminism must lay down its arms."[56] Although her reading is persuasive and counters that of Butler, Moi's self-proclaimed war against humanism and, in particular, its "Anglo-American" feminist adherents repeats a familiar divide and conquer strategy. Once the paper dragon of the humanist subject has been reduced to nothing but tattered colored streamers, Moi suggests, feminists can get on with the serious intellectual work that has yet to be done in the name of postmodernism.

My own position on the usefulness of Wittig's novels for rethinking problems of humanism, of the universal, and of the speaking subject approaches her fiction somewhat differently. The "performative theory of gender" articulated by Butler, I would argue, is not diminished but given an evocative political meaning in Wittig's texts. The lesbian subject cannot become a man to become a subject because to adopt the consciousness of a man assumes that one adopts "two 'natural' slaves": those constituted as Other in the terms race and gender.[57] In contrast, the lesbian is a thoroughly political subject, a provisional subject, an invented "epic" subject, that is created in Wittig's writings as a universal subject without a name, without an Other, and with no recourse to a presocial, prediscursive identity.[58]

If Wittig, in contrast to Beauvoir, refuses to say "I am a woman," it is because she understands that "woman" must always dissolve the "I" that makes a claim to subjectivity into the Other for the masculine subject — that colonizing "I" that "always has a tendency to lurk everywhere in language" ("Mark," 9). Choosing to work instead with pronouns, such as *j/e* and *on*, unqualified by nouns such as "woman" ("I am" rather than "I am a woman"), Wittig's novels give form to her theoretical claim that personal pronouns are "the only linguistic instances that, in discourse, designate its locutors and their different and successive situations in relationship to discourse" ("Mark," 4). As "the pathways and the means of entrance into language," such pronouns may be deployed by the writer to represent persons rather than a "fictive sex," which is represented by a noun such as "woman."

Thus *on*, in *The Opoponax*, she writes, allowed her to avoid the related problems of gendering and numbering because *on* is "neuter" and can represent a certain number of people successively or all at once while still remaining singular ("Mark," 6). By bending *on* to designate both the particular and the universal simultaneously, she uses it as "a delegate of a whole class of people, of everybody, of a few persons, of I (the *I* of the main character, the *I* of the narrator, and the *I* of the reader)" ("Mark," 8).

Similarly, the *j/e* of *Le Corps lesbien* like the *elles* of *Les Guérillères* are constituted in and through language but *not* through an individual speaking subject. This "I," attached to no person, but clearly detached from those persons called men, gives the lie to the naturalness of sex and to the universality of the universal, that is, whenever the category of sex is present. Wittig's critical comments about the English translation of *elles* as "the women" reveals the complexity of her deconstructive project. For "by turning my *elles* into *the women*," she writes, the translator destroyed the "effect of my attempt" by "destroying the process of universalization" ("Mark," 9).

"Femme and butch," which disrupt the naturalness of "masculine" and "feminine," cannot be construed as chimerical representations of originally heterosexual identities, writes Butler, "Gay is to straight not as copy [is] to original, but, rather, as copy is to copy" (*Gender Trouble*, 31). But if such mimicry in gesture, voice, and speech challenges and disrupts gender identity, as Butler persuasively contends, if the performance of the "butch" or "femme" does not underscore but contests heterosexuality as ontology, so too do Wittig's *on*, *elles*, and *j/e* contest through parody the Absolute Subject of heterosexual discourse. The parody is possible because the reader, much like Auerbach, awaits the entrance of familiar characters who speak, characters we can come to know, but who, in fact, we *already* know: "men" and "women." As part of a war machine, *on*, *elles*, and *j/e* insert themselves in language in the same way that gender has inserted itself in discourse: the reader is caught, so to speak, unawares.

So-called lesbian separatism, moreover, may be essential to this literary strategy. Like the Parisians who read Proust's *A la recherche du temps perdu*, the modern reader's search for a known "minority subject" that would diminish the social work of a text — that would console the reader, assure the reader that there is in fact a "woman" because there are recognizable "men" in Wittig's fictional worlds — is frustrated when the "particular subject" is made universal. But because that particular subject is a lesbian, and not, as it was for Proust, homosexuals, the need to construct worlds in which men have no existence may be more pressing for the writer who understands all too well the workings of the straight mind.

To set up the *elles*, for example, as the "absolute subject of the world," required some admittedly "draconian measures" ("Mark," 9). The first two parts of *Les Guérillères* eliminated the *il(s)* (he, they-he) so as to "shock" the reader, to force her or him to "see" the word *elles* differently. For in the absence of *il(s)*, *elles* cannot mean "they-she" and it most certainly cannot mean "the women." In order to challenge the binary of gender, in other words, the *elles*, to "become real," have to assume an "epic form." Indeed the point of the book, she insists, was not to "feminize the world but to make the categories of sex obsolete in language" ("Mark," 9). Similarly, the lesbian "I" (*j/e*) of Wittig's *Le Corps lesbien* does not assume the same position of the masculine "I," for the latter always presumes the Other of the (would-be) feminine "I." Instead, *j/e* simulates the universal; when spoken in a literary context whose subject is like Pascal's circle, this "I" flows into spaces yet unimaginable in heterosexual discourse.

When deployed as a war machine, then, Wittig's subversive pronouns appropriate first by inhabiting and then by displacing the fictional category of the universal subject constructed in and through heterosexuality. These pronouns work like the Trojan horse, that is, as simulacrums of that Absolute Subject that would deny those individuals called women the status of the subject while claiming to speak in their name. Wittig's "I," in short, forces the universal to live up to its promise by turning it upon itself, thus revealing its pretensions. In Wittig's hands, what Butler calls "doing gender" as performance becomes what might be called "doing universal." It is a strategy, literary and political, that ought not be reduced to naive humanist pipe dreams. If the "doer," as Nietzsche wrote, "is merely a fiction added to the deed—the deed is everything,"[59] so too is Wittig's lesbian "subject" one that demonstrates how the so-called ontological status of the "doer" is sustained through the ontology of heterosexuality. Thus, I would conclude, Wittig's deployment of the universal as a critique of heterosexuality invites feminists to reconsider the subversive acts that might yet be invented in the name of universality and its Absolute Subject.

NOTES

1. Monique Wittig, "The Mark of Gender," *Feminist Issues* 5, no. 2 (Fall 1985): 5.

2. There are several important exceptions here. See Judith Butler, *Gender Trouble: Feminism and the Subversion of Identity* (New York: Routledge, 1990); Namascar Shaktini, "Displacing the Phallic Subject, Wittig's Lesbian Writing," in *The Thinking Muse*, ed. Jeffner Allen and Iris Marion Young (Bloomington: Indiana University Press, 1989), 195–210; Susan Rubin Suleiman, "(Re)Writing the Body: The Politics and Poetics of Female Eroticism," in *The Female Body in Western Culture*, ed. Susan Rubin Suleiman (Cambridge, Mass.: Harvard University Press, 1986), 7–29, esp. 19–23; Heather Findlay, "Is There a Lesbian in This Text? Derrida, Wittig, and the Politics of the Three Women," in *Coming to Terms*, ed. Elizabeth Weed (New York: Routledge, Chapman and Hall, 1989), 59–69; Hélène Vivienne Wenzel, "The Text as Body/Politics: An Appreciation of Monique Wittig's Writings in Context," *Feminist Studies* 7, no. 2 (Summer 1981): 264–87.

3. Naomi Schor, "This Essentialism Which Is Not One: Coming to Grips with Irigaray," *Differences* 1, no. 2 (Summer 1989): 45.

4. Susan Okin, *Women in Western Political Thought* (Princeton, N.J.: Princeton University Press, 1979); Jean Bethke Elshtain, *Public Man, Private Woman* (Princeton, N.J.: Princeton University Press, 1981); Carole Pateman, *The Sexual Contract* (Stanford, Calif.: Stanford University Press, 1988).

5. Jean-François Lyotard, *The Postmodern Condition: A Report on Knowledge*, trans. G. Bennington and B. Massumi (Minneapolis: University of Minnesota Press, 1984).

6. Luce Irigaray, *Speculum of the Other Woman*, trans. Gillian G. Gill (Ithaca, N.Y.: Cornell University Press, 1985), 50.

7. For an engaged discussion of universalism and antifoundationalism see

especially the essays by Nancy Fraser collected in *Unruly Practices: Power, Discourse, and Gender in Contemporary Social Theory* (Minneapolis: University of Minnesota Press, 1989). For critical essays on postmodernism that are largely sympathetic toward but also wary of the antifoundationalist critique for feminism, see Linda Nicholson, ed., *Feminism/Postmodernism* (New York: Routledge, 1990) and Allen and Young, eds., *The Thinking Muse*. For a critique of social and political theories of community based on notions of the universal, see Iris Marion Young, "Impartiality and the Civic Public," in *Feminism as Critique*, ed. Seyla Benhabib and Drucilla Cornell (Minneapolis: University of Minnesota Press, 1987), 56–76.

8. Schor, "This Essentialism," 40.

9. See Martha N. Evans, "Murdering *L'Invitée*: Gender and Fictional Narrative," *Yale French Studies*, no. 72 (1986): 67–86 (special issue entitled "Simone de Beauvoir: Witness to a Century," ed. Hélène Vivienne Wenzel); Mary Evans, *Simone de Beauvoir: A Feminist Mandarin* (New York: Tavistock Publications and Methuen, 1985); Michèle Le Doeuff, "Simone de Beauvoir and Existentialism," and Mary Lowenthal Felstiner, "Seeing the Second Sex through the Second Wave," both in *Feminist Studies* 6, no. 2 (Summer 1980): 247–89; Schor, "This Essentialism," esp. 43–46.

10. Monique Wittig, "Mark of Gender," 6; Hélène Cixous and Catherine Clément, *The Newly Born Woman*, trans. Betsy Wing (Minneapolis: University of Minnesota Press, 1986); the works of Julia Kristeva, especially *Desire in Language*, ed. Leon S. Roudiez (New York: Columbia University Press, 1980), and "Stabat Mater," *The Kristeva Reader*, ed. Toril Moi (New York: Columbia University Press, 1986); Luce Irigaray, *Speculum of the Other Woman* and *This Sex Which Is Not One*, trans. Catherine Porter (Ithaca, N.Y.: Cornell University Press, 1985).

11. Carol Gilligan, *In a Different Voice: Psychological Theory and Women's Moral Development* (Cambridge, Mass.: Harvard University Press, 1982).

12. Monique Wittig, "The Straight Mind," *Feminist Issues* 1, no. 1 (Summer 1980): 103–11.

13. Quoted in Schor, "This Essentialism," 43. Page numbers in the text refer to this article.

14. Linda M. G. Zerilli, "I Am a Woman: Voice and Ambiguity in *The Second Sex*," *Women and Politics* 11, no. 1 (1991): 93–107.

15. On these debates see Wenzel, "Text as Body/Politics," esp. 272–75.

16. Wenzel, "Text as Body/Politics," 275.

17. Wenzel, "Text as Body/Politics," 276.

18. Monique Wittig, *Le Corps lesbien* (Paris: Minuit, 1973). English translation, *The Lesbian Body*, trans. David Le Vray (Boston: Beacon, 1975).

19. Shaktini, "Displacing the Phallic Subject," 198.

20. Ironically, Wittig herself warns about being identified as a lesbian writer. When one's work becomes a political symbol, she argues, it ceases to effect a radical transformation in language and politics. See the discussion of "committed literature" in Wittig's essay "The Trojan Horse," *Feminist Issues* 4, no. 2 (Fall 1984): 45–49 and the discussion in section IV of this chapter.

21. Donna Haraway, "A Manifesto for Cyborgs: Science, Technology, and Socialist Feminism in the 1980s," in Weed, *Coming to Terms*, 181.

22. For a similar argument about the all-female worlds of Wittig's novels, see Suleiman, "(Re)Writing the Body," 20–22.

23. "Mark of Gender," 6. Cited hereafter in the text as "Mark."

24. Butler, *Gender Trouble*, 117.

25. Butler, *Gender Trouble*, 20.

26. Simone de Beauvoir, *The Second Sex*, trans. H. M. Parshley (New York: Vintage, 1952), xviii.

27. Beauvoir, *Second Sex*, xvii.

28. Beauvoir, *Second Sex*, xvi.

29. Beauvoir, *Second Sex*, xvi–xvii.

30. See my "I Am a Woman."

31. Butler, *Gender Trouble*, 111–12. See also Judith Butler, "Sex and Gender in Simone de Beauvoir's *Second Sex*," *Yale French Studies*, no. 72: 35–50.

32. Adrienne Rich, "Compulsory Heterosexuality and Lesbian Existence," *Women, Sex, and Sexuality*, ed. Catherine Stimpson and Ethel Person (Chicago: University of Chicago Press, 1980). Wittig refers to Rich in her essay "The Social Contract," *Feminist Issues* 9, no. 1 (Spring 1989): 11.

33. Wittig, "Social Contract," 8.

34. Monique Wittig, "One Is Not Born a Woman, *Feminist Issues* 1, no. 2 (Winter 1981): 48.

35. Wittig, "Straight Mind," 107. Hereafter cited as "Straight" in the text.

36. Wittig, "Trojan Horse," 46.

37. On the question of difference, see especially Monique Wittig, "The Category of Sex," *Feminist Issues* 2, no. 2 (Fall 1982): 63–68.

38. Louis Althusser, *Lenin and Philosophy and Other Essays*, trans. Ben Brewster (London: New Left Books, 1971), 160.

39. Emile Benveniste, *Problems in General Linguistics* (Coral Gables, Fla.: University of Miami Press, 1971), 226. Derrida advances the insights of Saussure and Benveniste to argue that the meanings produced in language are themselves the products of differentiation. Language, argues Derrida, is "not a function of the speaking subject" but rather the speaking subject is "a 'function' of the language." One becomes a speaking subject "only by conforming his speech . . . to the system of linguistic prescriptions taken as the system of differences." Jacques Derrida, *Speech and Phenomena*, trans. David B. Allison (Evanston, Ill.: Northwestern University Press, 1973), 145, 146.

40. Jacques Lacan, "The Mirror Stage," in *Écrits*, trans. Alan Sheridan (New York: Norton, 1977), 1–7.

41. On this point see Catherine Belsey, "Constructing the Subject: Deconstructing the Text," in *Feminist Criticism and Social Change*, ed. Judith Newton and Deborah Rosenfelt (New York: Methuen, 1985), 50.

42. On Lacan's theory of language, of course, the "it" could stand as well for the I that speaks, the subject of the enunciating, whatever its gender.

43. Butler, *Gender Trouble*, 122. Hereafter cited with page numbers in the text.

44. Quoted in Butler, *Gender Trouble*, 25. See Friedrich Nietzsche, *On the Genealogy of Morals*, trans. Walter Kaufman (New York: Vintage, 1969), 45.

45. *Les Guérillères* (Paris: Minuit, 1969). English translation by David Le Vay (Boston: Beacon, 1985).

46. Wittig, "Trojan Horse," 45.

47. Wittig, *L'Opoponax* (Paris: Minuit, 1964).

48. Suleiman, "(Re)Writing the Body," 22.

49. Wittig, "Trojan Horse," 45–46. Hereafter cited as "Trojan" in the text.

50. "The Point of View: Universal or Particular?" *Feminist Issues* 3, no. 2 (Fall 1983): 65. Hereafter cited as "Point" in the text.

51. This point is made as well by Suleiman, "(Re)Writing the Body," 20.

52. Monique Wittig, *Les Guérillères* (Boston, Mass.: Beacon, 1985), 59.

53. Nina Auerbach, *Communities of Women: An Idea in Fiction* (Cambridge, Mass.: Harvard University Press, 1978), 190–91.

54. Toril Moi, *Sexual/Textual Politics* (New York and London: Methuen, 1985), 80.

55. Auerbach, *Communities of Women*, 191.

56. Moi, *Sexual/Textual Politics*, 80.

57. Wittig, "One Is Not Born a Woman," 49

58. On this point, see my "Rememoration on War? French Feminist Narrative and the Politics of Self-Representation," *Differences* 3, no. 1 (Spring 1991): 1–19.

59. Nietzsche, *Genealogy of Morals*, 45.

National Brands/National Body: *Imitation of Life*
Lauren Berlant

*Advertising ministers to the spiritual side of trade. It is a great power
that has been entrusted to your keeping which charges you with the
high responsibility of inspiring and ennobling the commercial world.
It is all part of the greater work of the regeneration and redemption
of mankind.*

— Calvin Coolidge, 1929[1]

Every normal female yearns to be a luminous person.
— Fannie Hurst, *Today Is Ladies' Day*[2]

In Nella Larsen's *Passing* (1929), two light-skinned American women
of African descent bring each other to mutual crisis. The gaze of one
woman virtually embodies the other, calling her back from her
absence-to-her-body, an absence politically inscribed by the legal
necessity to be nonblack while drinking iced tea at the Drayton Hotel
in Chicago in 1927. Lost in thought about domestic matters, abstracted from her juridicoracial identity, Irene Redfield senses the
gaze of the alluring blond, "ivory"-skinned woman who watches her:
"Feeling her colour heighten under the continued inspection, she
slid her eyes down. What, she wondered, could be the reason for
such persistent attention? Had she ... put her hat on backwards? ...
Perhaps there was a streak of powder somewhere on her face. She
made a quick pass over it with her handkerchief. Something wrong
with her dress?"[3]

Something must be wrong with her, she suddenly has a body. She
associates this sensation with the colonizing gaze whites wield when

trying to detect whether a light-skinned person is white (a white icon) or black (a white hieroglyph): "White people ... usually asserted that they were able to tell; and by the most ridiculous means, finger-nails, palms of hands, shapes of ears, teeth."[4] Yet Irene has already similarly catalogued and policed the body of her nemesis, disapproving her explicitly sexual display, her "peculiar caressing smile," "those dark, almost black eyes and that wide mouth like a scarlet flower against the ivory of her skin ... a shade too provocative."[5] It turns out that the women, Irene Redfield and Clare Kendry, are childhood friends. But they share more than this, in mutually usurping the privilege white Americans have, to assume free passage within any public space they can afford to lease or own — like a taxicab, a table in a restaurant, rooms in a hotel, a private home.

The whiteness of blackness here requires the light-skinned African-American woman to produce some way to ameliorate the violation, the pain, and the ongoing crisis of living fully within two juridically defined, racially polarized bodies — and perhaps, if Hortense Spillers is right that American genders are always racially inflected, two genders as well.[6] Passing for nonblack allows these women to wear their gender according to a particular class style. Irene affects the bourgeois norm of good taste, which means submitting her body to a regime of discipline and concealment; Clare wears the exotic sexuality of the privileged woman as her style of publicity. One style of femininity tends toward the invisible or the "abstract," which involves a wish to cast off the visible body, and the other, toward the erotic, the sensational, which hyperemphasizes the visual frame.[7] Nonetheless, each of these styles of femininity aims to deflect the racializing scrutiny of white culture, as it abstracts the woman's public identity from the complex juridical, historical, and memorial facts of her "racialized" body. Thus each woman returns the other to her legally "other" body by seeing her, and seeing through her — not to another "real" body, but to other times and spaces where the "other" identity might be inhabited safely. To Clare, who passes racially in her marital, familial, and everyday life relations, it is a relief to leave the specular erotics of the white female body under the gaze of a similarly racialized friend. But for Irene the embodiment resulting from their encounter thwarts her desire — which is not to pass as a white person, but to move unconsciously and unobstructed through the public sphere (which is, in this case, a marketplace where people participate through consumption).

Deborah McDowell has recently argued that these two women desire each other, sexually. *Passing*, in her view, is a classically closeted narrative, half concealing the erotics between Clare and Irene.[8] But there may be a difference between wanting someone sexually and wanting someone's body, and I wonder whether Irene's xenophilia is not indeed a desire to occupy, to experience the privileges of Clare's body, not to love or make love to her, but rather to wear her way of wearing her body, like a prosthesis, or a fetish.[9] What Irene wants is relief from the body she has: her intense class identification with the discipline of the bourgeois body is only one tactic for producing the corporeal "fog" in which she walks. "It was, she cried silently, enough to suffer as a woman, an individual, on one's own account, without having to suffer for the race as well."[10] This ideal model of bodily abstraction is understood, by Irene, to be nationally endorsed: despite suffering as a twice-biologized and delegitimated public subject — a "woman," a "Negro" — she displaces her surplus body onto the metaphorical logics of American citizenship, which become the "truth" of her body, her "person." Even though Irene desperately wants to save her rocky marriage, she refuses to emigrate to Brazil with her husband, where national alienation would replace racial: "She belonged in this land of rising towers. She was an American. She grew from this soil, and she would not be uprooted."[11] Married to this constellation of pain, her body the register for brands of race and of gender that specifically refer to the American context from which she has, apparently, parentless sprung, Irene embraces the nation in what seems to be a pathetic misrecognition. But what kind of body does American national identity give her, and how does the idea of this body solve or salve the pain that the colonized body experiences? And if a desire to be fundamentally American marks one field of fantasy for Irene, how does this intersect her other desire, to be incorporated in another woman's body?

In Irene's case, as often happens in bourgeois-identified "women's literature," this moment of political consciousness takes place in desperation,[12] and rather than think systemically about the state she is in, she reverts to the tendency to faint and fade out that has served her so well, and so analgesically, in the course of her life. But political theory has investigated more extensively the complex relation between local erotics and national identity, between homosociality and political abstraction.[13] So far almost all of this work, for clear historical reasons, has circulated around the construction of the male citizen in the political public sphere. Feminist political theorists, for instance, are reconsidering Enlightenment constitutionality, and how specifically white male privilege has been veiled by the rhetoric of the bodiless citizen, the generic "person" whose political identity is a priori precisely because it is, in theory, noncorporeal. Before moving to *Imitation of Life*, where a narrative of profound female identification is interarticulated with the national public sphere, it is worth spelling out specifically how such a model of political affiliation has figured the American male body, setting up a peculiar dialectic between embodiment and abstraction in the post-Enlightenment body politic.

The Constitution's framers constructed the "person" as the unit of political membership in the American nation; in so doing, they did not simply set up the public standard of abstract legitimation on behalf of an implicit standard of white male embodiment — technically, in the beginning, property ownership was as much a factor in citizenship as any corporeal schema. Nonetheless, we can see a real attraction of abstract citizenship in the way the citizen conventionally acquires a new body by participation in the political public sphere. The American subject is privileged to suppress the fact of his historical situation in the abstract "person": but then, in return, the nation provides a kind of prophylaxis for the person, as it promises to protect his privileges and his local body in return for loyalty to the state. As Pateman, Landes, MacKinnon, and others have argued, the implicit whiteness and maleness of the original American citizen is thus itself protected by national identity:[14] this is a paradox, because if in practice the liberal political public sphere protects and privileges the "person's" racial and gendered embodiment, one effect of these privileges is to appear to be disembodied or abstract while retaining cultural authority. It is under these conditions that what might be an erotics of political fellowship passes for a meritocracy or an order defined by objective mutual interests.[15] The white, male body is the relay to legitimation, but even more than that, the power to suppress that body, to cover its tracks and its traces, is the sign of real authority, according to constitutional fashion.

Needless to say, American women and African-Americans have never had the privilege to suppress the body, and thus the "subject who wants to pass" is the fiercest of juridical self-parodies as yet created by the American system. While this system prides itself liberally on the universal justice it distributes to its disembodied or "artificial" citizen, the mulatta figure is the most abstract and artificial of *embodied* citizens. She gives the lie to the dominant code of juridical representation by repressing the "evidence" the law would seek — a parent, usually a mother — to determine whether the light-skinned body claimed a fraudulent relation to the privileges of whiteness. By occupying the gap between official codes of racial naming and scopic norms of bodily framing conventional to the law and to general cultural practices, the American mulatta's textual and juridical representation after 1865 always designates her as a national subject, the paradigm problem citizen — but not only because she is indeterminate, and therefore an asterisk in the ledger of racial and gendered binarism that seems to organize American culture, as some critics have argued.[16] Irene Redfield's case suggests another way of looking at the national reference of the juridically problematic body: her will-to-not-know, to misrecognize, and to flee her body by embracing the Liberty Tree suggests that she experiences herself as precisely not abstract, but as imprisoned in the surplus embodiment of a culture that values abstraction; and that her affinity for the bourgeois, the individual, the subjective, and the unconscious symptomatize her desire to shed her two racially marked gendered bodies in fantasies of disembodiment, self-abstraction, invisibility. The very vulnerability she feels in her body would be solved by the state's prophylaxis: identification with state disembodiment might suppress or deflect what Spillers calls the "pornotroping" of racist patriarchy.[17] I do not mean to say that embodied subjects in the culture of abstraction always seek invisibility; following Scarry and Spillers we see that abstraction from the body's dignity and the subject's autonomy has been a crucial strategy of political oppression.[18] Moreover, we see in "camp," in youth, in sexual, and in ethnic subcultures strategies of corporeal parody that recast and resist the public denigration of the nonhegemonic "other" body. But sometimes a person doesn't want to seek the dignity of an always-already-violated body, and wants to cast hers off, either for nothingness, or in a trade for some other, better model.

In *Passing*, when women drink iced tea, shop, and have parties, and in *Imitation of Life*, when women make pancakes, picnics, and movies, the colonized female body is not abstract, but hyperembodied, an obstacle and not a vehicle to public pleasure and power. At the same time, the erotic sensation released in the conjunction of women with each other affirms and reasserts the body, in a way more in line with the oft-used feminist and colonial studies interest in the transition from invisibility to presence and from margin to center. It is the logic of this dialectic between abstraction in the national public sphere and the surplus corporeality of racialized and gendered subjects — its discursive expressions, its erotic effects, its implications for a nationalist politics of the body — that I want to engage in this paper. What would it take to produce the political dignity of corporeal difference in American culture, where public embodiment is in itself a sign of inadequacy to proper citizenship?

Imitation of Life — which exists in three versions, the Fannie Hurst novel and the films of John Stahl and Douglas Sirk — addresses these questions by linking the struggles of an Anglo- and an African-American woman, both single with a daughter, to a tale of economic success: in this complex text the women fight for dignity and pleasure by mutually exploiting the structures of commodity capitalism and American mass culture. As we trace the various embodiments of *Imitation of Life*, we will see its "stars" transformed into trademarks and corporate logos, prosthetic bodies that ideally replace the body of pain with the projected image of safety and satisfaction commodities represent. From some angles these commercial hieroglyphs look like vehicles of corporeal enfranchisement; but we will also see the failure of the erotic utopia of the female commodity, since the success montage of one American generation cannot reframe the bodies of the next.

Specifically, in every version of the text the white woman struggles to achieve economic success and national fame, while living in a quasi-companionate couple with the black woman, who does the domestic labor; the black woman, who is also instrumental in the white woman's mastery of commodity culture, remains a loyal domestic employee, even in the wealthy days. But once the women have leisure and security, their bodies reemerge as obstacles, sites of pain and signs of hierarchy: the white daughter falls in love with her mother's love object; the light-skinned African-American daughter wants to pass for white, and so disowns her dark-skinned mother, whose death from heartbreak effectively and melodramatically signals the end of this experiment in a female refunctioning of the national public sphere.[19]

For purposes of economy, my discussion of these narratives will be organized around the form of commodity aesthetics through which they trace the American female body: the trademark. Hurst's 1933 novel represents the business and life history of a white person named Bea Pullman, who assumes professionally her husband's name and gender after his death, and, "passing" for male, opens a hugely successful pancake franchise named "B. Pullman." The visual logo that accompanies her masculine signature, however, represents not the pseudobody of its white, male producer (whose race and gender are deceptively presumed by the concealment of "his" given name), but is displaced onto yet another corporeal other, her African-American housemate, Delilah Johnson. As a visual icon, Johnson is known, not surprisingly, as "Aunt Delilah." In contrast to Hurst's novel, Stahl's 1934 film associates the pancake business only with the trademark and brand name "Aunt Delilah." Miming the passing from novel to film, he honors her with both a logo and a huge, hieroglyphic neon sign; finally, Sirk's 1959 film isolates the white woman in the neon sign and the public body. Sirk renames the trademark characters and some of their professions: Bea Pullman, "the pancake queen," turns into Lora Meredith, actress, with her name up in lights on Broadway. Delilah turns into Annie Johnson and remains a domestic laborer, but with no cachet in popular culture. Thus more changes than names in these interpretations of *Imitation of Life*. I will not attempt to do full readings of these texts, but to see how they collectively imagine the American body politic from the points of view of the overembodied women who serve it.[20]

"B. Pullman" and "H. Prynne": The Feminine Uses of Camouflage

Fannie Hurst's *Imitation of Life* occurs in the midst of carnival. It opens in summertime, in Atlantic City, in 1911. But the crisis of the body we witness there has, at first, nothing to do with leisure culture, nor with the service industry that lives on the cycles of its pleasure.

Instead, in the novel's first scene we witness a paradigm moment of sentimental fiction, a daughter's private response to her mother's death. But the content of this moment is remarkable in its grotesque embodiment of the feminine:

> It struck Bea, and for the moment diverted her from grief, that quite the most physical thing she had ever connected with her mother was the fact of her having died. She found herself, crying there beside the bier, thinking of her mother's legs ... her arms and legs and breasts and her loins there, under the bengaline dress ... stiff and dead.[21]

"There had been so little evidence, during her lifetime," she thinks, "of any aspect of her [mother's] physical life," and yet "the physical fact of [Bea's own] coming of menstrual age" (1) revealed to her the repulsive and upsetting fact that her mother had "committed the act of sex" with "that crumpled figure over there in the corner of the darkened parlor, his back retching as he cried" (4). This primal scene, of sex after death, is unbearable to Bea: her response is mentally to dismember her mother, to protect her after the fact from the embodiment that had made her whole, and therefore penetrable. This style of mourning, and of preserving the memory of the maternal form by breaking it apart in a kind of catalogue, is not only Bea's awakening to her mother's body.[22] It is also her initiation to sexual self-consciousness: mourning "had felt like wine" to Bea, "fizzing down into, and exciting and hurting her" (5).

The erotics of female identification, then, are here tied up with a sublime amalgam of pleasure, pain, and physical defamiliarization that comes from Bea's mother's death. Bea's attraction to this mix of sensations is reinforced by her father's subsequent domination of her life: not only is she, at 17, forced to replace her mother functionally in the household, she is also pressured into marriage to Mr. Pullman, a man her father chooses. This idea in itself does not upset Bea, who is rightly accused of "marrying marriage" rather than marrying a man, for love (42). Marriage, with its usual transformations of a woman's name and sexual practice, is the conventional mode of female self-abstraction, and in marriage, Bea experiences abstraction doubly. While sex with Benjamin Pullman is simply a "clinical sort of something, apparently, that a girl had to give a man," "it was amazing what feeling secure did to the front one put up in the world" (55, 57). Being fit with the false front and the mental prophylaxis of marriage also admits Bea into the world of "girl-talk," as she and the neighborhood women now speak frankly about deviously managing men and faking orgasms (58). This is to say that her entry into marriage provides Bea with a prosthetic identity, estranges her from her body in both an alienating and a pleasing way, and consolidates her relations to other women. Bea wishes that marriage were not physically self-alienating, but this, she learns, is a fact about marriage. Her intuition is further confirmed by her father's tyranny: debilitated by a stroke soon after her marriage, he is physically brutal to Bea throughout her entire life, making him an ever-present "symbol of littleness from which she needed emancipation" (177).

But there is something good about her association with men, and this is in their connection to the national public sphere, specifically the activity of national politics and of capitalist enterprise. Men sit around the bourgeois home speaking their political opinions, which Bea registers but has no interest in; but Hurst's narrator provides a counterconsciousness to Bea's mental limits. She repeatedly draws analogies between the personal choices Bea makes and the political agency of the American citizen: for example, "Thus in the year when men were debating whether a college professor was of sufficient stamina for Presidency of the United States, Bea lifted her face, which intimated yes, for the betrothal kiss of Mr. Pullman" (33). They marry two days before the election, in the the midst of a raucous political parade; the house in which she marries is bedecked with the double symbology of a wedding bell and the American flag. Since these events take place before women had the national franchise, Bea's private acts are the only "votes" she has; and insofar as her later successes mark her *for other women* as a protofeminist, this self-abstracting private event becomes, in retrospect, the first of a set of steps she takes into national existence.[23] It should be said that the historical and ideological pressure of feminism on American women's public self-presence explicitly follows Bea everywhere throughout this book; but, like Irene Redfield, Bea needs to see herself as acting without agency under the pressure of necessity and has no affective relation to collective life, to politics, or history. Indeed, women's history is always in advance of Bea, who only belatedly understands her position in a symptomatic way. Hurst stages this isolate sentimentality as a problem Bea has, a mental blockage symptomatic of her sex class.

Along with gaining closer proximity to the political life of the nation, Bea's affiliation with Pullman brings her closer to the capitalist public sphere.[24] Hurst's representations of the capitalist presence in American everyday life are quite institutionally specific, as if she had contracted to advertise commodities in her narrative the way Hollywood films do now.[25] But the status of brand names and well-known corporations in *Imitation of Life* is not simply referential or commercial: by the turn of the century, product consciousness had become so crucial a part of national history and popular self-identity that the public's relation to business took on a patriotic value. As political parties became less powerful, and as capitalism became less local and more national, the imagined copresence of a consuming public in the emerging and transforming mass culture became a central figure of America, and crucial for its intelligibility;[26] indeed, Robert Westbrook writes that around this time political parties began using the strategies of advertising to encourage American citizens to participate in the political public sphere by characterizing it as consumer behavior.[27]

Like Bea's father, Mr. Pullman works for the great "Pickle and Relish Company." Daily he stands on "Amusement Pier" lecturing on "the life history of the tomato from the vine to the ketchup bottle," while handing out pickle stickpins and samples (13). His authorized biography of the tomato, which exists in an ironic linkage to a plagiarized biography of Abraham Lincoln's life he also delivers (14–15), discloses a corporate strategy to posit the commodity form and the brand name as the last stage of natural and national growth. By 1911, this form of suturing nation and nature was also associated with the sexual and commodity desire traversing Atlantic City, an interpenetration that makes Bea feel uncomfortably sexualized: pictures of Heinz Pier, to which Hurst clearly refers here, reveal scantily clad advertising beauties in the space of national/commodity history and distribution, linking up food and women in a public erotics of consumption, leisure, and knowledge.[28]

This conjunction of leisure culture and its servants subverts the discriminations of the bourgeois domestic economy. The capitalist public sphere absorbs the erotic investments of bodies in proximity, of contact through public exchange, and even of information culture, which emerges here as the new history of the nation, seen through its commodities. Meanwhile, the conventional topographical distinction between the home and the work spaces of the bourgeoisie does not hold: when the family travels, it travels to company functions; when the family moves, it is passively "transferred"; and a side business Mr. Pullman runs, selling maple syrup to local hotels, takes place within the home's instrumental space. In addition, Bea attends to the little "economies" of domestic labor with the zeal of an entrepreneur; but she is a formalist, and she needs to see the home she runs as a sentimental nexus of consolation and escape. Bea does not live a split between domestic ideology and practical social relations, but she sees it as her job to maintain and intensify its reality at the level of theory. Then tragedy strikes. Soon after their marriage, Mr. Pullman dies in a train wreck. Bea is pregnant, then, and gives premature birth to a girl, Jessie; she is also thrown into poverty, burdened by a child and an invalid father.

Simultaneously Bea is imbricated more deeply into separate spheres: the domestic/maternal and the public/capitalist. For her this is an impossible subject position, mapped out according to two mutually reified gender logics. Hurst stages Bea's mutation serially: first, her ether-inspired corporeal dissolution in the pain of childbirth evokes the sublimity of mortality the specter of her mother raised — "and when they started to try and amputate her legs by pulling them out from the sockets, she screamed, and there was the upper half of her separating from the something going from her" (72). She emerges from this event reconstructed and regendered, in a new, maternal body. In the next chapter, Bea is startled out of sleep, as if the sleep of childbirth, inspired to look at her husband's business cards: they reveal graphically that she can assume Pullman's business and gender identity because they share a first initial, B (73). This initial solves a problem she has been having on the job market, where her bourgeois female body has been exposed to the indignity of being all wrong for all the public positions she seeks. But the maple syrup business (run, suggestively, by H. Prynne of Vermont) is mail order, and so her female body would be suppressed, nonknowledge: Bea thinks of her paper transvestism as simply a wedge into the capitalist public sphere, but it is an identity she never fully relinquishes.[29] Bea emerges, then, from the first stage of female abstraction, marriage, to the second stage, where identity is marked by labor and self-alienation. Maternal and masculine employment work the same way on Bea's body, however — she is exhausted, anesthetized. Both labor in the family and labor for money absorb her libidinal energy, or, as Hurst puts it, "countless little budding impulses seemed to have been nipped in the frozen garden of her expectations" (88). She nonetheless retains her theoretical commitment to producing an unalienated domestic scene, but her need to earn wages disrupts the separate spheres on which her theory was based, and she displaces her need onto the capitalist public sphere, where she goes from serving her husband's leisure to serving as her husband, in the leisure industry. The contradictions of Bea's position threaten to disembody her permanently, an outcome she both wants and does not want.

For the next fifteen years, Bea "buckles herself" into the worker's body as though into a suit of "armor" (186). At first, she lives, "on a minus sign" (93), selling maple syrup in the back alleys of Atlantic City. At the height of Bea's exhaustion, she walks up to an "enormously buxom figure of a woman with a round black moon face that shone above an Alps of bosom, privately hoping that the scrubbed, starchy-looking negress would offer herself" as a sleep-in maid (91). This woman, Delilah Johnson, tenders the offer and comes not only to run the house, but also to provide Bea with the candy and pancake recipes she soon turns into commodities, in search of a franchise and a fortune. Later, selling "Delilah Delights" brand pancakes and candies in hotels, and then in her own restaurants, Bea becomes more like a classic capitalist, increasingly distant from the public scene of consumption. As the brains and the name behind the business, Bea remains almost entirely behind the veil of the male moniker. In addition, Bea uses "Aunt Delilah's" body to stand in for her own. When she imagines Delilah as a mammylike trademark, Delilah protests and says she wants to dress beautifully, to create a stylish image inheritance for her daughter to remember her by (105). But Bea forces Delilah to play the mammy, and in this coerced guise she becomes the prosthetic public body of "B. Pullman," the store, and Bea Pullman, the woman.

Bea relies on Delilah to do much more than to protect Bea's body: the "social hieroglyphic" or trademark representing Delilah serves to create consumer desire for the products of the "B. Pullman" restaurants. As Stahl's film displays, when Delilah stands framed in the store's plate-glas window making her authentic pancakes, the mise-en-scène of capitalist aesthetics merges with actual production. Bea relies on Delilah's double embodiment as icon and laborer to engender public "need" for her commodity. Delilah can do this because she is a professor in the true religious sense, one who trains "imitations" or "replicas" of herself in the "University of Delilah" (184): there, she teaches "Jemimesis," or how to commodify the "mammy's" domestic aura, which each waffle, pancake, and candy she makes is supposed to install in the consumer, like a communion wafer. In Delilah the religious aura of the commodity and the everyday imitation of God merge, in an uncanny repetition of Marx's analysis of how commodities become invested with soul and pseudo-agency: to Bea, this is imitation in the good, the best sense.[30] But Bea displaces onto Delilah more than her need to manage the public sphere. Delilah is also Bea's private maternal supplement, raising Jessie and caring for Bea's father. And finally, she is Bea's wife and mother, the only person who touches her body during the 1920s, massaging her back and feet after the long day at the office. In short, Delilah solves for Bea "the corporeal problem of being two places simultaneously," both in everyday life and in the capitalist public sphere (140). Because Delilah can "be" both places, Bea has to "be" in neither. In Delilah, Bea achieves the condition of prophylaxis she has sought since her mother's death.

Never for a moment does Bea question her structural relation to Delilah: to Bea, their cohabitation is a given, as untheorized as are their different places in the racial and class hierarchies of the dominant culture. Because Bea herself is so desperately liminal, masquerading as the difference between the white man's name and the black woman's body, she has no consciousness of her privilege. Rather, like Delilah's mulatta daughter, Peola, Bea has the perverse opportunity to capitalize on racist patriarchal culture, by creating a compensatory "body" to distract from the one already marked by the colonial digit. Peola "passing" creates a juridically fraudulent white body, while Bea incorporates public "persons" — companies and copyrighted trademarks — who sublate history and the violence of the colonized body.

Then one day Bea awakens to the distance she has traveled from the sensational body in which she might live. This is, in part, because fame and money eroticize her in the public eye, which is curious about how she pleasures her body under the stress of success. Second, she discovers the body as a site of potential pleasure because it is "sex o'clock in America," and the New Woman of the 1920s reveals to Bea another way to negotiate the public female body: in an armor not of bodiless abstraction, but of cosmetic masquerade. And finally, because capitalist practice carries its own erotic charge, its processes of abstraction are homoeroticized by Bea: she is openly attracted to other women who engage in what she calls "the racy ingredient of competition" (244) within the national public sphere. These feelings are congealed when Bea meets Virginia Eden — a beauty magnate, her own name a hieroglyph (a means of passing) that condenses the erotics of "sex solidarity," the American/Jeffersonian *locus amoenus*, and a Jewish background (she was born Sadie Kress). Eden opens the erotic floodgates in Bea: dates her, makes her a business "proposition," and seduces her into a contractual collaboration. "You and me ought to work together, Pullman. You make women fat and comfortable. My job is to undo all that and make them beautiful. You're grist to my mill. I want to be grist to yours" (193).

Awakened in the garden of Eden, Bea then becomes an erotic object for her female employees (she opens a gym so that they might also turn their bodies into erotic armor, and they fall so in love with Bea that her male secretary starts intercepting their "obnoxious" gifts and love letters [189]). But when the business deal with Eden falls through, Bea experiences the erotic pain of female alliance once again, for "Virginia Eden's teeth were as pointed and polished and incisive as a terrier's, and with them, when she sank, she drew blood" (201). Then, the feeling of being embodied and excited by Eden scares Bea: she immediately hyperheterosexualizes herself and falls in love with an unattainable man, Frank Flake.[31] After this embodied interlude, she returns to the life of abstraction. For Bea has not finally attained her national position by identifying with women, or with anything sensual. She has achieved success, within the self-containment of the commodity form, by reinforcing the very apparatus whose practices she flees: in hiding behind the colonial simulacrum of a "male" employer who owns the copyrighted image and labor of an African-American woman.

A trademark is supposed to be a consensual mechanism. It triangulates with the customer and the commodity, providing what W. F. Haug calls a "second skin" that enables the commodity to appear to address, to recognize, and thereby to "love" the consumer.[32] Bea repeatedly turns to this abstract erotics for love and protection. This is what Delilah is, and represents. And in this sense, Delilah's fractured public identity — as herself, as an autonomous iconic image, as a servant of "B. Pullman" — foregrounds the irregular operations of national capitalism on the bodies of racially and sexually gendered subjects. In other words, at the same time that Delilah brings dispersed fields of exchange into proximity and intimacy, she also shows their nonanalogousness. While Bea is protected by hiding behind Delilah's tremendous public body, Delilah's status as a living trademark takes over her own meaning and history: she married a bigamist and gave birth to a daughter cursed with Ham's opposite — light skin in a racist culture; she escaped the South to protect her daughter from the most brutal forms of racism. But when Delilah dies, the press reports that "her people" love her because the popularity of her facsimile legitimated blackness in public white culture; she is also, the press says, a constant reminder to white "national consciousness" of the dignity of her race. During World War I she becomes a domestic icon of the doughboys, who dream of a safe domestic political space after the most horrible of wars. It matters not to the public that she dies a most humiliating, lonely, and grotesque death "in her huddle on the floor, a heterogeneous twist of pain, her back in an arch, her torso writhing" (319–20), for "Delilah" has become the trademark who lives on, interminably. Through her forced abstraction, and not her biographical person, Delilah reconfigures the capitalist and the national public spheres to include, even to foreground, the American class of overembodied, colonized subjects. In this she provides an alternative image to the logics of liberal culture. At least this is someone's liberal fantasy of what such a trademark might do.

Aunt Jemima and Uncle Sam

It is, for sure, the fantasy condensed in the face and history of Aunt Jemima, whose aura in American culture Hurst borrows for "Aunt Delilah" in *Imitation of Life*. Aunt Jemima was introduced to America at the Columbian Exposition in 1893. This links her with the origin of American progressive modernism, the alliance between industry and the state to produce new "frontiers" of production and invention, and the induction of advertising itself as an arm of American sovereignty: it was to promote this event, after all, that the Pledge of

Allegiance was written.[33] A huge success, Aunt Jemima became associated with a line of new products that included the "skyscraper, the long-distance telephone, the X-ray, the motion picture, the wireless telegraph, the automobile, the airplane, and radium."[34] She herself was an example of state-of-the-art technologies: the invention of the halftone printing process at the turn of the century that enabled advertisers to install a new realism in the human trademark; the emergence of a new "logocentric" style, which encouraged consumers to link products with personalities;[35] the invention of ready-mix convenience foods, of which her pancake mix is the first to "emancipate" the housewife.[36] She did not, however, contain the promise of further racial emancipation: as Hazel Carby's recent discussion of the fair's contempt for African-Americans shows, the exoticization of Aunt Jemima would surely mark the limit of what the consuming public could bear in the linkage of African and American.[37]

The "promise" of Aunt Jemima thus went much further than household convenience: her condensation of racial nostalgia, national memory, and progressive history was a symptomatic, if not important, vehicle for post–Civil War national consolidation. At the fair she was embodied by a woman, Nancy Green, who lived in an enormous flour barrel. Periodically she would come out to sing and tell tales: "Some of her script was drawn from the words of the old vaudeville Aunt Jemima song, some from [pseudo]memories of her own plantation days in the Deep South," and some from her own invention.[38] The association of exotic, primitive women with pancakes and domestic consolation was reinforced by popular fantasy, as the renown of *Little Black Sambo* suggests. One other context is relevant to Aunt Jemima's phantom presence in *Imitation of Life*: the analogy embedded in the trademark's address to the notion of the bourgeois housewife's domestic "slavery." In one 1919 advertisement, for example, the copy is explicit: Jemima's pancakes were the last hope this side of Abraham Lincoln to maintain the union of the North and the South; housewives who buy Aunt Jemima will not only be emancipated from labor, but will keep the family together by keeping politics out.[39] In this way the trademark itself bridges the nuclear household and national history, along with helping to produce the kinds of historical amnesia necessary for confidence in the American future.

Something like this amnesiac activity is narrated in Hurst's *Imitation of Life*. The accumulated "pancake wealth" of the nation does not transform the injurious conditions of the national/capitalist public sphere. But since the commodity is the modern embodiment of the legitimate "artificial person," Americans in the text equate personal emancipation through it with shedding the collectively shared body of pain to gain a solitary protected self. This is Bea's strategy, which works so well that she ends up alone, enfranchised but not empowered. But John Stahl's 1934 *Imitation of Life* reads the text's utopian potential. Without looking away from the culture of abuse that saturates even American leisure, Stahl imagines *Imitation of Life* within an affirmative female economy. This utopia is not the abstract "paradise" of heterosexual, natural bliss her lover, Steven Archer, offers Bea (Claudette Colbert), on an island "elsewhere," outside of the frame; nor is it in sentimental womanhood, where differences dissolve through maternal identification — as in Delilah's (Louise Beavers) cry to Peola (Fredi Washington), "I'm your Mammy, child! I ain't no white mother!" Instead, Stahl derives from Hurst's text the positivity of difference: of female households and workplaces that protect the hyperembodied frame; of an unalienated capitalist public sphere; and of an identity in labor that eases the psychic burdens of gender and race. These "spaces," however, are really temporalities, moments in time when certain possibilities coalesce. This means that the film's "solution" is also framed as failure — in Delilah's commercial and Peola's racial hieroglyphic, and the impossibility of their suture, in American culture.

Delilah enters Stahl's *Imitation of Life* by accident, misreading the address in an advertisement, and ending up at Bea Pullman's door. To convince Bea that Bea has indeed asked for her, Delilah reads her the ad's text, which describes her own subject position in the marketplace: she is a "girl," "a housemaid, colored, not afraid of hard work." She says that she has been looking for jobs, answering ads like this, but no one will take her because she has a child, and the ads do not call for a child. Then she advertises her child: she has been "brung up right, not drug up, like most of 'em is." Peola comes in and performs for Bea: she says "Good Morning" in patrician diction, an act she has clearly practiced. While at first Bea protests that she cannot afford financially to succumb to Delilah's hard sell, seeing Peola induces her to revise the terms of the ad and to fold this female

family into her own equally impoverished unit: no longer a "girl,"
Delilah becomes to Bea "200 pounds of mother fighting to keep her
baby."

This scene is extraordinary in the way it shows Delilah textualiz-
ing, characterizing herself, in sound bites: it is apparently the lot of
the marginal subject to self-commodify verbally, to objectify and promote her own qualities, in a culture that, corporealizing, presumes
her insufficiency. Advertising rhetoric, then, starts to look like a
mode of colonized discourse. Delilah's insertion of Bea into the generic slot of the white housewife who consumes "colored" domestic
labor is misguided, however. To rent the abandoned Boardwalk pool
hall that turns into "Aunt Delilah's," Bea is forced to sell herself in
roughly the same way: without capital, as she later says, "All I had
was talk."

These two contradictory structures mark the relations of Bea and
Delilah in Stahl's film: in one mode, the traditional nomenclature
and spatialization of the domestic worker in the private home still
obtains, especially as the women achieve leisure. Delilah is always
"Delilah," while the other is "Miss Bea"; when they can afford a spa-
cious house, the "domestic" lives beneath and the employer above.
In addition, as they gain leisure, their bodies diverge, becoming
more socially proper to the public iconography of race, class, and
gender in early-twentieth-century America. The African-American
woman grows larger, and darker, and her clothes get slightly better;
the Anglo-American woman becomes a vital "new woman," wearing
corsets and bobbed hair and slinky things.[40] But during the first ten
years of struggle to gain financial stability and public dignity, the
women live in the closest of quarters. In physical style they are
equivalent, dressing in uniforms appropriate to their work. At that
point they inhabit their bodies in much the same way — both are
exhausted — and they are shot at the same respectful distance by
Stahl. But the film occasionally violates its accent on their shared
class and maternal difficulties. The recurrent success montage that
traces Delilah's transformation into a trademark emits the same odor
of racist expropriation that permeates Hurst's novel.

For Bea takes Delilah's pancake recipe, her maternal inheritance,
and turns it into a business; she takes Delilah's face and turns it into
a cartoon trademark. Stahl stages Delilah in this scene as a buffoon,
a position that provides her an opportunity for both ironic commen-

tary and objectification. On hearing Bea manipulate the rhetoric of credit to bilk businessmen into advancing their wares so that she might transform a boardwalk pool room into a women's domestic business space ("Aunt Delilah's Pancakes"), Delilah acts as a comic soundtrack, singing "I puts my trust in Jesus" in a worried tone as she washes the windows. But her disbelief in the efficacy of the capitalist logic she hears Bea using is turned back on Delilah too, as Bea aggressively frames and installs her within that logic.

When Bea asks Delilah to smile for the trademark sign, Delilah smiles a small and hesitant smile. But Bea forces her to assume and to freeze a "blackface" pose, which she dutifully maintains long after Bea needs her, to Bea's great delight. Stahl shoots the huge face of smiling Delilah in extreme close-up and uses shot/reverse shot cutting back to her frozen, smiling, saucer-eyed face as if to underscore how mentally insufficient Delilah is to her situation in the white patriarchal capitalist public sphere. But the grotesque hyperembodiment of Delilah in this sequence violates her own and the film's aesthetic codes: I feel certain that her graphic decontextualization is specially designed to allude to and to ironize Aunt Jemima, in her role as a site of American collective identification.

The film's interference with the Aunt Jemima in Delilah is reinforced elsewhere: after Delilah's visual degradation, we see her making pancakes in the store, dressed as her trademark likeness; then the film depicts a mass of imitation Delilahs, originating in her human face and fulfilled in her neon sign. But these women, who are shown packaging and mass producing Aunt Delilah's Original Pancake Mix, are explicitly industrialized, associated frame by frame with the disembodied human labor that generates their "product"; bodies without heads, they are filmed in an expressionist and not a cartoonish mode. They are surrounded by history: they are produced in history.[41] And when Delilah's product finally makes it into boxes, which are shown repetitiously moving along the production line, the soundtrack refers to the humanity abstracted by and condensed into the commodity, playing a sharply escalating series of the musical phrase "Nobody Knows the Trouble I've Seen," which is also featured in the opening moments of the film, over the credits.

In Delilah, Stahl gives Aunt Jemima a body dignified by labor and inscribed by struggle; but, distorted by racist magnification, she is "very deceivin' as to proportion." Indeed, in this seemingly stereotypical guise, Delilah utters the film's most political sentences. In that sense too she is decommodified, an anti-Aunt Jemima. She ironizes the tradition of grotesque African-American representations in American consumer culture, which includes the distortions of the Hurst novel itself; and, most important, Delilah talks back to the nation from within her fictive frame, in the mammy's costume. No tales of the sunny South from her, or sweet memories of the plantation: when she steps out of her flour barrel she speaks of the political brutality of the national public sphere. When Peola explodes in rage at being called "black" by Jessie, Delilah, on screen in uniform, tells Peola to "submit" to the cross her light-skinned father bore, and in an intense close-up that reflexively undermines the comic quality of the earlier caricature of her "trademarked" face, she faces the question of who is to blame for the pain of racist embodiment:

> It ain't her fault, Miss Bea. It ain't yourn, and it ain't mine. I don't
> know rightly where the blame lies. It can't be our Lord's. Got
> me puzzled.

At the moment Delilah settles on her perplexity, she looks away from the people on the screen and turns her face toward the camera. Thus the unspoken word in this speech is national, as she looks directly out at the audience: here, in her white, fluted chef's cap, she addresses her audience specifically as Americans. Delilah is generally read as an apologist for the discriminations of racist culture because she argues that Peola must reconcile herself to the pain of her embodiment. Despite the manifest power of religious belief that ameliorates her own experience of racial violation, Delilah also engages in political analysis; in fact, this entire scene reveals, in brief asides, the rage at the other side of her resignation. Two comments in particular frame both Delilah's reading of her own history and her desire to protect Peola from repeating it by way of spiritual and financial support. Just before Peola's first public outburst against identification with her mother's blackness, Bea and Delilah work in the store and fantasize about what they want for their own lives and the lives of their daughters. Bea comments that Peola is smarter than Jessie; Delilah replies, "Yesm. We all starts that way. We don't gets dumb till later on." What is "dumbness" here, if not Delilah's name for the mental blockages to rage and pain—what I earlier called "the-will-to-not-know"—that distinguish the colonized subject? Delilah's personal wish is just to get off her feet; but before then she will make certain that Peola is prepared, financially and educationally, to become a teacher, never to do housework for anyone. Teachers are "smart": not dumb, not full of sublimated rage, not sentenced to the life of the body as Delilah is, although she says she accepts the burden of her frame as part of the Lord's work.

The irony, of course, is that Delilah can pass through American culture because she has given her body over to its representation of what her subject position is: her very darkness, which overembodies her in the national public sphere, also domesticates her, because she is entirely intelligible to the juridical satisfaction of the white mind. The film's pictographic move from her surplus body to her gigantic neon luminosity emphasizes her objectification: it always seems to be night in the sky behind her luminous body. In contrast, Peola's resistance to the official and popular rule of racial classification makes her body a different kind of obstacle: Peola would have to choose to be "black," to submit to a colonial corporeal regime, according to her own agency. But to choose to be visible in a culture of abstraction, to be a racial hieroglyph in everyday life, would be to choose a form of slavery. She simply cannot inherit her mother's strategies of passing, because she does not have her mother's body — as juridically defined, and culturally staged. She looks, and dresses, much more like Bea.

Thus, one way of reading the racialized sign in this film is to see the contradictions, within its regime of visual representation, between the commercial and the personal racial hieroglyph: the cultural capital of the mother's public hyperembodiment versus the juridically constructed enigma of the daughter's, which can and cannot be registered in the mirror and the film. Each racialized corporeality requires a special kind of self-licensing: thus Delilah looks forward to leaving her body completely, because it is so saturated by unrequited cultural fantasy; while Peola wants to be "white," which means she wants to relinquish one of her bodies, to become less meaningful, more American. Since Bea and Jessie share the same frame, the same color, the same class style, they will not have this problem, and can affirm themselves while choosing each other.

But the contradictory and fracturing logics of race here produce another form of homosocial fantasy, which requires relinquishing the individual body as the primary unit of social meaning. When

Delilah asks Peola to be a good girl and go to a high-toned college, we might think, as many critics do, that the film endorses the racial assimilation of African-Americans. But she is also asking Peola to understand and to live her class interests, as a member of a contested collectivity. Delilah herself did not have the privilege to do this in the 1920s; like many of her race class, she was dependent on the national market for "colored" domestic work. But for a film that takes place on the New Jersey Boardwalk and then in New York City, *Imitation of Life* records almost nothing of American leisure culture or the political public sphere; for a film that takes place during the depression, we hear only fleeting references to unemployment. In contrast to the novel, which is manifestly national and institutional in its scope, Stahl's film does not seem to believe in the value of an abstract, coherent national or capitalist space. He finds America directly on the body, its surfaces; but the surfaces of the body are marked almost solely with collective signs, which map out the subject's vulnerabilities, the routes her pain travels. This kind of pain is not the individuating, isolating kind; it is the source of a political confederation, the public world women might make. But female alliance across race is not the film's solution to the fragmenting effects of American hierarchy. Rather, the film offers this alliance as a first step in effecting a shift away from the centrality of national identity as such. Delilah's funeral reveals on screen a concealed but vital and ongoing public sphere within the black community. In contrast to the novel, where all of America melts into the public space of mourning for Delilah, this funeral is run by the black churches and lodges that specialize in, among other things, ritualizing the passing of an individual person from a world where pain is a collective burden. The emergence of this suppressed locus of costume and ceremony is not merely a species of colonialist "artifacting" on Stahl's part:[42] it deconstructs the simulacrum of "one" American public sphere and reveals that the notion of one dominant culture is one of the culture's most powerful myths. What if *Imitation of Life* were told from Delilah's point of view? The film approaches this by excluding the elements of cultural life to which she has no access. And by having her speak from within the trademark, it creates a space for political agency that exists elsewhere, and here in her death as well. As Bea's final embrace of Jessie under the neon gaze of Delilah confirms, one must recognize that the body wrought by pain, memory, history, and ritual is collective. It is not aberrant or objectively in excess. In so shifting the public meaning of the "overembodied" body, the Stahl text imagines a crucial victory over the abstract and individualizing lure of paradise, whether in America or elsewhere. This antinationalist message is, paradoxically, brought to us by a national trademark. Perhaps this was the only voice to which the audience would listen.

White Neon, Black Gold: The Sirkean System[43]

In the thirties versions of *Imitation of Life*, national nostalgia for a safe domestic space was played out in commodity culture through the production and transcendence of a black trademark. The idea was that public investment in a commodity form, with its humanoid skin and soul, would consolidate a nation shaken by a monstrous war and debilitating depression: and so Aunt Jemima, who had served so well after the Civil War, was "modernized" in "Aunt Delilah," displacing Uncle Sam. In the novel, this trademark is appropriated callously from the body of a black domestic worker as part of a white woman's emancipatory strategy. In Stahl's film this trademark is given public speech, and speaks from the political place of surplus embodiment and the personal rage of collective suffering. Twenty-five years later, Douglas Sirk pulls back the black trademark's curtain, and reveals the white woman hovering there: in one of the great *tu quoque* sequels of our time, his *Imitation of Life* exposes the form of the white woman to the commodification she has for so long displaced onto the black woman's body.

As in Stahl's version, the narrative of female commodification hinges on a woman's relation to publicity in Sirk's 1959 film. Advertisements do much of the critical work: the opening shot of Lora Meredith's (Lana Turner) face, which is repeated later for emphasis, shows her bending over a sign that announces the "1947 Coney-Island Mardi-Gras." This frame reasserts the film's situation in Carnival, on the "fat Tuesday" of public culture that portends Lent's impending melodrama. But this film occupies the very public spaces excluded in Stahl's rendition — as if in a shot/reverse shot relation, Sirk shoots the boardwalk from the beach that Stahl never represents. Sirk puts the masses back in mass culture and condenses the national identity of their taste and their desire in the surplus corpo-reality of Lora Meredith. While in the thirties texts of *Imitation of Life* an ethic of bourgeois propriety motivated light-skinned women to escape the hyperdetermination of the public body, in the fifties the culture so embraces spectacular things that to be American means to want more body, more presence. But since presence, in mass culture, is signified by the image, Lora Meredith's stardom merges her embodiment and her abstraction — in a way peculiar to women but symptomatic of the gaudy culture at large. And so Lora Meredith becomes her own prosthesis, projecting herself into si-mulacral public spaces where the commodity, representation, and the body meet. That her fraudulence is America's has been widely discussed, by Sirk himself and by every critic who writes on this film. My interest here is to show specifically how Sirk determines the fe-male trademark, transforming its public iconicity, its stereotypicality, into a national problem.

The transformation of Lora Meredith into "Lora Meredith" involves a self-instrumentalizing contract with her director, David Edwards. The montage sequence in which he proposes to make her sexually and professionally generic involves photographically removing her body from his apartment, moving the shot across the public space he calls her "empire" and scattering her across the nation. In the ten years that this sequence covers, Lora's body becomes progressively reified: her name replaces Edwards's name in the lights and in-creases in prominence; her face floats, separated from her body, amid overlapping marquees; her image is peeled from her face and splayed on national magazine covers; and, toward the end, women in the audience mime her look, so that projection of her visual image is no longer necessary to transmit to us her dominion in the national/capitalist space of fantasy consumption.

Although the montage transmits a ridiculous brightness, and al-though all the evidence is that Lora is a shallow actress — since Broadway and Hollywood apparently seek only a "girl with a certain *Je ne sais quoi* ... that something [she] managed to get with the dog" — the humiliation to which she is exposed is mainly not profes-sional, but domestic. The film establishes its disciplinary home econ-omy in its very first scene, when Lora loses her daughter — now named Susie — on the beach. This loss introduces Lora both to Steve Archer, her soon-to-be-suffering-lover, and to Annie (rather than Delilah) Johnson, her soon-to-be-suffering-"maid": they themselves are linked by their spatial proximity to a policeman, whose job is also to find the mother who has lost her young blond child. Everyone in her household polices Lora, including the children. Each pronounces a monologue that catalogues explicitly Lora's inadequacy as a lover, mother, employer — in part because she really does lie and deceive herself to further her career, but mainly because public life is "imitation" and private life is "real" where women are concerned.

Yet there is something odd and ambivalent and even masochistic about the family's compulsion to repeat the argument for domesticity. More than anyone, Steve Archer brings this message to Lora. When they meet, he aspires to hang his photographs in the Museum of Modern Art — for example, the picture he takes of Lora on the Mardi Gras sign titled "Mother in Distress." But falling in love with Lora compels him to give up his dream, and to ask her to give up hers. He tells her: "What you're after isn't real." What's "real" to him is "the nicest looking green folding money," and sex, besides. When she says, "What about me? What about the way I feel?" in defense of her lifelong dream to act, he replies, "Stop acting." (In a later scene, when she offers to give up Steve for her daughter's sake, as Bea does in the Stahl film, Susie repeats this: "Stop acting, Mother.") Yet Steve returns repeatedly to the scenes of her acting: twice we see him in loving audience, both on the stage and off. He is addicted to consuming her product. He says, "You know, I still have you in my blood . . ."

This dynamic of attraction, rejection, discipline, and performance has its uncanny "blood" repetition in the maternal relation of Annie to her daughter, now named Sarah Jane. Sarah Jane is light-skinned, an inheritance from her father, who "was practically white" (as is Susan Kohner, the actress, in fact, white). Throughout her youth Sarah Jane blames her mother (rather than, say, the state or the law) for her condition and chooses a style of racial passing that negates her mother's "servile" mentality and manner, featuring instead libidinous, assertive physicality. Sarah Jane's racial passing is simultaneously sexual and theatrical, but in this she is typical of women. For in this film a woman who lives with difference — either gendered or racial — enjoys no prophylactic private sphere, no space safe from performance or imitation. This internal estrangement is as real for Annie as it is for her daughter: Annie comments that Lora's home has got to be better than the racist brutality of the South, but this is the closest she comes to saying that she feels at home where she lives. In any case, Sarah Jane mimes Lora in understanding that physical allure is the capital a woman must use to gain a public body. But this capital turns out to be as counterfeit for Sarah Jane as it is for Lora.

The writing on the wall in the scene where Frankie beats up Sarah Jane for camouflaging the "trouble" with her mother (she tells Frankie that she is the daughter of rich, conservative parents, but the "trouble" with her mother is that Sarah Jane is ashamed of her) stages Sirk's negative homage to Stahl's *Imitation of Life*. The empty store in front of which the young lovers meet sports a prominent FOR RENT sign, but this empty store will not provide a secure space for a female affective and economic unit. Rather, it reflects the brutality that takes place outside that unit — in the public space. Moreover, the plate-glass window that had contained the authentic embodiment of Delilah's icon now reflects the public truth of American culture: the word *liberty*, reflected backwards off a marquee from across the street meets the word *bar*. In conjunction — or in "disjunction" — they condense the story and the conclusion of both of the narratives Sarah Jane lives, in her Anglo- and her African-American frames.

After Frankie rejects Sarah Jane, she takes to the life of the white showgirl. She is not good enough to achieve the self-iconicity of mass culture: she earns no success montage. Instead, Sarah Jane's mode of self-instrumentality is to hyperemphasize her body in the present tense of performance, in the mode of the naked gold figurine that is the trademark of the Moulin Rouge, where she works. By making herself a thing, she takes over her own cultural objectification as a racialized subject, relying on male narcissism to separate her sexual "value" from her juridical body. Both of her performance scenes are extremely carnal, although opposite in their mode of allure: in the first, she dresses and sings raunchily about her need to embody herself sexually, so that she might avoid the fate of passive, feminine women who have "empty, empty arms";[44] in the second, at the Moulin Rouge, she is one of a chain of indistinguishable mute showgirls on a conveyor belt. They mime en masse a scene of seduction, drinking, and intercourse. You might even say they mime a success montage, in its mix of seriality and repetition, but the success belongs to the audience, whose mastery is one with the privilege of consuming, not to the persons who embody it. In contrast, the audience of Sirk's film is very differently positioned. The film routes these scenes through Annie's maternal eyes. Twice we and Annie see Sarah Jane in a sexual and racial performance: we watch Annie have an inverted primal scene, transfixed and sickened as her daughter does a "number." As with Steve and Lora, Sarah Jane is in Annie's "blood": it is as if the light-skinned female body in performance is irresistible to its consumers, even when it produces pain rather than arousal of the theater's Aristotelian emotions or the girlie show's carnal sensations.

If Lora and Sarah Jane produce the "unreal" simulations, what does Sirk hold out for authenticity? I have already suggested that Annie and Steve, who police imitation with an unwavering moral passion, become implicated in female fraudulence by their addiction to it. Steve and Annie assume pain the way Lora and Sarah Jane want pleasure, and if the star-crossed women overinvest in the ecstasy and value of being public objects, the star-crossed blood lovers turn their pain into its own kind of spectacle. In short, though the film concentrates most explicitly on the "problem" of the prosthetic public female body, it also shows how the problem of the female body itself becomes a commodity.

The paradoxes involved in this double commodification come together at Annie's opulent funeral. As the final scene in the film, the funeral might look like a privileged site of authentic public display, as I have argued that it does in the Stahl film. For like Delilah, Annie has a secret nondiegetic life in the black community. Annie says plainly that this life has not made it on screen because, "Miss Lora, you never asked." The funeral scene at the church brims with pomp and costume, but the ornate procession seems to reclaim the potential for dignified public spectacle. And the song Mahalia Jackson sings, "Trouble of the World," describes the weary one's relief at leaving for the Lord's house, where presumably there is no back room or basement. Compared to the rest of the film the funeral is unfrenetic, measured, subdued. It is also the only time we see men in costume, as if perhaps signaling a patriarchal reclaiming of public spectacle. But as the procession rolls down the street, the camera pulls back behind a frosted window: the window reads "costume rentals."

This ironizing text is authentic, like graffiti. On the walls of consumer America, as in this film of *Imitation of Life*, public advertising seems to be the only "agent" of truth. Sirk himself has said that he intended to undercut the funeral by making it bizarre and embarrassing; he also deliberately shot Mahalia Jackson to look grotesque. He could not understand why Jackson moved the audience, in her luminous cry for relief from her body, and, suspicious of public culture and popular expression, Sirk could not imagine that a representation of public female dignity might seem emancipating, after all the corporeal humiliation his characters endure.[45] Sirk preserves in his *Imitation of Life* the American loathing of the public body; he plays out, even in his own irony, how the ethic of universal and abstract dignity embodies the citizens it wants to humiliate.

I have argued that in American culture legitimacy derives from the privilege to suppress and protect the body; the fetishization of the abstract or artificial "person" is constitutional law, and is also the means by which whiteness and maleness were established simultaneously as "nothing" and "everything."[46] In *Passing* and in *Imitation of Life*, Anglo- and African-American women live the effects of their national identity directly on the body, which registers the subject's legitimacy according to the degree to which she can suppress the "evidence." One of the main ways a woman mimes the prophylaxis of citizenship is to do what we might call "code-crossing." This involves borrowing the corporeal logic of an other, or a fantasy of that logic, and adopting it as a prosthesis. The way women have usually tried this is heterosexual, but marriage turns out to embody and violate the woman more than it is worth. Thus other forms of bodily suppression have been devised. This is how racial passing, religion, bourgeois style, capitalism, and sexual camp have served the woman; indeed, in *Imitation of Life* this ameliorative strategy has become the "trademark" of female existence, across race and class and sexual preference.

What does this tell us about the potential national identity holds for the subjects it has historically burdened with bodies? We have seen that in modern America, the artificial legitimacy of the citizen has merged with the commodity form: its autonomy, its phantasmatic freedom from its own history, seem to invest it with the power to transmit its aura, its "body," to consumers. We have seen, in *Imitation of Life*, light-skinned women embracing the commodity's promise, although this embrace itself results in many different forms of embodiment. Sometimes the commodity becomes a prosthetic body, an apotropaic shield against penetration and further delegitimation; sometimes the body itself becomes the object of public consumption, protected by the distance between the image, performance, and actual form. But the films and the novel give the lie to the American promise that participation in the national/capitalist public sphere has emancipatory potential for the historically overembodied. First, the strategy of abstraction that distinguishes white bourgeois style "solves" the problem by disciplining and shedding the public body, which forces the woman to live with the torture of its perennial return. Second, the body of the dark-skinned African-American woman is apparently unabstractable on her own behalf. Even Aunt Delilah's nostalgic public form represents a history of violence that is simultaneously personal and national in scope. This is why the amelioration of religion is so crucial to the black mothers of these texts, for there is no imaginable space in America, not even in the most benign white woman's house, where she will see relief from the body's burden. In Stahl's version, Bea and Delilah do escape into the sisterhood of the laboring body, but once leisure is achieved they revert to the default forms of their culture. For light-skinned African-American women, then, the choice of public identity comes to be between two bodies of pain, not two possible modes of relief from indeterminacy.

There is a moment in Hurst's *Imitation of Life* that crystallizes the distances between the nation's promise of prophylaxis to the "person" and the variety of female genders it creates. At the moment before Bea has her first experience of intercourse with her husband, she goes upstairs to put on the nighttime garb of the virginal bride on her way to the hymenal altar. She has never before entered their "master bedroom": the "darkies" put it together during the wedding day. Bea, frightened, thinking of her mother, catalogues the objects on Pullman's mantel:

Framed photographs of an exceedingly narrow-faced pair of parents, deceased. One of quite an aged aunt, deceased. A framed program of the Pleiades Club, the one on which Mr. Pullman was announced to read his paper on Abraham Lincoln. And of all things! Dear knows from where, the black girl had unearthed a picture which must, in some way, have got mixed up with his other belongings. A horrid cabinet-sized thing of a woman, which Bea turned face

down, in stockings and no clothes, trying on a man's high hat
before a mirror. With what seemed like actual malice, that picture
had been propped up against one of the china pugs. Those
darkies ... (50)

At the moment when Bea is to leave her ignorant girlish body behind
for the sexual knowledge of womanhood, she finds her husband's
pornography. The "thing" of a woman violates everything she knows
about her proper New England husband, and Bea understands that
this woman has preceded her in his fantasy life. Bea turns the picture
face down because she does not want to face it. She wants instead to
blame it on the "black girl" who set up the room; she wants to displace her disgust at the masculine embodiment of women onto the
black women who serve her. I have suggested that Hurst's version of
Bea habitually relies on black women to be embodied, but along
with revealing her own racial and class instrumentality, the picture
suggests a politically "malicious" correspondence between Anglo-
and African-American women.

The "thing" of a woman in the picture is having a wonderful time.
She is fantasizing in a mirror, which itself frames the genitaled trunk
of her body for the husband's pornographic gaze. The text does not,
however, consider what the man wanted from the picture. Let us
imagine, then, for a moment, what this woman might be thinking.
Surely, her costumed appendages signify a fantasy of agency: I might
assume a male body, or masquerade as another kind of woman. But
the hat this "thing" of a woman wears is not just any hat: it is Lincoln's
hat. The text clues us in to this by referring to Pullman's speech about
Lincoln, which he plagiarized from the *Encyclopaedia Britannica*.
This 1911 article about Lincoln reminds us that he was for white
woman suffrage, as well as reluctantly for the emergence of black
slaves from property to personhood; the article also characterizes
Lincoln as the most feminine of presidents, because of his sensitive
heart.[47] In conjunction with the prop of the hat, the woman wears
most likely a pair of dark stockings. Perhaps she is enjoying imagining how an amalgam of races and genders might look, if legitimately
embodied as citizens, or even as president, within the national
frame. Bea is certainly not thinking this: she is too busy blaming the
"darkies." Or maybe the "thing" of a woman parodies Lincoln's
promise, revealing the bodies of light and dark women to be
"things" his proclamation did not liberate. Thus Lincoln's hat re-

minds us that the nation holds out a promise of emancipation and a pornographic culture both. And that, as Delilah says of Peola's picture, "It never done her justice."[48]

NOTES

My special thanks to Andy Parker, Corey Creekmur, Laura Kipnis, Michael Warner, Tom Stillinger, and to many members of the English Institute audience for their inspiring and challenging conversation.

1. Frank Presbrey, *The History and Development of Advertising* (New York: Doubleday, Doran, 1929), 625.

2. Fannie Hurst, *Today Is Ladies' Day* (Rochester: Home Institute, 1939), 3.

3. Nella Larsen, *Passing*, in *Quicksand and Passing*, ed. Deborah E. McDowell (New Brunswick, N.J.: Rutgers University Press, 1986), 149.

4. Larsen, *Passing*, 150.

5. Larsen, *Passing*, 148–49.

6. Hortense J. Spillers, "Mama's Baby, Papa's Maybe: An American Grammar Book," *Diacritics* 17, no. 2 (Summer 1987): 77–80.

7. For an elaboration on the regimes of discipline (as concealment, as grotesque or carnivalesque display) that have expressed the bourgeois body, see Peter Stallybrass and Allon White, *The Politics and Poetics of Transgression* (Ithaca, N.Y.: Cornell University Press, 1986).

8. Deborah E. McDowell, "Introduction," *Quicksand and Passing*, xxvi–xxxi.

9. I take the notion of xenophilia (and much inspiration, besides) from Cameron Bailey, "Nigger/Lover: The Thin Sheen of Race in *Something Wild*," *Screen* 29, no. 4 (Autumn 1988): 30.

10. Larsen, *Passing*, 225.

11. Larsen, *Passing*, 235.

12. Elsewhere I elaborate on how American "women's culture" constructs literary "modes of containment"—notably in sentimental and melodramatic narrative—that both testify to women's colonization within a racist/patriarchal/capitalist culture and mark the self-construed obstacles to specifically political thought and action toward social change by bourgeois-identified women. See "The Female Complaint," *Social Text* 19/20 (Fall 1988): 237–59.

13. See, for example, Paula Baker, "The Domestication of Politics: Women and American Political Society, 1780–1920," *American Historical Review* 89, no. 3 (June 1984): 620–47.

14. Some major attempts to dissect masculine/Enlightenment citizenship are: Ruth H. Bloch, "The Gendered Meanings of Virtue in Revolutionary America," *Signs* 13, no. 1 (1987): 37–58; Mary G. Dietz, "Citizenship with a Feminist Face: The Problem with Maternal Thinking," *Political Theory* 13, no. 1 (February 1985): 19–37; Jean Bethke Elshtain, *Public Man, Private Woman* (Princeton, N.J.: Princeton University Press, 1981); Moira Gatens, "Towards a Feminist Theory of the Body," in *Crossing Boundaries: Feminisms and the Critique of Knowledges*, ed. Barbara Caine, E. A. Grosz, and Marie de Lepervanche (Winchester, Mass.: Allen and Unwin, 1988), 59–70; Joan B. Landes, *Women and the Public Sphere in the Age of the French Revolution* (Ithaca, N.Y.: Cornell University Press, 1988); Catherine A. MacKinnon, *Toward a Feminist Theory of the State* (Cambridge, Mass.: Harvard University Press,

1989); Anne Norton, *Reflections on Political Identity* (Baltimore: Johns Hopkins University Press, 1988); Carole Pateman, *The Sexual Contract* (Stanford, Calif.: Stanford University Press, 1988); Hanna Fenichel Pitkin, *Fortune Is a Woman: Gender and Politics in the Thought of Niccolò Machiavelli* (Berkeley: University of California Press, 1984); Iris Marion Young, "Polity and Group Difference: A Critique of the Ideal of Universal Citizenship," *Ethics* 99, no. 2 (January 1989): 250–74.

15. Powerful arguments against these quasi-objective appearances of masculine American political culture can be found in Iris Marion Young, "Impartiality and the Civic Public: Some Implications of Feminist Critique of Moral and Political Theory," in *Feminism as Critique*, ed. and introduced by Selya Benhabib and Drucilla Cornell (Minneapolis: University of Minnesota Press, 1987), 57–76, and Nancy Fraser, "What's Critical about Critical Theory? The Case of Habermas and Gender," in *Feminism as Critique*, 31–56.

16. Casting the mulatta as an Ur-figure of political and rhetorical indeterminacy is the perspective of Jane Gaines, "White Privilege and Looking Relations: Race and Gender in Feminist Film Theory," *Screen* 8, no. 4 (Autumn 1988): 12–27, and Hortense J. Spillers, "Notes on an Alternative Model — Neither/Nor," in *The Difference Within: Feminism and Critical Theory*, ed. Elizabeth Meese and Alice Parker (Philadelphia: John Benjamins, 1989), 165–87.

17. Spillers, "Mama's Baby, Papa's Maybe," 67.

18. Elaine Scarry, *The Body in Pain: The Making and Unmaking of the World* (New York: Oxford University Press, 1985), 108–9; Spillers, "Mama's Baby, Papa's Maybe."

19. The vast majority of critical work on *Imitation of Life*, which almost always reads the Stahl and Hurst versions through the lens of the vastly successful Sirk narrative, focuses on maternal and familial relations (to the exclusion of specifically political ones) as the central "problem" for which the narrative provides an answer. This is, in part, because of the generic (over)emphasis of film criticism, which marks this complex text as melodrama and therefore as generated by contradictions within the family. This criticism tends to denigrate Hurst's and Stahl's texts for "giving in" to sentimentality, and to elevate Sirk's more explicitly critical stance toward American culture. I think each side of these valuations is extremely limited. See Christine Gledhill's (otherwise excellent) "The Melodramatic Field: An Investigation," in *Home Is Where the Heart Is: Studies in Melodrama and the Woman's Film*, ed. Christine Gledhill (London: BFI, 1987), 5–39; E. Ann Kaplan, "Mothering, Feminism and Representation: The Maternal in Melodrama and the Woman's Film, 1910–40," in *Home Is Where the Heart Is*, 113–37; and Marina Heung, " 'What's the Matter With Sara Jane?': Daughters and Mothers in Douglas Sirk's *Imitation of Life*," *Cinema Journal* 26, no. 3 (Spring 1987): 21–43. Lucy Fischer's introduction to her critical edition of Sirk's screenplay gathers the most comprehensive bibliography available on this complex text and moves beyond the auteurist and generic impasses of the criticism. See "Three Way Mirror: *Imitation of Life*," in *Imitation of Life*, ed. Lucy Fischer (New Brunswick, N.J.: Rutgers University Press, 1991).

20. Other crucial transformations within this "complex text" (the "work" in its three versions) also take place over time. For example, the domestic plot about the rivalry between the white daughter and the white mother finds three different resolutions: in the novel, the daughter marries the mother's love interest; in Stahl's

film, there is no marriage and the two women "choose" each other; in Sirk's film, the love plot works, with the older woman settling in with the man. Also, the mulatta daughter becomes progressively pathetic, insufficient, and submissive to the dominant order over the course of the complex text. The aggregate narrative fate of both daughters, unable to benefit directly from their mothers' successes, suggests some obstacles to thinking/effecting a postpatriarchal female mode of inheritance in American culture and constitutes a counternarrative to the mothers' confidence in labor and capital's liberatory possibilities. I bracket these concerns here, focusing instead on the adult women, who are already living the overembodiment into which their daughters are only emerging.

21. Fannie Hurst, *Imitation of Life* (New York: Harper and Brothers, 1933), 1, 5. The bodily cataloguing to which I refer occurs throughout the chapter: this hybrid passage from its first and last sentences is its most economic formulation. Future references to the novel will be contained in the text.

22. The relation between cataloguing the woman's body and national identity has been beautifully worked out, from the point of view of its service to patriarchal national cultures, by Patricia Parker, "Rhetorics of Property: Exploration, Inventory, Blazon," in *Literary Fat Ladies: Rhetoric, Gender, Property* (New York: Methuen, 1987), 126–54. Bea's strategies of female identification are ambiguously related to the patriarchal strategies of control Parker sees, because her will-to-disembodiment and abstraction proleptically subverts the procedures she mimes.

23. The social history of women's movement into the American political public sphere follows the half-conscious Bea through the novel: Hurst taps not only the history of suffrage, of women's emergence as citizen-consumers, and of women's increased participation in the work force during World War I, but also the fear of women in the depression that their ideological and material gains would be lost. The bibliography on these coterminous movements is enormous: for general histories, see Martha Banta, *Imaging American Women: Idea and Ideals in Cultural History* (New York: Columbia University Press, 1987); Nancy F. Cott, *The Grounding of Modern Feminism* (New Haven, Conn.: Yale University Press, 1987); Robert L. Daniel, *American Women in the 20th Century* (Harcourt Brace Jovanovich, 1987); Sara M. Evans, *Born for Liberty: A History of Women in America* (New York: Free Press, 1989). For Hurst's reading of the complex movement toward female "personhood" and economic and sexual legitimacy during this period, see Fannie Hurst, "Are We Coming or Going?" *Vital Speeches of the Day*, December 3, 1934, 82–83; *Today Is Ladies' Day* (Rochester: Home Institute, 1939); "A Crisis in the History of Women: Let Us Have Action Instead of Lip-Service," *Vital Speeches of the Day*, May 15, 1943, 479–80.

24. I describe the national public space as fundamentally "capitalist" following Simon Frith, who argues that the notion of "capitalist culture" addresses the "ideological experience" of capitalism not fully accounted for by traditional formulations of economic practice. Simon Frith, "Hearing Secret Harmonies," in *High Theory/Low Culture: Analyzing Popular Television and Film*, ed. Colin MacCabe (New York: St. Martin's, 1986), 53–70.

25. There is a story yet to be told about the way advertising appears differentially in novels and films of the 1920s and 1930s. Film historians show that very early on, the frame of the movie screen, the shop window, and the product package borrowed one another's functions in the circuit of production and consumption and

of creating social value. On the early history of cinematic and commodity coordi-
nation, see Jeanne Allen, "The Film Viewer as Consumer," *Quarterly Review of Film
Studies* 5, no. 4 (Fall 1980): 481–99; Charles Eckert, "The Carole Lombard in Macy's
Window," *Quarterly Review of Film Studies* 3, no. 1 (Winter 1978): 1–21; Elizabeth
Ewen, "City Lights: Immigrant Women and the Rise of the Movies," *Signs* 5, no. 3,
Supplement (Spring 1980): S45-S65; Mary Ann Doane, "The Economy of Desire:
The Commodity Form in/of the Cinema," in "Female Representation and Con-
sumer Culture," ed. Jane Gaines and Michael Renov, *Quarterly Review of Film and
Video* 11, no. 1 (1989): 23–33; and Jane Gaines, "The Queen Christina Tie-Ups:
Convergence of Show Window and Screen," in "Female Representation and Con-
sumer Culture": 35–60. Jennifer Wicke argues that literature and advertising car-
ried on a similar (although less capital intensive) mutual dependency earlier, at
the turn of the century. See *Advertising Fictions: Literature, Advertisement, and
Social Reading* (New York:" Columbia University Press, 1988).

26. Peter Dobkin Hall, *The Organization of American Culture, 1700–1900:
Private Institutions, Elites, and the Origins of American Nationality* (New York:
New York University Press, 1984), 209–81; T. J. Jackson Lears, "From Salvation
to Self-Realization: Advertising and the Therapeutic Roots of the Consumer Culture, 1880–1930," in *The Culture of Consumption: Critical Essays in American
History, 1880–1980*, ed. Richard Wightman Fox and T. J. Jackson Lears (New
York: Pantheon, 1983), 1–38; Garth S. Jowett, "The Emergence of the Mass Society: The Standardization of American Culture, 1830–1920," *Prospects* 7 (1982):
207–28.

27. Robert B. Westbrook, "Politics as Consumption: Managing the Modern American Election," in Fox and Lears, *Culture of Consumption*, 1–38.

28. Vicki Gold Levi, ed., *Atlantic City: 125 Years of Ocean Madness*, text by Lee
Eisenberg (New York: Clarkson N. Potter, 1979), 28–31.

29. "H. Prynne" is really "Hiram Prynne," a Vermont businessman who uses his
initial in his business dealings for "Prynne and Company." I gather that the text
posits a genetic relation between Hawthorne's Hester and Hurst's Bea: Bea "inherits" from Hester the tactic of giving herself over to the name of the father (the A,
the "B.") in order to "pass" through public culture in a relatively dignified way.

30. Karl Marx, *Capital*, in *The Marx-Engels Reader*, ed. Robert C. Tucker (New
York: Norton, 1978), 320–21.

31. Earlier I linked Bea's tendency to link sexual desire with women (her
mother), pain, and bodily abstraction, but the scary return of this form of desire
in her bond with Virginia Eden may also respond to the "heterosexual revolution"
that accompanied the emergence of modern consumer culture and the modern
female consuming body. While capitalism made it possible to live outside of economic dependence on the nuclear family, the twenties witnessed strong ideological pressure on women to choose heterosociality as a component of the new consumer narcissism. "Beauty culture" (and here Eden surely suggests Helena
Rubenstein) was administered by women to women—but *for* men. See Mike Feath-
erstone, "The Body in Consumer Culture," *Theory, Culture and Society* 1, no. 2
(September 1982): 18–33; Rayna Rapp and Ellen Ross, "The Twenties' Backlash:
Compulsory Heterosexuality, the Consumer Family, and the Waning of Feminism,"
in *Class, Race, and Sex: The Dynamics of Control*, ed. Amy Swerdlow and Hanna
Lesinger (Boston: G. K. Hall, 1983), 93–107; John D'Emilio, "Capitalism and Gay

Identity," in *Powers of Desire: The Politics of Sexuality*, ed. Ann Snitow, Christine Stansell, and Sharon Thompson (New York: Monthly Review Press, 1983), 100–13.

32. W. F. Haug, *Critique of Commodity Aesthetics: Appearance, Sexuality and Advertising in Capitalist Society*, trans. Robert Bock, introduction by Stuart Hall (Minneapolis: University of Minnesota Press, 1986), 50.

33. Robert W. Rydell, *All the World's a Fair: Visions of Empire at American International Expositions, 1876–1916* (Chicago: University of Chicago Press, 1984), 46.

34. Presbrey, *Advertising*, 360.

35. Presbrey, *Advertising*, 356, 382–84.

36. Arthur F. Marquette, *Brands, Trademarks and Good Will: The Story of the Quaker Oats Company* (New York: McGraw-Hill, 1967), 137–41; Joseph Boskin, *Sambo: The Rise and Demise of an American Jester* (New York: Oxford University Press, 1986), 139.

37. Hazel V. Carby, *Reconstructing Womanhood: The Emergence of the Afro-American Woman Novelist* (New York: Oxford University Press, 1987), 3–6. See also Robert W. Rydell, "The World's Columbian Exposition of 1893: Racist Underpinnings of a Utopian Artifact," *Journal of American Culture* 1, no. 2 (Summer 1978): 253–75; Ann Massa, "Black Women in the 'White City,'" *Journal of American Studies* 8, no. 3 (December 1974): 319–37; Elliott M. Rudwick and August Meier, "Black Man in the 'White City': Negroes and the Columbia Exposition, 1893," *Phylon* 26, no. 4 (Winter 1965): 354–61. For a discussion of how African-American women's particular marginality at the fair linked up to its production of the modern/American/woman, see Banta, *Imaging American Women*, 499–550.

38. Marquette, *Brands, Trademarks and Good Will*, 146.

39. This ad is taken from Robert Atwan, Donald McQuade, and John W. Wright, *Edsels, Luckies, and Frigidaires: Advertising the American Way* (New York: Delta, 1979), 92.

40. While Stahl's *Imitation of Life* was vastly popular in African-American communities (Thomas Cripps, *Slow Fade to Black: The Negro in American Film, 1900–1942* [New York: Oxford University Press, 1977], 303), its depiction of the reproduction of American racist and class hegemonies in the household of Bea and Delilah has provoked a long tradition of negative criticism. The paradigm text is Sterling Brown, "*Imitation of Life*: Once a Pancake," *Opportunity* 13 (March 1935): 87–88. Following Brown's example: William Harrison, "The Negro and the Cinema," *Sight and Sound* 8, no. 29 (Spring 1939): 17; Peter Noble, *The Negro in Films* (London: Skelton Robinson, 1948), 61–63; Donald Bogle, *Toms, Coons, Mulattoes, Mammies and Bucks: An Interpretive History of Blacks in American Film* (New York: Viking, 1973), 57–60; Cripps, *Slow Fade to Black*, 301–3; Jeremy G. Butler, "*Imitation of Life*: Style and the Domestic Melodrama," *Jump Cut* 32 (1987): 25–28; Donald Bogle, *Blacks in American Films and Television: An Encyclopedia* (New York: Garland, 1988), 113–15. For a brief history of the film's production and reception, see Thomas Schatz, *The Genius of the System: Hollywood Filmmaking in the Studio Era* (New York: Pantheon, 1988), 231–32.

41. Another facet to the film's cultural work in this scene is the metonymic linkage of Delilah to the body of white ethnic American immigrants. The man for whom Delilah produces her cartoon image is an Italian actor who engages in his own grotesque comic physical performance, complete with thick accent: Stahl shoots him as a direct parallel to Delilah, with Bea in the spatial center. Since

Delilah is explicitly an "immigrant" from the South, her juxtaposition with him and
their equivalent service functions (helping Bea produce a business, performing
slapstick comedy) signify yet another relay the film makes among social margin-
alities in non-melting-pot America.

42. Bailey, "Nigger/Lover," 40.

43. This is Paul Willemen's phrase and idea, founding *Screen*'s revival of Sirk's
reputation in the 1970s. Following this line, many cinema theorists and historians
valorize Sirk's avant-garde exploitation of Hollywood's laws of genre: he is said to
have worked so excessively within the melodrama as to have saturated it with irony
(along with the American culture that requires its consoling release). While I do
not disagree with this general reading of Sirk's political position, this section of
the essay explores the limits of his irony as it circulates around the female body.
Paul Willemen, "Towards an Analysis of the Sirkean System," *Screen* 13, no. 4
(Winter 1972/3): 128–34; see Fischer, *Imitation*, for the extensive Sirk bibliography.
My reading of Sirk's irony is more in line with that of Michael E. Selig, "Contradiction and Reading: Social Class and Sex Class in *Imitation of Life*," *Wide Angle* 10,
no. 4 (1988): 14–23.

44. The lyrics to this song signify that the discursive, erotic, and political space
between Sarah Jane and Annie is entirely an effect of Sarah Jane's "white" skin,
which can approximate for her a fantasy of racial invisibility. "The loneliest word I
heard of is 'empty,' and anything empty is sad. An empty purse can make a good
girl bad, you hear me Dad? The loneliest word I heard of is 'empty,' empty things
make me so mad. So fill me up with what I formerly had. Now Venus, you know,
was loaded with charms, and look at what happened to her. Waitin' around, she's
minus two arms—could happen to me, no sir! Now is the time to fill what is empty,
fill my life brim full of charms. Help me refill these empty, empty, empty arms."
The first time we see Sarah Jane dance erotically to its score is in her bedroom—
where, during the dance, she not only kicks a stuffed animal (a lamb) but steps
threateningly near a record of *Porgy and Bess* lying on the floor.

45. James Harvey, "Sirkumstantial Evidence," *Film Comment* 14, no. 4 (July–
August 1978): 55. Here is the entire passage:

HARVEY: Or the funeral scene.

SIRK: The funeral itself is an irony. All that pomp.

HARVEY: But surely there is no irony when Mahalia Jackson sings. The emotion is
large and simple and straightforward.

SIRK: It's strange. Before shooting those scenes, I went to hear Mahalia Jackson at
UCLA, where she was giving a recital. I knew nothing about her. But here on the
stage was this large, homely, ungainly woman—and all those shining, beautiful
young faces turned up to her, and absolutely smitten with her. It was strange and
funny, and very impressive. I tried to get some of that experience into the picture.
We photographed her with a three-inch lens, so that every unevenness in the face
stood out.

HARVEY: You don't think the funeral scene is highly emotional?

SIRK: I know, I know but I was surprised at that effect.

46. Richard Dyer, "White," *Screen* 29, no. 4 (Autumn 1988): 49.

47. *Encyclopaedia Britannica*, 11th ed., 703–10.

48. This is from Stahl, 1934.

For a Practical Aesthetics
George Yúdice

The neoconservative agenda to dismantle the National Endowment for the Arts (NEA) is, unsurprisingly, part of a larger strategy to reverse the gains made in the past two decades by gays and lesbians, racial and ethnic minorities, women, and other subordinated and subaltern groups. Why attack the aesthetic now? With civil rights on the retreat, the relatively protected sphere of the aesthetic has been foregrounded as a major terrain of political contestation, especially since it has provided forums for addressing crucial ethical concerns in ways that the mass media are disinclined to adopt. Up to now it has proven easier to withdraw advertising from a television station to pressure it to change its programming than to convince a panel of peers and experts what criteria they should use to judge what is or is not art. Of course, the powers that be can appoint one of their own to the NEA, but even that attempt to coopt is fraught with many indeterminacies, evident in John Frohnmayer's flip-flops on NEA grants to "offensive" artists. This observation does not, however, provide support for any claims for aesthetic autonomy. The belief, if not the rhetoric, that art appeals to a universal human spirit beyond the reaches of particular interests is unlikely to survive the soft cynicism of a Warhol soup can, the gendered politics of representation of a Cindy Sherman pose, the muckraking installations of a Hans Haacke, an ACT UP zap, or a Guerrilla Girls blitzkrieg on a gallery or museum, not to speak of the sexual politics of Women Against Pornography or the censorious grumblings of the religious right. Given the politicization and commodification of art, few people today can seriously identify the aesthetic with the realm of freedom.

The new contestatory movements have provoked a counteroffensive by various sectors of the right: fundamentalists (anti-obscenity and anti-abortion), nationalists (antiflagburning and English Only advocates), and political conservatives (anti–affirmative action and anti–civil rights). Having learned from the new social movements that the personal and the cultural are political, the right has openly declared itself the ideological foe not only of subaltern groups seeking enfranchisement but also of liberal, humanistic expressions of universality, such as the "aesthetic," that guarantee freedom of practice to their enemies.[1] In what follows, I focus on the reasons why these political, moral, and economic issues have converged on the question of the aesthetic, a dimension of social practice that the social sciences have largely ignored. I also pay particular attention to how current conservative attempts to maintain hegemony do so at the expense of gays and lesbians, who in turn have repoliticized their cultural practices.

The conservative backlash to the politicization of sexuality and other "intimate matters"[2] reached the pinnacle of high-handedness in the summer of 1989 when Jesse Helms proposed a ban on public funding for " 'obscene and indecent' art and for any work that 'denigrates, debases or reviles a person, group or class of citizens on the basis of race, creed, sex, handicap, age or national origin.' "[3] The motive was, as everyone no doubt remembers, the offense that Mr. and Mrs. Helms took at the flagrant display of homoeroticism in an exhibition of Robert Mapplethorpe's photographs, which was canceled by the Corcoran Gallery. "This Mapplethorpe fellow," said Helms, "was an acknowledged homosexual. He's dead now, but the homosexual theme goes throughout his work."[4] It is not the art work per se that Helms finds offensive; it is the group ethos conveyed by it. That Helms objected to grants awarded to "three acknowledged lesbian writers," without having even read their work, bears this out.[5] (Also provoking the proposed funding ban was Andrés Serrano's exhibit at the Southeastern Center for Contemporary Art in Winston-Salem, North Carolina, which included a "blasphemous" photograph of Christ in the artist's urine: *Piss Christ*.)

When I read the *New York Times* that summer morning, I wanted to be outraged but I could not help feeling fascinated by the "logic" of Helms's ploys. If all these contestatory groups could challenge the sacrosanct category of the aesthetic by insisting on questions of "content" — their lifestyle or group ethos — why shouldn't the right also participate in the dismantling of the universal by advocating its own ethos: fundamentalism, homophobia, nationalism? If blacks and other minorities protested against defamation, why shouldn't the right protest the defamation of its values? The very language of the proposed ban was a parody of civil rights legislation and the rhetoric of subject positions around which contemporary social movements wage their struggles. Helms twisted the arguments to the advantage of conservatives. Recognizing that federally sanctioned public avenues of expression legitimize the current practice of making rights claims on the basis of group ethos, Helms moved to close off those avenues. For two decades feminists, gay and lesbian activists, and racial and ethnic minorities had waged a politics of identity by which they sought self-determination over their "intimate matters." They had sought to participate actively in those public spheres in which decisions on such matters are made. The conservative counterattack, by appropriating their language, ironically made it more difficult for these movements to set the agenda of public discourse.

The irony of Helms's actions was not lost on professional philistine Hilton Kramer. In a *New York Times* article entitled "Is Art Above the Laws of Decency?" Kramer pried open the contradictions of an artistic sphere falsely perceived as autonomous. "Is art now to be considered such an absolute value," he asked, "that no other standard — no standard of taste, no social or moral standard — is to be allowed to play any role in determining what sort of art it is appropriate for the government to support?"[6] Against the likes of the senators, artists, and art critics who defended the "freedom of expression" protected by the Constitution — Christo, for example, wrote to the House subcommittee on civil rights that "as an artist and a citizen, I feel that nothing may ever inhibit or threaten the First Amendment right of speech and dissent"[7] — Kramer retorted that such a freedom does not guarantee public subvention. Knowing full well that the means of public participation of many subaltern groups has been recently facilitated by certain state agencies (most notably those dealing with the arts and education), Kramer argued for a public sphere in which the state does not intervene on behalf of any groups. This, in effect, amounts to a reprivatization of many of the issues that have entered public debate since civil rights, for without the resources provided by the state, many subaltern groups would not have a spitting chance against those groups that "privately" dominate the public.

As regards the institution of art, Kramer advocated that public policy should be to endorse, by funding, only those expressions that meet the standards of arbiters who answer to the public. On the basis of this criterion Kramer argued that the arbiters of public funding for the Mapplethorpe and Serrano exhibitions proved to be irresponsible. Among other reasons, he found them to be either hopelessly naive or disingenuously hypocritical in permitting "false avant-garde" promoters of "*an attitude toward life*" to be confused with the "authentic avant-garde . . . which everyone knows no longer exists."[8] Echoing the position of the Frankfurt School and more recent cultural theorists like Peter Bürger, Kramer's diagnosis of the situation of art in late capitalist society is really a postmortem: art died because it was absorbed by the logic of capitalism, it became pure commodity. Another contributor to the demise of its autonomy is "that famous 'cutting edge' that looks more and more to an *extraartistic content* for its raison-d'être."[9] Consequently, if artists themselves have abjured the sanctity of autonomy, it can only be "sheer hypocrisy" that "we are being asked to accept the unacceptable in the name of art."

Philistine that he is, Kramer would, of course, allow any "attitude toward life" in private. But even such a concession cannot save contemporary artistic practice because the art world has failed, according to Kramer, to effectively police the public/private divide; consequently, other arbiters of taste — namely Congress — will have to police the "autonomous" institution of art. The new arbiters will have to "distinguish between art and life" because the art world no longer demonstrates that ability. The entry of "life" into the hitherto protected sphere of art has made art a "threat to public decency."

There were many oppositional responses to Congress's invasion of artistic autonomy. Most, like the *New York Times*'s Olympian editorial of July 28, 1989, sought to protect "the process carefully legislated to insulate art from *crude politics*."[10] If the liberal response can be expected from the *Times*, it is somewhat more surprising for alternative institutions to strip the art they exhibit from its political reality. This is in fact what Susan Wyatt, director of Artists Space in

New York, attempted to do with respect to the exhibition "Witnesses: Against Our Vanishing" by alerting John Frohnmayer, then recently appointed chairman of the NEA, to the potential controversy that artist and AIDS activist David Wojnarowicz might set off with his catalogue essay "Post Cards from America: X-Rays from Hell." In it he excoriated Helms, Representative William Dannemeyer, and Cardinal O'Connor for their opposition to safe-sex education. Wyatt's action led to a hasty withdrawal of funding, which was subsequently restored. The catalogue, however, was not supported, thus complying with the injunction to keep art and "dirty politics" separate. The outcome demonstrated that even alternative institutions cannot be relied on to press the political-aesthetic claims of contestatory groups and social movements. They are, after all, part of the official art world and must look after their own assets.

As I stated earlier, most responses to the conservative attack have been liberal affirmations of freedom of expression and other civil rights and liberties whose most salient embodiment is the aesthetic. In order to understand why the aesthetic has been singled out for attack, it is essential to review, at least briefly, its role as an intermediary instance — between the individual and the state apparatuses — in which citizens are formed and, putatively, identify with the given national culture. In his recent *The Ideology of the Aesthetic*, Terry Eagleton argues that the notion of an autonomous, self-regulating, autotelic mode like the aesthetic negotiates a tenuous balance between, on the one hand, the rule of reason and state and, on the other, sensual inclination, intimately linked to the "irrational" and unruly manifestations of desire, will, and pleasure.[11] In the Kantian version, for example, aesthetic judgment strikes this balance by inscribing in the subject a "lawfulness without a law" that parallels the Rousseauian "authority which is not an authority" of the ideal political state.[12] As such, the aesthetic is a major ideological instrument by which the bourgeoisie constructed and maintained hegemony throughout modernity. In the eighteenth century it reconciled self-determination, the "casual, affable, taken-for-granted style of the stereotypical aristocrat,"[13] with the law of instrumental reason by which the bourgeoisie exercises the will to power. The aesthetic, in fact, was conceived of as the sensuous inscription of the law. In the nineteenth century it struck an "uneasy alliance of patrician and philistine, culture and society," as a "spiritually disabled bourgeoisie [was] constrained to go to school with an aestheticizing Right which speaks of organic unity, intuitive certainty and the free play of the mind."[14]

In keeping with the negotiated conflictuality at the heart of the concept of hegemony, the aesthetic, since its initial theoretical articulations in the eighteenth century, has had to confront challenges from those sectors the contingency of history has moved into contestatory positions: the working class,[15] rival sectors of the industrial and commercial bourgeoisie, and, more recently, new subject positions — immigrant, anti- and postcolonialist, gender and ethnically based, and so on. "Standards of taste," to use Hilton Kramer's phrase, constitute the cement of hegemony. Such a "cement," of course, begs the question of foundations, for the value projected by aesthetic hegemony is ultimately premised on a series of exclusions, clearly recognized by those most likely to lose out. Any person, object, or practice found to be offensive to prevailing standards of taste will have no legitimate place within the public sphere.[16] Social harmony is bought at the expense of those whose own tastes are not only aesthetically unacceptable but also, more importantly, potentially contestatory. Thus, when artistic practices are not perceived as contributing to the hegemony of the prevailing order — as in the current attacks on homoeroticism and obscenity — the law must manifest itself overtly in order to quash them.

The present conjuncture finds us in a struggle of conservative morals not only against contestatory groups that do not conform to liberal standards of taste but also against the consumer culture that has catered to them as targeted audiences. Now lacking conviction in universal categories of human value as a result of civil rights successes and the inroads made by new social movements that threaten the hegemony of the patriarchal, white, heterosexual status quo, liberals even find it hard to defend their political label, as Michael Dukakis failed to do, to his chagrin, in the 1988 presidential election. The liberal stance tends to bracket questions of moral judgment. But contestatory groups on the left and the right have forced such concerns onto the political agenda. It is for this reason that the question of aesthetics has been foregrounded, forced to emerge from its "immediate" and spontaneous workings to be scrutinized. Its very mediatory role is now challenged. Whenever such a struggle for hegemony occurs, culturalist or aesthetic arguments are no longer naturalized; they no longer make unquestioned common sense. Under these circumstances, the very notion of hegemony is put into crisis; perhaps we have entered a posthegemonic phase in which it is beside the point to seek to "cement" the heterogeneity of social actors in the medium of the cultural or the aesthetic.

Given the weakness of the liberal position on the edifying quality of aesthetic practice—recent *New York Times* editorials favoring reauthorization of the NEA make the perennial aesthetic arguments that "art touches the soul," civilizes us, and gives us access to a "universal language"[17]—a new and more convincing argument must be found. In a culture riven by increased social stratification (as the problem of the homeless and the class-linked intraracial conflict over the Thomas nomination to the Supreme Court make all too evident), ethnic controversy (which belies the "gorgeous mosaics" of multiculturalism), gender and sexuality struggles (which have driven a wedge between equally conservative women and men over sexual harassment and reproductive rights), and so on, the appeal to the universal confirmation of human dignity through artistic practice and reception is convincing to few. It is the feeble weapon of those vested interests—the major arts organizations—that have more or less supported the status quo of propriety and market criteria. As a Guerrilla Girls poster states: "Relax, Senator Helms, the art world *is* your kind of place!"[18] Out of expediency, fear, or indifference to the claims of subaltern groups made via "extra-artistic" means (Kramer's phrase again), the art world has opted for policing the offending elements. Institutional self-censorship[19] is a corrective to those artists who sneaked through the cracks, advocating an "attitude toward life" in their practice. As the *New York Times* editorial quoted earlier states, the NEA need not be scrapped, only "cleaned up."

What, then, are the viable contestatory responses? To be frank, nothing viable is forthcoming from the institutions themselves. This, despite bold gestures like Joseph Papp's rejection of NEA funding for the Public Theater. Through such a gesture a moral point is driven home about the autonomy of the aesthetic sphere. But that is precisely what can no longer be tolerated in a multicultural democracy in which certain groups have been consistently stereotyped, censored, and excluded. Social injustice must be addressed directly and not solely in the name of autonomy. Viable responses, however, may be found among the contestatory groups themselves, among whom many artists have chosen to work no longer just as artists but also as creative promoters of an "attitude toward life."

A painter friend of mine, active in GLAAD (Gay and Lesbian Alliance Against Defamation), ACT UP (AIDS Coalition to Unleash Power), and Gran Fury (ACT UP's art collective), felt that his long-standing policy of boycotting arts organizations was vindicated by this public funding fiasco. Not that he has anything against the idea of an institutionally sanctioned public sphere in which freedom of expression is guaranteed; on the contrary, he argues, the problem is that arts organizations have only constrained such a public sphere, at least as regards art that projects a gay "attitude toward life." Given the two complementary systems in which the art world operates — the market (galleries and auction houses tacitly supported by museum practice) and the nonprofit/public foundation overseen by "expert" panels — there is little chance that a truly contestatory art will be funded. These are systems of exclusion that work for the benefit of the status quo. His own practice — posters and other public works incorporating explicitly homoerotic reworkings of classical iconography in response to homophobic representations, especially as a result of the AIDS epidemic — which projects this group ethos, has not been deemed acceptable (except at AIDS art exhibitions, quite frequently sponsored by groups not usually involved in the art world). If art were truly autonomous, "extra-artistic content" would be of no consequence. This is not, however, the reality. The art world, which accepts even the harshest challenges to its institutional framework so long as they continue to nourish the frame, that is, *textualize* the institution, excludes those challenges that dispense with the frame itself because that is the most effective means to dissolve it, thus opening up aesthetic practice to decisions over which the institution has no control. Art history and criticism, even when they get beyond the disciplinary criteria of masters, national formations, and so on, nevertheless reinforce this neutralization of the political by reliance on textualization.

Take, for example, Cindy Sherman's deconstruction of socially constructed representations of women in patriarchal society. Despite the challenge to the authority of representation, her work is easily accommodated within the art world. To the extent that she works with subject matter that has always been in the public eye of Western modernity her work inherits its legitimacy. Not so with gay sexuality, especially in the age of AIDS. The advantage accorded to work that questions the institutional frame so as to expand it and nourish it — often unwittingly celebrating it — is a point cogently put forth by David Trend. The textualization of the institutional frame cannot "chang[e] the terms by which works are made, distributed, and received" because it "implicitly supports the system by speaking its language and replicating its rules."[20] The "politics of representation" engaged in by this type of art can even end up "fetishizing the very signifiers of taste and connoisseurship that lie on the surface of class-bound racism, misogyny, and greed." Of course, as such fetishized deconstructions become commodified — Sherman's images, like Madonna's, produce the same kind of pleasure that the original reifications did — they reach wider audiences who may or may not gain insight from the flouting of stock representations. This play on the constructedness of images, however, does not necessarily lead to changing the conditions that produced them in the first place.

Such a politics of representation would not seem to further very much the agenda of AIDS activists. Imagine representations that cited, in a Cindy Shermanesque way, the stock images of people with AIDS. What impact would such images have on our attitude toward pain and suffering? The problem would be, of course, that their textualization would preclude imagining alternatives to the current compulsion to represent AIDS, to give it a human face, which has resulted in mass media representations that merely stereotype. Countless news specials, panel discussions, documentaries, and docudramas follow the conventions of the adventure or human interest story, the melodrama or the naturalist tale of dissolution: protagonists are either researchers on the trail of the "magic bullet" that will garner a Nobel prize; "innocent victims" like Ryan White who can rally the support of a nation; or the wasting horrors (gays and intravenous drug users) dying in overcrowded hospital wards.[21]

Short of scuttling the whole system, Trend, like my friend, recommends transforming the material conditions of the institution: means of production, distribution, reception, publicity, and so on. The groups that have taken up this challenge — Feminists in Exile, Guerrilla Girls, Mothers of Medusa, PESTS, and others like GLAAD and ACT UP — do not engage in abstract or distanced deconstructions of the frameworks of representation. Instead, they work to open up new "unofficial" spaces both outside and within institutions, combating stigmatizing representations, developing "nontraditional audiences," serving the needs of particular communities, and simultaneously publicizing their practice for wider access. In this process, according to Trend, such groups serve two important functions: "coalition building" and "recovering the 'public' function of art."

I should like to emphasize that in recovering this public function, the practices of these groups are no longer "art" in its modern, institutionally autonomous sense. Without rehearsing the full argument regarding the autonomy of different value spheres (cognitive, moral, aesthetic), as posited by Peter Bürger, Jürgen Habermas, and others and summarized by Eagleton, it suffices to point out that the cultural legitimacy that undergirded such autonomy seems to have reached an irreconcilable crisis. The practices of new social actors have put pressure on institutions to break frame and deal with individuals in ways that do not reproduce the separation of spheres. Thus the boundaries between the aesthetic, the political, the legal, the biomedical, and so forth have been blurred.

Both the conservative and the new social movements deny that any practice is apolitical. On the one hand, morality, for conservatives, is the legitimizing principle. It is precisely for that reason that even the relative autonomy of liberal ideology is untenable for them; it enables emerging groups to erode their ascendancy by contesting representations in the name of art — what Kramer objected to in the article quoted earlier. Hence their politics of reprivatization. The new social movements, on the other hand, challenge autonomy on the basis of exclusionary practices that have always responded to the interests and morality of institutional gatekeepers. Hence their politics of making public hitherto depoliticized (i.e., privatized) needs and "intimate matters."

The public sphere celebrated by Habermas, in which there was "no authority beside that of the better argument,"[22] was founded, as he himself recognizes, on the authority of patriarchy (and we should add class privilege, racism, and colonialism). That is, the "public" presupposed a sphere of privacy rooted in the patriarchal conjugal family.[23] On this account, the novel emerged as the aesthetic form that publicly represented subjectivity as "the innermost core of the private."[24] This grounding for the public/private divide has, of course, changed. And the novel, an art form rooted in bourgeois institutions, is no longer the form through which the hegemonic totality of the social formation is inscribed in the constitution of subjectivity. On the contrary, the novel, like autobiography and the diary, is used by subaltern groups to construct particular rather than overarching hegemonic identities. It is not the entire social formation that reads Zora Neale Hurston or Ed Vega or Paula Gunn Allen, nor has a latter-day, multicultural Lukács emerged to argue that "the complex, capillary factors of development of the *whole* society"[25] are embodied in the particularity of the subaltern rather than the "higher consciousness" of the "world historical individual."

Is it possible, then, to speak of an aesthetic dimension that can contribute to change across the terrain of the social formation? I think so, but in this sense the aesthetic could only be understood outside of the dominant accounts of autonomy in which it has been straitjacketed throughout modernity. It could be understood, for example, in terms of the "community counter-practices" that Trend advocates not only as something that art *brings to* a community but also as aesthetic practices *by which group identity and ethos are formed*.

But what do I mean by this aesthetic dimension of the process of group formation? Taking as a point of departure Bakhtinian and Gramscian understandings of the cultural and ideological space in which all forms of consciousness necessarily take shape, it can be said that the aesthetic dimension is constituted by what I call, after Bakhtin, an "authoring process." It consists of the ways in which sets of individuals, marked by certain features socially recognized as common to them, negotiate and manage the heterogeneity of perspectives by which they are variously imaged, valued, and devalued, in this way or that, on the basis of class, sex, race, religion, regional provenance, and other "subject positions." This process, of course, is specific to the ensemble of institutions that make up a social formation. Furthermore, given the constraints imposed by such institutional configurations, individuals and groups of individuals are not free to simply construct their identities. That is why I use the words *negotiate* and *manage*, which belong to the conceptual repertoire of Gramsci's notion of hegemony but are useful in thinking through what may be a posthegemonic condition.

Gramsci posited that class identity can never be assumed a priori because it is the result of a complex struggle fought out on many terrains, in relation to diverse institutions. Class unity is an effect of the overall hegemony—the "compromise equilibrium" the group that holds moral and cultural leadership strikes with "the groups over which hegemony is to be exercised"[26]—and thus is never possible on its own terms. On a more microanalytical level, Bakhtin argues that the very materiality of consciousness, discourse, is never the property of the individual or group because it is always "populated—overpopulated—with the intentions of others."[27] The particular style and ethos of an individual or group is the result of an "authoring process" by which a "speech will" is manifested in the choice and manipulation of particular genres.[28] Identity, then, is not a given but a *practice*, a *deployment* across the institutionalized terrain of a social formation because the genres through which such "authorship" takes place are institutionally bound. Social change is thus a function of circumstances that alter the generic arrangements of institutions—especially those of identity, on the basis of which individuals are given access or excluded—which in turn alter the institutional arrangements of a social formation.

A parenthetical commentary is in order here. Although Bakhtin has important insights on the social constitution of discursive identity, his work focuses on the novel as the aesthetic form that "orchestrates the heteroglossia" or discursive diversity that is the condition of possibility of authorial identity. Unlike Habermas, who turns to the bourgeois novel to help explain the public sphere of the eighteenth century, Bakhtin construes the novel as a modality that undermines the generic constraints of any institutionalized discourse. Furthermore, he attributes a transformative, if not emancipatory, capacity to this process, for it projects the image of a society in which institutional arrangements have been disarticulated and reaccentuated in new ways.[29]

Of course, in my reading of Bakhtin I take the novel-as-authoring-process to be a metaphor of identity formation mediated by the discursive formations of others. Bakhtin himself provides a precedent for this metaphorical interpretation in "Forms of Time and Chronotope in the Novel."[30] In this essay he argues that different chronotopes—historically specific forms of social time-space arrangements—are discernible in the novel and stand for particular arrangements of public/private relations. Among these, he privileges the absolute publicity or "public wholeness" (i.e., with no forms of privacy, hence of depoliticization) of the chronotope that he reconstructs for ancient Greek romance.[31] Such a reconstruction is open to criticism, especially for its idealized construal of a society that excluded women, children, and slaves from the personhood provided by publicity (they were "private" individuals, relagated to an inferior status). Nonetheless, despite this oversight and despite the tendency to construe, as Lukács does, the novel as the image, albeit heteroglossic, of the "whole of society," it is important that Bakhtin posits an (admittedly utopian) possibility of reprojecting, through the "authoring process," the absolute publicity that enables an ongoing contestation of the institutional arrangements by which public/private relations are fixed, to the political disadvantage of some groups.

In the context of my discussion of group ethos, a posthegemonic adaptation of Gramsci's and Bakhtin's ideas helps explain how the constitution of identity takes place through means that are simultaneously aesthetic (authoring) and political (reconfiguring institutional arrangements). But the particular relationship (opposition, overlap, complementation, coincidence, etc.) of these spheres can be dealt with only in relation to specific historical conjunctures. Knee-jerk proclamations of the essential goodness or freedom of heterogeneity miss this point. Such a heterogeneity is an idealistic abstraction that eludes the social significance, which is always relational, of particular practices. It is, indeed, another idealized, culturalist form of the bourgeois aesthetic, which both progressive and conservative social movements reject.[32] Which brings me now to the problem of a *politics of identity* under circumstances, generally proclaimed to be postmodern, that place legitimacy and hegemony in question.

Habermas offers a universal pragmatics based on the idealistic premise of a "communicative rationality," which putatively legitimizes forms of democratic self-government that negotiate the reciprocal influence of "system" (economy and state administration) and "lifeworld" ("culture" broadly conceived).[33] The problem, as many critics have pointed out, is that this model of rationality relies a priori on a series of dichotomies (e.g., the *structural* nature of the system and the *hermeneutic* character of the lifeworld) that cannot account for the value that social interaction takes on when construed as partaking in *both* elements of the dichotomies. Nancy Fraser, for example, demonstrates that "the domestic sphere has a structural as well as an interpretive dimension and . . . the official economic and state spheres have an interpretive as well as a structural dimension."[34] By so doing she unveils the "gender subtext" that Habermas fails to discern in the system/lifeworld paradigm. For example, the system, insofar as it includes the welfare state, is internally dualized and gendered. It includes

> two basic kinds of programs — "masculine" social insurance
> programs tied to primary labor force participation and designed to
> benefit principal breadwinners, and "feminine" relief programs
> oriented to what are understood as domestic "failures," in short, to
> families without a male breadwinner. Not surprisingly, these two
> welfare subsystems are separate and unequal.[35]

The arts funding controversy and the ways in which it involves the politics of gay identity cannot be fully understood without taking into account that the late capitalist welfare state translates the interpretations of people's needs into legal, administrative, and therapeutic terms, thus reformulating the political reality of those interpretations.[36] According to Fraser, the conflicts among rival interpretations of needs in contemporary society reveal that we inhabit a "new social space" unlike the ideal public sphere posited by Habermas in which the better argument prevails. We have already confronted the contestants of this social sphere in the controversies brought on by the intrusion of a gay "attitude toward life" into the domain of state bureaucracies (arts foundations) established to adjudicate entitlements based on merit, needs, and other criteria. The controversies involve the viability of the "experts" who oversee these institutions, the legitimacy of claims made by groups on the basis of an ethos, and the " 'reprivatization' discourses of constituencies seeking to repatriate newly problematized needs to their former domestic or official economic enclaves."[37] To the latter we have to add the *aesthetic* enclave that remains acceptable to liberals even at the expense of censorship and policing ("no need to scrap the NEA, just clean it up") and that conservatives like Helms and Kramer would dismantle so that contestatory groups cannot avail themselves of it to transform their ethical claims into rights and entitlements. In this new social context, and given the conservative move to impede the access to rights, the grounds for entitlement have shifted to a paradigm of interpretability. In any case, classic liberal discourse accords rights to individuals and not groups. Group entitlement must take place, then, in a *sur-*

rogate terrain such as language (for Latinos and other ethnic minorities) or the family and sexuality (for gays and lesbians and women's groups) — that is, the particular experience around which groups, especially subordinated and stigmatized groups, constitute their identity.

Such a politics of identity has to be understood in the specificity of U.S. culture, which is not to say that a politics of identity does not operate, in different ways, in other national formations.[38] "Racial" movements could be understood to be the first of the "new social movements" or "new antagonisms" that call into question forms of subordination (bureaucratization and consumer commodification of "private" life) in the post–World War II United States.[39] Among their challenges is the push to legitimize the adjudication and legislation of rights on the basis of group need rather than the possessive individualist terms that traditionally define rights discourse. Martha Minow gives the following explanation of the shift to a politics of identity:

> One predictable kind of struggle in the United States arises among religious and ethnic groups. Here, the dominant legal framework of rights rhetoric is problematic, for it does not easily accommodate groups. Religious freedom, for example, typically protects individual freedom from state authority or from oppression by private groups. Ethnic groups lack even that entry point into constitutional protection, except insofar as individuals may make choices to speak or assemble in relation to a chosen group identity.[40]

This latter choice, which entails all the aesthetic dimensions of Bakhtin's "authoring process," helps explain why some gays and lesbians have adopted an "ethnic" self-characterization. According to Steven Epstein, "it has permitted a form of group organization that is particularly suited to the American experience."[41] Rather than language or "ethnic culture," however, sexuality provided the terrain of "self-fulfillment" and "personal actualization" throughout the seventies and early eighties.[42] AIDS, of course, has changed things, which is *not* to say that it has removed sexuality as the basis of gay identity. It has, rather, shifted its emphasis, which is now "less on seeing sex as a form of celebration and community and more on seeing it as a means of finding security and commitment."[43] And it is for the advancement of commitment that gay ethos has creatively come up with new means — safe sex — to check the spread of the epidemic,[44] as well as rallied to recognize its own diversity (traversed by racial and ethnic as well as gender and age differences) and to act politically to entitle all of its diverse components.[45]

AIDS has reaccentuated gay identity by thrusting it into the purview of the most important social institutions: public health, housing, and insurance systems, national and state legislatures, the media, religious institutions, self-help and grass-roots organizations, and so on. In each case, gay identity has been involved in struggles of validation, recognition, control, and self-reflection. Next to struggles for survival, these have been above all political struggles of identity whereby "new forms of discourse for interpreting ... needs" are invented.[46] These new forms of discourse emanate from the reaccentuations by which groups confront particular circumstances and institutional gatekeeping. For example, it is on the basis of the redefinition of the family, based in part on the shift of emphasis within gay discourse from sex to caring and commitment, that lesbian women and gay men in New York are now permitted to take over rent-stabilized apartments upon the death of their partners.[47] The redefinition of family also extends to medical and life insurance benefits. A bill has been introduced in the New York legislature to extend these and other spouse benefits to all "domestic partners," gay or otherwise.[48]

On the other hand, the construal of AIDS as a "gay disease" is coming into contention among gay groups — who have had relative success in transforming needs claims into benefits — as well as non-gay groups (not necessarily mutually exclusive with the former), who for reasons of racism or the stigma attached to drug use have not had such success. Even as we enter the second decade of the epidemic it is still largely perceived as a gay problem. This has created an onerous situation, especially for blacks and Latinos, who increasingly and justifiably contest gay-oriented interpretations of the needs of people with AIDS, whether projected by gays themselves or by the media and other institutions.[49]

Limiting ourselves to the terrain of the media, we can see that this is a complex struggle involving which spokespersons contribute to framing the terms of discussion, how the problems are defined, how the agenda is set, what is considered newsworthy, and so on.[50] It is possible to see how these circumstances make for an "authoring process" in which the discourse on AIDS is not any one group's property, not even that of the media or other dominant institutions. The negotiation of needs and identity and the construal of the disease/ epidemic itself involves medical and therapeutic experts, legislators, clergy, media workers, representatives of support organizations, and so on. And it is in this negotiation that the gay ethos that infuses ACT UP has proven most successful.

A coalition of white gay men, black and Latino gay men, lesbians, and straight women and men, New York ACT UP had more than 600 members as of June 1990. They engage in activities to advocate the expansion of treatment and drug therapies, to educate, to protest prejudicial representations, to distribute clean needles to intravenuous drug users, to advertise in all forums, and to participate in civil disobedience in order to reach the widest possible range of publics. In a recent *Village Voice* article, Donna Minkowitz described the group as an AIDS lobby, a gay liberation front, and a New Left collective. It has "evolved into a structure that seeks to incorporate political differences without tearing apart the whole."[51]

But the "whole" is not the "totality" underwritten by a bourgeois aesthetics in the business of seeking hegemony. Current struggles cannot be resolved by appeal to a practice — the aesthetic — that helped achieve hegemony under conditions in which the totalization of the social was guaranteed by the overarching power of the state. Eagleton's thesis that a radical politics can salvage hegemony-building aspects of the bourgeois aesthetic seems wrongheaded. Today, the state is just as powerful as ever but liberal ideology, under pressure, has opened itself to the partial enfranchising of many contestatory groups who seek to further consolidate their gains. Since these groups do not subscribe to the same aesthetic, given that their respective aesthetics derive from their particular group ethos, the aesthetic is not the mediating ground upon which hegemony can be established. Are we to accede to a hegemony based on the ethos of one group?

At best there are several diffuse competing rhetorics of diversity at odds with the conservative attempt to maintain a stratified diversity under the thumb of one nation under God: (1) the equal-potential-but-not-equal-distribution discourse of cultural pluralism, which works in tandem with consumer capitalism's appeal (audience targeting) to all possible subject positions by means of stereotyping representations; (2) the separatist discourses of certain sectors of current social movements (whether gay, ethnic, gender, even deep ecologist) that see the world as a Hobbesian scramble of hungry eaters divvying up an ever-shrinking pie; and (3) the multicultural paradigm that projects a new hegemonic ideal of continual redefinition of "America" in accordance with the changing configuration of its constituencies.

Each of these rhetorics of diversity is in a relationship of reciprocal constitution with respective sets of aesthetic practices. The first, liberal pluralism, with its appeal to our common soul, humanity, edification, and so on, is hardly convincing, either to conservatives or to marginalized and increasingly disenfranchised groups. The second plays right into the hands of the conservative push to dismantle the welfare state and the Constitution. Conservatives can say look here, we were right, give any group the opportunity for favoritism (*viz.* affirmative action) and it will take the largest slice of the pie in total disregard for other groups. The third rhetoric of diversity, multiculturalism, is the most threatening because it has a certain backing from consumer capitalism (rock music, fashion, television, film, etc.), politics (Jackson's rainbow and Dinkins's mosaic coalition), and the university. According to this paradigm, such programs as the welfare state, affirmative action, and institutions like the NEA and the National Endowment for the Humanities should be salvaged, but not at the cost of maintaining the exclusionary practices of the past.

On the other hand, even this "threatening" bid for a multicultural hegemony has been partly coopted by the state; there is probably no better pitched advertisement for multiculturalism than the representations of the racial and gender makeup of the U.S. armed forces during the invasion of Iraq, otherwise known as the Gulf War, and in subsequent recruitment commercials. And multiculturalism is the name of the game in Coke and Pepsi commercials as well as most MTV programming. The state, the market, and the army, then, may transform this potentially contestatory discourse into a new form of cultural pluralism, perhaps no longer a liberal one, but certainly a vacuously utopian rhetoric.

And yet, in the particular struggle to which I have been referring, the very structure of institutions is what is being challenged, including the policies of the media and the army. Under liberal pluralism these democratizing institutions were constrained by criteria founded on hegemonic constructions of value: gender and racial subtexts traversed the distribution of services by welfare state agencies; propriety and the market dictated what art could be displayed; economic factors determined who could go to college. As pressures were brought to bear on the processes of selection and distribution, these institutions were forced to expand their criteria of eligibility. Not only political pressures, which relied on liberal political representatives to pass progressive legislation and on a liberal Supreme Court to uphold these measures; there were also the cultural politics of these groups, from the first Earth Day twenty years ago and the sexual politics of feminists and gays and lesbians, to the self-affirmative practices of racial and ethnic groups today.

To repeat, then, aesthetics is not what it was in the heyday of liberal bourgeois hegemony. It is no longer an indifferent, totalizing definition of value. Or perhaps it would be more accurate to say that it was never indifferent; it promoted an ideology of freedom when in fact it circumscribed that freedom by setting conditions of participation (such as levels of knowledge, education, tastes, etc.), thus favoring certain classes, genders, sexual orientations, races, and ethnicities. The liberal bourgeois aesthetic, as Eagleton points out, "is incapable of generating positive affective bonds between individuals."[52] This is not the case with the current politics of identity. Precisely because groups marginalized or excluded on the basis of some subject position *must* struggle (politically and culturally in the arena of representation) to be economically and socially enfranchised, to have their value recognized (which means redefining the criteria by which value is construed), affective bonds are created. These bonds do not, however, span the range of all individuals in the nation-state. Consequently, there is no *one* alternative hegemony, but there are alternative aesthetics rooted in concrete ethical and cultural struggles.

The politics of identity, as I have sketched it out here, is where aesthetics and ethics meet. Understood thus, aesthetics is not defined as a "purposeless purposiveness" (Kant) but as Keith Haring's ACT UP fund-raising letter (sent in late 1989, a few months before his death) put it, an ethical practice by which "the *conscience* of our community [is] the *primary catalyst* for AIDS-related policy change." There is no one viable cultural politics in our posthegemonic condition, and identity politics is only one form that has proven enabling in many contexts by legitimizing new forms of agency, although if it were modeled after any given form (say, ethnic or racial groups, or women, or in other geopolitical contexts the peasantry, and so on) such a politics could prove oppressive for other groups. Michael Warner cautions against the ready crossover from one model of identity experience to another:

> The family may be a site of solidarity and value for racial or ethnic struggles, but current definitions of the family are abysmally oppressive for lesbians and gays. Familial language deployed to describe sociability in race- or gender-based movements (sisterhood, brotherhood, fatherland, mother tongue, etc.) can be a language of exile for queers. Similarly, notions of alternative traditions or canons have been very useful for African-American and feminist scholars. But because queer politics do not obey the member/nonmember logics of race and gender, alternative canons and traditions cannot be opposed to the dominant ones in the same way. Indeed, the emphasis on reproductive continuity in such models can produce an extreme homophobia, and the tension resulting from such unrecognized disparities can make alliance politics difficult.[53]

Queer politics is not an attempt to establish hegemony, which may suture in a group to the detriment of its ethos. Despite Warner's claims to the contrary, queer politics is identity politics, if by identity is meant a particular ethos that rejects the normal, that is, "rejects a minoritizing logic of toleration or simple political interest-representation in favor of a more thorough resistance to regimes of the normal."[54] As I understand it, identity politics does not have to mean minoritization, but rather pressure upon the rest of society not just to tolerate, but also to come to terms with a given ethos, to change in relation to it. In the process, aesthetic practices, redefined as *practical aesthetics*, break loose from the straitjacket of representation and act to change our circumstances by seizing the public realm. This is, indeed, what Gran Fury's political-aesthetic practice is all about:

> We consistently attempt to situate our work in the "public realm" in an effort to include a diverse, non-homogeneous audience. Through appropriating dominant media's techniques, we hope to make the social and political subtexts of the AIDS epidemic visible and to incite the viewer to take the next step.[55]

NOTES

1. Richard Bernstein, "Arts Endowment's Opponents Are Fighting Fire with Fire," *New York Times*, May 30, 1990, C13, C15.

2. The phrase is taken from John D'Emilio and Estelle B. Freedman, *Intimate Matters: A History of Sexuality in America* (New York: Harper & Row, 1988).

3. Maureen Dowd, "Jesse Helms Takes No-Lose Position on Art," *New York Times*, July 28, 1989, A1, B6. The word *indecent* was subsequently omitted in the "compromise" wording of the obscenity ban.

4. Dowd, "Jesse Helms Takes No-Lose Position."

5. Barbara Gamarekian, "White House Opposes Restrictions on Arts Grants," *New York Times*, March 22, 1990, A1, B4. The opposition referred to in this report has given way to political expediency as conservatives mounted a public campaign that has frightened Republican "moderates" and the White House into ceding ground on restrictions rather than lose conservative support. See Andrew Rosenthal, "Bush's Balancing Act over Financing of Arts," *New York Times*, June 19, 1990, C14.

6. *New York Times*, July 2, 1989, H1.

7. Quoted in Grace Glueck, "Senate Vote Prompts Anger, but Some Approval, in the Art World," *New York Times*, July 28, 1989, B6.

8. Glueck, "Senate Vote," emphasis added.

9. Glueck, "Senate Vote," emphasis added.

10. "The Helms Process," *New York Times* editorial, July 28, 1989, A26; emphasis added.

11. Terry Eagleton, *The Ideology of the Aesthetic* (Oxford: Basil Blackwell, 1990).

12. Eagleton, *Ideology*, 20–21.

13. Eagleton, *Ideology*, 36.

14. Eagleton, *Ideology*, 62.

15. David Lloyd and Paul Thomas—in "Culture and Society or 'Culture and the State'?" *Social Text* 30 (1992): 49–78—give the example of the English working-class radicals of the 1820s and 1830s who rejected the cultural criteria (*viz.* education) for citizenship and political representation on the grounds that there is a "close relationship between being represented, being educated and being appropriated" (61). In focusing on this working-class rejection of culture and representation, Lloyd and Thomas provide an important corrective to those Marxist and contestatory positions (they single out Raymond Williams but their critique could also be extended to Eagleton) that, although critical, approach social history as if its main protagonists were Culture and the Aesthetic, thus contributing to their hegemony as privileged concepts within contemporary theory.

16. This is the basis of Henry Louis Gates, Jr.'s, argument in defense of the rap group 2 Live Crew whose album *As Nasty As They Wanna Be* was banned on the grounds of obscenity. Gates contends that it is the group's threatening cultural ethos, and not obscenity per se, that brought on the reprisals by the courts. See "2 Live Crew, Decoded," *New York Times*, June 19, 1990, A23.

17. Cf. Letters to the Editor, "Art Agency Needs Cleaning Up, Not Scrapping," *New York Times*, June 13, 1990, A30.

18. Cf. Roberta Smith, "Waging Guerrilla Warfare Against the Art World," *New York Times*, June 17, 1990, H1, H31. See also Richard Regen, "Flinching and Fear:

Is the Art World Doing Jesse Helms's Work For Him?" *Village Voice*, October 17, 1989, 29.

19. See Carole Vance, "Misunderstanding Obscenity," *Art in America*, May 1990, 49–55, and C. Carr, "War on Art: The Sexual Politics of Censorship," *Village Voice*, June 5, 1990, 25–30.

20. David Trend, "Beyond Resistance: Notes on Community Counter-Practice," *Afterimage*, April 1989, 4.

21. For insightful analyses of such misrepresentations, see Timothy Landers, "Bodies and Anti-Bodies: A Crisis in Representation," in *Global Television*, ed. Cynthia Schneider and Brian Wallis (New York: Wedge, 1988); Simon Watney, "Photography and AIDS," *Ten* 8, no. 26 (1987); Douglas Crimp, "How to Have Promiscuity in an Epidemic," *October* 43 (Winter 1987).

22. Jürgen Habermas, *The Structural Transformation of the Public Sphere: An Inquiry into a Category of Bourgeois Society*, trans. Thomas Burger with Frederick Lawrence (Cambridge, Mass.: MIT Press, 1989), 41.

23. Habermas, *Public Sphere*, 43.

24. "Subjectivity, as the innermost core of the private, was always already oriented to an audience [*Publikum*]. . . . Thus, the directly or indirectly audience-oriented subjectivity of the letter exchange or diary explained the origin of the typical genre and authentic literary achievement of that century: the domestic novel, the psychological description in autobiographical form." Habermas, *Public Sphere*, 49.

25. Georg Lukács, *The Historical Novel*, trans. Hannah Mitchell and Stanley Mitchell, preface Fredric Jameson (Lincoln: University of Nebraska Press, 1983), 127.

26. This "compromise equilibrium" entails that a social group or class must "transcend the corporate limits of the purely economic class, [such that its interests] can and must become the interests of other subordinate groups too. . . . To propagate itself throughout society [the hegemonic group must] bring[] about not only a unison of economic and political aims, but also intellectual and moral unity, posing all the questions around which the struggle rages not on a corporate but on a 'universal' plane, and thus creating the hegemony of a fundamental group over a series of subordinate groups."

Antonio Gramsci, "The Modern Prince," in *Selections from the Prison Notebooks*, ed. and trans. Quintin Hoare and Geoffrey Nowell Smith (New York: International Publishers, 1971), 161, 181–82.

27. M. M. Bakhtin, "Discourse in the Novel," in *The Dialogic Imagination*, ed. Michael Holquist, trans. Caryl Emerson and Michael Holquist (Austin: University of Texas Press, 1981), 294.

28. M. M. Bakhtin, "The Problem of Speech Genres," in *Speech Genres and Other Late Essays*, ed. Caryl Emerson and Michael Holquist, trans. Vern W. McGee (Austin: University of Texas Press, 1986), 79.

29. "What conditions this re-accentuation of images and languages in the novel? It is a change in the background animating dialogue, that is, changes in the composition of heteroglossia. In an era when the dialogue of languages has experienced great change, the language of an image begins to sound in a different way, or is bathed in a different light, or is perceived against a different dialogizing background. . . .

In re-accentuations of this kind there is no crude violation of the author's will. It can even be said that this process takes place *within the image itself*, i.e., not only in the changed conditions of perception. Such conditions merely actualize in an image a potential already available to it (it is true that while these conditions strengthen some possibilities, they weaken others). We could say with justification that in one respect the image has become better understood and better 'heard' than ever before. In any case, a certain degree of incomprehension has been coupled here with a new and more profound comprehension." "Discourse in the Novel," 420.

30. In *Dialogic Imagination*, 84–258.

31. *Dialogic Imagination*, 137.

32. So long as "heterogeneity" remains a metaphysical concept, homogenizing the differences of dominant and subaltern, privileged and disenfranchised, liberals can take comfort. Contestatory groups, on the other hand, need to point up unequal distributions of value. The difference between progressive and conservative attacks on liberal homogenization is that the former characterize the unequal distribution masked by homogenization as a form of injustice; the right, on the contrary, appeals to the difference entailed by inequality as proof that the motor of history is *might*.

Alain de Benoist sums up the rightist position on diversity quite clearly: "By 'rightist' I mean (to be sure we understand each other) the attitude that holds that *diversity* in the world and the *relative* inequalities it necessarily produces are a good, while the progressive homogenization of the world advocated and implemented by the bimillennial discourse of egalitarian ideology is an evil. I call *rightist* those doctrines that consider that relative inequalities of existence motivate *relationships of strength* from which *historical change* results, and which believe that *history should continue*. . . . From my viewpoint, then, the enemy is not 'the left,' 'Communism' or even 'subversion.' It is simply that *egalitarian ideology* which (whether in religious, secular, metaphysical or ostensibly 'scientific' formulation) has flourished without interruption for two thousand years, of which the 'ideas of 1789' have been only one stage, and of which present-day subversion and Communism are an inevitable consequence." (Alain Benoist, *Les idées à l'endroit* [Paris: Libres-Hallier, 1979]; quoted in Agustín Cuevas, "La derechización de occidente: señas y contraseñas," in *Tiempos conservadores: América Latina en la derechización de Occidente* [Quito: El Conej, 1987]. The translation into English of Cuevas's article is by Holly Staver.)

33. See Jürgen Habermas, *The Theory of Communicative Action*, Vol. 1, *Reason and the Rationalization of Society*, and vol. 2, *Lifeworld and System: A Critique of Functionalist Reason*, trans. Thomas McCarthy (Boston: Beacon, 1984 and 1987).

34. Nancy Fraser, "What's Critical about Critical Theory? The Case of Habermas and Gender," in *Unruly Practices: Power, Discourse and Gender in Contemporary Social Theory* (Minneapolis: University of Minnesota Press, 1989), 142, n. 34.

35. Fraser, "What's Critical?" 132.

36. See Fraser, "Women, Welfare, and the Politics of Need Interpretation," in *Unruly Practices*, 144–60.

37. Fraser, "Women, Welfare," 157.

38. In many Latin American countries, for example, new kinds of politics of identity emerged *not* in relation to the welfare state but, rather, in relation to the

absence of civil society as in the Southern Cone during the dictatorships of the seventies, which saw the rise of a "mothers' movement" (e.g., The Mothers of the Plaza de Mayo), and in relation to the absence of viable state action to remedy egregious social disparities and the enormous cost in human life and property due to natural disasters such as the 1985 earthquake in Mexico City, which catalyzed the formation of self-help communities and even the creation of a self-help hero, Superbarrio.

39. On the "new social movements," see Ernesto Laclau and Chantal Mouffe, *Hegemony and Socialist Strategy: Towards a Radical Democratic Politics* (London: Verso, 1985), and Stanley Aronowitz, "Postmodernism and Politics," in *Social Text* 18 (Winter 1987/88), reprinted in Andrew Ross, ed., *Universal Abandon? The Politics of Postmodernism* (Minneapolis: University of Minnesota Press, 1988).

For a social movement account of racial and ethnic movements, see Michael Omi and Howard Winant, *Racial Formation in the United States: From the 1960s to the 1980s* (New York: Routledge & Kegan Paul, 1986) and Juan Flores and George Yúdice, "Living Borders/Buscando America: Languages of Latino Self-Formation," *Social Text* 24 (Spring 1990).

40. Martha Minow, "We, the Family: Constitutional Rights and American Families," in *The Constitution and American Life*, ed. David Thelen (Ithaca, N.Y.: Cornell University Press, 1988), 319.

41. Steven Epstein, "Gay Politics, Ethnic Identity: The Limits of Social Constructionism," *Socialist Review* 1987: 20.

42. Dennis Altman, *The Homosexualization of America* (Boston: Beacon, 1982), 82; quoted in Epstein, "Gay Politics," 31.

43. Dennis Altman, *AIDS in the Mind of America: The Social, Political, and Psychological Impact of a New Epidemic* (Garden City, N.Y.: Anchor, 1987), 189.

44. See Crimp, "How to Have Promiscuity," 250–51.

45. All the representatives of gay and lesbian organizations participating in the discussion program "Out! New York/San Francisco Town Meeting of Gay and Lesbian Pride" (New York: WNET, Channel 13, June 23, 1990) stressed the recognition of this diversity and endorsed political activism to entitle it as the most important aspect of their new agenda.

46. Fraser, *Unruly Practices*, 171.

47. See Philip S. Gutis, "New York Housing Officials Redefine the Family to Block Evictions," *New York Times*, November 9, 1989, B1, B7; "Should Gays Have Marriage Rights?" *Time*, November 20, 1989, 101–2; and "Massachusetts Acts to Permit Homosexual Foster Parents," *New York Times*, April 6, 1990, A18.

48. Cf. Philip S. Gutis, "Gay Teachers Sue for Benefits for Longtime Companions," *New York Times*, November 7, 1989, B2.

49. See Nat Hentoff, "Silence = Black and Hispanic Deaths," *Village Voice*, February 27, 1990, 22, and Richard Goldstein, "The Myth of the Powerful Gay Man. Why Nat Hentoff Can't Be Trusted on AIDS," *Village Voice*, March 20, 1990, 37–40. For a review of the polemic between Hentoff and Goldstein, see Ed Sikov, "Out of Control: Fear, Loathing, Hentoff and Goldstein," *New York Native*, April 16, 1990, 16–19.

50. See Ronald Bayer, *Private Acts, Social Consequences: AIDS and the Politics of Public Health* (New York: Free Press, 1988), and David C. Colby, Timothy E. Cook, and Timothy B. Murray, "Social Movements and the Sickness on the Air: Agenda Control and Television News on AIDS," paper delivered at the 1987 annual

meeting of the American Political Science Association, The Palmer House, Chicago, September 3–6, 1987.

51. Donna Minkowitz, "ACT UP at a Crossroads," *Village Voice*, June 5, 1990, 19–21.

52. *Ideology*, 110.

53. Michael Warner, "Introduction: Fear of a Queer Planet," *Social Text* 29 (1991): 12–13.

54. Warner, "Introduction," 16.

55. Gran Fury, "International AIDS Information," *The Act* 2, no. 1 (1990) 5–9.

The Mass Public and the Mass Subject
Michael Warner

for Lauren Berlant

The Egocrat coincides with himself, as society is supposed to coincide with itself. An impossible swallowing up of the body in the head begins to take place, as does an impossible swallowing up of the head in the body. The attraction of the whole is no longer dissociated from the attraction of the parts.

> — Claude Lefort, "The Image of the Body
> and Totalitarianism" (1979)[1]

During these assassination fantasies Tallis became increasingly obsessed with the pudenda of the Presidential contender mediated to him by a thousand television screens. The motion picture studies of Ronald Reagan created a scenario of the conceptual orgasm, a unique ontology of violence and disaster.

> —J. G. Ballard, "Why I Want to Fuck Ronald Reagan"(1969)[2]

As the subjects of publicity — its "hearers," "speakers," "viewers," and "doers" — we have a different relation to ourselves, a different affect, from that which we have in other contexts. No matter what particularities of culture, race, gender, or class we bring to bear on public discourse, the moment of apprehending something as public is one in which we imagine — if imperfectly — indifference to those particularities, to ourselves. We adopt the attitude of the public subject, marking to ourselves our nonidentity with ourselves. There are any number of ways to describe this moment of public subjectivity — as a universalizing transcendence, as ideological repression, as utopian wish, as schizocapitalist vertigo, or simply as a routine difference of register. No matter what its character for the individual subjects who come to public discourse, however, the rhetorical contexts of publicity in the modern Western nations must always mediate a self-relation different from that of "personal life." This becomes a point of more than usual importance, I will suggest, in a period such as our own when so much political conflict revolves around identity and status categories.

Western political thought has not ignored the tendency of publicity to alter or refract the individual's character and status. It has been obsessed with that tendency. But it has frequently thought of publicity as distorting, corrupting, or, to use the more current version, alienating individuals. The republican notion of virtue, for example, was designed exactly to avoid any rupture of self-difference between ordinary life and publicity. The republican was to be the same as citizen and as man. He was to maintain continuity of value, judgment, and reputation from domestic economy to affairs of public nature. And lesser subjects — noncitizens such as women, children, and the poor — were equally to maintain continuity across both realms, as nonactors. From republicanism to populism, from Rousseau to Reagan, self-unity has been held to be a public value, and publicity has not been thought of as requiring individuals to have discontinuous perceptions of themselves. (Hegel, it is true, considered the state as a higher-order subjectivity unattainable in civil society. But because he considered the difference both normative and unbridgable within the frame of the individual, a historical and political analysis of discontinuous self-relations did not follow.)

One reason why virtue was spoken about with such ardor in the seventeenth and eighteenth centuries was that the discursive conventions of the public sphere had already made virtuous self-unity archaic. In the bourgeois public sphere, talk of the citizen's virtue was already partly wishful. Once a public discourse had become specialized in the Western model, the subjective attitude adopted in public discourse became an inescapable but always unrecognized political force, governing what is publicly sayable. Inescapable, because only when images or texts can be understood as meaningful to a public rather than simply to oneself, or to specific others, can they be called public. Unrecognized, because this strategy of impersonal reference — in which the subject might say, "The text addresses me" *and* "It addresses no one in particular" — is a ground condition of intelligibility for public language. The "public" in this sense has no empirical existence, and cannot be objectified. When we understand images and texts as public, we do not gesture to a statistically measurable series of others. We make a necessarily imaginary reference to the public *as opposed to* other individuals. Public opinion, for example, is understood as belonging to a "public" rather than to scattered individuals. (Opinion polls in this sense are a performative genre. They do not measure something that already exists as public opinion; but when they are reported as such they *are* public opinion.) So also it is only meaningful to speak of public discourse where it is understood as the discourse of a public rather than as an expansive dialogue among separate persons.

The public sphere therefore presents problems of rhetorical analysis. Because the moment of special imaginary reference is always necessary, the publicity of the public sphere never reduces to information, discussion, will formation, or any of the other scenarios by which the public sphere represents itself. The mediating rhetorical dimension of a public context must be built into each individual's relation to it, as a meaningful reference point against which something could be grasped as information, discussion, will formation. To ask about the relation between democracy and the rhetorical forms of publicity, we would have to consider how the public dimension of discourse can come about differently in different contexts of mediation, from official to mass cultural or subcultural. There is not simply "a" public discourse and a "we" who apprehend it. Strategies of public reference have different meanings for the individuals who suddenly find themselves incorporating the public subject, and the rhetorics that mediate publicity have undergone some important changes.

Utopias of Self-Abstraction

In the eighteenth century, as I have argued elsewhere, the imaginary reference point of the public was constructed through an understanding of print.[3] At least in the British American colonies, a style of thinking about print appeared in the culture of republicanism, according to which it was possible to consume printed goods with an awareness that the same printed goods were being consumed by an indefinite number of others. This awareness came to be built into the meaning of the printed object, to the point that we now consider it simply definitional to speak of printing as "publication." In print, understood this way, one surrendered one's utterance to an audience that was by definition indefinite. Earlier writers might have responded with some anxiety to such mediation, or might simply have thought of the speaker-audience relation in different terms. In the eighteenth century the consciousness of an abstract audience became a badge of distinction, a way of claiming a public disposition.

The transformation, I might emphasize, was a cultural rather than a technological one; it came about not just with more use of print, but also as the language of republicanism was extended to print contexts as a structuring metalanguage. It was in the culture of republicanism — with its categories of disinterested virtue and supervision — that a rhetoric of print consumption became authoritative, a way of understanding the publicness of publication. Here for example is how the Spectator, in 1712, describes the advantage of being realized in the medium of print:

> It is much more difficult to converse with the World in a real than a personated Character. That might pass for Humour, in the *Spectator,* which would look like Arrogance in a Writer who sets his Name to his Work. The Fictitious Person might condemn those who disapproved him, and extoll his own Performances, without giving Offence. He might assume a Mock-Authority; without being looked upon as vain and conceited. The Praises or Censures of himself fall only upon the Creature of his Imagination, and if any one finds fault with him, the Author may reply with the Philosopher of old, *Thou dost but beat the Case of* Anaxarchus.[4]

The Spectator's attitude of conversing with the world is public and disinterested. It elaborates republican assumptions about the citizen's exercise of virtue. But it could not come about without a value placed on the anonymous subjectivity here associated with print. The Spectator's point about himself is that he is different from the person of Richard Steele. Just as the Spectator here secures a certain liberty in not calling himself Richard Steele, so it would take a certain liberty for us to call the author of this passage Richard Steele — all the more so since the pronoun reference begins to slip around the third sentence ("those who disapproved *him*"). The ambiguous relation between Spectator and Writer, Steele says, liberates him. The Spectator is for Steele a prosthetic person, to borrow a term from Lauren

Berlant — prosthetic in the sense that it does not reduce to or express the given body.[5] By making him no longer self-identical, it allows him the negativity of debate — not a pure negativity, not simply reason or criticism, but an identification with a disembodied public subject that he can imagine as parallel to his private person.

In a sense, however, that public subject does have a body, because the public, prosthetic body takes abuse for the private person. The last line of the passage refers to the fact that Anaxarchus was pummeled to death with iron pestles after offending a despotic ruler. In the ventriloquistic act of taking up his speech, therefore, Steele both imagines an intimate violation of his person and provides himself with a kind of prophylaxis against violation (to borrow another term from Berlant). Anaxarchus was not so lucky. Despite what Steele says, the privilege that he obtains over his body in this way does not in fact reduce to the simple body/soul distinction that Anaxarchus's speech invokes. It allows him to think of his public discourse as a routine form of self-abstraction, quite unlike the ascetic self-integration of Anaxarchus. When Steele impersonates the philosopher to have the Spectator (or someone) say, "Thou dost but beat the case of Anaxarchus," he appropriates an intimate subjective benefit of publicity's self-abstraction.

Through the conventions that allowed such writing to perform the disincorporation of its authors and its readers, public discourse turned persons into a public. In *The Structural Transformation of the Public Sphere*, Jürgen Habermas makes a similar point. One of the great virtues of that book is the care it takes to describe the cultural-technical context in which the public of the bourgeois public sphere was constituted. "In the *Tatler*, the *Spectator*, and the *Guardian* the public held up a mirror to itself.... The public that read and debated this sort of thing read and debated about itself."[6] It is worth remembering also that *persons* read and debated this sort of thing, but in reading and debating it *as* a public, they adopted a very special rhetoric about their own personhood. Where earlier writers had typically seen the context of print as a means of personal extension — they understood themselves, in print, essentially to be speaking in their own persons — people began to see it as an authoritative mediation. That is clearly the case with the Steele passage, and pseudonymous serial essays like the *Spectator* did a great deal toward normalizing a public print discourse.

In the bourgeois public sphere, which was brought into being by publication in this sense, a principle of negativity was axiomatic: the validity of what you say in public bears a negative relation to your person. What you say will carry force not because of who you are but despite who you are. Implicit in this principle is a utopian universality that would allow people to transcend the given realities of their bodies and their status. But the rhetorical strategy of personal abstraction is both the utopian moment of the public sphere and a major source of domination. For the ability to abstract oneself in public discussion has always been an unequally available resource. Individuals have to have specific rhetorics of disincorporation; they are not simply rendered bodiless by exercising reason. And it is only possible to operate a discourse based on the claim to self-abstracting disinterestedness in a culture where such unmarked self-abstraction is a differential resource. The subject who could master this rhetoric in the bourgeois public sphere was implicitly — even explicitly — white, male, literate, and propertied. These traits could go unmarked, even grammatically, while other features of bodies could only be acknowledged in discourse as the humiliating positivity of the particular.

The bourgeois public sphere claimed to have no relation to the body image at all. Public issues were depersonalized so that any person would, in theory, have the ability to offer an opinion about them, submitting that opinion to the impersonal test of public debate without personal hazard. Yet the bourgeois public sphere continued to rely on features of certain bodies. Access to the public came in the whiteness and maleness that were then denied as forms of positivity, since the white male qua public person was only abstract rather than white and male. The contradiction is that, even while particular bodies and dispositions enabled the liberating abstraction of public discourse, those bodies also summarized the constraints of positivity, the mere case of Anaxarchus, from which self-abstracion can be liberating.

It is very far from being clear that these asymmetries of embodiment were merely contingent encumbrances to the public sphere, residual forms of illiberal "discrimination." The difference between self-abstraction and a body's positivity is more than a difference in what has officially been made available to men and to women, for example: it is a difference in the cultural/symbolic definitions of masculinity and femininity.[7] Self-abstraction from male bodies confirms masculinity. Self-abstraction from female bodies denies femininity. The bourgeois public sphere is a frame of reference in which it is supposed that all particularities have the same status as mere particularity. But the ability to establish that frame of reference is a feature of some particularities. Neither in gender nor in race nor in class nor in sexualities is it possible to treat different particulars as having merely paratactic or serial difference. Differences in such realms already come coded as the difference between the unmarked and the marked, the universalizable and the particular. Their own internal logic is such that the two sides of any of these differences cannot be treated as symmetrical — as, for example, they are in the rhetoric of liberal toleration or "debate" — without simply resecuring an asymmetrical privilege. The bourgeois public sphere has been structured from the outset by a logic of abstraction that provides a privilege for unmarked identities: the male, the white, the middle-class, the normal.

That is what Pier Paolo Pasolini meant when he wrote, just before he was murdered, that "tolerance is always and purely nominal":

> In fact they tell the "tolerated" person to do what he wishes, that he has every right to follow his own nature, that the fact that he belongs to a minority does not in the least mean inferiority, etc. But his "difference" — or better, his "crime of being different" — remains the same both with regard to those who have decided to tolerate him and those who have decided to condemn him. No majority will ever be able to banish from its consciousness the feeling of the "difference" of minorities. I shall always be eternally, inevitably conscious of this.[8]

Doubtless it is better to be tolerated than to be killed, as Pasolini was. But it would be better still to make reference to one's marked particularities without being specified thereby as less than public. As the bourgeois public sphere paraded the spectacle of its disincorporation, it brought into being this minoritizing logic of domination. Publicness is always able to encode itself through the themes of universality, openness, meritocracy, and access — all of which dehetoricize its self-understanding, guaranteeing at every step that difference will be enunciated as mere positivity, an ineluctable limit imposed by the particularities of the body, a positivity that cannot translate or neutralize itself prosthetically without ceasing to exist.

This minoritizing logic, intrinsic to the deployment of negativity in the bourgeois public sphere, presents the subjects of bodily difference with the paradox of a utopian promise that cannot be cashed in for them. The very mechanism designed to end domination is a form of domination.

The appeal of mass subjectivity, I will suggest, arises largely from the contradiction in this dialectic of embodiment and negativity in the public sphere. Public discourse from the beginning offered a utopian self-abstraction, but in ways that left a residue of unrecuperated particularity, both for its privileged subjects and for those it minoritized. Its privileged subjects, abstracted from the very body features that gave them the privilege of that abstraction, found themselves in a relation of bad faith with their own positivity. To acknowledge their positivity would be to surrender their privilege, as for example to acknowledge the objectivity of the male body would be feminizing. Meanwhile, minoritized subjects had few strategies open to them, but one was to carry their unrecuperated positivity into consumption. Even from the early eighteenth century, before the triumph of a liberal metalanguage for consumption, commodities were being used — especially by women — as a kind of access to publicness that would nevertheless link up with the specificity of difference.[9]

Consumption offered a counterutopia, precisely in a balance between a collectivity of mass desires and an unminoritized rhetoric of difference in the field of choices among infinite goods. A good deal of noise in modern society comes from the inability to translate these utopian promises into a public sphere where collectivity has no link to the body and its desires, where difference is described not as the paratactic seriality of illimitable choice but as the given constraints of preconscious nature. Where consumer capitalism makes available an endlessly differentiable subject, the subject of the public sphere proper cannot be differentiated. It can represent difference as other, but as an available form of subjectivity it remains unmarked. The constitutional public sphere, therefore, cannot fully recuperate its residues. It can only display them. In this important sense, the "we" in "We the People" is the mass equivalent of the Spectator's prosthetic generality — a flexible instrument of interpellation, but one that exiles its own positivity.

From the eighteenth century, we in the modern West have inherited an understanding of printing as publication, but we now understand a vast range of everyday life as having the reference of publicity. The medium of print is now only a small part of our relation to what we understand as the public, and the fictitious abstraction of the Spectator would seem conspicuously out of place in the modern discourse of public icons. So although the bourgeois public sphere continues to secure a minoritizing liberal logic of self-abstraction, its rhetoric is inceasingly complicated by other forms of publicity. At present the mass-cultural public sphere continually offers its subject an array of body images. In earlier varieties of the public sphere, it was important that images of the body *not* figure importantly in public discourse. The anonymity of the discourse was a way of certifying the citizen's disinterested concern for the public good. But now public body images are everywhere on display, in virtually all media contexts. Where printed public discourse formerly relied on a rhetoric of abstract disembodiment, visual media — including print — now display bodies for a range of purposes: admiration, identificaion, appropriation, scandal, and so forth. To be public in the West means to have an iconicity, and this is true equally of Muammar Qaddafi and Karen Carpenter.

The visibility of public figures, for the subject of mass culture, occurs in a context in which publicity is generally mediated by the discourse of consumption. It is difficult to realize how much we observe public images with the eye of the consumer. Nearly all of our pleasures come to us coded in some degree by the publicity of mass media. We have brand names all over us. Even the most refined or the most perverse among us could point to his or her desires or identifications and see that in most cases they were public desires, even mass public desires, from the moment that they were our desires. This is true not only in the case of salable commodities — our refrigerators, our sneakers, our lunch — but also in other areas where we make symbolic identifications in a field of choice: the way we bear our bodies, the sports we follow, or our erotic objects. In such areas, our desires have become recognizable through their display in the media; and in the moment of wanting them, we imagine a collective consumer witnessing our wants and choices.

The public discourse of the mass media has increasingly come to rely on the intimacy of this collective witnessing in its rhetorics of publicity, iconic and consumerist alike. It is a significant part of the ground of public discouse, the subjective apprehension of what is public. In everyday life, for one thing, we have access to the realm of political systems in the sarne way that we have access to the circulation of commodities. Not only are we confronted by slogans that continually make this connection for us ("America Wears Hanes," "The Heartbeat of America"); more importantly, the contexts of commodities and politics share the same media and, at least in part, the same metalanguage for constructing our notion of what a public or a people is. When the citizen (or noncitizen — for contemporary publicity the difference hardly matters) goes down to the 7-Eleven to buy a Budweiser and a *Barbie Magazine* and scans from the news headlines to the tabloids' stories about the Rob Lowe sex scandal, several kinds of publicity are involved at once. Nevertheless, it is possible to speak of all of these sites of publicity as parts of a public sphere, insofar as each is capable of illuminating the others in a common discourse of the subject's relation to the nation and its markets.

In each of these mediating contexts of publicity, we become the mass public subject, but in a new way, unanticipated within the classical bourgeois public sphere. If mass-public subjectivity has a kind of singularity, moreover, an undifferentiated extension to indefinite numbers of individuals, those individuals who make up the "we" of the mass public subject might have very different relations to it. It is at the very moment of recognizing ourselves as the mass subject, for example, that we also recognize ourselves as minority subjects. As participants in the mass subjeet, we are the "we" that can describe our particular affiliations of class, gender, sexual orientation, race, or subculture only as "they." This self-alienation is common to all of the contexts of publicity, but it can be variously interpreted within each. The political meaning of the public subject's self-alienation is one of the most important sites of struggle in contemporary culture.

The Mirror of Popularity

In an essay called "The Image of the Body and Totalitarianism," Claude Lefort speculates that public figures have recently begun to play a new role. He imagines essentially a three-stage history of publicity's body. Drawing on the work of Ernst Kantorowicz, he sketches first a representative public sphere in which the person of the prince stands as the head of the corporate body, summing up in his person the principles of legitimacy, though still drawing that legitimacy from a higher power. Classical bourgeois democracy, by contrast, abstracted the public, corporate body in a way that could be literalized in the decapitation of a ruler. "The democratic revolution, for so long subterranean, burst out when the body of the king was destroyed, when the body politic was decapitated and when, at the same time, the corporeality of the social was dissolved. There then occurred what I would call a 'disincorporation' of individuals."[10]

According to Lefort, however, the new trend is again toward the display of the public official's person. The state now relies on its double in "the image of the people, which ... remains indeterminate, but which nevertheless is susceptible of being determined, of being actualized on the level of phantasy as an image of the People-as-One." Public figures increasingly take on the function of concretizing that phantasmatic body image, or in other words of actualizing the otherwise indeterminate image of the people. They embody what Lefort calls the "Egocrat," whose self-identical representativeness is perverse and unstable in a way that contrasts with the representative person of the feudal public sphere:

> The prince condensed in his person the principle of power ... but he was *supposed* to obey a superior power.... That does not seem to be the position of the Egocrat or of his substitutes, the bureaucratic leaders. The Egocrat coincides with himself, as society is supposed to coincide with itself. An impossible swallowing up of the body in the head begins to take place, as does an impossible swallowing up of the head in the body.[11]

Lefort sees the sources of this development in democracy, but he associates the trend with totalitarianism — presumably in the iconographies of Stalin and Mao. But then Lefort wrote this essay in 1979; since that time it has become increasingly clear that such phantasmatic public embodiments have come to be the norm in the Western democratic bureaucracies.

Jürgen Habermas has an interestingly similar narrative. He too describes a first stage of a representative public sphere, in which public persons derived their power in part from being on display. The idealizing language of nobility did not abstract away from the body: "Characteristically, in none of [the aristocracy's] virtues did the physical aspect entirely lose its significance, for virtue must be embodied, it had to be capable of public representation."[12] For Habermas as well as for Lefort, this ceased to be the case with the bourgeois public sphere, in which the public was generalized away from physical, theatrical representation. It was relocated instead to the mostly written contexts of rational debate. And Habermas, again like Lefort, speaks of a more recent return to the display of public representatives, a return that he calls "refeudalizing": "The public sphere becomes the court *before* [which] public prestige can be displayed — rather than *in* which public critical debate is carried on."[13]

Why should modern regimes so require a return to the image of the leader, in the peculiar form that Lefort calls the Egocrat? We can see both how powerful and how complicated this appeal in mass publicity can be by taking the example of Ronald Reagan's popularity. Reagan is probably a better example than others because his figure, more than any other, blurs the boundary between the iconicities of the political public and the commodity public. George Bush, Michael Dukakis, and other national politicians have been less adept at translating their persons from the interior of the political system to the surface of the brand-name commodity. The Reagan-style conjunction of these two kinds of appeal is the ideal-typical moment of national publicity against which they are measured. So regardless of whatever skills they have within the political system, Bush and others like him have not been able to bring to their superbureaucratic persons the full extended reference of publicity. Reagan, by contrast, was the champion spokesmodel for America, just as he had earlier been a spokesmodel for General Electric and for Hollywood. It is easy to understand why the left clings to its amnesia about the pleasures of publicity when confronted with a problem like the popularity of a Ronald Reagan. But we do not have a clear understanding of the nature of the public with which Reagan was popular, so to speak; nor do we have a clear understanding of the attraction of such a public figure.

One report in *The Nation* has it that Reagan was not a popular president at all. Gallup opinion polls, over the duration of his two terms, rated him far less favorably than Roosevelt, Kennedy, or Eisenhower. He was not appreciably more popular than Ford or Carter. For the left-liberal readership of *The Nation*, this surprising statistic spells relief. It encourages us to believe that the public might not be so blind, after all. Indeed, in the story that presents the statistics, Thomas Ferguson claims exactly this sort of populist vindication. For him, the point of the story is simply that journalists who genuflect before Reagan's popularity are mistaken and irresponsible. The people, he implies, know better, and politics would be more reasonable if the media better represented the public. Not without sentimentality, *The Nation* regards the poll as the public's authentic expression, and the media picture as its distortion.[14]

But even if the figures represent an authentic public, it is far from clear how to take reassurance from the fact of such a poll. What could it mean to say that Reagan's popularity was simply illusory? For Congress discovered that it was not. And so did the media, since editors quickly learned that the journalistic sport of catching Reagan in his errors could make their audiences bristle with hostility. Reagan in one sense may have had no real popularity, as polls record it. But in another sense he had a substantial and positive popularity that he, and others, could deploy both within the political system and within the wider sphere of publicity. So if we characterize the poll as the authentic opinion of the public, while viewing the media reports of Reagan's popularity as a distortion, then both the genesis and the force of that distortion become inexplicable. It would be clearly inadequate to say, in what amounts to a revival of old talk about the conspiracy of the bosses, that the media were simply "managed" or "manipulated," despite the Republicans' impressive forensics of spin control.[15]

The Nation, then, gives a much too easy answer to the question of Reagan's attraction when it claims that there simply never was any. If that answer seems mistaken, the poll shows that it would be equally mistaken to see the public as successfully recruited into an uncritical identification with Reagan and an uncritical acclamation of Reaganism. It might otherwise have been comforting to believe, by means of such explanations, that Reagan really *was* popular, that the people were suckered. Then, at least, we could tell ourselves that we knew something about "the people." In fact, we have no way of talking about the public without theorizing the contexts and strategies in which the public could be represented. If we believe in the continued existence of a rational-critical public, as *The Nation* does, then it is difficult to account for the counterdemocratic tendencies of the public sphere as anything other than the cowardice or bad faith of some journalists. On the other hand, if we believe that the public sphere of the mass media has replaced a rational and critical public with one that is consumerist and acclamatory, then we might expect it to show more consumer satisfaction, more acclaim.

The media construction "Reagan" owes its peculiar character in large part to the appeal of the one that is offered jointly with it: "the public." In publicity, we are given a stake in the imaginary of a mass public in a way that dictates a certain appeal not so much for Ronald Reagan in particular, but for the kind of public figure of which he is exemplary. Different figures may articulate that appeal differently, and with important consequences, but there is a logic of appeal to which Reagan and Jesse Jackson equally submit. Publicity puts us in a relation to these figures that is also a relation to an unrealizable public subject, whose omnipotence and subjectivity can then be figured both on and against the images of such men. A public, after all, cannot have a discrete, positive existence; something becomes a public only through its availability for subjective identification. "Reagan" bears in his being the marks of his mediation to a public; and "the public" equally bears in its being the marks of its mediation for identification. Indeed, the most telling thing of all about the story in *The Nation* is Ferguson's remark that the myth of Reagan's popularity is itself "ever-popular." The problem is not Reagan's popularity, but the popularity of his popularity. "Reagan," we might even say, is a relay for a kind of metapopularity. The major task of Western leaders has become the task of performing popularity, which is not the same as being popular.

What makes figures of publicity *attractive* to people? I do not mean this to be a condescending question. It is not a matter of asking simply how people are seduced or manipulated. It is a matter of asking what kinds of identifications are required or allowed in the discourse of publicity. The rhetorical conditions under which the popular can be performed are of consequence not only for policy outcomes but also, more importantly, for who we are.

Self-Abstraction and the Mass Subject

Part of the bad faith of the res publica of letters was that it required a denial of the bodies that gave access to it. The public sphere is still oriented enough to its liberal logic that its citizens long to abstract themselves into the privilege of public disembodiment. And when that fails, they can turn to another kind of longing, which, as Lauren Berlant shows, is not so much to cancel out their bodies as to trade in for a better model. The mass public sphere tries to minimize the difference between the two, surrounding citizens with trademarks through which they can trade marks, offering both positivity and self-abstraction. This has meant, furthermore, that the mass public sphere has had to develop genres of collective identification that will artic-ulate both sides of this dialectic.

Insofar as the two sides are contradictory, however, mass identifi-cation tends to be characterized by what I earlier called noise, but which typically appears as an erotic-aggressive disturbance. Here it might be worth thinking about a genre in which the display of bodies is also a kind of disembodiment: the discourse of disasters. At least since the great Chicago fire, mass disaster has had a special relation-ship to the mass media. Mass injury can always command a headline; it gets classed as immediate reward news. But whatever kind of re-ward makes disaster rewarding, it evidently has to do with injury to a *mass* body — an already abstracted body, assembled in simultaneity, but somewhere other than here. When massive numbers of separate injuries occur, they fail to command the same fascination. This dis-crepancy in how seriously we take different organizations of injury is a source of never-ending frustration for airline executives. They never tire of pointing out that, although the fatality rate for automo-biles is astronomically higher than for airplanes, there is no public panic of supervision about automobiles. In the airline executives' interested exasperation, that seems merely to prove the irrationality of journalists and members of Congress. But I think this fondness of the mass media for a very special kind of injury makes rigorous sense. Disaster is popular, as it were, because it is a way of making mass subjectivity available, and it tells us something about the desir-ability of that mass subject.

John Waters tells us in *Shock Value* that one of his hobbies in youth was collecting news coverage of disasters. His all-time favorite pho-tograph, he claims, is a famous shot of the stadium collapsing at the Indianapolis 500 — a photograph he proudly reproduces. But despite his pride in the aura of perversion that surrounds this disclosure, he is at some pains (so to speak) to point out that his pleasure is a normal feature of the discourse. "It makes the newspapers worth the quarter," he writes, and "perks up the local news shows." What could be the dynamic of this link between injury and the pleasures of mass publicity? Waters stages the intimacy of the link in the following story about his childhood, in what I think of as a brilliant corruption of Freud's *fort/da* game:

> Even as a toddler, violence intrigued me.... While other kids were out playing cowboys and Indians, I was lost in fantasies of crunching metal and people screaming for help. I would sweet-talk unsuspecting relatives into buying me toy cars — any kind, as long as they were new and shiny.... I would take two cars and pretend they were driving on a secluded country road until one would swerve and crash into the other. I would become quite excited and start smashing the car with a hammer, all the while shouting, "Oh, my God, there's been a terrible accident!"[16]

Exactly what kind of pleasure is this? It is not just the infantile recuperation of power that the *fort/da* game usually represents. The boy-Waters, in other words, is not just playing out identification and revenge in the rhythm of treasuring and destroying the cars.

Nor is Waters simply indulging the infantile transitivism of which Jacques Lacan writes: "The child who strikes another says that he has been struck; the child who sees another fall, cries."[17] In fact, Waters's pleasure in the scene seems to have little to do with the cars at all. Rather, it comes about largely through his identification with publicity. Not only does Waters have access to auto disaster through the public discourse of news; he dramatizes that discourse as part of the event. Whose voice does he take up in exclaiming, "Oh, my God, there's been a terrible accident!"? And just as important, to whom is he speaking? He turns himself into a relay of spectators, none of whom is injured so much as horrified by witnessing injury. His ventriloquized announcer and his invisible audience allow him to internalize an absent witness. He has been careful to imagine the cars as being on "a secluded country road," so that his imaginary audience can be anywhere *else*. It is, in effect, the mass subject of news.

In this sense, the story shows us how deeply publicity has come to inform our subjectivity. But it also reveals, through Waters's camp humor, that the mass subject's absent witnessing is a barely concealed transitivism. The disaster audience finds its body with a revenge. Its surface is all sympathy: there has been a terrible accident.

The sympathetic quality of its identification, however, is only half the story since, as Waters knows, inflicting and witnessing mass injury are two sides of the same dynamic in disaster discourse. Being of necessity anywhere else, the mass subject cannot have a body except the body it witnesses. But in order to become a mass subject it has left that body behind, abstracted away from it, canceled it as mere positivity. It returns in the spectacle of big-time injury. The transitive pleasure of witnessing/injuring makes available our translation into the disembodied publicity of the mass subject. By injuring a mass body — preferably a really massive body, somewhere — we constitute ourselves as a noncorporeal mass witness. (I do not, however, mean to minimize Waters's delirious perverseness in spelling out this link between violence and spectatorship in mass subjectivity. The perverse acknowledgment of his pleasure, in fact, helps him to violate in return the minoritizing disembodiment of the mass subject. It therefore allows Waters a counterpublic embodied knowledge in the mode of camp.) The same logic informs an astonishing number of mass publicity's genres, from the prophylaxes of horror, assassination, and terrorism to the organized prosthesis of sports. (But, as Waters writes, "Violence in sports always seemed so pointless, because everyone was prepared, so what fun could it possibly be?")[18] The mass media are dominated by genres that construct the mass subject's impossible relation to a body.

In the genres of mass-imaginary transitivism, we might say, a public is thinking about itself and its media. This is true even in the most "vulgar" of the discourses of mass publicity, the tabloid pastime of star puncturing. In the figures of Elvis, Liz, Michael, Oprah, Geraldo, Brando, and the like, we witness and transact the bloating, slimming, wounding, and general humiliation of the public body. The bodies of these public figures are prostheses for our own mutant desirability. That is not to say that a mass-imaginary identification is deployed with uniform or equal effect in each of these cases. A significant subgenre of tabloid publicity, for instance, is devoted not to perforating the iconic bodies of its male stars, but rather to denying them any private power behind their iconic bodies. Johnny Carson, Clint Eastwood, Rob Lowe, and others are subjected to humiliating forms of display, not for gaining weight or having cosmetic surgery, but for failing to exercise full control over their lives. By chronicling their endless romantic/matrimonial disasters, publicity keeps them available for our appropriation of their iconic status by reminding us that they do not possess the phallic power of their images: we do.

In this respect we would have to say that Ronald Reagan stands in partial contrast to these other male icons of publicity. He does not require a discourse of star puncturing because he seems to make no personal claim on the phallic power of his own image. His body, impossible to embarrass, has no private subject behind it. The gestures stay the same, undisturbed by reflection or management. Reagan never gives a sense of modulation between a public and private self, and therefore remains immune to humiliation. That is why it was so easy for news reports to pry into his colon without indiscretion. His witless self-continuity is the modern equivalent of virtue. He is the perfect example of Lefort's Egocrat: he coincides with himself, and therefore concretizes a fantasy image of the unitary people. He is popularity with a hairdo, an image of popularity's popularity.

The presentation of Reagan's body was an important part of his performance of popularity. J. G. Ballard understood that as early as his 1969 story called "Why I Want to Fuck Ronald Reagan." In that story, every subject of publicity is said to share the secret but powerful fantasy of violating Reagan's anus. In sharing that fantasy, Ballard suggests, we demonstrate the same thing that we demonstrate as consumers of the Kennedy assassination: the erotics of a mass imaginary. Like Waters's perverse transitivism, Ballard's generalized sadistic star cult theorizes the public sphere and ironizes it at the same time. His characters, especially in *Crash*, are obsessed with a violent desire for the icons of publicity. But theirs is not a private pathology. Their longing to dismember and be dismembered with Ronald Reagan or Elizabeth Taylor is understood as a more reflective version of these public icons' normal appeal. In the modern nations of the West, individuals encounter in publicity the erotics of a powerful identification not just with public icons, but also with their popularity.

Given the outcome of such a metapopularity in the realm of policy, it is important to stress that the utopian moments in consumer publicity have an unstable political valence. Responding to an immanent contradiction in the bourgeois public sphere, mass publicity promises a reconciliation between embodiment and self-abstraction. That can be a powerful appeal, especially to those minoritized by the public sphere's rhetoric of normative disembodiment. Mass subjectivity, however, can result just as easily in new forms of majoritarian tyranny as it can in the claims of rival collectivities. Perhaps the clearest example now is the discourse on AIDS. As Simon Watney and others have shown, one of the most hateful features of AIDS discourse has been its construction of a "general public."[19] A spokesman for the White House, asked why Ronald Reagan had not even mentioned AIDS or its problems until late in 1985, explained, "It hadn't spread into the general population yet."[20] The mass media have pursued the same logic, in the pursuit of a public demanded by good professional journalism, interpellating their public as unitary and as heterosexual. Moreover, they have deployed the transitivism of mass identification in order to exile the positivity of the body to a zone of infection; the unitary public is uninfected but threatened. In this context, it is heartbreakingly accurate to speak of the prophylaxis held out by mass publicity to those who will identify with its immunized body.

Hateful though it is to those exiled into positivity by such a discourse, in a sense everyone's relation to the public body must have more or less the same logic. No one really inhabits the general public. This is true not only because it is by definition general, but also because people bring to such a category the particularities from which they have to abstract themselves in consuming this discourse. Of course, some particularities, such as whiteness and maleness, are already oriented to that procedure of abstraction. (They can scarcely even be imagined as particularities; think for example of the asymmetry between the semantics of "feminism" and "masculinism.") But the given of the body is nevertheless a site of countermemory, all the more so since statistically everyone will be mapped into some minority or other, a form of positivity minoritized precisely in the abstracting discourse with which everyone also identifies.

So in this sense, the gap that gay people register within the discourse of the general public might well be an aggravated form — though a lethally aggravated form — of the normal relation to the general public. I am suggesting, in other words, that a fundamental feature of the contemporary public sphere is this double movement of identification and alienation: on one hand, the prophylaxis of general publicity; on the other hand, the always inadequate particularity of individual bodies, experienced both as an invisible desire with a visible body and, in consequence, as a kind of closeted vulnerability.

The centrality of this contradiction in the legitimate textuality of the videocapitalist state is, I think, the reason why the discourse of the public sphere is so entirely given over to a violently desirous speculation on bodies. What I have tried to emphasize is that the effect of disturbance in mass publicity is not a corruption introduced into the public sphere by its colonization through mass media. It is the legacy of the bourgeois public sphere's founding logic, the contradictions of which become visible whenever the public sphere can no longer turn a blind eye to its privileged bodies.

For the same reasons, the public sphere is also not simply corrupted by its articulation with consumption. If anything, consumption sustains a counterpublicity that cuts against the self-contradictions of the bourgeois public sphere. One final example can show how. In recent years, graffiti writing has taken a new form. Always a kind of counterpublicity, it has become the medium of an urban and mostly black male subculture. The major cities all devote millions of dollars per year to obliterate it, and to criminalize it as a medium, while the art world moves to canonize it out of its counterpublic setting. In a recent article, Susan Stewart argues that the core of the graffiti writers' subculture lies in the way it has taken up the utopian promise of consumer publicity, and particularly of the brand name. These graffiti do not say "U.S. Out of North America," or "Patriarch Go Home," or "Power to the Queer Nation"; they are personal signatures legible only to the intimately initiated. Reproduced as quickly and as widely as possible (unlike their canonized art equivalents), they are trademarks that can be spread across a nearly anonymous landscape. The thrill of brand name dissemination, however, is linked to a very private sphere of knowledge, since the signature has been trademarked into illegibility. Stewart concludes:

> Graffiti may be a petty crime but its threat to value is an inventive
> one, for it forms a critique of the status of all artistic artifacts, indeed
> a critique of all privatized consumption, and it carries out that threat
> in full view, in repetition, so that the public has nowhere to look, no
> place to locate an averted glance. And that critique is paradoxically
> mounted from a relentless individualism, an individualism which,
> with its perfected monogram, arose out of the paradox of all
> commodity relations in their attempt to create a mass individual; an
> ideal consumer, a necessarily fading star. The independence of the
> graffiti writer has been shaped by a freedom both promised and
> denied by those relations — a freedom of choice which is a freedom

among delimited and clearly unattainable goods. While that paradise of consumption promised the transference of uniqueness from the artifact to the subject, graffiti underlines again and again an imaginary uniqueness of the subject and a dissolution of artifactual status *per se*.[21]

The graffiti of this subculture, in effect, parodies the mass media; by appearing everywhere, it aspires to the placeless publicity of mass print or televisualization. It thus abstracts away from the given body, which in the logic of graffiti is difficult to criminalize or minoritize because it is impossible to locate. (The "no place to look . . . no place to locate an averted glance" exactly describes the abstraction of tele-visualized space.) Unlike the self-abstraction of normal publicity, however, graffiti retains its link to a body, in an almost parodic de-votion to the sentimentality of the signature. As Stewart points out, it claims an imaginary uniqueness promised in commodities but can-celed in the public sphere proper. Whenever mass publicity puts its bodies on display, it reactivates this same promise. And although emancipation is not around the corner, its possibility is visible everywhere.

Obviously, the discursive genres of mass publicity vary widely. I group them together to show how they become interconnected as expressing a subjectivity that each genre helps to construct. In such contexts, the content and the media of mass publicity mutually de-termine each other. Mass media thematize certain materials — a jet crash, Michael Jackson's latest surgery, a football game — in order to find a way of constructing their audiences as mass audiences. These contents then function culturally as metalanguages, giving meaning to the medium. In consuming the thematic materials of mass media discourse, persons construct themselves as its mass subject. Thus the same reciprocity that allowed the *Spectator* and its print medium to be mutually clarifying can be seen in the current mass media. But precisely because the meaning of the mass media depends so much on their articulation with a specific metalanguage, we cannot speak simply of one kind of mass subjectivity, or one politics of mass pub-licity. Stewart makes roughly the same observation when she re-marks that the imbrication of graffiti, as a local practice, with the systemic themes of access — "access to discourse, access to goods, access to the reception of information" — poses a methodological problem, "calling into question the relations between a micro-

and a macro-analysis: the insinuating and pervasive forms of the mass culture are here known only through localizations and adaptations."[22]

Nevertheless, some things are clear. In a discourse of publicity structured by deep contradictions between self-abstraction and self-realization, contradictions that have only been forced to the fore in televisual consumer culture, there has been a massive shift toward the politics of identity. The major political movements of the past half century have been oriented to status categories. Unlike almost all previous social movements — Chartism, Temperance, the French Revolution — they have been centrally about the personal identity formation of minoritized subjects. These movements all presuppose the bourgeois public sphere as background. Their rallying cries of difference take for granted the official rhetoric of self-abstraction. It would be naive and sentimental to suppose that identities or mere assertions of status will precipitate from this crisis as its solution, since the public discourse makes identity an ongoing problem. An assertion of the full equality of minoritized statuses would require abandoning the structure of self-abstraction in publicity. That outcome seems unlikely in the near future. In the meantime, the contradictions of status and publicity are played out at both ends of the public discourse. We, as the subjects of mass publicity, find a political stake in the difficult-to-recognize politics of our identity; and the ego-crats who fill the screens of national fantasy must summon all their skin and hair to keep that politics from getting personal.

NOTES

1. Claude Lefort, "The Image of the Body and Totalitarianism," in his *Political Forms of Modern Society*, ed. John B. Thompson (Cambridge, Mass.: MIT Press, 1986), 306.

2. J. G. Ballard, *Love and Napalm: Export U.S.A.* (New York: Grove, 1972), 149–51.

3. The arguments condensed here can be found in their full form in *The Letters of the Republic: Publication and the Public Sphere in Eighteenth-Century America* (Cambridge, Mass.: Harvard University Press, 1990).

4. [Richard Steele], *The Spectator*, no. 555, in *Selections from the Tatler and the Spectator*, ed. Angus Ross (New York: Penguin, 1982), 213.

5. Lauren Berlant, "National Brands/National Body: *Imitation of Life*," in this volume.

6. Jürgen Habermas, *The Structural Transformation of the Public Sphere*, trans. Thomas Burger (Cambridge, Mass.: MIT Press, 1989), 43.

7. The point here about the character of gender difference has been a common one since Simone de Beauvoir's *The Second Sex* (1949); its more recent extension to an analysis of the bourgeois public sphere is in Joan Landes, *Women and the Public Sphere in the Age of the French Revolution* (Ithaca, N.Y.: Cornell University Press, 1988).

8. Pier Paolo Pasolini, *Lutheran Letters*, quoted in Douglas Crimp, "Strategies of Public Address: Which Media, Which Publics?" *Discussions in Contemporary Culture, Number One*, ed. Hal Foster (Seattle: Bay Press, 1987), 33.

9. Timothy Breen, "Baubles of Britain," *Past and Present* 119 (May 1988): 73–104.

10. Lefort, "Image of the Body," 303.

11. Lefort, "Image of the Body," 304–6.

12. Habermas, *Structural Transformation*, 8.

13. Habermas, *Structural Transformation*, 201. The MIT translation reads "whose" where I have corrected the text to "which."

14. "F.D.R., Anyone?" *The Nation* 248, no. 20 (May 22, 1989): 689.

15. For a critique of the still-popular notion of media manipulation, see Hans Magnus Enzensberger, "Constituents of a Theory of the Media," in *Critical Essays* (New York: Continuum, 1982), 46–76.

16. John Waters, *Shock Value* (New York: Dell, 1981), 24.

17. "Aggressivity in Psychoanalysis," *Ecrits*, trans. Alan Sheridan (New York: Norton, 1977), 19.

18. Waters, *Shock Value*, 26.

19. Simon Watney, *Policing Desire: Pornography, AIDS, and the Media* (Minneapolis: University of Minnesota Press, 1987), 83–84 and *passim*.

20. Jan Zita Grover, "AIDS: Keywords," in *October* 43 (Winter 1987): 23. This issue has since been reprinted as *AIDS: Cultural Analysis, Cultural Activism*, ed. Douglas Crimp (Cambridge, Mass.: MIT Press, 1988).

21. Susan Stewart, "Ceci Tuera Cela: Graffiti as Crime and Art," in *Life after Postmodernism: Essays on Value and Culture*, ed. John Fekete (New York: St. Martin's, 1987), 161–80, at 175–76.

22. Stewart, "Ceci Tuera Cela," 163.

The Fine Art of Regulation
Andrew Ross

I am not at all sure if "censorship" is the most useful term to describe the recent clampdowns on cultural expression in North America. For reasons that will be explored only speculatively in this essay, the more general term "regulation" better serves the arguments I want to make about the relationships between the state and the cultural marketplace that have been at the forefront of recent public discussion about "censorship" and the arts. While the bulk of this discussion has focused on the National Endowment for the Arts flap, the Mapplethorpe and 2 Live Crew trials, and the debates about political correctness, its general context lies within the high-pressure area of conservative morality that has been building in strength since the rise of the New Right at the end of the seventies.

If the strident New Right morality offends more genteel or traditional codes of cultural conservatism, it may be because it has established its deepest influence within popular consciousness, setting up shop with an explicitly populist agenda that ties nationalism to a set of proscriptions about the bodily behavior of target groups. "Youth," the traditional postwar target group, is no longer an undifferentiated category, and so the policing of sex, drugs, and rock 'n' roll is more complex and various today than it was in the full flush of the sixties youth counterculture, when the official diet of "repressive tolerance" was still linked to the long consumerist boom of the postwar years. Just as new desires had to be tapped to create new markets, the destabilizing effects of these new desires on the social order were ultimately held up as an excuse for the creation of new regulatory powers. Consequently, sex, drugs, and rock 'n' roll are no longer simply useful as controlled stimulants for the consumer economy; they are now indispensable categories for controlling and policing the new ethnic, sexual, and economic identities that have become such an important feature of public and political life in the past twenty years.

The signals that control the traffic between economic and cultural life are never simple, and yet there are moments when the stop signs are more or less in alignment. At a time when sectors of the nation's debtor economy are being encouraged to go slow, the restraining power of more than a decade of "Just Say No" sloganeering has seized the day to extend its conscious and subjudicial influence over the whole realm of cultural expression. At least three objectives are accomplished in one fiercely moral campaign. First, the stabilization (even through the imposition of a temporary recession) of markets, circulating out of the orbit of the national economy along flow lines governed by the post-Fordist economy. Second, the opportunity to regulate and proscribe our bodily lives, and especially those of women, sexual minorities, and people of color. And third, the authorization of aggressive intervention: in the case of drug-producing countries (including the United States itself), especially those harboring leftist insurgency movements; in the instance of aid-receiving nation-states that provide publicly funded abortion; in the newly independent Eastern European states that are judged to be hungry for the messianic coming of *Playboy* magazine; or in the Middle East, where religious ideologies that oppress women are disregarded in the interests of oil imperialism. On the domestic front, things are no less clear. The combat-zone regulation of many practices concerning sex, drugs, and popular music — homosexuality; nonmonogamous or interracial sex; AIDS drugs, abortion drugs, or crack; Satanist metal, rap against police racism, or fetish rock — surely demonstrates that the "free" body has become the chief site for generating new forms of power relations in the "free" world.

Formerly enthusiastic, even naive, advocates of the *sexual revolution* have long had to confront the evidence that the "creation" of freedoms is not a simple linear process that can be guaranteed to constantly expand the limits of permissibility until the revolution can be said to be complete. Each liberatory step forward is also a step sideways (what Shklovsky called "the knight's move"), into an alternate world where new and often unforeseen relations of power come into play, and where what had been seen as "advances" at the previous stage now take on a different and less straightforward appearance. Narratives of the sort that are associated with the promise of a "sexual revolution" can no more be divorced from changing socioeconomic conditions than they can be expected to easily absorb the meaning of new diseases like AIDS that can change the way we think of our bodies in such a very short space of time. Who, seven years ago, could have foreseen the powerful moralizing and regulating presence of something called the "immune body," which now lies at the center of our political culture? Or that its pervasive authority would dovetail so easily with such familiar and shopworn historical discourses as the militarist obsession about the vulnerability of the national body, or the fundamentalist doctrine of the socially purified body, giving each a new lease on life into the bargain? Who could have foreseen that the immunity of a "body" within a body, the fetus, would be part of the same rhetorical package that characterizes the *dominant* image of the vulnerable body of today? The sexual revolution in our times cannot be recorded as a calendar of liberatory milestones, with each new advance in freedoms duly entered, nor even as a theater of war, fought on many different and complex fronts. It is more like a game with many different players, and with rules and stakes that are constantly changing.

While neither the Cincinnati trial of the Robert Mapplethorpe photography show nor the trial of Miami rappers 2 Live Crew produced a successful prosecution, the fact that they took place, in the current climate, was a sure sign that a mood of prohibition, rather than an apparatus of repression, was slowly being consolidated. Even when state censorship plays its (inevitably) losing hand, self-censoring is sure to follow. Almost as bad, at least in my mind, we have had to put up with knee-jerk libertarian responses to the recent crackdowns, as if it were all a "free speech" issue. Public discussion of these trials strategically steered the debate about sexuality and art onto classical grounds of threats to free speech and basic civil liberties concerning freedom of expression. Consequently, artists from all across the spectrum of age, gender, race, sexual preference, and aesthetic orientation responded with anger and as if with the unified voice of a class under siege. But this kind of response does art a disservice, since it assumes that art, even critical art, already enjoys immunity from external social and political regulation; it assumes that the social dialogue between art and politics ought ideally to be a polite, risk-free (and, perhaps, one-way) conversation, and that the existence of critical art is so fragile that it will crumble or wither away under the slightest scrutiny of the philistine gaze. If art were something that only needs to be protected, then it would deserve to be quarantined, and the museum, or the Rock 'n' Roll Hall of Fame, would be its only true home.

Similar issues and arguments have characterized the recent public debates in the media about "political correctness" within the universities. There, the defense of "free speech" has been perversely turned against those seeking to challenge entrenched orthodoxies and to make the academy into a more multicultural environment. While misrepresentation and disinformation are rife in the high-profile red-baiting campaign, there is every reason to welcome a public debate about the shape of "culture" as it is defined and reproduced within the academy. If nothing else, the debate has served to shatter the mythical perception of an ivory tower milieu that is comfortably removed from public life. Millions of citizens populate the world of colleges and universities, and thereby constitute a public in its own right. In spite of the powerful, and overly prestigious, influence of the private sector within higher education, internal conflicts can easily be defined as issues of public concern, at least if the stakes are high enough and are of consequence to right-wing interests. The actually existing left, within the universities, has at last gained recognition, but at the cost of becoming a visible, and potentially vulnerable, target. We may not welcome the conditions of our newfound visibility, but we ought to be prepared, in time-honored fashion, to make some history under conditions not of our own making.

It should be quite clear that the charge of political correctness now means something more than it used to. Let me join my voice with those who lament the loss of a good thing. Let me also join with those who are prepared to see the new arrangement as an opportunity to make some good politics. First of all, the nostalgia part. Generally speaking, "political correctness" was a term devised to humorously warn those whose authoritarian zeal for militant purity was pursued at the cost of a politics of pleasure. Emma Goldman probably kicked things off when she said, "If I can't dance, I don't want to be part of your revolution." Anti-antiporn feminists were exercising the same logic sixty years later, when they argued against the puritanical concept of "feminist" sexual desire — seen as an attempt to restrict womens' access to areas of sexual experience deemed incorrect. Some of the most important debates in cultural politics in recent years have revolved around the concept of correctness. Indeed, up until the recent switcheroo, the new cultural left took many of its cues from transgressing older codes of correctness in matters of fashion, style, and taste.

One of the most insurgent developments, for example, took place in the realm of popular culture, hitherto considered a no-go area for leftists unless they were in the reassuring company of acoustic guitars and protest lyrics. It was one giant leap (but still a knight's move) from Holly Near, Billy Bragg, and Tracy Chapman to Madonna, Prince, and the Pet Shop Boys. The jury is still out on the "incorrectness" of cases like Guns N' Roses and Ice Cube, but at least there are grounds today for a serious debate about the conditions of racism, sexism, and homophobia in popular culture. Fifteen years ago, it was still all mindless fodder and pap, the new opium of the masses. Nothing was more politically incorrect on the left than commercial popular culture, and, even today, it remains the most undigestible portion of the expanded scholarly body represented by the new multicultural canon, whose advocates may speak in the name of diversity but who all too quickly have made their peace with the principles of inclusion/exclusion espoused by any form of canonmaking. It is no surprise that "great" works by great authors of color and female gender have already passed the test of legitimacy; they are, after all, according to the self-fulfilling nature of the test, great. It is still easier for a camel to pass through the eye of a needle than it is for the guardians (and wannabes) of a disciplinary body of knowledge, dependent upon the isolation of discretely accredited cultural objects, to recognize the busy culture of daily life as a realm of activity fit for adult discussion and analysis. Hardly surprising, then, that it is still difficult for many fully subscribed PC-ers to imagine that daily culture might be a place where a radical democratic culture could be built. Popular culture will no doubt retain its degraded and marginal status even in a fully legitimate multicultural curriculum. Its placement within the context of "multicultural studies," however, opens up the treatment of popular culture to questions about race, sexuality, and gender that cut across, although they do not eradicate, the traditional class framework of high/low.

Evidence of this new configuration can be drawn from the public conduct of and response to the Mapplethorpe and 2 Live Crew trials. In the case of 2 Live Crew, defamed inside and outside the hip-hop community for the sexist profile of their music, liberal public opinion was hardly rock steady in its support. Generally speaking, the defense of their misogyny was seen as a necessary evil. Henry Louis Gates, Jr., a major defense witness at the trial, mounted an articulate case for viewing the band's performance as a parodic exaggeration of the oversexed, black, working-class male, and went so far as to suggest that white audiences may not have been capable of seeing the parody. Since no one wants to be exposed as a cultural dope, incapable of recognizing a parody, the predominantly white jurors took the bait and affirmed this interpretation by rejecting Gates's suggestion about a white/black culture divide, duly exonerating the rappers. In the trial of Dennis Barrie, the Cincinnati curator of the Mapplethorpe show, defense witnesses testified to the artistic value of the photographs, citing Mapplethorpe as a leading figure in the formalist mode of the eighties and calling attention to the formal details of classical composition in his work. Photographs that explicitly focused on gay practices were praised for their "opposing diagonals" and their framing of the tension between "lines" and "light." For the formalist art establishment, holding its nose for as long as it had to, defending Mapplethorpe may have been as much a necessary evil as the defense of 2 Live Crew would be for right-thinking liberals. As for the jurors, in Miami they were quite happy about their verdict, regretting only that it could not have been announced in the form of a rap song. By contrast, the Cincinnati jurors, few of whom had even been to an art museum, confessed that they felt truly browbeaten into delivering an acquittal, at least if we are to believe what they said to journalists after the trial. "Art" had been defined for them by the expert witnesses. Even though they all had strong opinions about Mapplethorpe's work, they had no opportunity, no language with which to question, let alone contest, the experts' definition of art. If it was the experts' testimony about art that impelled these jurors to return their verdict, the experts' statements had little to do with any conception of art as public dialogue.

No doubt many lessons could be drawn from the jurors' responses in these two trials, lessons, in the Cincinnati trial, about the exclusive policing of art and high culture by accredited experts, and lessons, in the Broward County trial, about the more openly participatory appeal of popular culture. The trial proceedings in Cincinnati created a good deal of class resentment among the jurors. The Broward County trial, by contrast, turned into an opportunity to transcend racial divisions and differences. But to focus only on the contrasts between the trials is to neglect what they initially shared as object lessons in the politics of regulation. While the verdicts in both trials were seen as victories for the civil libertarian cause, there was no mistaking the respective targets of the suits: the gay artist and the black popular performer. The civil libertarian stand on freedom of expression turns on the question of universal rights, and therefore cannot specifically address the central significance of homoeroticism and black male sexuality in these trials. So too, the counterallegations about cultural fascism, reinforced by references to the Nazi category of "degenerate art" (*entartete Kunst*), provide little in the way of historical aid in the task of explaining the delicacy of "content" in the new proscribed art. The Nazi category, like its social realist counterpart and the vestigial Zhdanovism in postwar socialist countries, was primarily about the politics of *form*, a politics that was shared, from a different perspective, of course, in North America by the cold war advocacy of abstract expressionism, especially as a cultural export. Some might still be prepared to split hairs over the legitimacy of distinguishing between form and content, but they would be missing the point — Jesse Helms had no problem with this distinction; he has focused quite directly on artistic content relating to homosexual practices.

Consider what may look like a rather obtuse comparison between the Helms position and the case of the sculptor Brancusi's "Bird in Flight," impounded by a U.S. Customs official in 1936 because it just did not look like a bird in flight. Helms's appeal to populist morality on questions of content seems to have little in common with the appeal to populist taste on questions of form made during the Brancusi trial. The argument that public money should not be used for the funding of homoerotic art is a far cry from the argument that the public is entitled to levy an import tax on abstract art, but there is a common principle at stake here about the public accountability of art, a political question on the face of it, but one that is clearly bound up with economic considerations. In fact, I will maintain here that such arguments might best be seen in the context of the *cultural economy* of their times; both are examples of the *regulation* of the market that is governed by prevailing economic demands but that depends upon cultural prohibitions and morality plays about the "public interest" to legitimate its work.

How exactly do the gay artist and the "oversexed" black performer pose a threat to the "public interest" in whose name these trials and other regulatory procedures were being conducted?[1] One of the answers to that question may lie in the nature of the cultural marketplace. Like all markets, the art market and the marketplace of popular culture depend upon regulatory features to offset their volatile, unstable, and anarchic tendencies. In the case of the art market, aesthetic taste is the preferred form of regulation; taste in the form of "decent" moral standards is less preferred but is still highly operative. Both function as cultural prohibitions that offset the amoral workings of a marketplace and thereby provide it with a stable, coherent appearance. In economic theory, regulation is required to ensure that the behavior of the market *looks* as if it is coherent, settled, and securely supported by an appropriate cultural consensus at any given time.[2] One could say, for example, that the art market depends precisely upon the assumption of such a consensus about matters of taste. The price fixing of any market has an anarchic and destabilizing effect that needs to be balanced by regulatory features if it is to maintain an ordered and coherent appearance: one of these economic features is the credit system (money bet on production that does not yet exist), another is state intervention in the form of fiscal aid, legal guarantees, credit creation, tax redistribution, control over wages and prices, restrictions on labor union power, military expenditure, and so on. When major shifts in the balance between capital accumulation and consumption are required by the market, these regulatory features extend to the whole "structure of feeling" of social and cultural life — including morality and sexuality (the recent shift, postdating the oil crisis of 1974, is often referred to as the move from Fordism to post-Fordism). When such a shift occurs, a new consensus about cultural values is created through this process of regulation. In the same way, the stability of price fixing on the art market depends not only upon the regulatory importance of investment in artists' reputations, but also upon state intervention, primarily in the form of legal and tax provisions relating to the "public" donation of art to museums. At the lower end of the art market, public funding of art primes the pump of the system by ensuring fresh production of value. Changes in the cultural consensus about taste and value require a step-up in the interventionist activity of regulatory features. It is at that point that the "public" or the "public interest" is opened up to debate, since visibly greater regulation is always introduced in the name of "the public interest." What we could term the Helms effect is to do precisely that — to redefine the "public interest" as a primarily moral interest, which then governs the fundability of aesthetics in the name of public standards of "decency." The politics of state intervention is thereby provided with an aesthetic/moral covering.

In free-market ideology, of course, state intervention is supposed to be the mark of Satan, and yet regulation of this kind, as I have argued, is essential to the stability of the otherwise anarchic market. This is why the Victorian public morality of the New Right and Christian fundamentalism has been such a godsend to the full revival of free-market ideology in the Reagan-Bush years. In principle, libertarian marketeering holds that anything that *can* be bought or sold *should* be bought and sold. If all market exchanges are legitimate, then homosexual exchanges are ultimately legitimate. Homosexual exchange is thus *the* name that the free market dare not speak, if only because it reveals too much the true (amoral) colors of free-market ideology. In the case of the current crackdown on gay and lesbian artists, the regulatory checks on a market (where "anything goes") are introduced in the name of "public interest," the best possible cover for state intervention. One could make a similar argument about the spectacle of "oversexed" black male sexuality in the case of the 2 Live Crew performance. Not only did it contravene long-standing moral prohibitions against black male access in the sexual marketplace, but the excessive misogynism of the rappers' performance also exposes what would otherwise be seen as normative — as everyday, institutionalized sexism within popular culture. Here again, public taste is brought to bear upon the regulation of taste in the popular marketplace of cultural goods.

Let us bear in mind that regulation of this sort, which is normative, takes the risk of looking like repressive censorship only if there are very large stakes involved. Let us also remember that even though the constitutionally lawful limits of the Helms crusade seem to have been reached, and a temporary retrenchment forced upon it, this should not blind us to the fact that the crusade has performed its regulatory work, leaving in place a new prohibitory mood that is exercising its sway over the whole realm of cultural expression and access. In conclusion, then, I would suggest that the Helms effect is not finally about the curtailment or the censorship of free (political) speech, nor about generalized homophobia, although these are two of the stable, and recognizable, forms in which the new repression has masqueraded. Rather, their restraining effect might be seen in the context of a larger cultural prohibition that helps to play the role of regulating the market balance between capital accumulation and cultural consumption, a balance that has been subject to redefinition in the past fifteen years of post-Fordism. The generalized regulation of the body that is the primary vehicle for these prohibitions has provided new authoritarian opportunities for controlling what our bodies produce and consume, ensuring a greater degree of predictive stability for the economy. This is what I mean by the fine art of regulation.

It may seem that I am taking the high ground in appealing to the largest economic contexts of these cultural imbroglios. But it is just as odd to have to apologize for reintroducing economic analysis into the cultural critique of problems that lie currently at the forefront of affairs of state. After all, economic recessionary measures have long been used to "discipline" the rising expectations of a populace by raising the specter of scarcity in the midst of relative affluence. In recent years, we have even seen how appeals to ecological limits have entered public consciousness in a similarly coercive way. Indeed, it is by now taken for granted that we live in an age of limits, where even the hard lessons of ecological arguments about "limits to growth" have found their way into the lexicon of capitalist economics, if only under the aegis of technocratic efficiency. But we cannot afford to see the rationality of ecological "limits" carried over into the realm of cultural and political restrictions. Ecologists have long insisted that there are "natural" limits to the carrying capacity of bioregions and that capitalism's grow-or-die ethic, founded on hidden social costs that are increasingly visible, has exceeded those limits in its exploitation of the world's biological capital. Some political theorists, like William Ophuls, argue that the return of "natural scarcity," after three hundred years of artificial abundance for the West, will put paid to the public sphere of liberal democracy.[3] This golden age of liberties was supported by assumptions about ecological abundance in nature that could apply only to a minority of the world's population for the limited space of time during which these resources could be profitably exploited. An ecological law of the minimum, not unlike the rule of diminishing returns that Marx called "the falling rate of profit," has come into play. Ophuls believes that the return of material scarcity and physical necessity seriously compromises the assumptions of libertarian individualism and necessitates fresh political institutions that can legislate ecologically minded limits and restrictions to libertarianism.

There is no doubt that this is a dangerous argument. Material scarcity has long been an excuse for imposing hierarchical structures within societies, and, in the context of global politics today, it is increasingly cited as a rationale for draconian measures within the developing world, where population measures — starvation, disease, forced sterilization — that will ensure the sustainability of the Western way of life are "introduced." Capitalism, moreover, has long relied upon repressive political measures on behalf of the state to support its own reliance on "free" resources, cheap energy, and cheap labor. Even if we acknowledge the thesis about a temporary period of Western growth, there is no necessary link between assumptions about natural abundance and the democratic "luxury" of public freedoms. Indeed, it is precisely because of the existence of public freedoms that limits on growth can be democratically chosen and agreed upon. To accept the authority of a "natural" or "biological" law of scarcity as a prior court of judgment is to sell political rationality short.

But it is just as clear that the "public interest," with its primarily anthropocentric worldview, can no longer be accepted as the highest court of appeal in ecological matters. Even more so since corporate environmentalism, engaged in its largest-ever public relations exercise, now wages its conservationist claims to be defending the earth in the name of accountability to a credulous public. As the contours of the "public" bend under pressure to assume a manageable corporate shape, the marginal and excluded voices that rise, as ever, to challenge this essentially humanist legacy include those that register the interests of nonhuman nature. But do not be alarmed by this. There are no rough beasts slouching toward the public sphere.

NOTES

1. I do not want to give the impression that the issues raised by the work of Mapplethorpe and 2 Live Crew are mutually exclusive. In fact, a good deal of controversy about Mapplethorpe's work within the gay community revolves around his commodification of black male sexuality for gay, white male spectators.

2. For a North American case study of the "regulation school," see Michel Aglietta, *A Theory of Capitalist Regulation: The US Experience*, trans. David Fernbach (London: Verso, 1979).

3. See William Ophuls, *Ecology and the Politics of Scarcity* (San Francisco: Freeman, 1977).

Disjuncture and Difference in the Global Cultural Economy
Arjun Appadurai

It takes only the merest acquaintance with the facts of the modern world to note that it is now an interactive system in a sense which is strikingly new. Historians and sociologists, especially those concerned with translocal processes (Hodgson 1974) and with the world systems associated with capitalism (Abu-Lughod 1989; Braudel 1981–84; Curtin 1984; Wallerstein 1974; Wolf 1982), have long been aware that the world has been a congeries of large-scale interactions for many centuries. Yet today's world involves interactions of a new order and intensity. Cultural transactions between social groups in the past have generally been restricted, sometimes by the facts of geography and ecology, and at other times by active resistance to interactions with the Other (as in China for much of its history and in Japan before the Meiji Restoration). Where there have been sustained cultural transactions across large parts of the globe, they have usually involved the long-distance journey of commodities (and of the merchants most concerned with them) and of travellers and explorers of every type (Helms 1988; Schafer 1963). The two main forces for sustained cultural interaction before this century have been warfare (and the large-scale political systems sometimes generated by it) and religions of conversion, which have sometimes, as in the case of Islam, taken warfare as one of the legitimate instruments of their expansion. Thus, between travellers and merchants, pilgrims and conquerors, the world has seen much long-distance (and long-term) cultural traffic. This much seems self-evident.

But few will deny that given the problems of time, distance and limited technologies for the command of resources across vast spaces, cultural dealings between socially and spatially separated groups have, until the last few centuries, been bridged at great cost and sustained over time only with great effort. The forces of cultural gravity seemed always to pull away from the formation of large-scale ecumenes, whether religious, commercial or political, towards smaller-scale accretions of intimacy and interest.

Sometime in the last few centuries, the nature of this gravitational field seems to have changed. Partly due to the spirit of the expansion of Western maritime interests after 1500, and partly because of the relatively autonomous developments of large and aggressive social formations in the Americas (such as the Aztecs and the Incas); in Eurasia (such as the Mongols, and their descendants, the Mughals and Ottomans); in island South-East Asia (such as the Buginese); and in the kingdoms of pre-colonial Africa (such as Dahomey), an overlapping set of ecumenes began to emerge, in which congeries of money, commerce, conquest and migration began to create durable cross-societal bonds. This process was accelerated by the technology transfers and accelerations of the late eighteenth and nineteenth centuries (e.g., Bayly 1989), which created complex colonial orders centered on European capitals and spread throughout the non-European world. This complex and overlapping set of Euro-colonial worlds (first Spanish and Portuguese, later principally English, French and Dutch) set the basis for a permanent traffic in ideas of peoplehood and selfhood, which created the imagined communities (Anderson 1983) of recent nationalisms throughout the world.

With what Benedict Anderson has called 'print capitalism', a new power was unleashed in the world, the power of mass literacy and its attendant large-scale production of projects of ethnic affinity that were remarkably free of the need for face-to-face communication or even of indirect communication between persons and groups. The act of reading things together set the stage for movements based on a paradox — the paradox of constructed primordialism. There is, of course, a great deal else that is involved in the story of colonialism and of its dialectically generated nationalisms (Chatterjee 1986), but the issue of constructed ethnicities is surely a crucial strand in this tale.

But the revolution of print capitalism, and the cultural affinities and dialogues unleashed by it, were only modest precursors to the world we live in now. For in the last century, there has been a technological explosion, largely in the domain of transportation and information, which makes the interactions of a print-dominated world seem as hard-won and as easily erased as the print revolution made earlier forms of cultural traffic appear. For with the advent of the steamship, the automobile and the aeroplane, the camera, the computer and the telephone, we have entered into an altogether new condition of neighborliness, even with those most distant from ourselves. Marshall McLuhan, among others, sought to theorise about this world as a global village, but theories such as McLuhan's appear to have overestimated the communitarian implications of the new media order. We are now aware that with media, each time we are tempted to speak of the 'global village', we must be reminded that media create communities with 'no sense of place' (Meyrowitz 1985). The world we live in now seems rhizomic (Deleuze and Guattari 1987), even schizophrenic, calling for theories of rootlessness, alienation and psychological distance between individuals and groups, on the one hand, and fantasies (or nightmares) of electronic propinquity on the other. Here we are close to the central problematic of cultural processes in today's world.

Thus, the curiosity which recently drove Pico Iyer to Asia (1988) is in some ways the product of a confusion between some ineffable McDonaldization of the world and the much subtler play of indigenous trajectories of desire and fear with global flows of people and things. Indeed Iyer's own impressions are testimony to the fact that, if 'a' global cultural system is emerging, it is filled with ironies and resistances, sometimes camouflaged as passivity and a bottomless appetite in the Asian world for things Western.

Iyer's own account of the uncanny Philippine affinity for American popular music is rich testimony to the global culture of the 'hyperreal', for somehow Philippine renditions of American popular songs are both more widespread in the Philippines, and more disturbingly faithful to their originals, than they are in the United States today. An entire nation seems to have learned to mimic Kenny Rogers and the Lennon sisters, like a vast Asian Motown chorus. But Americanization is certainly a pallid term to apply to such a situation, for not only are there more Filipinos singing perfect renditions of some American songs (often from the American past) than there are Americans doing so, there is, of course, the fact that the rest of their lives is not in complete synchrony with the referential world which first gave birth to these songs.

In a further, globalizing twist on what Jameson has recently called 'nostalgia for the present' (1989), these Filipinos look back to a world they have never lost. This is one of the central ironies of the politics of global cultural flows, especially in the arena of entertainment and leisure. It plays havoc with the hegemony of Euro-chronology. American nostalgia feeds on Filipino desire represented as a hyper-competent reproduction. Here we have nostalgia without memory. The paradox, of course, has its explanations, and they are historical; unpacked, they lay bare the story of the American missionization and political rape of the Philippines, one result of which has been the creation of a nation of make-believe Americans, who tolerated for so long a leading lady who played the piano while the slums of Manila expanded and decayed. Perhaps the most radical postmodernists would argue that this is hardly surprising, since in the peculiar chronicities of late capitalism, pastiche and nostalgia are central modes of image production and reception. Americans themselves are hardly in the present any more as they stumble into the mega-technologies of the twenty-first century garbed in the film noir scenarios of sixties 'chills', fifties diners, forties clothing, thirties houses, twenties dances, and so on ad infinitum.

As far as the United States is concerned, one might suggest that the issue is no longer one of nostalgia but of a social *imaginaire* built largely around re-runs. Jameson (1983) was bold to link the politics of nostalgia to the postmodern commodity sensibility and surely he was right. The drug wars in Colombia recapitulate the tropical sweat of Vietnam, with Ollie North and his succession of masks — Jimmy Stewart concealing John Wayne concealing Spiro Agnew and all of them transmogrifying into Sylvester Stallone who wins in Afghanistan — thus simultaneously fulfilling the secret American envy of Soviet imperialism and the re-run (this time with a happy ending) of the Vietnam War. The Rolling Stones, approaching their fifties, gyrate before eighteen-year-olds who do not appear to need the machinery of nostalgia to be sold on their parents' heroes. Paul McCartney is selling the Beatles to a new audience by hitching his oblique nostalgia to their desire for the new that smacks of the old. *Dragnet* is back in nineties drag, and so is *Adam-12*, not to speak of *Batman* and *Mission Impossible*, all dressed up technologically but remarkably faithful to the atmospherics of their originals.

The past is now not a land to return to in a simple politics of memory. It has become a synchronic warehouse of cultural scenarios, a kind of temporal central casting, to which recourse can be had as appropriate, depending on the movie to be made, the scene to be enacted, the hostages to be rescued. All this is par for the course, if you follow Baudrillard or Lyotard into a world of signs wholly unmoored from their social signifiers (all the world's a Disneyland). But I would like to suggest that the apparent increasing substitutability of whole periods and postures for one another, in the cultural styles of advanced capitalism, is tied to larger global forces, which have done much to show Americans that the past is usually another country. If your present is their future (as in much modernization theory and in many self-satisfied tourist fantasies), and their future is your past (as in the case of the Philippine virtuosos of American popular music), then your own past can be made to appear as simply a normalized modality of your present. Thus, although some anthropologists may continue to relegate their Others to temporal spaces that they do not themselves occupy (Fabian 1983), post-industrial cultural productions have entered a post-nostalgic phase.

The crucial point, however, is that the United States is no longer the puppeteer of a world system of images, but is only one node of a complex transnational construction of imaginary landscapes. The world we live in today is characterised by a new role for the imagination in social life. To grasp this new role, we need to bring together: the old idea of images, especially mechanically produced images (in the Frankfurt School sense); the idea of the imagined community (in Anderson's sense); and the French idea of the imaginary (*imaginaire*), as a constructed landscape of collective aspirations, which is no more and no less real than the collective representations of Emile Durkheim, now mediated through the complex prism of modern media.

The image, the imagined, the imaginary — these are all terms which direct us to something critical and new in global cultural processes: *the imagination as a social practice*. No longer mere fantasy (opium for the masses whose real work is elsewhere), no longer simple escape (from a world defined principally by more concrete purposes and structures), no longer elite pastime (thus not relevant to the lives of ordinary people) and no longer mere contemplation (irrelevant for new forms of desire and subjectivity), the imagination has become an organized field of social practices, a form of work (both in the sense of labor and of culturally organized practice) and a form of negotiation between sites of agency ('individuals') and globally defined fields of possibility. It is this unleashing of the imagination which links the play of pastiche (in some settings) to the terror and coercion of states and their competitors. The imagination is now central to all forms of agency, is itself a social fact, and is the key component of the new global order. But to make this claim meaningful, it is necessary to address some other issues.

Homogenization and Heterogenization

The central problem of today's global interactions is the tension between cultural homogenization and cultural heterogenization. A vast array of empirical facts could be brought to bear on the side of the homogenization argument, and much of it has come from the left end of the spectrum of media studies (Hamelink 1983; Mattelart 1983; Schiller 1976), and some from other perspectives (Gans 1985; Iyer 1988). Most often, the homogenization argument subspeciates into either an argument about Americanization, or an argument about commoditization, and very often the two arguments are closely linked. What these arguments fail to consider is that at least as rapidly as forces from various metropolises are brought into new societies they tend to become indigenized in one or another way: this is true of music and housing styles as much as it is true of science and terrorism, spectacles and constitutions. The dynamics of such indigenization have just begun to be explored systemically (Barber 1987; Feld 1988; Hannerz 1987, 1989; Ivy 1988; Nicoll 1989; Yoshimoto 1989), and much more needs to be done. But it is worth noticing that for the people of Irian Jaya, Indonesianization may be more worrisome than Americanization, as Japanization may be for Koreans, Indianization for Sri Lankans, Vietnamization for the Cambodians, Russianization for the people of Soviet Armenia and the Baltic Republics. Such a list of alternative fears to Americanization could be greatly expanded, but it is not a shapeless inventory: for polities of smaller scale, there is always a fear of cultural absorption by polities of larger scale, especially those that are nearby. One man's imagined community is another man's political prison.

This scalar dynamic, which has widespread global manifestations, is also tied to the relationship between nations and states, to which I shall return later. For the moment let us note that the simplification of these many forces (and fears) of homogenization can also be exploited by nation-states in relation to their own minorities, by posing global commoditization (or capitalism, or some other such external enemy) as more real than the threat of its own hegemonic strategies.

The new global cultural economy has to be seen as a complex, overlapping, disjunctive order, which cannot any longer be understood in terms of existing center-periphery models (even those which might account for multiple centers and peripheries). Nor is it susceptible to simple models of push and pull (in terms of migration theory), or of surpluses and deficits (as in traditional models of balance of trade), or of consumers and producers (as in most neo-Marxist theories of development). Even the most complex and flexible theories of global development which have come out of the Marxist tradition (Amin 1980; Mandel 1978; Wallerstein 1974; Wolf 1982) are inadequately quirky and have failed to come to terms with what Lash and Urry have called disorganized capitalism (1987). The complexity of the current global economy has to do with certain fundamental disjunctures between economy, culture and politics which we have only begun to theorize.[1]

I propose that an elementary framework for exploring such disjunctures is to look at the relationship between five dimensions of global cultural flow which can be termed: (a) ethnoscapes; (b) mediascapes; (c) technoscapes; (d) finanscapes; and (e) ideoscapes.[2] The suffix -scape allows us to point to the fluid, irregular shapes of these landscapes, shapes which characterize international capital as deeply as they do international clothing styles. These terms with the common suffix -scape also indicate that these are not objectively given relations which look the same from every angle of vision, but rather that they are deeply perspectival constructs, inflected by the historical, linguistic and political situatedness of different sorts of actors: nation-states, multinationals, diasporic communities, as well as subnational groupings and movements (whether religious, political or economic), and even intimate face-to-face groups, such as villages, neighbourhoods and families. Indeed, the individual actor is the last locus of this perspectival set of landscapes, for these landscapes are eventually navigated by agents who both experience and constitute larger formations, in part by their own sense of what these landscapes offer.

These landscapes thus are the building blocks of what (extending Benedict Anderson) I would like to call *imagined worlds*, that is, the multiple worlds which are constituted by the historically situated imaginations of persons and groups spread around the globe (Appadurai: in press). An important fact of the world we live in today is that many persons on the globe live in such imagined worlds (and not just in imagined communities) and thus are able to contest and sometimes even subvert the imagined worlds of the official mind and of the entrepreneurial mentality that surround them.

By ethnoscape, I mean the landscape of persons who constitute the shifting world in which we live: tourists, immigrants, refugees, exiles, guestworkers and other moving groups and persons constitute an essential feature of the world and appear to affect the politics of (and between) nations to a hitherto unprecedented degree. This is not to say that there are no relatively stable communities and networks, of kinship, of friendship, of work and of leisure, as well as of birth, residence and other filiative forms. But it is to say that the warp of these stabilities is everywhere shot through with the woof of human motion, as more persons and groups deal with the realities of having to move or the fantasies of wanting to move. What is more, both these realities as well as these fantasies now function on larger scales, as men and women from villages in India think not just of moving to Poona or Madras, but of moving to Dubai and Houston, and refugees from Sri Lanka find themselves in South India as well as in Switzerland, just as the Hmong are driven to London as well as to Philadelphia. And as international capital shifts its needs, as production and technology generate different needs, as nation-states shift their policies on refugee populations, these moving groups can never afford to let their imaginations rest too long, even if they wish to.

By technoscape, I mean the global configuration, also ever fluid, of technology, and of the fact that technology, both high and low, both mechanical and informational, now moves at high speeds across various kinds of previously impervious boundaries. Many countries now are the roots of multinational enterprise: a huge steel complex in Libya may involve interests from India, China, Russia and Japan, providing different components of new technological configurations. The odd distribution of technologies, and thus the peculiarities of these technoscapes, are increasingly driven not by any obvious economies of scale, of political control, or of market rationality, but by increasingly complex relationships between money flows, political possibilities and the availability of both un- and highly skilled labor. So, while India exports waiters and chauffeurs to Dubai and Sharjah, it also exports software engineers to the United States — indentured briefly to Tata-Burroughs or the World Bank, then laundered through the State Department to become wealthy resident aliens, who are in turn objects of seductive messages to invest their money and know-how in federal and state projects in India.

The global economy can still be described in terms of traditional indicators (as the World Bank continues to do) and studied in terms of traditional comparisons (as in Project Link at the University of Pennsylvania), but the complicated technoscapes (and the shifting ethnoscapes) which underlie these indicators and comparisons are further out of the reach of the queen of the social sciences than ever before. How is one to make a meaningful comparison of wages in Japan and the United States or of real estate costs in New York and Tokyo, without taking sophisticated account of the very complex fiscal and investment flows that link the two economies through a global grid of currency speculation and capital transfer?

Thus it is useful to speak as well of finanscapes, since the disposition of global capital is now a more mysterious, rapid and difficult landscape to follow than ever before, as currency markets, national stock exchanges, and commodity speculations move mega-monies through national turnstiles at blinding speed, with vast absolute implications for small differences in percentage points and time units. But the critical point is that the global relationship between ethnoscapes, technoscapes and finanscapes is deeply disjunctive and profoundly unpredictable, since each of these landscapes is subject to its own constraints and incentives (some political, some informational and some techno-environmental), at the same time as each acts as a constraint and a parameter for movements in the others. Thus, even an elementary model of global political economy must take into account the deeply disjunctive relationships between human movement, technological flow and financial transfers.

Further refracting these disjunctures (which hardly form a simple, mechanical global infrastructure in any case) are what I call mediascapes a these disjunctures (which hardly form a simple, mechanical global infrastructure in any case) are what I call mediascapes and ideoscapes, though the latter two are closely related landscapes of images. Mediascapes refer both to the distribution of the electronic capabilities to produce and disseminate information (newspapers, magazines, television stations and film production studios), which are now available to a growing number of private and public interests throughout the world, and to the images of the world created by these media. These images of the world involve many complicated inflections, depending on their mode (documentary or entertainment), their hardware (electronic or pre-electronic), their audiences (local, national or transnational) and the interests of those who own and control them. What is most important about these mediascapes is that they provide (especially in their television, film and cassette forms) large and complex repertoires of images, narratives and ethnoscapes to viewers throughout the world, in which the world of commodities and the world of news and politics are profoundly mixed. What this means is that many audiences throughout the world experience the media themselves as a complicated and interconnected repertoire of print, celluloid, electronic screens and billboards. The lines between the realistic and the fictional landscapes they see are blurred, so that, the further away these audiences are from the direct experiences of metropolitan life, the more likely they are to construct imagined worlds which are chimerical, aesthetic, even fantastic objects, particularly if assessed by the criteria of some other perspective, some other imagined world.

Mediascapes, whether produced by private or state interests, tend to be image-centered, narrative-based accounts of strips of reality, and what they offer to those who experience and transform them is a series of elements (such as characters, plots and textual forms) out of which scripts can be formed of imagined lives, their own as well as those of others living in other places. These scripts can and do get dis-aggregated into complex sets of metaphors by which people live

(Lakoff and Johnson 1980) as they help to constitute narratives of the Other and proto-narratives of possible lives, fantasies which could become prolegomena to the desire for acquisition and movement.

Ideoscapes are also concatenations of images, but they are often directly political and frequently have to do with the ideologies of states and the counter-ideologies of movements explicitly oriented to capturing state power or a piece of it. These ideoscapes are composed of elements of the Enlightenment worldview, which consists of a concatenation of ideas, terms and images, including 'freedom', 'welfare', 'rights', 'sovereignty', 'representation' and the master-term 'democracy'. The master-narrative of the Enlightenment (and its many variants in England, France and the United States) was constructed with a certain internal logic and presupposed a certain relationship between reading, representation and the public sphere (for the dynamics of this process in the early history of the United States, see Warner 1990). But their diaspora across the world, especially since the nineteenth century, has loosened the internal coherence that held these terms and images together in a Euro-American master-narrative and provided instead a loosely structured synopticon of politics, in which different nation-states, as part of their evolution, have organized their political cultures around different keywords (e.g., Williams 1976).

As a result of the differential diaspora of these keywords, the political narratives that govern communication between elites and followings in different parts of the world involve problems of both a semantic and a pragmatic nature: semantic to the extent that words (and their lexical equivalents) require careful translation from context to context in their global movements; and pragmatic to the extent that the use of these words by political actors and their audiences may be subject to very different sets of contextual conventions that mediate their translation into public politics. Such conventions are not only matters of the nature of political rhetoric (viz., what does the aging Chinese leadership mean when it refers to the dangers of hooliganism? What does the South Korean leadership mean when it speaks of discipline as the key to democratic industrial growth?).

These conventions also involve the far more subtle question of what sets of communicative genres are valued in what way (newspapers versus cinema, for example) and what sorts of pragmatic genre conventions govern the collective readings of different kinds of text. So, while an Indian audience may be attentive to the resonances of a political speech in terms of some keywords and phrases reminiscent of Hindi cinema, a Korean audience may respond to the subtle codings of Buddhist or neo-Confucian rhetorical strategy encoded in a political document. The very relationship of reading to hearing and seeing may vary in important ways that determine the morphology of these different ideoscapes as they shape themselves in different national and transnational contexts. This globally variable synaesthesia has hardly even been noted, but it demands urgent analysis. Thus democracy has clearly become a master-term, with powerful echoes from Haiti and Poland to the Soviet Union and China, but it sits at the center of a variety of ideoscapes (composed of distinctive pragmatic configurations of rough translations of other central terms from the vocabulary of the Enlightenment). This creates ever new terminological kaleidoscopes, as states (and the groups that seek to capture them) seek to pacify populations whose own ethnoscapes are in motion and whose mediascapes may create severe problems for the ideoscapes with which they are presented. The fluidity of ideoscapes is complicated in particular by the growing diasporas (both voluntary and involuntary) of intellectuals who continuously inject new meaning-streams into the discourse of democracy in different parts of the world.

This extended terminological discussion of the five terms I have coined sets the basis for a tentative formulation about the conditions under which current global flows occur: *they occur in and through the growing disjunctures between ethnoscapes, technoscapes, finanscapes, mediascapes and ideoscapes*. This formulation, the core of my model of global cultural flow, needs some explanation. First, people, machinery, money, images, and ideas now follow increasingly non-isomorphic paths: of course, at all periods in human history, there have been some disjunctures between the flows of these things, but the sheer speed, scale and volume of each of these flows are now so great that the disjunctures have become central to the politics of global culture. The Japanese are notoriously hospitable to ideas and are stereotyped as inclined to export (all) and import (some) goods, but they are also notoriously closed to immigration, like the Swiss, the Swedes and the Saudis. Yet the Swiss and Saudis accept populations of guestworkers, thus creating labor diasporas of Turks, Italians and other circum-Mediterranean groups. Some such guestworker groups maintain continuous contact with their home-nations, like the Turks, but others, like high-level South Asian mi-grants, tend to desire lives in their new homes, raising anew the problem of reproduction in a deterritorialized context.

Deterritorialization, in general, is one of the central forces of the modern world, since it brings laboring populations into the lower-class sectors and spaces of relatively wealthy societies, while some-times creating exaggerated and intensified senses of criticism or at-tachment to politics in the home-state. Deterritorialization, whether of Hindus, Sikhs, Palestinians or Ukrainians, is now at the core of a variety of global fundamentalisms, including Islamic and Hindu fun-damentalism. In the Hindu case, for example (Appadurai and Breck-enridge: forthcoming), it is clear that the overseas movement of In-dians has been exploited by a variety of interests both within and outside India to create a complicated network of finances and reli-gious identifications, in which the problem of cultural reproduction for Hindus abroad has become tied to the politics of Hindu funda-mentalism at home.

At the same time, deterritorialization creates new markets for film companies, art impresarios and travel agencies, who thrive on the need of the deterritorialized population for contact with its homeland. Naturally, these invented homelands, which constitute the mediascapes of deterritorialized groups, can often become suffi-ciently fantastic and one-sided that they provide the material for new ideoscapes in which ethnic conflicts can begin to erupt. The creation of Khalistan, an invented homeland of the deterritorialized Sikh pop-ulation of England, Canada and the United States, is one example of the bloody potential in such mediascapes, as they interact with the internal colonialisms (e.g., Hechter 1974) of the nation-state. The West Bank, Namibia and Eritrea are other theatres for the enactment of the bloody negotiation between existing nation-states and various deterritorialized groupings.

The idea of deterritorialization may also be applied to money and finance, as money managers seek the best markets for their invest-ments, independent of national boundaries. In turn, these move-ments of monies are the basis of new kinds of conflict, as Los Angelenos worry about the Japanese buying up their city, and people in Bombay worry about the rich Arabs from the Gulf States who have not only transformed the prices of mangos in Bombay, but have also substantially altered the profile of hotels, restaurants and other services in the eyes of the local population, just as they continue to do in London. Yet, most residents of Bombay are ambivalent about the Arab presence there, for the flip side of their presence is the absence of friends and kinsmen earning big money in the Middle East and bringing back both money and luxury commodities to Bombay and other cities in India. Such commodities transform consumer taste in these cities and often end up smuggled through air and sea ports and peddled in the gray markets of Bombay's streets. In these gray markets, some members of Bombay's middle classes and of its lumpenproletariat can buy some of these goods, ranging from cartons of Marlboro cigarettes, to Old Spice shaving cream and tapes of Madonna. Similar gray routes, often subsidized by the moonlighting activities of sailors, diplomats, and airline stewardesses who get to move in and out of the country regularly, keep the gray markets of Bombay, Madras and Calcutta filled with goods not only from the West, but also from the Middle East, Hong Kong and Singapore.

It is in this fertile ground of deterritorialization, in which money, commodities and persons are involved in ceaselessly chasing each other around the world, that the mediascapes and ideoscapes of the modern world find their fractured and fragmented counterpart. For the ideas and images produced by mass media often are only partial guides to the goods and experiences that deterritorialized populations transfer to one another. In Mira Nair's brilliant film *India Cabaret*, we see the multiple loops of this fractured deterritorialization as young women, barely competent in Bombay's metropolitan glitz, come to seek their fortunes as cabaret dancers and prostitutes in Bombay, entertaining men in clubs with dance formats derived wholly from the prurient dance sequences of Hindi films. These scenes cater in turn to ideas about Western and foreign women and their 'looseness', while they provide tawdry career alibis for these women. Some of these women come from Kerala, where cabaret clubs and the pornographic film industry have blossomed, partly in response to the purses and tastes of Keralites returned from the Middle East, where their diasporic lives away from women distort their very sense of what the relations between men and women might be. These tragedies of displacement could certainly be replayed in a more detailed analysis of the relations between the Japanese and German sex tours to Thailand and the tragedies of the sex trade in Bangkok, and in other similar loops which tie together fantasies about the Other, the conveniences and seductions of travel, the economics of global trade and the brutal mobility fantasies that dominate gender politics in many parts of Asia and the world at large.

While far more could be said about the cultural politics of deterritorialization and the larger sociology of displacement that it expresses, it is appropriate at this juncture to bring in the role of the nation-state in the disjunctive global economy of culture today. The relationship between states and nations is everywhere an embattled one. It is possible to say that in many societies, the nation and the state have become one another's projects. That is, while nations (or more properly groups with ideas about nationhood) seek to capture or co-opt states and state power, states simultaneously seek to capture and monopolize ideas about nationhood (Baruah 1986; Chatterjee 1986; Nandy 1989). In general, separatist transnational movements, including those which have included terror in their methods, exemplify nations in search of states: Sikhs, Tamil Sri Lankans, Basques, Moros, Quebecois, each of these represent imagined communities which seek to create states of their own or carve pieces out of existing states. States, on the other hand, are everywhere seeking to monopolize the moral resources of community, either by flatly claiming perfect coevality between nation and state, or by systematically museumizing and representing all the groups within them in a variety of heritage politics that seems remarkably uniform throughout the world (Handler 1988; Herzfeld 1982; McQueen 1988).

Here, national and international mediascapes are exploited by nation-states to pacify separatists or even the potential fissiparousness of all ideas of difference. Typically, contemporary nation-states do this by exercising taxonomic control over difference, by creating various kinds of international spectacle to domesticate difference, and by seducing small groups with the fantasy of self-display on some sort of global or cosmopolitan stage. One important new feature of global cultural politics, tied to the disjunctive relationships between the various landscapes discussed earlier, is that state and nation are at each other's throats, and the hyphen that links them is now less an icon of conjuncture than an index of disjuncture. This disjunctive relationship between nation and state has two levels: at the level of any given nation-state, it means that there is a battle of the imagination, with state and nation seeking to cannibalize one another. Here is the seed-bed of brutal separatisms, majoritarianisms that seem to have appeared from nowhere, and micro-identities that have become political projects within the nation-state. At another level, this disjunctive relationship is deeply entangled with the global disjunctures discussed throughout this essay: ideas of nationhood appear to be steadily increasing in scale and regularly crossing existing state boundaries; sometimes, as with the Kurds, because previous identities stretched across vast national spaces, or, as with the Tamils in Sri Lanka, the dormant threads of a transnational diaspora have been activated to ignite the micro-politics of a nation-state.

In discussing the cultural politics that have subverted the hyphen that links the nation to the state, it is especially important not to forget its mooring in the irregularities that now characterize disorganized capital (Kothari 1989; Lash and Urry 1987). It is because labor, finance and technology are now so widely separated that the volatilities that underlie movements for nationhood (as large as transnational Islam on the one hand, or as small as the movement of the Gurkhas for a separate state in the North-East of India) grind against the vulnerabilities that characterize the relationships between states. States find themselves pressed to stay 'open' by the forces of media, technology, and travel that have fuelled consumerism throughout the world and have increased the craving, even in the non-Western world, for new commodities and spectacles. On the other hand, these very cravings can become caught up in new ethnoscapes, mediascapes, and eventually, ideoscapes, such as democracy in China, that the state cannot tolerate as threats to its own control over ideas of nationhood and peoplehood. States throughout the world are under siege, especially where contests over the ideoscapes of democracy are fierce and fundamental, and where there are radical disjunctures between ideoscapes and technoscapes (as in the case of very small countries that lack contemporary technologies of production and information); or between ideoscapes and finanscapes (as in countries such as Mexico or Brazil, where international lending influences national politics to a very large degree); or between ideoscapes and ethnoscapes (as in Beirut, where diasporic, local and translocal filiations are suicidally at battle); or between ideoscapes and mediascapes (as in many countries in the Middle East and Asia) where the lifestyles represented on both national and international TV and cinema completely overwhelm and undermine the rhetoric of national politics: in the Indian case, the myth of the law-breaking hero has emerged to mediate this naked struggle between the pieties and the realities of Indian politics, which has grown increasingly brutalised and corrupt (Vachani 1989).

The transnational movement of the martial arts, particularly through Asia, as mediated by the Hollywood and Hong Kong film industries (Zarilli: forthcoming) is a rich illustration of the ways in which long-standing martial arts traditions, reformulated to meet the fantasies of contemporary (sometimes lumpen) youth populations, create new cultures of masculinity and violence, which are in turn the fuel for increased violence in national and international politics. Such violence is in turn the spur to an increasingly rapid and amoral arms trade which penetrates the entire world. The world-wide spread of the AK-47 and the Uzi, in films, in corporate and state security, in terror, and in police and military activity, is a reminder that apparently simple technical uniformities often conceal an increasingly complex set of loops, linking images of violence to aspirations for community in some imagined world.

Returning then to the ethnoscapes with which I began, the central paradox of ethnic politics in today's world is that primordia (whether of language or skin color or neighborhood or kinship) have become globalized. That is, sentiments whose greatest force is in their ability to ignite intimacy into a political sentiment and turn locality into a staging ground for identity, have become spread over vast and irregular spaces as groups move, yet stay linked to one another through sophisticated media capabilities. This is not to deny that such primordia are often the product of invented traditions (Hobsbawm and Ranger 1983) or retrospective affiliations, but to emphasize that because of the disjunctive and unstable interplay of commerce, media, national policies and consumer fantasies, ethnicity, once a genie contained in the bottle of some sort of locality (however large), has now become a global force, forever slipping in and through the cracks between states and borders.

But the relationship between the cultural and economic levels of this new set of global disjunctures is not a simple one-way street in which the terms of global cultural politics are set wholly by, or confined wholly within, the vicissitudes of international flows of technology, labor and finance, demanding only a modest modification of existing neo-Marxist models of uneven development and state-formation. There is a deeper change, itself driven by the disjunctures between all the landscapes I have discussed, and constituted by their continuously fluid and uncertain interplay, which concerns the relationship between production and consumption in today's global economy. Here I begin with Marx's famous (and often mined) view of the fetishism of the commodity and suggest that this fetishism has been replaced in the world at large (now seeing the world as one, large, interactive system, composed of many complex subsystems) by two mutually supportive descendants, the first of which I call production fetishism, and the second of which I call the fetishism of the consumer.

By production fetishism I mean an illusion created by contemporary transnational production loci, which masks translocal capital, transnational earning-flows, global management and often far-away workers (engaged in various kinds of high-tech putting-out operations) in the idiom and spectacle of local (sometimes even worker) control, national productivity and territorial sovereignty. To the extent that various kinds of Free Trade Zones have become the models for production at large, especially of high-tech commodities, production has itself become a fetish, masking not social relations as such, but the relations of production, which are increasingly transnational. The locality (both in the sense of the local factory or site of production and in the extended sense of the nation-state) becomes a fetish which disguises the globally dispersed forces that actually drive the production process. This generates alienation (in Marx's sense) twice intensified, for its social sense is now compounded by a complicated spatial dynamic which is increasingly global.

As for the fetishism of the consumer, I mean to indicate here that the consumer has been transformed, through commodity flows (and the mediascapes, especially of advertising, that accompany them), into a sign, both in Baudrillard's sense of a simulacrum which only asymptotically approaches the form of a real social agent; and in the sense of a mask for the real seat of agency, which is not the consumer but the producer and the many forces that constitute production. Global advertising is the key technology for the worldwide dissemination of a plethora of creative, and culturally well-chosen, ideas of consumer agency. These images of agency are increasingly distortions of a world of merchandising so subtle that the consumer is consistently helped to believe that he or she is an actor, where in fact he or she is at best a chooser.

The globalization of culture is not the same as its homogenization, but globalization involves the use of a variety of instruments of homogenization (armaments, advertising techniques, language hegemonies, and clothing styles) which are absorbed into local political and cultural economies, only to be repatriated as heterogeneous dialogues of national sovereignty, free enterprise and fundamentalism in which the state plays an increasingly delicate role: too much openness to global flows, and the nation-state is threatened by revolt — the China syndrome; too little, and the state exits the international stage, as Burma, Albania and North Korea in various ways have done. In general, the state has become the arbitrager of this *repatriation of difference* (in the form of goods, signs, slogans and styles). But this repatriation or export of the designs and commodities of difference continuously exacerbates the internal politics of majoritarianism and homogenization, which is most frequently played out in debates over heritage.

Thus the central feature of global culture today is the politics of the mutual effort of sameness and difference to cannibalize one another and thus to proclaim their successful hijacking of the twin Enlightenment ideas of the triumphantly universal and the resiliently particular. This mutual cannibalization shows its ugly face in riots, in refugee flows, in state-sponsored torture and in ethnocide (with or without state support). Its brighter side is in the expansion of many individual horizons of hope and fantasy, in the global spread of oral rehydration therapy and other low-tech instruments of well-being, in the susceptibility even of South Africa to the force of global opinion, in the inability of the Polish state to repress its own working classes, and in the growth of a wide range of progressive, transnational alliances. Examples of both sorts could be multiplied. The critical point is that both sides of the coin of global cultural process today are products of the infinitely varied mutual contest of sameness and difference on a stage characterized by radical disjunctures between different sorts of global flows and the uncertain landscapes created in and through these disjunctures.

The Work of Reproduction in an Age of Mechanical Art

I have inverted the key terms of the title of Walter Benjamin's famous essay (1969, orig. 1936) to return this rather high-flying discussion to a more manageable level. There is a classic human problem which will not disappear however much global cultural processes might change their dynamics, and this is the problem today typically discussed under the rubric of reproduction (and traditionally referred to in terms of the transmission of culture). In either case, the question is as follows: how do small groups, especially families, the classical loci of socialization, deal with these new global realities as they seek to reproduce themselves, and in so doing, as it were by accident, reproduce cultural forms themselves? In traditional anthropological terms, this could be phrased as the problem of enculturation in a period of rapid culture change. So the problem is hardly novel. But it does take on some novel dimensions under the global conditions discussed so far in this essay.

In the first place, the sort of trans-generational stability of knowledge which was presupposed in most theories of enculturation (or, in slightly broader terms, of socialization) can no longer be assumed. As families move to new locations, or as children move before older generations, or as grown sons and daughters return from time spent in strange parts of the world, family relationships can become volatile, as new commodity patterns are negotiated, debts and obligations are recalibrated and rumors and fantasies about the new setting are manoeuvred into existing repertoires of knowledge and practice. Often, global labor diasporas involve immense strains on marriages in general and on women in particular, as marriages become the meeting points of historical patterns of socialization and new ideas of proper behavior. Generations easily divide, as ideas about property, propriety and collective obligation wither under the siege of distance and time. Most important of all, the work of cultural reproduction in new settings is profoundly complicated by the politics of representing a family as 'normal' (particularly for the young) to neighbours and peers in the new setting. All this is, of course, not new to the cultural study of immigration.

What is new is that this is a world in which both points of departure and points of arrival are in cultural flux, and thus the search for steady points of reference, as critical life-choices are made, can be very difficult. It is in this atmosphere that the invention of tradition (and of ethnicity, kinship and other identity-markers) can become slippery, as the search for certainties is regularly frustrated by the fluidities of transnational communication. As group pasts become increasingly parts of museums, exhibits and collections, both in national and transnational spectacles, culture becomes less what Bourdieu would have called a habitus (a tacit realm of reproducible practices and dispositions) and more an arena for conscious choice, justification and representation, the latter often to multiple, and spatially dislocated audiences.

The task of cultural reproduction, even in its most intimate arenas, such as husband-wife and parent-child relations, becomes both politicized and exposed to the traumas of deterritorialization as family members pool and negotiate their mutual understandings and aspirations in sometimes fractured spatial arrangements. At larger levels, such as community, neighborhood and territory, this politicization is often the emotional fuel for more explicitly violent politics of identity, just as these larger politics sometimes penetrate and ignite domestic politics. When, for example, two offspring in a household split with their father on a key matter of political identification in a transnational setting, pre-existing localized norms carry little force. Thus a son who has joined the Hezbollah group in Lebanon may no longer get along with parents or siblings who are affiliated with Amal or some other branch of Shi'i ethnic political identity in Lebanon. Women in particular bear the brunt of this sort of friction, for they become pawns in the heritage politics of the household, and are often subject to the abuse and violence of men who are themselves torn about the relation between heritage and opportunity in shifting spatial and political formations.

The pains of cultural reproduction in a disjunctive global world are, of course, not eased by the effects of mechanical art (or mass media, if you will) since these media afford powerful resources for counter-nodes of identity which youth can project against parental wishes or desires. At larger levels of organization, there can be many forms of cultural politics within displaced populations (whether of refugees or of voluntary immigrants), all of which are inflected in important ways by media (and the mediascapes and ideoscapes they offer). A central link between the fragilities of cultural reproduction and the role of the mass media in today's world is the politics of gender and of violence. As fantasies of gendered violence dominate the B-grade film industries that blanket the world, they both reflect and refine gendered violence at home and in the streets, as young men (in particular) come to be torn between the macho politics of self-assertion in contexts where they are frequently denied real agency, and women are forced to enter the labor force in new ways on the one hand, and continue the maintenance of familial heritage on the other. Thus the honor of women becomes not just an armature of stable (if inhuman) systems of cultural reproduction, but a new arena for the formation of sexual identity and family politics, as men and women face new pressures at work, and new fantasies of leisure.

Since both work and leisure have lost none of their gendered qualities in this new global order, but have acquired ever subtler fetishized representations, the honor of women becomes increasingly a surrogate for the identity of embattled communities of males, while their women, in reality, have to negotiate increasingly harsh conditions of work at home and in the non-domestic workplace. In short, deterritorialized communities and displaced populations, however much they may enjoy the fruits of new kinds of earning and new dispositions of capital and technology, have to play out the desires and fantasies of these new ethnoscapes, while striving to reproduce the family-as-microcosm of culture. As the shapes of cultures grow themselves less bounded and tacit, more fluid and politicized, the work of cultural reproduction becomes a daily hazard. Far more could, and should, be said about the work of reproduction in an age of mechanical art: the preceding discussion was meant to indicate the contours of the problems that a new, globally informed, theory of cultural reproduction will have to face.

Shape and Process in Global Cultural Formations

The deliberations of the arguments that I have made so far constitute the bare bones of an approach to a general theory of global cultural processes. Focusing on disjunctures, I have employed a set of terms (ethnoscape, finanscape, technoscape, mediascape, and ideoscape) to stress different streams or flows along which cultural material may be seen to be moving across national boundaries. I have also sought to exemplify the ways in which these various flows (or landscapes, from the stabilizing perspectives of any given imagined world) are in fundamental disjuncture with respect to one another. What further steps can we take towards a general theory of global cultural processes, based on these proposals?

The first is to note that our very models of cultural shape will have to alter, as configurations of people, place and heritage lose all semblance of isomorphism. Recent work in anthropology has done much to free us of the shackles of highly localized, boundary-oriented, holistic, primordialist images of cultural form and substance (Appadurai: in press; Hannerz 1989; Marcus and Fisher 1986; Thornton 1988). But not very much has been put in their place, except somewhat larger if less mechanical versions of these images, as in Wolf's work on the relationship of Europe to the rest of the world. What I would like to propose is that we begin to think of the configuration of cultural forms in today's world as fundamentally fractal, that is, as possessing no Euclidean boundaries, structures, or regularities. Second, I would suggest that these cultural forms, which we should strive to represent as fully fractal, are also overlapping, in ways that have been discussed only in pure mathematics (in set theory for example) and in biology (in the language of polythetic classifications). Thus we need to combine a fractal metaphor for the shape of cultures (in the plural) with a polythetic account of their overlaps and resemblances. Without this latter step, we shall remain enmired in comparative work which relies on the clear separation of the entities to be compared, before serious comparison can begin. How are we to compare fractally shaped cultural forms which are also polythetically overlapping in their coverage of terrestrial space?

Finally, in order for the theory of global cultural interactions predicated on disjunctive flows to have any force greater than that of a mechanical metaphor, it will have to move into something like a human version of the theory that some scientists are calling 'chaos' theory. That is, we will need to ask how these complex, overlapping, fractal shapes constitute not a simple, stable (even if large-scale) system, but to ask what its dynamics are: Why do ethnic riots occur when and where they do? Why do states wither at greater rates in some places and times rather than others? Why do some countries flout conventions of international debt repayment with so much less apparent worry than others? How are international arms flows driving ethnic battles and genocides? Why are some states exiting the global stage while others are clamouring to get in? Why do key events occur at a certain point in a certain place rather than in others? These are, of course, the great traditional questions of causality, contingency and prediction in the human sciences, but in a world of disjunctive global flows, it is perhaps important to start asking them in a way that relies on images of flow and uncertainty, hence 'chaos', rather than on older images of order, stability and systemacity. Otherwise, we will have gone far towards a theory of global cultural systems but thrown out 'process' in the bargain. And that would make these notes part of a journey towards the kind of illusion of order that we can no longer afford to impose on a world that is so transparently volatile.

Whatever the directions in which we can push these macrometaphors (fractals, polythetic classifications and chaos), we need to ask one other old-fashioned question out of the Marxist paradigm: is there some pre-given order to the relative determining force of these global flows? Since I have postulated the dynamics of global cultural systems as driven by the relationship between flows of persons, technologies, finance, information and ideology, can we speak of some structural-causal order linking these flows, by analogy to the role of the economic order in one version of the Marxist paradigm? Can we speak of some of these flows as being, for a priori structural or historical reasons, always prior to and formative of other flows? My own hypothesis, which can only be tentative at this point, is that the relationship of these various flows to one another, as they constellate into particular events and social forms, will be radically context-dependent. Thus, while labor flows and their loops with financial flows between Kerala and the Middle East may account for the shape of media flows and ideoscapes in Kerala, the reverse may be true of Silicon Valley in California, where intense specialization in a special technological sector (computers) and specific flows of capital may well profoundly determine the shape that ethnoscapes, ideoscapes and mediascapes may take.

This does not mean that the causal-historical relationship between these various flows is random or meaninglessly contingent, but that our current theories of cultural 'chaos' are insufficiently developed to be even parsimonious models, at this point, much less to be predictive theories, the golden fleeces of one kind of social science.

What I have sought to provide in this essay is a reasonably economical technical vocabulary and a rudimentary model of disjunctive flows, from which something like a decent global analysis might emerge. Without some such analysis, it will be difficult to construct what John Hinkson calls a 'social theory of postmodernity' that is adequately global.

REFERENCES

Abu-Lughod, J. 1989. *Before European Hegemony: The World System A.D. 1250–1350*. New York: Oxford University Press.

Ahmad, A. 1987. "Jameson's Rhetoric of Otherness and the 'National Allegory.'" *Social Text* 17: 3–25.

Amin, S. 1980. *Class and Nation: Historically and in the Current Crisis*. New York and London: Monthly Review Press.

Anderson, B. 1983. *Imagined Communities: Reflections on the Origin and Spread of Nationalism*. London: Verso.

Appadurai, A. In press. "Global Ethnoscapes: Notes and Queries for a Transnational Anthropology." In R. G. Fox, ed., *Interventions: Anthropologies of the Present*.

———. Forthcoming. *Imploding Worlds: Imagination and Disjuncture in the Global Cultural Economy*.

Appadurai, A., and C. A. Breckenridge. Forthcoming. *A Transnational Culture in the Making: The Asian Indian Diaspora in the United States*. London: Berg.

Barber, K. 1987. "Popular Arts in Africa." *African Studies Review* 30, no. 3 (September): 1–78.

Baruah, S. 1986. "Immigration, Ethnic Conflict and Political Turmoil, Assam 1979–1985," *Asian Survey* 26 no. 11 (November): 1184–1206.

Bayly, C. 1989. *Imperial Meridian: The British Empire and The World, 1780–1830*. London and New York: Longman.

Benjamin W. 1969. "The Work of Art in the Age of Mechanical Reproduction." In *Illuminations*, ed. H. Arendt, trans. H. Zohn. New York: Schocken, 217–51.

Braudel, F. 1981–1984. *Civilization and Capitalism, 15th-18th Century* (3 vols.). London: Collins.

Chatterjee, P. 1986. *Nationalist Thought and the Colonial World: A Derivative Discourse*. London: Zed.

Curtin, P. 1984. *Cross-Cultural Trade in World History*. Cambridge: Cambridge University Press.

Deleuze, G., and F. Guattari. 1987. *A Thousand Plateaus: Capitalism and Schizophrenia*. Trans. B. Massumi. Minneapolis: University of Minnesota Press.

Fabian, J. 1983. *Time and the Other: How Anthropology Makes Its Object*. New York: Columbia University Press.

Feld, S. 1988. "Notes on World Beat." *Public Culture* 1, no. 1: 31–37.

Gans, E. 1985. *The End of Culture: Toward a Generative Anthropology*. Berkeley: University of California Press.

Hamelink, C. 1983. *Cultural Autonomy in Global Communications*. New York: Longman.

Handler, R. 1988. *Nationalism and the Politics of Culture in Quebec*. Madison: University of Wisconsin Press.

Hannerz, U. 1989. "Notes on the Global Ecumene." *Public Culture* 1, no. 2 (Spring): 66–75.

———. 1987. "The World in Creolization." *Africa* 57, no. 4: 546–59.

Hechter, M. 1974. *Internal Colonialism: The Celtic Fringe in British National Development, 1536–1966*. Berkeley and Los Angeles: University of California Press.

Helms, M. W. 1988. *Ulysses' Sail: An Ethnographic Odyssey of Power, Knowledge, and Geographical Distance*. Princeton, N.J.: Princeton University Press.

Herzfeld, M. 1982. *Ours Once More: Folklore, Ideology and the Making of Modern Greece*. Austin: University of Texas Press.

Hobsbawm, E., and T. Ranger, eds. 1983. *The Invention of Tradition*. New York: Columbia University Press.

Hodgson, M. 1974. *The Venture of Islam, Conscience and History in a World Civilization*. Chicago: University of Chicago Press.

Iyer, P. 1988. *Video Night in Kathmandu*. New York: Knopf.

Ivy, M. 1988. "Tradition and Difference in the Japanese Mass Media." *Public Culture* 1, no. 1: 21–29.

Jameson, F. 1983. "Postmodernism and Consumer Society." In *The Anti-Aesthetic: Essays on Postmodern Culture*, ed. H. Foster. Port Townsend, Wash.: Bay Press, 111–25.

———. 1986. "Third World Literature in the Era of Multi-National Capitalism." *Social Text* 15 (Fall): 65–88.

———. 1989. "Nostalgia for the Present." *South Atlantic Quarterly* 88 no. 2 (Spring): 517–37.

Kothari, R. 1989. *State against Democracy: In Search of Humane Governance*. New York: New Horizons.

Lakoff, G., and M. Johnson. 1980. *Metaphors We Live By*. Chicago and London: University of Chicago Press.

Lash, S., and J. Urry. 1987. *The End of Organized Capitalism*. Madison: University of Wisconsin Press.

Mandel, E. 1978. *Late Capitalism*. London: Verso.

Marcus, G., and M. Fisher. 1986. *Anthropology As Cultural Critique: An Experimental Moment in the Human Sciences*. Chicago: University of Chicago Press.

Mattelart, A. 1983. *Transnationals and Third World: The Struggle for Culture*. South Hadley, Mass.: Bergin and Garvey.

McQueen, H. 1988. "The Australian Stamp: Image, Design and Ideology." *Arena* 84 (Spring): 78–96.

Meyrowitz, J. 1985. *No Sense of Place: The Impact of Electronic Media on Social Behavior*. New York: Oxford University Press.

Nandy, A. 1989. "The Political Culture of the Indian State." *Daedalus* 118, no. 4: 1–26.

Nicoll, F. 1989. "My Trip to Alice." *Criticism, Heresy and Interpretation* (CHAI) 3: 21–32.

Schafer, E. 1963. *Golden Peaches of Samarkand: A Study of T'ang Exotics*. Berkeley: University of California Press.

Schiller, H. 1976. *Communication and Cultural Domination*. White Plains, N.Y.: International Arts and Sciences.

Thornton, R. 1988. "The Rhetoric of Ethnographic Holism." *Cultural Anthropology* 3, no. 3 (August): 285–303.

Vachani, L. 1989. "Narrative, Pleasure and Ideology in the Hindi Film: An Analysis of the Outsider Formula." M.A. thesis, University of Pennsylvania.

Wallerstein, I. 1974. *The Modern World-System* (2 vols.). New York and London: Academic Press.

Warner, M. 1990. *The Letters of the Republic: Publication and the Public Sphere in Eighteenth-Century America.* Cambridge, Mass.: Harvard University Press.

Williams, R. 1976. *Keywords.* New York: Oxford University Press.

Wolf, E. 1982. *Europe and the People without History.* Berkeley: University of California Press.

Yoshimoto, M. 1989. "The Postmodern and Mass Images in Japan." *Public Culture* 1, no. 2: 8–25.

Zarilli, P. Forthcoming. "Repositioning the Body: An Indian Martial Art and Its Pan-Asian Publics." In C. A. Breckenridge, ed., *Producing the Postcolonial: Trajectories to Public Culture in India.*

NOTES

1. One major exception is Fredric Jameson, whose work on the relationship between postmodernism and late capitalism has, in many ways, inspired this essay. However, the debate between Jameson and Ahmad in *Social Text* shows that the creation of a globalizing Marxist narrative, in cultural matters, is difficult territory indeed. My own effort, in this context, is to begin a restructuring of the Marxist narrative (by stressing lags and disjunctures) that many Marxists might find abhorrent. Such a re-structuring has to avoid the dangers of obliterating difference within the third world, of eliding the social referent (as some French postmodernists seem inclined to do) and of retaining the narrative authority of the Marxist tradition, in favor of greater attention to global fragmentation, uncertainty and difference.

2. These ideas are argued more fully in a book I am currently working on, tentatively entitled *Imploding Worlds: Imagination and Disjuncture in the Global Cultural Economy.*

Contributors

Robin Andersen is professor of communications at Fordham University.

Arjun Appadurai is Barbara E. and Richard J. Franke Professor in the Departments of Anthropology and South Asian Languages and Civilizations at the University of Chicago and director of the Chicago Humanities Institute as well as the associate editor of *Public Culture*. He is the editor of *The Social Life of Things* (1986) and is currently working on a book on global cultural flows.

Stanley Aronowitz is professor of sociology at the City University of New York Graduate Center and a coeditor of *Social Text*. He is the coauthor, with Henry Giroux, of *Education under Siege* (1985) and *Postmodern Education* (1991) and the author of *The Crisis in Historical Materialism* (1981) and *Science as Power* (1988).

Lauren Berlant teaches in the English department at the University of Chicago. She is the author of *The Anatomy of National Identity: Hawthorne, Utopia, and Everyday Life* (1991). The present essay is part of an ongoing project about the sentimental identity politics of American "women's culture" since the 1830s.

Paolo Carpignano is professor of communications at Fordham University.

William DiFazio is professor of sociology at St. John's University in Jamaica, New York. He is the author of *Longshoremen*.

Nancy Fraser is professor of philosophy and comparative literature and theory at Northwestern University. She is the author of "What's Critical about Critical Theory? The Case of Habermas and Gender" in *Feminism as Critique: Essays on the Politics of Gender in Late-Capitalist Societies*, edited by S. Benhabib and D. Cornell (1987), and of *Unruly Practices: Power, Discourse and Gender in Contemporary Social Theory* (1989).

Fredric Jameson is professor of comparative literature at Duke University and a founding member of *Social Text*. He is the author of, among other books, *The Signature of the Visible* (1990) and *Postmodernism; or, Cultural Logic of Late Capitalism* (1991).

Thomas Keenan teaches English at Princeton University. He is the author of *Fables of Responsibility* (1992) and coeditor of Paul de Man's *Wartime Journalism* (1988) and *Responses* (1989). In addition, he is coeditor of Jacques Derrida, *Negotiations*, forthcoming from University of Minnesota Press.

Dana Polan teaches film and theory at the University of Pittsburgh. He is the author of *The Poetical Language of Film and the Avant-Garde* (1985), *Power and Paranoia: History, Narrative, and the American Cinema, 1940–1950* (1986), and articles in *October*, *boundary 2*, *Camera Obscura*, and *Enclitic*, among other journals.

Bruce Robbins teaches in the English department at Rutgers University and is a coeditor of *Social Text*. He is the author of *The Servant's Hand: English Fiction from Below* (1986) and the editor of *Intellectuals: Aesthetics, Politics, Academics* (1990).

Andrew Ross teaches English at Princeton University and is a coeditor of *Social Text*. He is the author of *The Failure of Modernism* (1986), *No Respect: Intellectuals and Popular Culture* (1989), and *Strange Weather* (1991). He is the editor of *Universal Abandon? The Politics of Modernism* (1989) and coeditor of *Technoculture* (1991).

Michael Warner — teaches in the English department at Rutgers University. He is the author of *The Letters of the Republic: Publication and the Public Sphere in Eighteenth-Century America* (1990) and the coeditor, with Gerald Graff, of *The Origins of Literary Study in America* (1989).

George Yúdice is an associate professor of Romance languages at Hunter College, City University of New York, and a member of the editorial collective of *Social Text*. He is the author of *Vincente Hui-dobro y la motivacíon del languaje póetico* (1978) and "Cubist Aesthetics in Painting and Poetry," *Semiotica* 36 (1981). He is the coeditor of *On Edge: The Crisis of Contemporary Latin American Culture* (1992).

Linda M. G. Zerilli is an assistant professor in the political science department at Rutgers University. She has published in the areas of feminist political theory, Continental philosophy, and French feminist theory.

Index

Terms that are used on nearly every page of this book, such as *public*, *public sphere*, *private*, *domestic*, *capitalism*, and *politics*, are not included here.